High-Performance

JAVA

Platform Computing

ISBN 0-13-016164-0

9 780130 161642

90000

High-Performance
JAVA
Platform Computing

THOMAS W. CHRISTOPHER • GEORGE K. THIRUVATHUKAL

Prentice Hall PTR, Upper Saddle River, NJ 07458
www.phptr.com

Sun Microsystems Press
A Prentice Hall Title

Editorial/production supervision: *Rose Kernan*
Acquisitions editor: *Mary Franz*
Editorial assistant: *Noreen Regina*
Marketing manager: *Julie Tiso*
Manufacturing manager: *Alexis Heydt*
Manufacturing buyer: *Maura Zaldivar*
Art director: *Gail Cocker-Bogusz*
Interior designer: *Meg VanArsdale*
Cover director: *Jerry Votta*
Cover designer: *Nina Scuderi*

Sun Microsystems Press
Marketing manager: *Michael Llwyd Alread*
Publisher: *Rachel Borden*

10 9 8 7 6 5 4 3 2 1
ISBN 0-13-016164-0

Sun Microsystems Press
A Prentice Hall Title

Contents

....

Chapter 2
....

Threads, 19

Chapter 3

Race Conditions and Mutual Exclusion, 43

Chapter 6

Parallelizing Loops, 171

Preface

This is a book about programming high-performance multithreaded applications using the Java language.

Multithreading and multiprogramming, long heralded as useful ideas in the computing literature, have been the focus of numerous textbooks on operating systems, parallel and distributed computing, and, most, recently Java. Yet a key question remains unanswered: Why would one really use threads in the first place?

Our book attacks this question from the bottom up and the top down. Beginning with the bottom-up discussion, threads have been created with the primary goal of improving performance of software applications. At a low level, a thread is much like a process, but differs from processes in one key respect: resource consumption. This is because threads, unlike processes, share common code and data, thus having a lower cost of creation and context-switching overhead.

On the other hand, the low-level focus on threads–the mechanism–has much to do with why threads have not achieved widespread usage in applications. Threads *do* allow great advances in performance to be made, but not without some up-front program structuring. The fact that all threads share data structures can in many cases lead to poor performance, due to synchronization costs.

To answer the question posed earlier, we believe multithreading exists primarily to allow performance gains to be realized, particularly on scalable hardware platforms, such as parallel supercomputers, workstation clusters, and symmetric multiprocessor (SMP) systems. Our book emphasizes programming techniques and packages for high-end computing (often called the "server side" in the business world). We are concerned with using the power available on multiprocessor computers and computer networks to perform computations rapidly.

This book was conceived as a natural follow-up to a successful series of short courses we offered at the Illinois Institute of Technology and elsewhere to working professionals and graduate students alike. Additionally, between us we have approximately two decades of relevant teaching and research experience in the fields of high-performance computing, object-oriented systems, programming languages, and operating systems.

Our research in high-performance computing and languages has always focused on facilitating the development of concurrent, parallel, and distributed software, going back as far as 1988, when we first began working together on the Message Driven Computing (MDC) environment. We have developed a number of working programming languages and libraries to support such software development. All of the work we did in the past, however, was done in the C, Icon, and C++ programming languages. For this book, we have reworked many of our ideas into a form more suitable for the practicing software engineer, while fully exploiting the power of a true object language such as Java.

With its built-in support for concurrency via a monitorlike abstraction, Java makes concurrent programming easier for programmers than languages such as C and C++. We will discuss how monitors are adequate for solving many problems in concurrency, particularly the so-called classical synchronization problems, which have been well documented in operating-systems textbooks. As more complex libraries and software systems are developed, the evidence gathered supports the proposition that monitors, much like other low-level mechanisms for synchronization, break down. Monitors, despite being a higher-level mechanism for supporting concurrency, present the same problems as found in "less sophisticated" environments such as C and C++ (where low-level threads libraries, such as pthreads and Win32 threads, are used). We refer in the text to these problems (race conditions and deadlocks) as *enemies*. We present stategies for dealing with these enemies and a number of higher-level frameworks that enable the programmer to worry less often about them.

Java is one of the great programming languages of our time. Like many of the great programming languages, a company was behind its development, adoption, and popularity. The sensational marketing blitz was enough to make many of us think that all of the work on languages was now complete, so we could start packing our bags and look for other work. Now that the dust has settled, it is clear that Java does occupy an important space in the marketplace; however, there is a great deal of potential for exploring other programming languages and techniques. The environments in which Java is being considered will require at least a subset of the ideas presented in this book: network appliances, server-side computing, workstation clustering, and parallel systems, to name a few. In this book, our aim is to give the reader some insight into what Java does and does not provide, in terms of support for concurrency. What Java does not provide, we do provide with a working library of Java code that allows the programmer to "operate at a higher-level" (to borrow a phrase from IBM marketing from the OS/2 days).

This book, like all books, does not exist in a vacuum. There are a number of competing books, some of which are appearing in new editions during the next year. We believe our book will be the first of its kind in terms of multithreading and its application to real-world programming. It also provides the following benefits and features:

- It presents a human-understandable explanation of multithreading, its implementation, and how it works in Java.

- It helps the programmer to understand the very real problems encountered in concurrent systems, focused on race conditions, deadlock, and problems encountered when introducing parallelism and distribution. This particular aspect of our book brings to life the chapters on concurrency presented in "abstract" OS textbooks, wherein working code examples are seldom, if ever, provided.

- It helps the programmer to understand the classic synchronization problems, which have suddenly been placed in the spotlight as more and more code is (incorrectly) being written to exploit concurrency.

- It introduces high-level approaches to shared- and distributed-memory multithreading. This section will be of great interest to those who want to develop multithreaded applications but prefer to work at a higher level.

- It shows how to extend the threads concept to the network. It shows how to extend the threads model beyond the single Java Virtual Machine (JVM) to a network of JVMs.

We hope you enjoy this book. It has been written to address the needs of a broad audience. There is introductory, intermediate, and advanced material. The book is designed to be progressive and can be used either as a reference or as a companion to a variety of courses. Exercises are provided at the end of each chapter to reinforce the principles.

Speaking of Code

Code for the Tools of Computing thread package is available through our company Web site at `http://www.toolsofcomputing.com`. You will find links to it on the book sub-Web at `http://www.toolsofcomputing.com/JavaThreads`. We also provide a number of other useful, free packages via the sub-Web.

The example programs are working examples. We have run all of them. We hope the printed versions are as error free as possible; however, mistakes do occur and bugs are found. We actually use our code for development and will regularly update the site to include the latest code. All of the code is freely available under a GNU LGPL-style license.

The algorithm animations available include parallel sorting algorithms and simulations of multiple readers and writers synchronizing with the monitors shown in "The Multiple Reader–Writer Monitors" on page 110. These animations are applets.

We will maintain an errata forum to report errors and corrections found after publication.

Animations

The Multiple Readers–Writers Simulations Color Codes

The simulationes include an array of buttons that indicate the states of the threads accessing the shared structure. The colors of the buttons the threads states:

Red	Writing
Blue	Reading
Magenta	Waiting to write
Cyan	Waiting to read
White	Resting between reads or writes
Gray	Has finished its iterations.

How to Change the Parameters

You can change the parameters in the multiple readers–writers simulations.

You may choose to have a thread choose randomly each time whether to read or write (the default) or to be always be a reader or always a writer. The "% reads" and "# readers" radio buttons choose which option. You use the corresponding text fields to specify the percent probability of reading or the number of threads that are readers, respectively.

To change any number, edit the field and then type ENTER. The new value will not be stored until ENTER is pressed.

You can choose whether the actual read, write, and rest times are constants or whether they are generated from negative exponential distributions. You are able to specify the times' constant or mean values. If you change the mean read, write, or rest times, you should probably not go much below 200ms; smaller values don't give Java enough time to refresh the display. Constant times give simulations that are easier to understand.

You can change any of the values in the left column. The bottom four text fields on the right are output fields. Although you can change the lower four fields yourself, making manual changes won't have any influence on the simulation.

Experiments

There are several charts in this book showing the performance of parallel algorithms. These charts report experimental runs on an intel dual-processor system running Solaris located in the Java High Performance Computing laboratory at DePaul University in Chicago. The Java system has kernel threads, which allow both processors to execute threads in the same program simultaneously.

The experiments were run from scripts that executed, in random order, the algorithms, problem sizes, and number of threads. This was to avoid potential errors that could occur if the system had different loads at different times. If we did not randomize the order, we might not be seeing the effects of the parameters, but rather of system load. The runs in the scripts were separated with *sleep* calls in order to prevent Unix from "nicing" our priority down because our process is compute-bound.

Each algorithm–problem size–number of threads combination was run 32 times to allow the use of large-sample statistics.

In some of the summary charts, where we combine several runs, we did not run the experiments again with the same care for randomizing the runs; therefore, these comparisons may be viewed with suspicion, because they may show effects of differing system loads.

Running the Exercises

To run programs for most of the exercises, you will need a multiprocessor and a kernel-threads version of Java (at least if you want to see any kind of performance improvement). Intel dual-processor systems have become inexpensive. Solaris and Linux are reasonable operating systems, as are Windows NT and successors.

Acknowledgments

Thomas Christopher's Acknowledgments

I would like to acknowledge Mr. Nack Po Paik and his wife Sun Ja Paik (nee Kim), the proprietors of Cafe Express South at Main and Hinman in Evanston, Illinois. George and I have held many meetings there, and I spend hours working there several days each week.

I would like to thank the School of Computer Science, Telecommunications, and Information Systems of DePaul University in Chicago and its dean, Helmut Epp, who gave me a visiting associate professorship in the 1999–2000 academic year, which provided me with security while finishing this book. The school also provided support for the Java High Performance Computing laboratory, in which we tested the performance of the algorithms herein.

Thanks also go to the Department of Computer Science at Illinois Institute of Technology in Chicago, where I was a professor for about 20 years. I developed much of the material in this book teaching Java and parallel processing courses there.

Finally, I'd like to thank my wife, Patricia Guilbeault, and my son, Nick Guilbeault, for providing me with a sense of meaning and belonging that allowed me to devote my attention to other issues.

Thomas Christopher, Evanston, IL
March 15, 2000

George K. Thiruvathukal's Acknowledgments

I, too, wish to begin by acknowledging my favorite Java site, Intelligentsia, which, simply put, is one of the best places to enjoy coffee in Chicago (and possibly the world!) Anyway, if you are thinking about writing a book, I suggest ordering some right away from *http://www.intelligentsia.com* (they do deliver to non-Chicago addresses), and you'll have a book written in no time.

I also wish to acknowledge DePaul University, School of Computer Science, Telecommunications, and Information Sciences (CTI) and Helmut Epp for providing the Java and High-Performance Computing (JHPC) lab for us to carry out part of this work. I thank the members of JHPC, who have provided help in one way or another, including John Shafaee, Luiz C. de Oliveira, and Arti Singh. I also extend thanks to Andy Korczynski and Lovely S. Thomas (past members of JHPC), whose work on the Reflective RMI system led to a next-generation system called Generic Method Invocation (the subject of Chapter 12).

A special word of thanks is in order for Mary Franz of Prentice Hall. She has been enthusiastic about this project from day one, and she has shown extraordinary vision by understanding the importance of parallel computing in a distributed world, where server–side computing will play an increasing role in E-commerce and application servers. Thanks also to the reviewers for their inspiring feedback that helped us to finish the last 5% of this book, which often takes 95% of the time! A very special thanks to Rose Kernan, who has really helped us to catch the bugs that are the hardest to debug—writing bugs.

Last, but most certainly not least, I wish to acknowledge the loving support of my wife, Nina Wilfred. She has been most kind and patient, during our first year of marriage, to accommodate me and this project. Her love and patience are rarely found in life, and this book is much better simply by virtue of her presence. I think now is an excellent time for that European vacation.

Surf's up! And Go Cubs!

George K. Thiruvathukal, Chicago, IL

March 15, 2000

Chapter **1**

Foundations

▼ THE VON NEUMANN MACHINE

▼ FLYNN'S TAXONOMY

▼ SPEEDUP AND EFFICIENCY

▼ AMDAHL'S LAW

▼ SCALABILITY

▼ PROBLEMS OF PARALLELISM

▼ PROGRAMMING TECHNIQUES

▼ CHAPTER WRAP-UP

▼ EXERCISES

J ava is an object-oriented programming language, this much is true. It's also an Internet programming language. These two features of Java are enough to make it an exciting and compelling programming language in its own right. However, Java is successful to a large extent because it is the quintessential concurrent and distributed programming language.

Concurrency is a far-reaching topic. This book is primarily focused on the use of Java for programming the "server side" (symmetric multiprocessor systems) and clusters of workstations. This chapter provides an overview of the key principles behind concurrent and parallel systems with discussions of architecture, performance analysis, challenges and complications arising in concurrent systems, and a quick survey of some programming techniques. These discussions are intentionally generic in nature. If you absolutely must "take a sip" of Java, please proceed directly to Chapter 2. We strongly recommend, however, that you read this chapter throughout your travels with this book.

1

The von Neumann Machine

A discussion of parallel computing must begin with a discussion of sequential computing and the von Neumann machine—our sequential computer. The von Neumann machine is one of the computer designs of John von Neumann. A processor fetches instructions and data from a memory, operates on the data, and writes the results back into memory. Computation is accomplished by making small incremental changes in the global memory.

The problem with the von Neumann machine is that the design relies on making a sequence of small changes, a highly sequential process. Note that current programming languages are designed assuming that the von Neumann machine will be used. The assignment statement fetches data from memory on the right hand side, performs computations, and writes results back into the memory for the left-hand-side variable. The statements are executed sequentially, with control accomplished by branches. In the language, the branches are given the syntactic sugar of `if` statements, `while` statements, and so on.

There is a problem in trying to speed up von Neumann machines. They are inherently sequential in principle. Attempts may be made to execute several instructions at once (super-scalar execution), but that gives only a few times the speedup. Similarly, it is difficult to gain high speedup from a program written in a von Neumann language without doing an extensive rewrite of the program.

Flynn's Taxonomy

Flynn produced a taxonomy of parallel machines that is widely used. He classified computers with respect to how many different instruction streams they are fetching and executing at the same time, and by how many data sets (data streams) they are fetching and processing. His taxonomy is as follows:

- SISD—single instruction stream–single data stream: the familiar von Neumann machine. Fetching one sequence of instructions and fetching the data and the instructions address from one memory.

- MIMD—(pronounced "mim-dee") multiple instruction–multiple data stream: a multiprocessor or multicomputer (and the subject of this book). Here, several processors are fetching their own instructions and operating on the data those instructions specify. To gain speedup on individual programs, these processors must synchronize and communicate with each other.

- SIMD—(pronounced "sim-dee") single instruction stream–multiple data stream: These machines typically are used to process arrays. A single processor fetches instructions and broadcasts those instructions to a number of data units. Those data units fetch data and perform operations on them. The appropriate programming language for such machines has a single flow of control (like a Von Neumann language), but has operations that can operate on entire arrays, rather than on individual array elements. The hardware needs ways in which data units will not execute some operations based on tests of their own data (e.g., so that some units can turn off for the `then` and others for the `else` parts of `if-then-else` statements), and it needs to let the control unit read the `and` or the `or` of the results of data tests at the data units (e.g. to know when all units have finished executing a while loop).

- MISD—multiple instruction stream–single data stream: It's not totally clear what machines fit into this category. One kind of MISD machine would be designed for fail-safe operation; several processors perform the same operations on the same data and check each other to be sure that any failure will be caught.

  Another proposed MISD machine is a systolic array processor. Streams of data are fetched from memory and passed through arrays of processors. The individual processors perform their own operations on the streams of data passing through them, but they have no control over where to fetch data from.

MIMD machines are divided into two varieties: shared memory and distributed memory. Shared-memory machines have several processors accessing a common memory. Unless the machine is for a special purpose, the processors will be accessing the shared memory through some sort of address-mapping hardware. To be used for parallel processing, the software must let the processors actually share that memory in their address spaces. Shared-memory machines have significant advantages for programming. All of the processors working on a common problem can share the large data structures (e.g., large arrays) and cooperate by working on parts of the data structure, while other processors work on other parts.

The problems with programming shared-memory machines have to do with synchronizing the processors. Since the processors work by fetching and storing small data elements, a processor updating a large data structure cannot read or write it in one instant. This means that if one processor is reading and another writing the same data structure at the same time, the reader may be getting some old components and some new ones. The state will not be consistent, and the computation will therefore become confused ("confused," meaning there is an inconsistent state.) Similarly, if two processors are trying to write the same structure at the same time, parts of the two writes will be confused. Therefore, the software for shared-memory parallel machines must provide facilities for coordinating processors. The problem with programming is to make sure the coordination is done correctly.

There is another problem with shared-memory machines: It's hard to build them to be large. The switch between the processors and memory becomes a bottleneck, limiting the traffic between processors and memory, or it tends to become expensive or slow. This is particularly the problem with UMA machines (Uniform Memory Access). UMA machines take the same amount of time to get to all memory locations. As the UMA machines get larger, physical packaging alone dictates that some memory will get further from some processors than it will for smaller versions. When the problems of switching more processors to more memory chips are added, UMAs can be expected to get slower still.

An alternative to UMA is NUMA (nonuniform memory access) machines. Typically, NUMA machines have some memory attached to each processor, which the processor can access quickly. To get to the memory attached to another processor, the processor must go through some sort of switch, which slows down the access. By careful placement and replication of some data and subroutines, NUMA machines can have many of the programming conveniences of UMA machines, but with cheaper hardware, larger numbers of processors, and reasonable speed. However, programmers tend to discover that they can gain even better performance by copying entire data structures into local memory, operating on them locally, and writing them back to local memory. At this point, their code becomes more complex and less portable.Distributed-memory MIMD machines (MIMD-DM) are much easier to build, but much harder to program. The MIMD-DM machine is basically a collection of computers, called nodes, connected through a high-performance network. The major programming problem is that the individual machines must coordinate and communicate data by message passing; it often requires entire redesigns of programs to port them to MIMD-DM machines. The only way to access data on another node is to have that node send it to you. For that to happen, the other node must know that you need the data—or you must send it a request message, and it must be programmed to reply.

It is arguable that the change from shared-memory to distributed-memory machines is a radical shift; it goes to the root of how one thinks about computations. On the von Neumann machine, the most important entity is the process, the program in execution. The process fetches instructions and manipulates data, thereby embodying both control and data. On a shared-memory machine, the process is still the most important entity, although there are now multiple threads of execution within the data space. But at the global level, on a distributed-memory machine, messages convey data across the machine and the arrival of messages enables computations. At the global level of distributed-memory machines, it is the messages that embody control and data. Hence, the messages are more important than the processes that are running on the nodes.

Control–Memory Taxonomy

Flynn's taxonomy is usually applied to machines with von Neumann processors. Further insight may be gained by considering other control mechanisms. The von Neumann machines may be characterized as "control driven"; it is the flow of control represented by the program counter that schedules operations for execution.

"Data-driven" processors schedule operations for execution when their operands become available. In the paradigmatic variety of data-driven machines, scalar data values flow in tokens over an interconnection network to the instructions that work upon them (hence the term "data flow"). When a token arrives, the hardware checks that all operands are present and, if they are, schedules the instruction for execution. Data-flow machines are easily built distributed memory.

It is also possible to store the data in shared memory and signal each instruction whose operand is now available. Similarly, there is a technique for handling large data structures. An entire data structure cannot be passed in a token, so the structure is stored in a memory where components of the structure arrive as they are computed. Fetches of the elements arrive in tokens and wait for the value of the element to arrive, whereupon the value is sent on in a token to where the fetch specifies.

A "demand-driven" processor performs computations when values are demanded. For example, when the value of a binary operator is demanded, the operator, in turn, demands the values of its operands. A common implementation of demand-driven processors is based on "reductions," which occur when a functional program is repeatedly rewritten until the solution is computed. The rewritings include replacing an operator applied to data values with its result and replacing a function call with the function body, with the actual parameters substituted for the formal. Reductions are performed on an internal representation of the program. Two common representations are graphs and strings. Graphs consist of nodes linked together with pointers and hence work best with shared memory. Strings can be spread across a chain of processors so that an individual processor can reduce subexpressions contained entirely in its memory and neighboring processors can shift expressions falling across their boundary into one of them. "Pattern-driven" computation is typically done without specialized hardware and is implemented atop von Neumann machines. Shared-memory, pattern-driven programming usually means parallel-logic programming. Distributed-memory, pattern-driven programming is represented in this book by Active Messages and Concurrent Aggregates.

Speedup and Efficiency

We want to use parallelism to compute answers more quickly. How much more quickly? We define speedup as

$$S = \frac{T_1}{T_n}$$

where T_1 is defined as the execution time of the best sequential algorithm for the problem on a single processor, and T_n is the execution time of the parallel algorithm on n processors. Notice several things:

1. T_n should be smaller than T_1, since the parallel algorithm should run faster than the sequential algorithm.

2. The larger the value of S, the better. This is coherent with a cultural metaphor of bigger is better[1] (even though we want the smallest run time possible).

3. T_1 is supposed to be the run time of the best possible sequential algorithm, but in general, the best possible algorithm is an unknown quantity. Thus, it is often the case that T_1 is simply a version of the parallel program that is run sequentially.

4. We define linear speedup as

$$S = \frac{T_1}{T_n} = n$$

We would expect that speedup cannot be better (larger) than linear, and indeed should be smaller. If the entire work of the sequential program could be evenly divided among the n processors, they could all complete in $1/n$ the time. But it is unlikely that the work could be divided evenly; programs tend to have a sequential part, such as initialization or reading data from or writing results to sequential files. If the sequential part can only be done on a single machine, then only the rest can be run in parallel. We will examine this in more detail when we discuss Amdahl's law. Even if the program could be evenly divided among n processors, the processors would probably have to coordinate their work with each other, which would require extra instruction executions beyond the sequential program. Therefore, T_n may be $1/n$ of a larger value than T_1.

Moreover, T_1 is supposed to be the best known sequential algorithm.[2] If the parallel algorithm runs faster on a single machine, it would be a better sequential algorithm, and therefore, you'd use it. So you can expect the algorithm T_1 to be at least as good as the algorithm for T_n. You cannot expect any help from differences in the algorithms in achieving even linear speedup.

However, in practice, super-linear speedup ($S > n$) is sometimes observed. There are several reasons for this:

- The hardware is different. The parallel machine has more processors, and hence more cache memory, for one thing. Better locality and pipelining can also play a role.

---

[1] In our lab, we also are known to say that "working software is even better."

[2] Another way to think of this is to rewrite the program such that it has nothing concurrent about it. It is unlikely that the time of the concurrent program would beat the nonconcurrent program time, simply because of the overheads involved to run a concurrent program.

- The algorithm is different. For example, a depth-first search on a sequential machine might be translated into a collection of depth-first searches on the nodes of a parallel computer, but the parallel depth-first searches would have an element of a breadth-first search. A single depth-first search might spend a large amount of time on one fruitless branch, whereas with several searches, it is likely that another path might find the solution more quickly.

Efficiency is defined as

$$E = \frac{S}{n} = \frac{T_1}{nT_n} = \frac{T_1/n}{T_n}$$

The formula shows two ways to think about efficiency. Suppose you were to run the parallel program on a serial machine. The serial machine would have to execute all the parallel processes. If there are n processes, then the serial execution shouldn't take more than about nT_n (assuming that the time to swap the processor from one process to another is negligible). Efficiency, then, would measure the ratio of the actual sequential time to the worst expected time to execute the n processes sequentially.

Suppose that, on the other hand, you calculate how long you would expect it to take to run the sequential algorithm on n processors, assuming linear speedup. That gives you T_1/n. The efficiency would be the ratio of execution time with linear speedup to observed execution time. If speedup is no greater than linear, efficiency will be less than or equal to 1.

Amdahl's Law

Amdahl's law[3] does not really deserve the title of *law*. It is merely a back-of-the-envelope attempt (or conjecture) to prove that there are severe limits to the speedup that can be achieved by a parallel program. Amdahl's law asserts that there is a serial part of any parallel program that must be executed sequentially, and the time required for this part will be a lower limit on the time the program takes to execute. Consider a serial program that executes in time T. Let's calculate the best speedup we could achieve if a fraction f of the exe-

---

[3]Amdahl is the name of computer scientist–engineer, Gene Amdahl, who is one of the pioneers in the field of parallel-computing architecture. The Amdahl corporation is named after him.

cution time is taken up by sequential execution. If you divide the parallel execution time into the serial and parallel parts, you get speedup with an *upper bound* of

$$S = \frac{T}{fT + \frac{(1-f)T}{n}}$$

We get this equation by taking the definition of speedup and breaking down T_n into the time taken by the serial fraction (fT) and the time taken by the parallel fraction [$(1-f)T$]. We divide the parallel fraction by n to calculate the best we could expect from a linear speedup.

T appears as a factor in both the numerator and the denominator. Thus, it can be removed, which leads to an equation not involving T, or

$$S = \frac{1}{f + \frac{(1-f)}{n}}$$

As n approaches infinity (i.e., the number of processors is increased), we arrive at the folllowing limit:

$$\lim_{n \to \infty} S = \lim_{n \to \infty} \frac{1}{f + \frac{(1-f)}{n}} = \frac{1}{f}$$

So, no matter how many processors we use, we would not expect to gain any more speedup than the reciprocal of the serial fraction. If five percent of the program must run sequentially, speedup will never be better than 20.

Scalability

A flaw in the reasoning behind Amdahl's law is that it deals with fixed-sized problems and questions how much faster they can be run. This is not, however, the way massively parallel processors are used. Take the example of weather forecasting. The calculations are made by superimposing a mesh onto the atmosphere and calculating pressure, temperature, humidity, etc., at each mesh point, repeatedly using the values at the surrounding points at small time intervals. The more numerous the mesh points and the smaller the time intervals, the better is the forecast. But the more calculations that are required, the slower the program runs. And for weather forecasting, if the calculation takes too long, it loses all value. When presented with a faster machine, weather forecasters will use more grid points and a smaller step size. They increase the problem size to the largest possible value that allows the answer to be reached in the same amount of time.

Let's rephrase the calculation, starting with a parallel program with serial fraction g that runs in time R on n processors. If we ran the calculation on a single processor, how long would it take? The answer is

$$T = gR + n(1 - g)R$$

This equation follows, since the serial fraction will still take the same time $(g \times R)$ and the n parts of the parallel fraction $[(1-g) \times R]$ would have to be interleaved.

This results in the speedup calculation

$$S = \frac{gR + n(1 - g)R}{R} = g + n(1 - g)$$

a linear speedup with slope $(1 \times g)$. The efficiency is

$$E = 1 - g\frac{n - 1}{n}$$

which approaches the parallel fraction as the number of processors increases. In this formulation, there is no theoretical limit on speedup. As long as we scale the problem size to the size of the machine, we will not run into limits.

Another aspect of this argument against Amdahl's law is that, as the problem size increases, the serial fraction may decrease. Consider a program that reads in two N-by-N matrices, multiplies them, and writes out the result. The serial I/O time grows as N^2, while the multiplication, which is highly parallelizable, grows as N^3.

Problems of Parallelism

Grain Size

Grain size loosely refers to the amount of computation that is done between communications or synchronizations. Too large a grain size can result in an unbalanced load. Too small a grain size can waste too much time on system overhead. Consider eight processors that are to execute 10 independent tasks, each of which takes t time units. Suppose the system takes s time units to run a task. The schedule looks like this:

- Six processors execute one task completing in time $t + s$.

- Two processors execute two tasks completing in time $2t + 2s$.

- The overall completion time is the maximum of any processor's completion time: $2t + 2s$.

Suppose we divide each task into 10 independent tasks, giving us 100 tasks for the entire job. Each task now will take $t/10$ time units. The schedule now looks like this:

- Four processors execute 12 tasks completing at time $12t/10 + 12s$.

- Four processors execute 13 tasks completing at time $13t/10 + 13s$.

- The overall completion time is the maximum of any processor's completion time: $13t/10 + 13s$.

How do these compare? If s is negligible compared to t, then schedule (1) will complete in $2t$, and schedule (2) in $1.3t$. However, $13s$ is significantly larger than $2s$, so system overhead s, being even a small fraction of grain size t, might destroy all of the advantages of load balancing. What is the cutover point? That is, at what fraction of t does s cause schedule (2) to take as long as schedule (1)? The answer is

$$2t + 2s = 1.3t + 13s$$

$$s = (0.7/11)t = 0.064t$$

So, if s is even seven percent of t, the version with 100 tasks will be as slow as the version with 10. So how do you choose a good grain size? Folklore suggests that one millisecond of execution between communications is a reasonable amount. Other folklore suggests that processing 300–400 array elements between communications is good on some systems. What you will probably have to do is experiment for yourself to find a good grain size. By parameterizing your actual code, you can enable the possibility to experiment.

Starvation

Starvation results when some user computations do not get adequate processor time. Here's an example of starvation on a distributed-memory machine: For some distributed computations, it is difficult to determine if they are finished. There are some algorithms that send system probe messages around to inquire about the state of the computation. Starvation can result if the probe messages use up significant processor time, making processor time unavailable to the user computations. On shared-memory machines, processors lock and unlock resources. When a resource is unlocked, one of the processors waiting for it (if any) is allowed to proceed. If the resource allocation mechanism is unfair, some waiting processes may be long delayed, while other processes acquire the resource repeatedly.

Deadlock

A set of processes is deadlocked if each process is waiting for resources that other processes in the set hold and none will release until the processes have been granted the other resources that they are waiting for. There are four conditions required for deadlock:

- Mutual Exclusion: Only a process in possession of a resource may proceed.

- Hold and Wait: Processes will hold resources and wait for others.

- No Preemption: A resource may not be removed from one process to give to another.

- Circular Wait: There exists a cycle of processes holding resources and waiting for resources the next process in the cycle holds.

There are three things you can try to do about deadlock:

- You can try to detect when deadlock has occurred and then try to do something about it. For example, you may cancel one or more of the processes involved to free the resources they hold.Usually, this requires the presence of a monitor process that effectively acts as a proxy for any resource request.

- You can try to avoid creating a deadlock by checking before each resource allocation to determine whether the allocation might result in a deadlock and then allowing processes to proceed only if it is safe to do so.

- You can try to make it impossible for deadlock to occur. The easiest prevention is to eliminate circular waits by numbering the resources and requesting resources in ascending numeric order. That is, never request a resource if you already possess one with a higher number.

Flooding and Throttling

Strangely, one of the problems with parallelism is having too much rather than too little. For many parallel algorithms (especially divide and conquer and combinatoric search), a problem is repeatedly broken into smaller parts that can be run in parallel. Once the number of parallel parts significantly exceeds the number of processors available, it is sometimes detrimental to create more parallelism: All processors will be kept busy anyway, the time to create more parallel tasks will be wasted, and the storage for those task descriptions will tax the parallel machine's memory.

Preventing a flood of parallelism typically requires extra programming: The algorithm must be broken down into the code that is executed before enough parallel tasks are created, which creates more tasks, and the code that is executed after sufficient tasks are available, which does its work within a single task.

Choice of when to switch from creating more tasks to executing within tasks can be made statically, before the algorithm runs, or dynamically, in response to the system load. Dynamic switching requires additional information about the current state of the system, which is oftentimes not available or is highly imprecise.

Layout

The layout of a data structure on a distributed-memory machine can make a significant difference in performance. There are two interacting concerns. First, it is important to balance the load so that all nodes have approximately the same amount of work to do. Secondly, it helps to have most communication between neighboring nodes; there won't be as many queueing delays as messages contend for communication edges along longer paths.

Consider, though, a simulation of the cosmos: If you divide space into equally sized cubes and assign one cube to each node of a multicomputer, then communication of gravitation and movements of mass can be done between neighboring nodes on a mesh-connected computer. Unfortunately, there will be vast regions of nearly empty space mapped to some regions of nodes, while those parts of space with clusters of galaxies will be mapped into other nodes; that is, the load will be horribly imbalanced. A way to balance the load is to divide space into a larger number of regions and randomize their mapping onto the nodes, say, by hashing their coordinates to give the node number. Then you can count on the law of large numbers to balance the load, but communication between neighboring regions is no longer between neighboring nodes.

Suppose we have N rows of an array that must be processed. How can we divide them evenly among P nodes?

1. We could give floor $\lfloor N/P \rfloor$ rows to each of the first $P-1$ nodes and the remaining rows to the last node. If $N = 15$ and $P = 4$, nodes 0, 1, and 2 get three rows, and node 3 gets six. The load is imbalanced, and the completion time will be dominated by the last node.

2. We could give ceiling $\lceil N/P \rceil$ rows to each of the first $P-1$ nodes and the remaining rows to the last. If $N = 21$ and $P = 5$, we would assign five rows to each of the first four nodes and one row to the last. The last is underutilized, but it's not as severe as case (1), where the last node was the bottleneck.

3. We could try to assign the rows so that no node has more than one row more than any other node. An easy way to do this is to assign node i all rows j such that j mod $P = i$, assuming rows are numbered zero through $N-1$ and nodes are numbered zero through $P-1$. Node i will contain rows $i, i + P, i + 2P, i + 3P, \ldots$.

We can assign blocks of rows to nodes, as in (1) and (2), but guarantee that no node has more than one more row than any other node, as in (3). Assign node i the rows in the range L_i to U_i inclusive, where

$$L_i = \text{floor}(N/P) + \min(i, N \bmod P)$$
$$U_i = L_i + 1 - 1$$

Some algorithms divide arrays into regions that communicate along their edges, so messages will be shorter and faster if the perimeters of regions are smaller: Square regions tend to be better than long, rectangular regions.

Latency

As machines get larger, physical packaging itself requires that components get further apart. Therefore, it will take longer for information to flow between some components rather than others. This implies that the larger, shared-memory machines will be NUMA (nonuniform memory access). Data layout becomes increasingly important. Algorithms may benefit by being rewritten to fetch remote objects, operate on them locally, and then write them back, rather than just manipulating them in place.

Latency is also one of the considerations in laying out tasks and data on distributed-memory machines. On distributed-memory machines, one has the extra option of using asynchronous message passing to allow other computations to be performed while messages are being passed.

Scheduling

Scheduling assigns tasks to processors to be run in a particular order or at particular times. There is a large amount of literature devoted to process scheduling, the major import of which is this: Almost any scheduling of activities on processors is an *NP*-hard problem. For practical purposes, the meaning of *NP*-hard is this: The worst-case time to run an *NP*-hard algorithm grows so rapidly (e.g., doubling when you add one element to the input), that you may not get a solution for a modestly sized problem before the sun burns out. Do not seek perfect solutions to *NP*-hard problems. Instead, look for ways to quickly get solutions that are reasonably good most of the time. Static scheduling of tasks on processors would be done before the tasks are run. Dynamic scheduling assigns tasks during execution. Self-scheduling is a form of dynamic scheduling in which the processors themselves select which task to execute next.

The techniques for partitioning rows among nodes that we saw in the discussion of layout are also applicable to processor scheduling on shared-memory machines. For technique (3), an easy way to assign process i all rows j such that j mod $P = i$ is to handle the rows in a loop:[4]

```
for (j = my_id; j<n; j +=P) {
  process row j
}
where the rows are numbered 0 through N-1
my_id is the node number in the range 0..P-1
```

Rather than assign entire rows or columns to processors, better load balancing can sometimes be accomplished by assigning groups of elements. If there are K total elements in an array, we can assign them numbers 0 through $K-1$, assign ranges of those numbers to processors, and convert from the element number to the array indices when necessary. For an $M \times N$ matrix A with zero origin addressing, element A[i,j] would be given the number i*N+j in row major order. Similarly, the element with number q would correspond to A[i,j], where

```
i = floor(q/N)
j = q mod N
```

A simple form of self-scheduling for K elements is to keep the index C of the next element to be processed and to allocate items by incrementing or decrementing C. The following code is illustrative:

```
initially, C = K-1
i = 0;
while (i>=0) {
    lock C_lock;
    i = C;
    C = C-1;
    unlock C_lock;
    if (i >= 0) process item i;
}
```

However, if the processing of a single element takes little time, the grain size is too small. Of course the processor could allocate some constant number of elements greater than one at a time. This is clearly better for grain size, but may still have load balance problems. An improved self-scheduling algorithm has each of the P processors allocate ceiling (C/P) elements (i.e., allocate 1/P of the remaining elements):

---

[4]This technique is shown in the examples throughout the book and in Chapter 12.

```
initially, C = K
low = 0;
while (low>=0) {
        lock C_lock;
        t = ceiling(C/P);
        if (t == 0)
            low=-1;
        else {
            high = C-1;
            low = C = C-t;
        }
        unlock C_lock;
        if (low>=0)
            process items low through high inclusive;
}
```

Programming Techniques

There are a number of techniques for programming MIMD parallel processors. There are two general techniques based on SIMD and MIMD computers. Data-parallel computation is based on SIMD. This involves a common data structure which is divided up among the processors so that the processors perform the same operations at the same time, but on different data elements. Control-parallel computation is based on MIMD. Here, the processors execute different code at the same time. There are a number of ways to divide up the computations. In the job-jar (or processor farm) organization, the program keeps a list of jobs (or tasks, or chores, or whatever you wish to call them); we call this list the job jar. When a processor becomes free, it pulls a job out of the job jar and executes it. The job may place more jobs in the job jar. In the pipelined or stream organization, a stream of data passes down a chain of processes, each of which reads, transforms, and writes the stream.

A reactive object organization is based on message passing. All computation is performed by objects responding to messages. Similar to the reactive object system is the client–server organization: Client processes send requests to servers, which perform the services requested and send responses back.

Macro dataflow is based on the data-driven computation model. The presence of its operands triggers a computation that uses them. The "macro" refers to the operands being larger than individual scalars (e.g., sections of arrays).

Chapter Wrap-up

The intention of this chapter has been to provide a "crash-course" style introduction to parallel computing. The word "Java" has not been mentioned in this chapter, since this discussion is intended to be brief and to provide an essential overview. The remainder of this book is dedicated to putting the ideas into practice. This chapter gives you the information you'll need over the long haul to give a "report card" to Java as a programming language. Both authors believe that Java has the potential to be a great language for parallel computing. There are many issues that must be overcome in order for Java to be taken seriously as a high-performance computing language. We will not dedicate bandwidth in this book to explaining all of the issues. We have provided some performance data for selected algorithms to illustrate the good, the bad, and the ugly of Java performance. For an informed discussion of the issues, Java must address to become the grande langue for high-performance computing, an excellent source of information is the Java Grande Forum, of which one of the authors has served as Secretary General and contributor to the Java Grande Report. More information is available at *http://www.javagrande.org* on the Internet.

Exercises

1. Networks of workstations and rack-mounted CPUs connected with fast Ethernet are the dominant platform for parallel and distributed computing today. Why has this occured? Into which classification would you place such an architecture, using Flynn's taxonomy?

2. Why is linear speedup seldom achieved in practice?

3. Another interesting *law* is known as Moore's law, which essentially states that processor speed is doubling every year. In practical terms, your algorithm will run twice as fast as it does today—if you are willing to wait a year. Some have used Moore's law to suggest that parallel computing is dead and no longer has a place in the world. (We are inclined to disagree, since Prentice Hall published this book.) What is the potential flaw in the reasoning behind the law? Show an example of a problem that requires parallel computing to have any hope of being solved in a reasonable amount of time. Why will waiting a year not be acceptable for this problem?

4. Explain the flaw in the counterargument to Amdahl's law, which essentially showed that speedup and efficiency can be obtained simply by increasing the problem size?

5. Explain how processor pipelining and locality can play a role in the super-linear speedup effect that was discussed.

6. This problem requires you to study the manual pages of your operating system. How long does it take to acquire a lock in your operating system? How many multiplications (floating point or integer) of two scalar values can be done in the same period of time. Can a ratio be obtained? What are the implications on grain size when locking is involved?

7. Latency is a major problem in NUMA systems, as well as in ordinary networking. How long does it take for a zero-byte TCP/IP message to be transmitted from one computer to another on your local area network (Ethernet)? Using the same methodology as in the previous question, what are the implications on grain size when network latency is involved?

8. Flynn's taxonomy presents the entire gamut of known (and even unknown) computer architectures for high-performance computing. What architectures are in use today? Which ones are not in use? Are there any architectures that have been out of use that are now coming back into use? Is there anything that Flynn's architecture has left out? Which architecture makes the most economical sense?

9. In the 1990s and the rolling 0s (2000s), the field of parallel computing could more aptly be described as clustered computing. What is a cluster? What kinds of machines make up a cluster? What kind of network is needed to support a cluster adequately? Is "cluster" just a euphemism for commodity parallel machine?

10. You don't need to read this book to determine that Java programs run slower than hand-coded FORTRAN and C (or C++). Considering the discussion in this chapter about T_1, the serial performance, pick one of your favorite codes (say, matrix multiplication of integers/floats). Write the program in C and again in Java, making every effort to make best use of the language. How does the performance compare? This would appear to be a major strike against Java. How would you justify the lower performance to someone antagonistic to the Java cause? Will waiting a year (assuming processor speed doubles) make the Java version faster than the FORTRAN- or C-equivalent's performance (using today's performance numbers)?

## Chapter 2

Threads

▼ WHY IS MULTITHREADING USEFUL?

▼ OVERVIEW OF THE JAVA THREADS CLASSES

▼ OTHER EXAMPLES

▼ CONCEPTS

▼ EXAMPLE QUICK TOUR OF JAVA THREADS FUNCTIONS

▼ EXERCISES

T hreads are the fundamental unit of concurrency in the Java programming language. This chapter provides a very light introduction to Java threads programming. If you are already familiar with the concept of a thread, it is safe to skip ahead to the next section; however, the last section of this chapter provides a quick overview of the methods provided in the `Thread` class. We will presume that you understand the basics of these methods in the many examples presented in the next chapter.

The chapter opens with a discussion of why you should care about multithreading. Although this book is mostly about high-performance Java computing, multithreading is useful even in applications that do not require the best possible performance (e.g., making a GUI more responsive). A quick overview of the essential classes and interfaces is presented, followed by a more detailed overview of the methods found in these classes. A few small examples are presented so that you may become familiar with threads. In the next chapter, we will assume that you understand the skeletal structure of a threaded class—a class that either inherits `Thread` or implements the `Runnable` interface.

19

Why is Multithreading Useful?

When faced with using a language feature that does not appear to be very easy to use, this is often a perfectly valid opening question (one often asked by our students, in fact). Multithreading is the vehicle to concurrency in the Java programming language. This term has been defined in the preceding chapter. Of course, this usually leads to the next most common question: Why is concurrency useful?

At this point we usually turn to the confused students and, after a bit of hand waving, are prompted to come up with examples.

Consider the Web browser. Web browsers are used to view Web pages, among other interesting things. Web pages, in fact, are not usually single pages, but instead consist of text, embedded images, or pages (in the case of frames). In order to construct what looks like a perfectly beautiful (or atrocious) looking Web page in your browser window, the Web browser may, in fact, have to issue multiple so-called HTTP requests to obtain all of the parts needed to construct your Web page. Early Web browsers (e.g., Mosaic, the mother of Netscape) would issue HTTP requests serially in order to obtain each of the parts. The executive summary is that it would take a long time to actually *get* the Web pages.

It may not be immediately obvious why the performance is so bad; however, consider that each of the requests is posted separately *and* the Web browser must wait for each result separately. Sometimes, the requests are not even going to the same site, which is very common when browsing pages today. If you watch the status bar carefully while visiting a commerce site, observe how many pages contain embedded advertising links. These are usually coming from a different Web site than the one being contacted initially. In any event, a network request takes a short amount of time, and waiting for a response takes a long time. Why not post a set of requests at the same time and then wait for the results to come back?

By answering this innocent question, the usefulness of threads becomes almost immediately apparent. It also becomes apparent that the waiting game becomes a bit more complicated, too. One advantage of processing one request at a time is that the response is known to belong to a particular request. When posting multiple requests concurrently, the responses must be properly sorted out. This is not only to ensure the proper display of a page, but also to know that a particular request for part of a page has been completely fulfilled.

There are other situations where threads and concurrency appear to be particularly useful:

- The example just presented can be applied to a number of network programming problems in general. Network programming is used extensively in distributed-systems applications, such as transaction processing and other network services (of which a Web server is a specific example).

- Parallel processing (a subject of great interest to the authors) is used in science and business to solve large-scale problems with the help of multiple processors. Using threads, parts of your program can run on multiple processors and, if done properly, reduce the program run time considerably.

Later chapters of this book are concerned with applications of threads to parallel processing and network computing.

Overview of the Java Threads Classes

The use of threads is pervasive to the entire design of Java. The following list defines the various classes and interfaces that are provided, and an executive summary of the role played by each in the Java design:

- `Thread`—the class that is responsible for creating and managing a thread.

- `ThreadGroup`—a class that allows all operations that apply to a `Thread` object to be generalized to a group of `Thread` instances.

- `Runnable`—an interface that can be implemented by a class that in turn will be used as a thread. Because `Runnable` is an interface, it is the preferred way of turning a class into a thread, in particular when the class already has a superclass (which is very common in practical applications).

- `Object`—this class is familiar to all Java programs. It is the ultimate superclass of any class. Java automatically extends the `Object` class whenever a class is being defined. Among its other features, `Object` provides the support needed for *thread synchronization* and *thread conditions*. These features are introduced much later, when *race conditions* are presented; however, it is very important to know that `Object` is a vital part of the threads' abstraction presented by Java to the programmer.

`Thread`: *The Class Responsible for Thread Creation and Execution*

The `Thread` class is usually the first class a Java programming student learns to write. For more experienced programmers, think of the `Thread` class as the way to model a thread control block. An instance of a Thread must be created for each thread you want to run.

Example 2-1 shows how to extend the `Thread` class to create your own threaded class. The class has been named `ThreadSkeleton` to indicate that this class represents a good starting point for making your own threaded classes.

Although this code is a "skeleton" class that does not appear to do much, it is, in fact, a complete working Java program. The static method `main()`—the entry or starting point in a Java program—is provided and creates an instance of the class `ThreadSkeleton`. It then starts the thread, using the `start()` method of class `Thread`. This will eventually result in the `run()` method being called when the thread is actually scheduled for

Example 2-1 `ThreadSkeleton`: Making Your Own `Thread` Subclass

```
public class ThreadSkeleton extends Thread {
    public ThreadSkeleton() {

    }

    public void run() {

    }

    public static void main(String[] args) {
        ThreadSkeleton t = new ThreadSkeleton();
        t.start();
    }
}
```

execution. The `run()` method provided here is not so interesting, since it contains an empty body, which performs something called a **NOP**—a term which means *no operation,*

Thread scheduling is a topic that is discussed in detail later; however, the separation of the `start()` and `run()` methods does merit a brief discussion. Why is it not the case that a thread is started immediately upon creation? The answer is one often used in the discussion of object-oriented design: separation of concerns. Creating a `Thread` class and defining a `run()` method establishes the potential for running a thread. It is not always the case that, when a concurrent activity is being defined, the intention is to run the activity right away. In addition to the `start()` method of the `Thread` class, there are other methods of interest, such as `setPriority()`. This method allows a thread to be scheduled at a different priority level, which should be done before actually starting the thread. This will ensure that the thread gets scheduled at the selected priority level. In later chapters, we will discuss other situations where it is *not* desirable to start a thread right away.

One example in which the `setPriority()` method would be desirable is the notion of a task graph. In a task graph, activities are arranged in a hierarchical fashion to indicate that a particular activity is dependent on other activities being completed. When the activities are actually completed, this triggers the execution of the waiting activity. Ideally, each activity in the graph is a thread (or a `Runnable`). The activities that are not awaiting other activities to be completed can be started immediately [with the `start()` method]. Activities that are waiting will not be started until explicitly started. The concept of a task graph is relatively straightforward. There are many possible implementations, and this example itself is enough to cause many headaches. It is mentioned here strictly to provide a preview of later discussion in this text.

Runnable: *Making Threads Without Extending the Thread Class*

An alternative to creating a subclass of Thread is to use the Runnable interface. This is usually the preferred method used to create a class that will be run as a thread, since Java only allows the use of single inheritance. (That is, you can only extend a single class.) In practical applications of object-oriented programming, a class other than Thread typically will be used as a superclass.

A sidebar will appear on how you decide when to inherit or not.

Example 2-2 provides an example of how a class can implement the Runnable interface, and then be run as a Thread. This class, RunnableSkeleton, can also be used as a building block to create your own multithreaded classes. The difference in this example pertains primarily to creation. Contrasted with the ThreadSkeleton class (which only required a single object to be instantiated and could subsequently be started as a thread with the start() method), one must first create an instance of RunnableSkeleton and then create an instance of Thread—which has a special constructor that requires a single Runnable parameter.

Example 2-2 RunnableSkeleton: Making Your Own Runnable Thread

```
public class RunnableSkeleton implements Runnable {
    public RunnableSkeleton() {

    }

    public void run() {

    }

    public static void main(String[] args) {
        RunnableSkeleton r = new RunnableSkeleton();
        Thread t = new Thread(r);
        t.start();
    }
}
```

Because the Thread class provides the actual implementation of the start() method, only instances of class Thread or a subclass of Thread may call this method. In the earlier example, in which Thread was being inherited, the class being defined (Thread-Skeleton) picked up all of the methods that are defined in the Thread class. The same is not true when the Runnable interface is implemented. An interface defines a precise contract of what methods must be implemented by the class that is declared to *implement* an interface. The interface `Runnable` is a contract to provide an implementation of a method called `void run()`.

The Relationship Between `Thread` and `Runnable`

There is an important relationship between `Runnable` and `Thread`, which can be studied more closely by looking at the Java Core API documentation on the Web, or by browsing the CD-ROM.

The class `Thread` is declared to implement the interface `Runnable`. Because it is declared as such, by definition, class `Thread` is required to do one of two things: implement the interface by providing either a definition for `run()` or an abstract method. The former has been adopted in Java, which means that you can extend class `Thread` without providing a definition for the `run()` method. In this case, a method will be inherited that "does nothing" in much the same way as our `ThreadSkeleton` class' `run()` method does.

Regardless of whether the `Thread` class is extended or the `Runnable` interface is implemented, it is always necessary to have an instance of `Thread` (or a subclass thereof) in order to actually start a thread in Java. Simply having an object that implements `Runnable` will not suffice.

In our experience, it is clearly preferable to implement the `Runnable` interface than it is to extend the `Thread` class; however, implementing `Runnable` can cause problems for programmers.

The first and foremost problem is that of convenience. When a subclass of `Thread` is created, any protected or public method of class `Thread` can be called directly. This same convenience is not available to a class that implements `Runnable`, since `Runnable` is not a subclass of `Thread`. In fact, if the class does not extend any class and instead implements `Runnable`, the only methods the class inherits are from the Java `Object` class.

The problem of convenience introduces a second, but related, problem. If a class implements `Runnable`, how does it actually get a reference to the `Thread` instance that has actually started it? The following box shows the definition of a static method, provided in the `Thread` class, that can help to address the problem:

```
public static native Thread currentThread()
```

This static method can be called at any time (even if a program has not explicitly created a `Thread` instance) in order to get a reference to the currently running thread. (There is at least one currently running thread by the time the `main()` method is called in your program.)

Any class that implements `Runnable` but does not extend `Thread` must make use of this static method in the event that there is a need to perform finer control on the currently running thread (something we will be doing extensively in later examples). An example of "finer control" would be `setPriority()`—a method provided by the `Thread` class to adjust the scheduling priority of a `Thread`—assuming that the platform being used actually supports preemptive scheduling, which is more or less true in all modern operating systems.

Hello World: A First Example of Multithreading

The intention of the foregoing discussion has been to introduce, with a bare minimum (skeleton) code example, two key ways in which threads are created in Java. Both examples, `ThreadSkeleton` and `RunnableSkeleton`, can, in fact, be run with your Java compiler. Also, they will run to completion, print no output, and exit normally.

We now proceed with a discussion of the "Hello World" multithreaded program. It suffices as a good introductory example to multithreading, but raises a number of interesting questions at the same time. Thus, this example should not be considered the banal example it usually is. You will want to understand what is going on in this example before proceeding to more advanced examples.

Example 2-3 shows the code for a multithreaded "Hello, World" program, which really does not print "Hello, World." Instead, the words "Hi" and "Lo" are printed on separate lines.

The `main()` method creates a second `Thread` that will be responsible for printing "Lo" to `System.out` (which is the "standard output" stream in Java). This thread will run concurrently with the `main()` method, and we expect to see the words "Hi" and "Lo" appear on the console without much ado.

It all seems very simple—perhaps too simple. The first question that comes to mind is, why would "Hi" be printed before "Lo"? Is it possible for the inverse situation to arise (i.e., "Lo" before "Hi")?

The answer all depends on thread scheduling. A detailed discussion of thread scheduling is presented much later in the book; however, a brief explanation is now in order.

As mentioned earlier, when a Java program starts, there is guaranteed to be at least one thread of execution in your program; otherwise, your program would not be able to run at all. This thread is responsible for managing the `main()` method. A thread typically runs until the underlying scheduler determines that another thread needs to run. This determination is usually made when a thread is no longer performing a "CPU-bound" activity, such as Input/Output (I/O). In the Hello-World example, the `main()` method does indeed start another thread by creating a "Hello" and then issuing the `start()` method call to schedule the thread for execution; however, the thread does not start immediately. (Recall the earlier discussion in the section entitled "`Thread`: The Class Responsible for Thread

Example 2-3 **Multithreaded Hello World**

```
/*
 * HelloThread.java - a threaded Hello World example.
 */

class Hello extends Thread {
    public static void main(String[]x) {
        Thread lo=new Hello();
        // lo.setPriority(Thread.MAX_PRIORITY);
        lo.start();
        System.out.println("Hi!");
    }

    public void run() {
        System.out.println("Lo!");
    }
}
```

Creation and Execution" on page 21). Thus, the `main()` method keeps running while the thread `lo` is in limbo, awaiting the opportunity to run. The point where the `main()` method does a `System.out.println("Lo!")` is where the main thread can get blocked. At this point, the `lo` thread can be scheduled. Unfortunately, when the `run()` method is called, it immediately encounters a `System.out.println("Lo!")`, which raises the possibility of the `lo` thread being blocked.

"Hi" will always be printed before "Lo" for two reasons. The first reason has to do with the queuing of requests. The request to output "Hi" precedes the request to output "Lo." The second reason has to do with blocking. Blocking causes a thread to be put on a waiting list. If the main thread got blocked awaiting I/O, the `lo` thread will also be blocked awaiting I/O. Assuming a FIFO ordering of queueing, (an assumption that is valid on all operating systems), the main thread, having been lucky enough to get its request queued first, is guaranteed to complete first if the operation can be completed at all (a safe assumption, most of the time, for sending output to standard output).

In short, the Hello World example is rather straightforward, but highlights many of the problems encountered when writing concurrent programs. In the case of this example, it is easy to prove or argue that the outcome is reasonable. In many other examples, it is sometimes difficult (if not impossible) to prove that the outcome will always be the same. The following is a glimpse of the problems you may encounter when writing concurrent programs. The rest of this chapter and the next are dedicated to exploring these issues in detail.

Implementing Interfaces and Extending Classes: What's the Deal?

The decision of whether to implement an interface or to extend a class is undoubtedly one of the most confusing decisions a Java programmer ever has to make. Unfortunately, much of the confusion is due to the term "interface" having been overloaded with multiple meanings. In the past, the notion of an interface was generically applied to mean "function prototypes" (in the case of C) and "public methods" (in C++, Java, and other OOL). Now an interface is defined in yet another way as a type that can indicate that a class fulfills a contract by actually providing implementations of a list of named methods.

Interfaces have proven to be particularly useful in one aspect of Java related to multi-threading and concurrency called event handling. The use of interfaces is pervasive to both the Abstract Windowing Toolkit (AWT) and Java Beans. AWT is Java's "low-level" framework for creating graphical user interfaces (GUIs). Interfaces are an important bridge between GUI classes (which generate events) and other classes (which handle the events). When an object needs to be notified of a certain event (e.g., a button was pressed, which resulted in an `ActionEvent` instance being created), it can subscribe to the event by registering itself with the GUI object that generates the event. In order to do this, however, the class of the object must be declared to implement the appropriate interface (i.e., `ActionListener`) and provide the function that will actually process the event (`ActionEvent`). This allows for the safest possible implementation of event handling, since there is an explicit contract that must be fulfilled before the object can actually subscribe to the event(s) in question.

It is beyond the scope of this book to cover GUI and AWT in detail; however, this brief example illustrates that interfaces are a prized possession of the Java language and are highly useful.[1]

The following tip is intended for you to decide when to use inheritance (subclassing) or interfaces. You will find it helpful to refer to this box often, whenever you create a class.

Class Inheritance vs. Interface Implementation: The Litmus Test

When defining a class `Y` that extends `X`, ask yourself the question, "Is `Y` an `X`?"

Object-oriented design textbooks often refer to this test as the `IS-A` test. If the answer is no, class inheritance probably does not apply.

Thus, implementing an interface is the preferred option when the `IS-A` test does not pass, but there is a need to enforce a certain contract. A contract is a statement of behavior (which could be called the `MUST-DO` test) that must be fulfilled in order for a class to be used with other classes.

---

[1] As it turns out, we couldn't resist using graphical interfaces completely. Chapter 11 (Networking) shows the use of AWT to implement a simple SMTP mail client.

Inheritance has also proven to be very useful in Java. Inheritance allows the possibility of factoring out common elements that characterize every object. Consider the `Object` class in the Java language package (java.lang.Object). The `Object` class is often called the "root" of the hierarchy of classes in Java, because all classes (both built-in and your own) are ultimately descendents of the `Object` class. This means that there are certain things that all objects can do, regardless of how the class was defined. A few examples are provided below:

- **`String toString()`**: A method that will allow any object to be turned into a `String`. This method can be overridden to print the details of your own objects in a different format.

- **`boolean equals(Object another)`**: A method that allows two objects to be quickly compared to one another, usually with the intention of being placed in an indexed collection such as a Hashtable.

- **`Class getClass()`**: A method that allows any object to find out what its type is (so-called reflection or introspection). This can be useful in situations in which we don't know the actual type of an object and need a way to "discover" the type. For example, the declaration `Object var = new Integer(5)` causes the actual type of the object, Integer, to appear to be lost. One could find the actual (dynamic) type of var by calling `var.getClass()`. `var.getClass().getName()` would return the type "java.lang.Integer" as a `String`.

These are just a sampling of the methods that can be found in the `Object` class. It is worthwhile to study this class in detail, as it provides a good example of the benefits of inheritance. At first glance, virtually all of the given methods provide functionality that you would want every object to be able to do. You can study the additional methods in the `Object` class documentation at JavaSoft to learn about the other important methods.

The box, "Inheritance Gone South," provides an example of poorly done inheritance.

Concepts

Having provided a brief introduction to threads and how to make your own thread classes, we now return to a discussion of some essential principles that you will need to understand before continuing with "hard-core" multithreading.

We will cover the following topics here:

- a bit about history—where threads came from

- a bit about processes and threads in modern operating systems

- a bit about the Java threads model

- a bit about user vs. kernel scheduling

Inheritance Gone South.

In textbooks on OOP, inheritance (subclassing) has long been argued as one of the great accomplishments of the object paradigm. Recent examples of inheritance being misused may convince you to take a second look.

Consider the `Stack` class, which is provided in the Java utilities package (java.util.Stack). The `Stack` class is implemented as a subclass of the `Vector` class.

The notion of a `Stack` has always been rather well defined, especially if one considers the myriad of textbooks on data structures in which the interfaces of a `Stack` are always the same:

push—push an object onto the stack;

pop—pop an object from the stack;

empty—is the stack empty;

top—retrieve the object atop the stack.

Anyone using a `Stack` is expecting to get these methods, and the Java Stack class delivers exactly what is expected. Unfortunately, it also delivers functionality, which is not expected. This added functionality precisely violates the definition of what a Stack *is*.

To make this clear, the `Stack` class inherits all of the methods of `Vector`, which in turn inherently violate the clean semantics of a `Stack`. For example, the `removeElement()` method (a `Vector` method) allows objects to be removed from any position in the `Stack`, which results in a loss of transparency.

How does one fix the `Stack` class to restore transparency to the implementation? The answer is simple. Remove `Vector` as a superclass and use a *private* `Vector` instance to delegate the operations push, pop, empty, and top to the equivalent functions in *class* `Vector`. By so doing, the other `Vector` methods cannot be called without adding methods to the public methods in class `Stack`.

These issues are essential to understand what is really happening "behind the scenes" when you write a multithreaded program. Many operating systems cover these topics at a rather abstract level. Our discussion will center around concepts that are backed up by examples throughout the book.

A Little Bit of History

The earliest computers were huge and expensive, but they were essentially personal computers, since only one programmer at a time could use them. The very expense of the hardware led to the development of operating systems. One of the first innovations was batch systems—a batch of programs that are put on magnetic tape and executed by the expensive computer, one after another, thus saving the time of human programmers signing up for time and running their own programs. Another innovation was multiprogramming. This involves the machine's memory becoming partitioned into several areas, each executing a different program stream. The processor could be switched from one to another, so that it could work on one program while another was waiting for I/O.

As operating systems became more complex, it became more difficult to program them, especially using interrupts (which behave like asynchronous subroutine calls).

The great breakthrough in operating-system design came with Dijkstra's development of the T.H.E. system. He showed how to develop the system in layers (with each layer able to use the facilities of the layers below—these days called application program interfaces, or APIs), how to handle multiprogramming, how to write the system using concurrent processes, and even how to convert interrupts into process synchronization.

Some Definitions

To start, we need to remember some distinctions between hardware and software, and between software as code and software being executed.

A *processor* refers to the central processing unit (or units) of a computer. It is a piece of hardware that is usually part of a larger piece of hardware—the computer. A *multiprocessor* system is a computer with two or more processors. There are too many multiprocessor architectures to be listed here. A common multiprocessor in the marketplace is the so-called symmetric multiprocessor or SMP. An SMP is typically formed from 2–16 processors, all of which share a global memory and I/O devices through a common and arbitrated bus.

A *program* is a list of instructions to be executed by a processor. Traditionally, programs have been written in a number of ways: hand-coded machine language (not very common nowadays), assembler language, compiled languages (FORTRAN, C, and C++), and now, Java. In the case of Java, the program is always the same. The Java Virtual Machine is a program that can load user-defined classes to behave differently from session to session. Programs are generally created in one way or another as a result of *compilation*, which is the process of turning a source language into an executable form.

A *process*, or task, is the program in execution—that is, the processor actually carrying out the instructions. Processes support the principle of multiprograming (discussed shortly) and are managed by an operating system. The operating system itself is a process that allows other processes to run every so often, usually at some computed unit of time, known as a time slice.

These definitions are provided in this very concise form to give a quick primer of terminology that should be familiar to most readers. If any of these terms seems unfamiliar or shady, we recommend that you refer to one of the textbooks on operating systems.[2]

---

[2] Silberschatz and Galvin provide one of the best overall discussions of operating-systems concepts.

Multiprogramming vs. Multitasking

Multiprogramming consists of running several programs in the same computer at the same time. This does *not* require a multiprocessor; a single processor can execute a few instructions in one program and then switch to another program and execute a few of *its* instructions.

Multiprogramming does imply multitasking. Multitasking is the execution of more than one process at the same time. (We would like to call it multiprocessing, but that word has already been used for multiple processors.)

With multitasking, more than one process is in the computer and all the processes are making progress—that is, they are all executing. A single processor can be switching back and forth among processes, giving a little time to each one, or each process could have its own processor. Each process could be executing a different program (multiprogramming), or they all could be executing the same program (presumably with different data).

Java Support for Multiprogramming. Java supports multiprogramming (running several programs) through the `Process` class. Instances of the `Process` class can be created by using the `Runtime` class—a singleton, platform-specific class that can handle a number of runtime issues that simply cannot be done in a platform-independent way, yet are essential to programming in general.

This book focuses on multithreaded execution; however, multiprogramming and multitasking are highly useful for supporting parallel and distributed computing. There are many situations one faces in Java programming in which the use of multiprogramming and multitasking may be necessary. Here, we name just a few such situations:

- You want to take advantage of a symmetric multiprocessor. A good number of Java threads implementations *still* do not support SMP. By using a `Process` instance, the operating system will physically allocate a process to execute the instance.

- You want to take advantage of a distributed environment. Threads in Java currently (and for the foreseeable future) provide only local semantics. This means that it is generally not possible to use a single Java Virtual Machine that runs coherently on a network of workstations. It is possible, however, to run the JVM on multiple computers (or virtual computers) and make use of a remote procedure-calling framework (such as RMI or one of the systems described in this book) to manage a remote thread or a collection of threads.

- You want to make use of some legacy code (most likely, a native code written in FOR-TRAN or C) that makes use of a number of shared data structures and that was never intended for use in a concurrent environment. It is better to create processes than threads in this case, because processes introduce the possibility of sharing nothing while simultaneously providing the benefits of concurrency. It is notable that most concurrent server applications on the Internet (telnet, ftp, and Web servers, to name but a few) have been written to make use of heavyweight processes. Only recently have some of these "legacy" Internet services migrated to a threads approach.

Concurrency vs. Parallelism vs. Distribution

We have said that, with multitasking, the processes could be either sharing a single processor or executing on different processors at "the same time." This represents the fundamental difference between simple concurrency and parallelism.

Both concurrency and parallelism involve several processes running at the same time. The difference lies in what we mean by the same time. If "the same time" means at the same *instant* of time, we are talking about parallelism. If "the same time" means over the same *period* of time, we are talking about concurrency. In actual operating systems running on a uniprocessor (single processor) machine, no two processes actually run simultaneously. This even includes the operating system scheduler, which itself must be considered a process responsible for scheduling the execution of other processes. When a process is ready to run, the scheduler must run (briefly) in order to pick another process to be suspended, so that the ready process can be executed. Scheduling is a very delicate operation and requires a fair amount of bookkeeping to be done by the operating system (such as managing virtual memory and file descriptors, as well as saving and restoring the CPU state). It is beyond the scope of this book to address the subject of scheduling in detail, but this overview represents, in a nutshell, how concurrency is achieved. It is done this way even on your home computer running Windows, MacOS, or Linux (and others).

Parallelism is the opportunity to schedule ready processes on multiple CPUs. Symmetric multiprocessors (so-called SMP architecture) represent the most common class of machines that are able to support parallel process scheduling, given the right operating system. (Note that there are other "alternative" architectures that can support parallel scheduling that differ radically in design from SMP architecture; however, they are somewhat obscure and will not be considered in this book.) A typical SMP architecture features multiple CPUs and shares all resources (memory and I/O) among them. There are a number of reasons this kind of architecture is popular, but most noteworthy is the fact that everything is shared. Such sharing *does* have the effect of simplifying the programming model, since a memory address or I/O port always has the same meaning regardless of which CPU tries to access a particular address or memory port. From an operating system point of view, the bookkeeping task is no more difficult for a uniprocessor machine. Of course, there are some additional bookkeeping tasks required, simply because there are more CPUs (which means that summary information is maintained for more than one CPU). Scheduling on an SMP is not all that difficult either, since any processor can, in fact, be chosen to run a ready process. This means that a process which has previously run on one CPU can run on a different CPU the next time it is ready to run.

Distributed systems have become enormously popular, especially with mounting interest in the Internet. A distributed environment can be built from virtually any kind of component systems. One thing that is universally agreed upon is that a distributed system must feature some form of interconnection network. Most networks today are built from Ethernet and Asynchronous Transfer Mode (ATM) technologies. Distributed systems are typically not controlled by a single operating system (although many researchers have tried to achieve it), and usually interact with the help of higher level protocols and services.

Java provides varying degrees of support for these concepts. Concurrency is the only feature that is directly supported by the Java language proper. Parallelism and distribution are, to some extent, natural extensions of concurrency; however, some problems manifest themselves in distributed systems that are beyond the scope of this book.

First, we will consider parallelism. Parallelism is the ability to schedule tasks on two or more CPUs simultaneously. This can only happen on symmetric multiprocessors and other novel parallel architectures. The Java language proper does not *directly* address parallelism. This should come as no major surprise, since parallel architectures remain the exception and not the rule, and Java is designed with the notion of being platform independent. However, the fact that parallelism is not addressed does present some problems:

- Little or no support exists for controlling parallelism. An application could conceivably create thousands of threads and therefore be completely at the mercy of the underlying scheduler and threads implementation.

- Thread affinity is not supported. The `ThreadGroup` class provides a mechanism for grouping threads to facilitate performing a common operation on all threads in a group of threads; however, this class appears to play no role in the underlying scheduling of the threads.

Java has many features designed to easily support distributed computing. Most of these features exist as add-ons to the language in the form of libraries. Remote Method Invocation (RMI) is a framework for Java-to-Java client–server computing. RMI itself does not provide any facilities for transparently managing remote thread references. In the second half of this book, we will discuss how transparent thread handling can be achieved through an experimental message-passing system called `Memo`.

Threads vs. Processes

In the computing literature, threads are often called *lightweight* processes. This is perhaps a bit of a misnomer, because the term "process" in most operating systems usually addresses a number of key aspects, such as the following:

- processor state,

- separate memory image, and

- separately held resources.

The more significant aspect that threads and processes have in common is the need to maintain processor state information. Processor state information includes the program counter, registers, and the execution stack pointer. The actual details are somewhat platform-specific; however, most modern processors provide direct support for maintaining such state information.

Aside from processor state information, threads are not processes. This does not imply that no relationship exists between threads and processes. Threads do, in fact, have the ability to share the memory image and resources belonging to a particular process. Without this sharing ability, threads would have to be processes, which would militate against having processes at all.

There are two questions that arise at this time:

- Why do threads exist?

- Why do we still need processes?

We will make every effort to address these two questions throughout the book by presenting a number of examples. Consider the first question, "Why do threads exist?" Threads exist to lower the cost of task creation. Process creation time takes much longer than that of thread creation. Why? First of all, a memory image must be created when a program is loaded by the operating system. This usually results in an interaction with the operating system's virtual memory subsystem, which usually involves I/O requests. This cost, when all is said and done, amounts to seconds of elapsed time (according to the wall clock). Thread creation represents a small fraction of process creation time, because, in most operating systems, a thread can only be created from an existing *and* running process. The newly created thread will share the memory image and resources with its *parent*.

The second question, "Why do we still need processes?" has a more difficult answer. The answer to the question can be "yes" or "no," depending on how you view the entire subject of programming. Programmers who have not worked with object technology are more likely to say "yes," while others are more likely to say "no." Let's first consider the group that would say "yes." A typical representative of this group would be a seasoned FORTRAN or C programmer who comes from the school of programming without robust data structures and the need to share global data between subroutines. As will be discussed in the next chapter on race conditions and mutual exclusion, shared data structures are one of the key suspects in any concurrent program that does not work correctly. Before threads existed, processes were used to run such programs concurrently. Instead of having to worry about whether the global variables were or were not shared, processes allowed concurrency to be achieved by copying the memory image of the process, thereby guaranteeing that no conflicts arose from access to a global data structure. Sometimes this is truly the best way to achieve concurrency. This is because the cost of protecting the shared data (even when it is not really being shared) is greater than the cost of creating a separate process in the first place. In this book, we choose to use threads predominantly for achieving concurrency; however, processes do have their place. As we will discuss in the chapters addressing parallelism, there are simply occasions in doing Java (or any other) programming where the process is the only vehicle to ensure that one can actually take advantage of all of the processors on a particular system or network of computers.

Java Support for Parallel Execution

Java provides direct support for concurrency in its multithreading framework. Often, concurrency and parallelism are mistakenly thought of as being equivalent ideas.

The support for parallelism depends heavily on the Java implementation being considered. Most Java implementations do not provide support for scheduling threads on multiple CPUs, although there is some work in progress for specific platforms, like Solaris and AIX.

Many of the frameworks discussed in the second half of this book will allow you to take advantage of parallel processing, even if your Java implementation does not support scheduling on multiple CPUs. You can run multiple JVM sessions on your machine and then take advantage of a parallel framework, such as the Memo system (presented in the last chapter).

Programmers who are more familiar with object technologies are likely to answer "no" to the second question posed earlier. After all, object-oriented thinking and programming strongly discourage the use of shared and global data structures, except within the bounds of the object paradigm. Java programmers are used to passing references to objects whose use is intended to be shared. Global data are typically limited to "public static final" variables assigned initial values that never change (i.e., they are constants). Any other type of variable is accessed by appropriate "get" and "set" (or other kinds of mutator) methods. The absence of global data makes a strong case against using heavyweight processes; however, as we shall see later, it simply does not make engineering sense. Thread scheduling and synchronization cost can sometimes overwhelm a multithreaded program. When this happens, it is sometimes better to divide threads among multiple processes (possibly running on different machines), giving more threads an opportunity to run.

Unix Processes. This is where it all started. In a classic UNIX process, there is a process control block in the system area that has information about the process and links to information about the open files. The address space that the process can see is in the user area.

The program's instructions are loaded into low memory and can be in read-only storage. Above the program is static storage (e.g., variables declared static or global in C programs). Beyond that, and growing upwards, is the *heap,* where dynamic storage is allocated (by `malloc()` in C or new in C++).

Growing down from the top of memory is the stack where information about procedure activations is allocated. A procedure-activation record contains the parameters, local variables, return address, pointer back to the caller's activation record, and any other needed information.

When a UNIX process creates another process (subprocess) by using the `fork()` system call, a new process control block is allocated for the subprocess. The entire contents of the user space are copied into a new user space for the subprocess. (The read-only program can be shared.) In UNIX, the relationship between a process and the newly created process is called a parent–child relationship. Despite the fact that all data is copied when the child process is created, the open files are shared between the parent process and the child process. This is because files are accessed with opaque *handles* and the variable holding the handle, albeit copied, contains the same handle value.

Whereas only the parent process is called `fork()`, both the parent and the child return from it. In the parent, `fork()` returns the child's process id—an integer identifying the child process. In the child process, `fork()` returns zero. Examining the value `fork()` returns is the way in which a process can tell whether it is the parent or the child.

If the child process is supposed to execute a different program, it calls the `exec()` system function (which loads the new program from a file and sets it running). This will empty the contents of the user's memory, replacing it with the loaded program's contents. This means that the copying of the parent's memory that `fork()` did was wasted. It is notable that Windows NT, using the `CreateProcess()` system call, does not require the child process to be created as a copy of the parent process.[3]

But whether the child continues executing the same program as the parent or loads a new one instead, it is still expensive to set another process running in UNIX (or in any system where a process runs in a separate memory space). Threads, however, are much less expensive to start, because they execute in the same memory space and henceforth share all memory and code with a parent process.

Kernel-level vs. User-level Threads

There are basically two kinds of multithreading systems: user threads and kernel threads. User threads are totally within a user process. The user process shares the processor among the several threads within its user space. Kernel threads have thread control blocks within the operating-system kernel. The operating system allocates processors directly to kernel threads.

The way in which processors are allocated in an operating system is as follows: When a processor becomes free, it pulls the next process (or thread) control block off of the queue

---

[3] System V derivatives of UNIX provide the vfork() system call, which behaves similarly to CreateProcess in Windows NT.

of runnable processes and starts executing it. Since user threads are within a single process, and the single process has a single-process control block in the kernel, user threads can be concurrent, but not parallel. Because kernel threads have their thread control blocks in the kernel, more than one processor can execute the threads in the same process at the same time. Thus, kernel threads can run in parallel on a multiprocessor.

The Java language proper does not address the underlying thread scheduling issues. This is not a major disadvantage, since most thread libraries (such as pthreads and Win32 threads) do not directly address underlying thread scheduling. In fact, these policies are very platform specific. Most Java implementations only allow multithreading issues to be controlled by defining appropriate environment variables and specifying command-line switches. Thus, the entire issue of determining whether your code is running in multithread (and in parallel) may represent one of the biggest challenges you will face in programming with threads in Java or any other programming language.

Java implementations usually provide some degree of support for controlling what threads are actually being used to support Java threads. Typically, JDK ports allow the user to select from green threads (a user-level threads library developed by the Javasoft team) and native threads. Native-threads JDK implementations are available for all of the major platforms that support threads proper, including Win32, Solaris (SPARC and x86), Linux, and some versions of UNIX (AIX and Irix). Now, it is a good idea to investigate the threads support provided with your Java tool set.

Quick Tour of Java Threads Functions

We conclude the chapter with a quick overview of the different methods supported in the Java `Thread` class. Much like other Java classes, the `Thread` class provides a number of static methods (class methods that do not require an instance) and instance methods.

Construction

The `Thread` class contains many constructors. We will not enumerate all of them here; however, we will discuss each of the parameters that can be specified in the various constructors and why you might want to use them.

`Runnable` target

> We have already discussed the connection between `Runnable` and `Thread`. The preferred way to work with the `Thread` class is to contain a reference to an object that is `Runnable`. This does create extra work for you as a programmer but provides the convenience of being able to save inheritance for "a rainy day." More often than not, in real OOP applications, you will need to inherit from a class other than `Thread`.

ThreadGroup group

A `ThreadGroup` is useful when you have a collection of threads that you need to operate on as a whole. You would create a `ThreadGroup` instance and then pass a reference to this instance to each `Thread` you wish to include in the `ThreadGroup`. This might appear backwards in comparision to the use of other containers, such as `AWT` and `Collection` classes.

String name

If you are working with a large number of threads, consider using a constructor that has this option. Providing a name for a thread will make it considerably easier for debugging, especially if the thread causes an unhandled exception and a spewage of the runtime stack to the console.

Daemon Threads

Daemon threads are threads that are created with the intention of running for the lifetime of a particular JVM "session." After creating a `Thread` instance, you should call the `setDaemon()` method to enable this possibility. Note that it is not an option to specify a thread as a Daemon thread at construction time. It is possible to test whether a particular thread instance is a Daemon thread by using the `isDaemon()` method after the thread is constructed.

Thread Control

Thread control methods have been available in Java 1.0 and 1.1 implementations. These control methods were primarily provided to support Java applet development (which, interestingly, has similarly named methods). Most of these methods, except for `start()` and `interrupt()`, have officially been deprecated, because of troublesome interactions with the garbage collector.

start()

This method must be called to actualy start a `Thread`. A common mistake Java programmers make when programming with threads is to forget to call the method. Until this happens, an instance of `Thread` is not much different than any other Java object. (i.e., the `Thread` object will only do what it is told by calling one of its public methods.)

stop() and **stop(Throwable o)**

This method is deprecated in Java 1.2. Nonetheless, current Java implementations will stop a particular thread when this method is called. The default implementation of `stop()` causes a `ThreadDeath` object to be thrown. (You can think of this as being like an exception, but its more like a signal.) Optionally, a user-specified `Throwable` can be specified.

It is not recommended to use this method. Instead, you should consider using the `interrupt()` method, which will be supported (most likely) in Java 1.2 and its afterlife.

suspend() and **resume()**

> This method is deprecated in Java 1.2. The idea here is that a thread is temporarily halted until explicitly resumed (with the `resume()` call).

> Again, it is not recommended to use this method. It is better to gracefully "stop" a running thread and design the thread such that it could be started again later. Consider using `interrupt()` and then restarting the thread again with `start()`.

interrupt(), **interrupted()**, and **isInterrupted()**

> This method can be called to interrupt a thread. Conceivably, threads can be in two states when this method is called (assuming that the thread has already been started). These are waiting (possibly sleeping—a form of waiting) and running. Waiting and sleeping are examples of blocking calls (which are discussed in the next chapter), and must be surrounded by a try–catch block. When a thread is in the running state, an interrupted flag is set. This can be tested by the running thread at any time.

> This is likely to become the preferred method for being able to start and stop threads, but has (as a major disadvantage and annoyance) the property that the running thread must explicitly poll for whether it has been interrupted. This is done using the `interrupted()` method. It is also possible to test whether another thread has been interrupted using `isInterrupted()`.

Very Useful Static Methods

sleep(long millis), **sleep(millis, nanos)**

> This method puts the currently running thread to sleep. It is not necessary to have a reference to an actual thread instance in order to call this method. Java knows what thread is running. See the discussion of nanosecond resolution in the discussion of the `join()` method, which is covered under Thread Synchronization.

currentThread()

> If you have created a class that implements `Runnable` instead of extending `Thread`, the noticeable disadvantage will be that many of the methods [i.e., instance methods, such as `join()`] cannot be called. Any object can obtain a reference to the currently running thread (since Java always knows what the currently running thread is) simply by calling the `currentThread()`. To change the name of the currently running thread, you could do this:

> `currentThread().setName("My New Name");`

> To reiterate, code such as the foregoing only needs to be done in classes that are not subclasses of `Thread`. You will see code like this in various examples presented throughout the book.

Thread Synchronization

join() throws InterruptedException

join(long millis) throws InterruptedException

join(long millis, long nanos) throws InterruptedException

> This important method will be used throughout this book. The method join(), in its various forms, allows a currently running thread to wait for another thread to terminate. As with most blocking calls, InterruptedException instances can be thrown. It is also possible to specify the number of milliseconds and nanoseconds you want the program to wait before starting the thread to terminate. There are two problems associated with the use of these "timed" join() calls. First, most operating systems do not support nanosecond-resolution timing functions (the only one of which the author is aware is the Solaris operating system, among major OS contenders). The second and perhaps more serious problem is that the timed versions give you no easy way of determining whether the thread has actually terminated. Your only way of doing this is to call one of the status functions, isAlive(), which is discussed shortly.

Cooperative Multitasking

yield()

> Layering Java threads atop an operating system that does not support bona fide threads (user-level or kernel-level) requires the presence of the yield() method to support cooperative multitasking. This method will cause the currently running thread to yield the CPU to another runnable thread at the same priority level.

Prioritized Scheduling

getPriority() and **setPriority()**

> In Java, it is possible to adjust a thread's priority level prior to starting it. The priority values must be between MIN_PRIORITY and MAX_PRIORITY, inclusive. These two constants, along with NORM_PRIORITY, are all defined in the Thread class.

> A close examination of these priority values reveals that Java only supports 10 priority levels. We will discuss this issue a bit later. This limited range of priority values does present problems for implementing certain kinds of parallel algorithms, such as branch and bound problems (and other search problems, such as computer games).

> A word of warning is in order. The value MAX_PRIORITY should be used very sparingly, if at all. We will show an interesting use for this priority level later. If you are not careful, it is possible to prevent any thread from running (other than the ones set to MAX_PRIORITY). This phenomenon is called *starvation* and represents a classic problem in operating systems—one that supports prioritized scheduling of processes and threads. Nonetheless, there are valuable uses for thread priorities. Most modern operating systems support prioritized scheduling, including Windows, Solaris, and Linux, just to name a few.

Miscellaneous Status Methods

`getName()` and `setName()`

As mentioned earlier, a `Thread` can be given a name. Naming is useful for debugging. At any time, this name can be obtained by using the `getName()` method, or changed with `setName()`.

`getThreadGroup()`

This method is used to find out the `ThreadGroup` to which a particular thread belongs. All threads belong to the default system `ThreadGroup`, so you can rest assured that every thread belongs to a group, regardless of whether the thread was explicitly constructed to belong to a `ThreadGroup`.

`isAlive()`

This method allows you to figure out whether a thread is alive. A thread is alive if it is running; otherwise, it is not. Note that it is not a sign of a problem if a thread is not alive. The thread may never have been started, may have terminated gracefully, or may have been interrupted. Of course, another exception may have occurred that must be handled in the body of the thread [i.e., its `run()` method], except in the case of runtime exceptions (e.g., `NullPointerException`, etc.)

Methods Not Covered Here

`activeCount()`

`static enumerate(Thread[] tarray)`

`checkAccess()`

`countStackFrames()`

`destroy()`

Exercises

1. Explain the advantages and disadvantages of implementing `Runnable` instead of extending `Thread`.

2. If a class implements `Runnable`, can it execute all `Thread` methods?

3. Using your Java Development Kit (JDK) or other Java implementation and the associated documentation, determine what level of threads support is provided. Are the threads user-level or kernel-level?

4. Can Java work on a platform, such as MS-DOS, that does not directly support multiprogramming, multitasking, and multithreading?

5. Show how to implement a `Stack` with the familiar operations and no use of inheritance, `push()`, `pop()`, or `top()`.

6.   Implement an AWT application that has two buttons, "Go" and "Stop." When the "Go" button is pressed, the event handler should execute something that takes a long time, such as a long-running loop. When the "Stop" button is pressed, the long-running task should be stopped. Once this is done, modify the code to create a thread when the "Go" button is pressed (be sure to keep a reference to this thread object), but only if a thread is not already running. When the "Stop" button is pressed, the long-running activity should be stopped. [To do this, you can call the stop() method on the currently running thread. This is a deprecated method; however, it *will* stop the currently running thread. Later, we will discuss ways to gracefully terminate threads in the absence of a stop() method.] What do you observe about the responsiveness of your interface when threads are used vs. when they are not?

## Chapter 3

Race Conditions and Mutual Exclusion

▼ KNOW YOUR ENEMY!

▼ RACE CONDITIONS

▼ CONDITIONS

▼ CLASSIC SYNCHRONIZATION MECHANISMS

▼ EXERCISES

Java is, without a doubt, popular because of its extensive support for multithreading and networking. It is also among an elite group of languages that directly support concurrent and distributed computing right out of the box. Despite this support, Java is plagued by the same problems that have traditionally affected programmers who write concurrent programs. This chapter is dedicated to *race conditions*, which undoubtedly account for most of the problems that occur in concurrent programming.

We will begin with a discussion of the general "enemies" that manifest themselves in concurrent programming, and follow it with a discussion of a specific enemy—the race condition. We then turn to a discussion of how to eliminate race conditions by using mutual exclusion and built-in object synchronization (which are supported by each and every Java object, regardless of whether it is used or not). The chapter concludes with a discussion of the need for more complex synchronization control with conditions and a brief tour of some classic high-level synchronization mechanisms found in computer science literature on operating systems, programming languages, and parallel processing.

Know Your Enemy!

Concurrency creates problems unlike those you encounter with single processes. You must know how to counteract these problems in order to use threads successfully. There are three problems in particular to worry about:

- *Race conditions*: Threads can try to update the same data structure at the same time. The result can be partly what one thread wrote and partly what the other thread wrote. This garbles the data structure, typically causing the next thread that tries to use it to crash.

- *Deadlock*: To avoid updating the same data structure at the same time, threads lock a data structure until they have finished making their modifications to it. Other threads are forced to wait to modify a data structure until it is unlocked. However, if threads try to modify two data structures at the same time, they will also try to lock them both. Thread *A* can lock data structure *X,* and thread *B* can lock data structure *Y.* Then, if *A* tries to lock *Y* and *B* tries to lock *X*, both *A* and *B* will wait forever—*B* will wait for *A* to unlock *X* and *A* will wait for *B* to unlock *Y.* This deadlock occurs easily, and you must find ways to prevent it.

- *Starvation*: In its effects, starvation is similar to deadlock in that some threads do not make progress. But the causes of starvation are different from those of deadlock: The threads could, in theory, execute, but they just don't get time on a processor, perhaps because they don't have a high enough priority.

- Other forms of *nondeterminism*: Race conditions are the most common form of non-determinism encountered in practical multithreading problems; however, other forms of nondeterminism also occur in practice. For example, two different executions of a multithreaded program may run correctly, but produce output or traces that appear to be different from one another (i.e., sometimes called different serializations). This is a case that occurs in transaction systems.

Race Conditions

Egoist: A First Study in Race Conditions

To motivate the problem of race conditions, consider the example shown in Example 3-1, which presents two classes, `Egoist` and `OutChar`. An egoist is an object that has a name and contains a reference to an `OutChar` instance. When executed, the `run()` method (the body of the thread) will simply print the name of the egoist repeatedly (300 times) to the output stream.

The `OutChar` class is a wrapper class that is used to print characters one at a time and limit the output to 50 characters per line. The `out()` method is marked "synchronized," because the `OutChar` instance will be shared by multiple threads.

Example 3-1 presents a class, `Sched`, that makes use of both `Egoist` and `OutChar`. Three `Egoist` instances (A, B, and C) are created in the `main()` method. A single `OutChar` instance is also created, which is referenced by the three `Egoist` instances. Once the `Egoist` has been instantiated, its priority level is set. (See "A Word on Priorities" on page 46.)

This example shows the effect of thread scheduling on the outcome of a given program's execution. Recall that, in the introductory discussion about "knowing your enemy," we discussed how concurrent programming with threads introduces the possibility of "other forms of nondeterminism." In this case, the output can be in any order, because the `OutChar` object (variable C in the code) only guarantees synchronized access to its state when a single character is output. It is possible to serialize the accesses of the individual `Egoist` objects to the single `OutChar` object; however, that has not been done in this code.

However, there is a question, that arises as a result of this example:

Why isn't the output always the same?

The answer is not a simple one and raises several additional questions:

- **Just exactly what *does* happen when the code `sleep(5)` is executed?** This code is used in the thread class to put the currently running thread to sleep for 5 milliseconds. Is it possible that the thread "sleeps" for more than 5 milliseconds? The answer is yes and ultimately depends on the operating system being used. Time-sharing operating systems (UNIX and WindowsNT) make no guarantees about how long a thread (or a process) will be away from the CPU once it yields to the CPU. The sleep call results in the current thread blocking immediately, thus yielding to the CPU.

- **What role, if any, is played by the `setPriority` calls?** Again, the answer depends on the operating system. Thread scheduling priorities are a highly OS-dependent phenomenon. Windows NT thread scheduling is limited to five priority levels (at least in Version 4.0 and earlier releases). Some versions of UNIX don't support threads, at all. Solaris and Linux, which both support the `pthreads` standard, support at least 255 priority levels. Most thread implementations do support the notion of a highest-priority thread, which, if running, is allowed to run until it yields to the CPU.

- **Is thread scheduling preemptive?** This is an important question. Most operating systems that support threads do support preemptive thread scheduling.

- **Is there kernel-level or user-level scheduling?** It turns out that this is an important question to answer in a general sense. The answers most likely will not affect your view of the outcome. However, if you run this code on a machine with multiple CPUs, the outcome could be very different, because it is possible that more than one thread can be running on two different CPUs. Most Java implementations do not yet support the notion of symmetric scheduling; but by the time you are reading this, it is more than likely that Java implementations will exist that support parallel hardware well.

Example 3-1 `Sched` - **The Driver for** `Egoist` **to Demonstrate Scheduling**

```
class Sched extends Thread {
    public void run(){
        for(;;) {
            try {
                sleep(5);
            }
            catch(InterruptedException e) { }
        }
    }

    public static void main(String[] s) {
        Thread q; int i;
        OutChar C=new OutChar();
        for (i='A';i<='C';i++) {
            q=new Egoist((char) i,C);
            q.setPriority(Thread.NORM_PRIORITY-1);
            // try commenting the above out
            q.start();

        }
        q=new Sched();
        q.setPriority(Thread.MAX_PRIORITY);
        q.setDaemon(true);
        q.start();
    }
}
```

A Word on Priorities

Before continuing with the discussion of race conditions and presenting more examples, a few words are warranted about Java thread priority levels. The `Thread` class provides the definitions of two constants: `MIN_PRIORITY` and `MAX_PRIORITY`. If you check the Java Development Kit source code, the values of these constants are set to 1 and 10, respectively. The choice of these particular numbers is somewhat curious, since the use of thread priority levels is somewhat common in actual programming practice.

In parallel algorithms (e.g., branch-and-bound problems or game trees, as in chess), there may be situations in which hundreds of possible alternatives can be evaluated concurrently. Some of the alternatives are likely to require further exploration, while others clearly do not. Suppose you have the resources (i.e., dozens of processors) to evaluate many alternatives. You would clearly want the ability to evaluate the alternatives that are most likely to yield a good result. (In chess, your hope as a programmer is to choose alternatives that lead to victory.) Based on an evaluation function, you could assign a priority value to the thread that will explore the alternatives further. Priorities allow the alternatives to be scheduled dynamically, working from the best to the worst. As more alternatives are discovered, it is possible that more threads will be created, again with dynamically assigned priorities. As desirable alternatives are discovered, they will be scheduled ahead of undesirable alternatives.

Now, let us return to the point: Thread priorities *are* useful! Since they are known to be useful, it would be convenient if Java supported more than 10 priority levels, though there does seem to be a reason for the low number. As mentioned earlier, Windows NT supports five levels. and `pthreads` (the UNIX threads standard) supports many. There is no clear explanation provided in the Java specification; however, the choice of 10 seems particularly close to Windows NT. This fact, in and of itself, might provide some insight as to why there are so few, since Java has been designed for platform independence. Platform independence sometimes comes at the cost of utilizing the full power of a particular platform. Later in this book, we will return to the issue of thread priorities and examine how one can support an arbitrary number of priority levels for certain kinds of tasks, similar to Example 3-1.

What is a Race Condition?

The `Egoist` example showed the results of a race condition in which the output depended on the scheduling of the execution of the concurrent threads. A *race condition* typically is a result of nondeterministic ordering of a set of external events. In the case of `Egoist`, the events were the ticks of a computer clock that caused rescheduling. The ticks of a computer clock are used in most operating systems (like UNIX and Windows NT) to support preemptive task scheduling. A time slice (discussed earlier) is usually computed as a function of so many clock ticks. In dealing with networking applications, the external events include the speed and scheduling of both the remote computers you are linked to and queueing delays on the network.

In a concurrent application, race conditions are not always a sign of problems. There may be many legitimate execution orders (often referred to in the computing literature as *serializations* or *schedules*) for the same program, all of which produce an equivalent and correct result. Consider the concept of sorting an array or list of values, to be rearranged such that the elements are in either ascending or descending order. One way to perform a concurrent sort is to break up the array into small chunks, sort each chunk using a well-known sequential algorithm (like selection sort), and then merge all of the small arrays, in pairwise fashion, until there are no more merges to be performed. There are many possible schedules for performing the merge, all of which will lead to the correct result (provided the merging algorithm is correct). This conceptual example, which actually appears as a programming example later in the book, leads to an important observation about concurrent programming in general: Proving the correctness of a concurrent program is harder than doing so for one that is not concurrent, or sequential. For a concurrent program to be correct, all serializations of the program must yield a correct result. The notion of a correct result is something we will be addressing throughout this book. Clearly, if any serialization leads to the values of the array not being sorted for some reason, the program is not correct. Another example of an incorrect result is if the program does not terminate. This could occur in the presence of deadlock, the subject of a later chapter.

The most dangerous race conditions, however, involve access to shared data structures. If two threads are updating the same data structure at the same time, the changes may be made partially by one thread and partially by the other. The contents of the data structure can then become garbled, which will confuse threads that access it later, thereby causing them to crash. The trick is to force the threads to access the data structure one at a time, so-called mutual exclusion, so that each thread can complete its update and leave the structure in a consistent state for the next thread.

To do this, threads must be able to lock the data structure while it is being accessed and then unlock it when they are finished. Code that updates a shared data structure is called a *critical section.*

Consider again the `Egoist` example. This code showed an example of a harmless race condition. Each `Egoist` instance outputs a single character (its name) to the output stream a total of 300 times. One expects to see the letters "A," "B," and "C" each appear 300 times. If, for some reason, each of the letters did not appear 300 times, it could be concluded that there is, indeed, a bug in the code. The way the sample code has been written, there is no implicit or explicit design that will make the output appear in any particular order (or be grouped in any particular way). The only thing that is assured is that each `Egoist`'s name appears 300 times and that no fewer (or greater) than 50 characters per line is output.

Race0 *Class*

Let us now consider an example in which race conditions can cause something unexpected to occur. Example 3-2 demonstates an example of two threads that are created to both be able to access a common data structure. The data structure to be shared between the two threads is aptly named `Shared0`, shown in Example 3-3. As the name indicates, an instance of this class will be somehow shared. `Shared0` consists of two instance variables, x and y, both of type integer, and two methods:

Example 3-2 A Simple Example of Race Conditions (`Race0.java`)

```java
class Race0 extends Thread {
    static Shared0 s;
    static volatile boolean done=false;

    public static void main(String[]x) {
        Thread lo=new Race0();
        s=new Shared0();
        try {
            lo.start();
            while (!done) {
                s.bump();
                sleep(30);
            }
            lo.join();
        } catch (InterruptedException e)
            { return; }
    }

    public void run() {
        int i;
        try {
            for (i=0;i<1000;i++) {
                if (i%60==0)
                    System.out.println();
                System.out.print(".X".charAt(s.dif()));
                sleep(20);
            }
            System.out.println();
            done=true;
        } catch (InterruptedException e)
            { return; }
    }
}
```

- **`bump()`**: When called, this method increments the value of x, puts the currently running thread to sleep for awhile, and then increments the value of y. The outcome of the bump() method is that both variables are incremented by one.

- **`dif()`**: When called, this method returns the difference between the current values of x and y.

The class responsible for accessing the instance of Shared0 is Race0. Race0 has no instance variables but does declare two static variables. Static variables are variables that are shared (and visible) among all instances of the class Race0, as well as the main()

Example 3-3 A Class That will be Used to Create a Shared Data Objects.

```
class Shared0 {
    protected int x=0,y=0;

    public int dif() {
        return x-y;
    }

    public void bump() throws InterruptedException {
        x++;
        Thread.sleep(9);
        y++;
    }
}
```

method defined in `Race0`. (That is, an instance is not even required to access the variable `s`, as the `main()` method illustrates.) There are two methods here:

- `main()`: The method is the main thread of execution. It creates the shared object, starts a second thread, and immediately enters a loop that executes until a variable done is set true (by the other thread). Inside the loop, the `bump()` method is repeatedly called on by the shared object `s`, and then the thread goes to sleep for awhile. Once the loop is done, the `join()` method is called on the other thread to await its completion. `join()` is a very convenient way to wait for a thread to finish its execution, but it must be used with care. We give more details on this later.

- `run()`: the routine that is called when a thread is scheduled for execution. Recall that the `main()` method called `lo.start()` to start the other thread. The other thread is an instance of `Race0`. Thus, `Race0` must have a run method to ensure that some task is actually performed. This method enters a loop that, similar to the `Egoist` program, executes a certain number of times and formats the output such that only 60 characters per line are written. The `dif()` method is called to determine the difference between `x` and `y`, as explained earlier, and prints "." or "X." Then this thread sleeps for awhile. When the loop is finished, the done variable is set so that the main thread can terminate its `while` loop.

The box titled "A First Run of `Race0`" illustrates the race condition clearly. Sometimes the difference is 0 and other times 1. The difference is never a value other than 0 or 1. Why is this the case?

A First Run of `Race0`

```
java Race0
```

```
.....X.X.X......X.X.X........X.......X.X.X.X.X.X.X.......
........X.X.X.X.X.X.........X.X.X.X.X.X.........
X.X.X.X............X.X.X.X.X.X.............X.X.X.X.......
......X.X.X.........X.X.X.X.X.X.............X.X.X.X.X...
.......X.X.X.X.X........X.X.X.X.X..............X
.X.X.X.X............X.X.X.X.X..........X.X.X.X
.X................X.X.X.X.X............X.X.X.X.X....
.............X.X.X.X.X..........X.X.X.X.X.X.........
..X.X.X.X..............X.X.X.X.X.X.........X.X.X.X.
X.X.............X.X.X.X.X.........X.X.X.X............X
.X.X.X.X.X...........X.X.X.X.X...........X.X.X.X......
.......X.X.X.X.X.X...X...X.X.X.X.X.X..............X.X.X.X
...............X.X.X.X..........X.X.X.X.X.........X.
X.X.X.X...............X.X.X.X.X.X...........X.X.X.X.X.X...
..........X.X.X.X.X.............X.X.X.X.X.............
.X.X.X.X.X...........X.X.X.X.X.X.............X.X.X.X.X.X
```

- A key to understanding concurrency is to fully understand what would happen if all traces of concurrency were removed. For example, what would happen if we called `bump()` and `dif()`, guaranteeing in the process that the two could never execute at the same time? The difference between x and y would always be 0. The fact that it is sometimes 1 implies that `dif()` must somehow be able to execute in the middle of the execution of the `bump()` method.

- The `bump()` method always increments x and y. The value of y can never be different from that of x by more than 1.

- The `dif()` method never updates x or y. `bump()` is the only method that does so.

- Furthermore, in this example, only one call of `bump()` or `dif()` is active at any given time; however, due to multithreading, both `bump()` and `dif()` may sometimes be running simultaneously.

The bottom line is that in order to fully understand a concurrent program, even one as simple as this, you must consider the serial behavior and understand exactly what could be happening. In the preceding code, it is possible for the value of x or y to be read by the thread calling `dif()` in the middle of the `bump()` call. This is why the difference is sometimes 1 and at other times 0.

The box titled "A Second Run of Race0" shows a second run of the Race0 code. This example demonstrates that attempting to predict the pattern is somewhat of an exercise in futility.

A Second Run of Race0

```
java Race0
```

```
.....X.X.X......X.X.X......X.X..X.X.X.X...............X.X.
X.X.X.X...............X.X.X.X...............X.X.X...........
.....X.X.X.X.X.X.................X.X.X.X...............X.X.X.X
.X.X...............X.X.X.X...............X.X.X.X...........
..X.X.X.X.X.X.................X.X.X.X.X.X...............X.X.
X.X.X.X...............X.X.X.X.X.X...............X.X.X.X.X.
X...............X.X.X.X.X.X.X...............X.X.X.X.X.X...
...............X.X.X.X.X.X...............X.X.X.X.X.X...........
.....X.X.X.X.X.X.X...............X.X.X.X.X...............X
.X.X.X.X.X...............X.X.X.X.X.X...............X.X.X.X
...............X.X.X.X.X.X...............X.X.X.X.X.X........
........X.X.X.X.X.X...............X.X.X.X.X.X...........
...X.X.X.X.X.X...............X.X.X.X.X.X...............X.X.X.X.
X...............X.X.X.X.X.X...............X.X.X.X.X.X......
.....X.X.X.X.X.X...........X.X.X.X.X...............X.X.X.X
.............X.X.X.X.X.X...........X.X.X.X.X...........
```

A cursory look at the output might lead you to think that the results of the two runs are the same. The output patterns are similar but not the same. This is clearly an artifact of scheduling. The long stretches of dots (".") indicate that often, scheduling strictly alternates between the thread causing the bump and the thread computing the difference. At other times there is a pattern of strict alternation between equal and unequal values of x and y. To fully understand the patterns, you would need to consider how the operating system schedules threads and how the sleep time is computed. The fact that there are patterns is not entirely coincidental, but is not predictable either.

Critical Sections and Object Locking

What we have shown in Example 3-2 and 3-3 demonstrates a concept known as a *critical section*. A critical section is a section of code that accesses a common data structure. Shared0 was the class used to create an object that is shared between the two running threads. Because Java is object oriented, the data structures are usually encapsulated in individual objects. It is not always a requirement that an object be used. Scalar values (e.g., int, float, and char variables) may also be used without being "wrapped" by using a class.

The term "critical section" has its origins in the operating systems community. As mentioned in Chapter 1, problems of concurrency go all the way back to programming with multiple processes. (UNIX, an operating system with a design that goes back to the late 1960s and early 1970s, has provided full support for concurrent programming from its inception.) In many respects, the term "section" is a bit of a misnomer. As is often the case in actual practice, multiple "sections," or blocks, of code access common variables or shared data structures. As you are reading, bear in mind that a critical section will usually be guarded by a common synchronization mechanism.

Java handles critical sections by allowing threads to lock individual objects. In Java, every object has a lock which can be accessed by any piece of code that merely holds a reference to an object. To lock an object, Java has synchronized statements and declarations, which are easily spotted in code with the keyword `synchronized`. If you use the synchronized statement, the object is locked for the duration of your execution of the statement.

It is very common to use synchronization (in particular the Java programming library itself) in method declarations. Methods that are declared to be synchronized will result in the entire object being locked for the duration of the call. There are some subtleties to understanding what "the duration of a call" means, primarily due to exceptions. An exception may cause transfer of control to leave a function in much the same way as an explicit return statement or reaching the end of a `void` method call does. All forms of exiting a procedure call result in proper release of the lock, which is very convenient for programmers. In other languages, such as C and C++, which require the use of an external threads library that is not part of the language proper, a great deal of care was once required to ensure that a lock was explicitly released *prior* to leaving the function.

Race1 *Class—Fixing* Race0 *with Synchronization*

Example 3-4 shows a reworked version of class Race0, which has been renamed Race1. Aside from making use of class Shared1, Race1 remains fundamentally unchanged from Race0. The major changes have taken place in class Shared1, which is the reworked version of the class Shared0, found in Example 3-5. The key difference between Race0 and Race1 is that the methods bump() and dif() are now synchronized methods. This means that the shared object is now locked whenever bump() or dif() is executed. Again, this means that bump() and dif() will not be able to "use" the shared object simultaneously, since they are each declared synchronized. If either the bump() or dif() method is called while the other is executing, the called method cannot proceed until the other one has completed its work.

Note that both bump() and dif() must be declared synchronized. If a method or statement is not declared synchronized, it won't even look at the lock before using the object. Note also that there is no convenient shorthand to indicate that all of the methods in a class are to be synchronized (i.e., there is no such thing as a synchronized "class").

Example 3-4 Eliminating Race Condition in `Race0` (`Race1.java`)

```java
class Race1 extends Thread {
    static Shared1 s;
    static volatile boolean done=false;

    public static void main(String[] args) {
        Thread lo=new Race1();
        s=new Shared1();
        try {
            lo.start();
            while (!done) {
                s.bump();
                sleep(30);
            }
            lo.join();
        } catch (InterruptedException e) {return;}
    }

    public void run() {
        int i;
        try {
            for (i=0;i<1000;i++) {
                if (i%60==0) System.out.println();
                System.out.print(".X".charAt(s.dif()));
                sleep(20);
            }
            System.out.println();
            done=true;
        } catch (InterruptedException e) {return;}
    }
}
```

Example 3-5 Eliminating Race Condition in Shared1 (Race1.java)

```java
class Shared1 {
    protected int x=0,y=0;
    public synchronized int dif() {
        return x-y;
    }
    public synchronized void bump() throws
      InterruptedException {
        x++;
        Thread.sleep(9);
        y++;
    }
}
```

The box entitled "Third Run of `Race0`" shows the output that appears when executing this example. Note that the difference between x and y is always 0 when `dif()` is called.

Third Run of `Race0`

```
java Race0
```

. . . .
. . . .
. . . .
. . . .
. . . .
. . . .
. . . .
. . . .
. . . .
. . . .
. . . .
. . . .
. . . .
. . . .
. . . .

Conditions

Motivating the Need for Conditions

Synchronization is useful for ensuring that shared data structures are mutually exclusive, as illustrated in the earlier examples; however, at times, synchronization can be unwieldy in applications in which the shared data is not something as simple as two integers being incremented.

Examples of such a need abound with the most common example being a producer–consumer problem. Consider such an example. A file of size *N* bytes is to be copied. The copying is to take place *K* bytes at a time. (*K* will usually be some power of two, because the underlying block size in a file system is usually something like 1,024, 2,048, or 4,096 bytes—and getting larger with all of the huge disk drives flooding the marketplace.) Example 3-6 shows a single-threaded implementation of how this algorithm would be implemented.

Copying a file is a good application for multithreading. One thread—the producer—reads bytes from a file (*K* at a time) and then writes the blocks to a shared data structure (an array or simple queue will do). The other thread—the consumer—waits for a block to

Example 3-6 `FileCopy0`: **A Single-Threaded File Copying Program**

```java
import java.util.*;
import java.io.*;

public class FileCopy0 {

    public static final int BLOCK_SIZE = 4096;

    public static void copy(String src, String dst)
        throws IOException {
        FileReader fr = new FileReader(src);
        FileWriter fw = new FileWriter(dst);
        char[] buffer = new char[BLOCK_SIZE];
        int bytesRead;

        while (true) {
            bytesRead = fr.read(buffer);
            System.out.println(bytesRead + " bytes read");
            if (bytesRead < 0)
                break;
            fw.write(buffer, 0, bytesRead);
            System.out.println(bytesRead + " bytes written");
        }
        fw.close();
        fr.close();
    }

    public static void main(String args[]) {
        String srcFile = args[0];
        String dstFile = args[1];
        try {
            copy(srcFile, dstFile);
        } catch(Exception e) {
            System.out.println("Copy failed.");
        }
    }
}
```

appear in the shared data structure, then writes bytes to the destination (copy) file. The producer and consumer are to be concurrently started as threads.

This type of application is difficult to write by simply relying on the basic synchronization features (locking) found in Java. Recall that both the producer and consumer are started as threads. This means that either thread has a chance of being scheduled first (in general), which results in a race to access the shared data structure. From the onset, there is the possibility that the consumer gets there first. The consumer locks the shared data structure and tests whether there is a block to be written. If there is, the block is removed from the shared data structure and appended to the destination file. If there is no block to be written, the data structure is left alone. In either case, the shared data structure is unlocked, giving the producer a chance to write a block. The producer must go through the similar lock and unlock maneuver. When the producer acquires the lock, it can write a block into the shared data structure, assuming that there is room to write the block. (There will be room if the data structure is dynamic as opposed to fixed.) Assuming that the producer was able to write the block, the consumer will eventually be able to read a block from the shared data structure.

This example shows the unwieldy nature of working exclusively with synchronization. Synchronization itself allows you to protect shared data, but does very little for elegantly passing control between the producer and consumer. This is because the consumer needs to be able to test whether a block has, in fact, been written. Instead of going through the endless cycle of acquiring the lock, testing the condition, and then releasing the lock, it would be nice if the consumer could temporarily give up the lock and wait until (hopefully) another thread runs and causes the state of the shared data structure to change in a favorable way to the consumer.

Key Object Methods Needed to Work with Conditions in Java

Java provides built-in support awaiting this "change in state" via the notion of a condition. A condition is a bit of a misnomer, however, because it is entirely up to the user whether or not a condition actually occurred. Furthermore, a condition need not be specifically true or false.

To use conditions, one must become familiar with three key methods of the `Object` class:

- `wait()`: This method is used to await a condition. It is called when a lock is presently being held for a particular (shared) object.

- `notify()`: This method is used to notify a single thread that a condition has (possibly) changed. Again, this method is called when a lock is presently being held for a particular object. Only a single thread can be awakened as a result of this call.

- `notifyAll()`: This method is used to notify multiple threads that a condition has (possibly) changed. All threads that are running at the time this method is called will be notified.

`notify()` and `notifyAll()` are *memoryless* operations. If no threads are waiting, then none are awakened. Java does not remember a `notify()` and therefore cannot use it to awaken a thread that waits later.

These three methods are available to any class, since all classes, in one way or another, are derived from the standard Java `Object` class.

Although a thread may be waiting for a particular condition to become true, there is no way to specify the condition in the `wait()` or in the `notify()`. Even if there were only one condition a thread could wait for in a particular object, it is not guaranteed that the condition will be true when the thread starts executing again: After it has been notified, a thread still may not start executing immediately. Another thread may lock the object and make the condition false before the notified thread can run.

This is sometimes called the "false wakeup problem." It can be a potentially confusing problem on an SMP system, since on these systems, there is a real possibility that two or more threads are awakened simultaneously.

On a condition variable, the proper way to wait is to wait inside a loop. This is done as follows:

```
while (!condition) wait();
```

At first, this technique appears to be awkward; however, it is the safest way to work with threads. Most of the time, the loop only executes for one iteration. When the loop is exited, it is without doubt that the condition being tested is true.

Also, `wait()` can be terminated by an `interrupt` from another thread, so you will have to put the command in a `try` statement.

File Copying: A Producer–Consumer Example

Until now, we have considered only many small examples of important conceptual value, but somewhat limited practical value. Here, we consider a more practical example of how threads, synchronization mechanisms, and conditions all come together in order to support a practical need: file copying.

While this example has been structured to be useful for a reference textbook, it demonstrates a number of useful building blocks that could be adapted for more sophisticated applications. In the approach to file copying presented here, concurrency is used with the hope of improving file copying performance, especially in an environment in which resources may enable this possibility. (e.g., multiprocessor systems, multiple I/O devices, multiple I/O buses, etc.)

If you want to take advantage of concurrency, more often than not it pays to have multiple processors; however, in the case of file copying, you may even benefit from concurrency on a single-processor architecture. Traditionally, file copying is done either a byte at a time (a naive implementation) or a block at a time (somewhat more sophisticated). Copying one byte at a time is not efficient, because block devices themselves communicate (via device drivers) with the operating system one block at a time. (Common block sizes are 512 and

1,024 bytes.) However, even when file copying is done a block at a time, there are some important aspects to consider:

- Reads are typically faster than writes. This tends to be true of most devices and is more obvious in the case of floppy disks and recordable compact discs.

- In both reading and writing, the process of finding the block tends to cause a zigzag pattern of accesses.

In short, the reader and writer are usually not working at the same rate. When you approach this problem serially, the process of alternating between reading a block and writing a block is simply not the way to go.

By reworking the problem as a concurrent problem (i.e., the reader and writer are both allowed to read and write blocks at whatever rate they can), performance can significantly be improved, thus addressing both aspects mentioned previously. It may not be obvious how the issue of "seek time" can be tamed by moving to a concurrent design. This will become apparent when you see (in the discussion and code) that it is possible for the reader to read (queue) several blocks from the source file before the writer is actually able to write the blocks to the destination file.

Before we turn to the details of the various classes used to implement concurrent file copying, the following list presents an overview of the classes and how they collaborate to implement the solution to the file-copying problem (we address each of these classes in detail later):

- **Buffer**: This class is an example of a wrapper class. Wrapper classes are often used in Java to make it easier to put data that belong together in a container. A `Buffer` is used to store a block of data that has been read from the source file and is to be written to the destination file.

- **Pool**: This class shows a useful pattern for minimizing the overhead associated with "garbage collection." A `Pool` is simply a fixed collection of `Buffer` instances. These instances are borrowed from the `Pool` and returned as needed. This class actually makes use of conditions.

- **BufferQueue**: This class is used to maintain, in first-in-first-out (FIFO) order, a list of `Buffer` instances waiting to be written to the destination file. Unlike the `Pool`, any number of instances can appear on the `BufferQueue`. Conditions are also used by `BufferQueue` to provide flow control between the reader and the writer.

- **FileCopyReader1**: An instance of this class (which is a subclass of `Thread`) will read blocks from a file one at a time and write them to a `BufferQueue` that is shared with an instance of `FileCopyWriter1`. A `Pool` is also shared between an instance of this class and an instance of `FileCopyWriter1`.

- **FileCopyWriter1**: An instance of this class (which is a subclass of `Thread`) will read blocks from a `BufferQueue` instance and write them to the destination file. It is this class that is actually responsible for doing the final copying.

- **FileCopy1**: This is the main class that drives the entire application. This class is not used to create instances; it simply contains a `main()` method that processes the parameters and properties (we will talk about this shortly) and then creates the worker threads to copy a source file to a destination file.

This is intended to be an executive summary to help you understand at a high level how the code is actually assembled. We will now explore each of the classes in detail.

Example 3-7 shows the code for the `FileCopy1` class. This class contains the `main()` method and is used to drive the entire process of performing the file copy. Two command-line arguments are expected: the source and destination file names. Optionally, an "rc" file can be specified with a list of property bindings:

- **buffers**: These are the number of fixed buffers to be allocated *a priori* for file copying.

- **bufferSize**: This represents the number of characters (`char`) to be allocated per buffer.

Properties

`Properties` is a Java class that supports an environment mechanism (similar to environment variables) in a platform-independent manner.

`Properties` can be read from any stream (not just files). A property is defined as follows: `name=value`

One property may be defined per line of input, separated by new lines. There is no limit on how many times a name can be used on the left-hand side.

There is more to the `Properties` class. It can inherit a set of default properties, so you never really have to hard code anything.

Once the command line arguments and properties have been processed, the real work begins. An instance of `Pool` (`pool`) is created, using the values `buffers` and `bufferSize` to do the allocation. An instance of `BufferQueue` (`copyBuffers`) is created to hold blocks that are to be copied to the destination file. Classes `Pool` and `BufferQueue` appear at first to be redundant; however, we emphasize they both have an important role in the design and are intentionally different to separate the concerns.

The `FileCopyReader1` and `FileCopyWriter1` classes are then instantiated (as `src` and `dst`, respectively) to perform the actual file copying. Note that `pool` and `copyBuffers` are shared object references being contained by both `src` and `dst` objects. Both objects are then started as threads; the `main()` thread simply awaits the completion of these two threads by performing a `join()` operation.

Example 3-7 `FileCopy1`: Multithreaded Version of `FileCopy0`

```
import java.io.*;
import java.util.*;

public class FileCopy1 {
    public static int getIntProp(Properties p, String key
                                 int defaultValue) {
        try {
            return Integer.parseInt(p.getProperty(key));
        } catch(Exception e) {
            return defaultValue;
        }
    }

    public static void main(String args[]) {
        String srcFile = args[0];
        String dstFile = args[1];

        Properties p = new Properties();
        try {
            FileInputStream propFile =
              new FileInputStream("FileCopy1.rc");
            p.load(propFile);
        } catch(Exception e) {
          System.err.println("FileCopy1: Can't load Properties");
        }
        int buffers = getIntProp(p, "buffers", 20);
        int bufferSize = getIntProp(p, "bufferSize", 4096);
        System.out.println("source = " + args[0]);
        System.out.println("destination = " + args[1]);
        System.out.println("buffers = " + buffers);
        System.out.println("bufferSize = " + bufferSize);
        Pool pool = new Pool(buffers, bufferSize);
        BufferQueue copyBuffers = new BufferQueue();

/* code continues on next page */
```

Example 3-7 `FileCopy1`: Multithreaded Version of `FileCopy0` (Continued)

```
/* continuation of main() method on previous page */

        FileCopyReader1 src;
        try {
            src = new FileCopyReader1(srcFile, pool, copyBuffers);
        } catch(Exception e) {
            System.err.println("Cannot open " + srcFile);
            return;
        }
        FileCopyWriter1 dst;
        try {
            dst = new FileCopyWriter1(dstFile, pool, copyBuffers);
        } catch(Exception e) {
            System.err.println("Cannot open " + dstFile);
            return;
        }
        src.start();
        dst.start();

        try {
            src.join();
        } catch(Exception e) {}
        try {
            dst.join();
        } catch(Exception e) {}
    }
}
```

Example 3-8 shows the `Pool` class. This class is used as a storage manager and represents a useful techique for minimizing interactions with the garbage collector in Java programming. The `Pool` class employs the `Buffer` class (shown in Example 3-9), which is simply a wrapper class used both to maintain a reference to a `char` array (`char[]`) and to keep track of the number of characters actually being used in the array. To understand why the `Buffer` class exists, recall that the copying is performed by using fixed-size blocks to do the reads and writes. More often than not, copying the very last block results in only a fraction of the actual character array being used. The `Buffer` class exists to elegantly handle this condition, as well as the end-of-file (EOF) condition. When EOF occurs, a Buffer of length zero is used to indicate the end-of-file boundary condition.

Example 3-8 `Pool`**: A Shared Pool of Buffer Structures**

```
import java.util.*;
import java.io.*;

public class Pool {
    Vector freeBufferList = new Vector();
    OutputStream debug = System.out;
    int buffers, bufferSize;

    public Pool(int buffers, int bufferSize) {
        this.buffers = buffers;
        this.bufferSize = bufferSize;
        freeBufferList.ensureCapacity(buffers);
        for (int i=0; i < buffers; i++)
            freeBufferList.addElement(new Buffer(bufferSize));
    }

    public synchronized Buffer use()
      throws InterruptedException {
        while (freeBufferList.size() == 0)
            wait();
        Buffer nextBuffer =
          (Buffer) freeBufferList.lastElement();
        freeBufferList.removeElement(nextBuffer);
        return nextBuffer;
    }

    public synchronized void release(Buffer oldBuffer) {
        if (freeBufferList.size() == 0)
            notify();
        if (freeBufferList.contains(oldBuffer))
            return;
        if (oldBuffer.getSize() < bufferSize)
            oldBuffer.setSize(bufferSize);
        freeBufferList.addElement(oldBuffer);
    }
}
```

The `Pool` class supports two key methods:

- **use**: This method is used to obtain a reference to the next available buffer. The method is always called by the reader thread (i.e., `FileCopyReader1`).

• **release**: This method is used to return an existing `Buffer` object to the `Pool`. This method is always called by the writer thread, after the contents of a given buffer have been written to the destination. No check is performed to determine whether the object originally came from the `Pool` (i.e., an honor system is assumed here); however, a check *is* performed to ensure that the object has a correct block size for the `Pool`. This requires that every `Buffer` object satisfies the invariant on `buffer-Size`.

Example 3-9 Buffer

```java
public class Buffer {
    private char[] buffer;
    private int size;

    public Buffer(int bufferSize) {
        buffer = new char[bufferSize];
        size = bufferSize;
    }

    public char[] getBuffer() {
        return buffer;
    }

    public void setSize(int newSize) {
        if (newSize > size) {
            char[] newBuffer = new char[newSize];
            System.arraycopy(buffer, 0, newBuffer, 0, size);
            buffer = newBuffer;
        }
        size = newSize;
    }

    public int getSize() {
        return size;
    }
}
```

The `BufferQueue` class (shown in Example 3-10) is used to maintain a list of `Buffer` objects in FIFO order. Since the `Vector` class of Java already supports FIFO functionality, the `BufferQueue` class can be construed as a wrapper class; however, it is also the

Example 3-10 **BufferQueue**

```java
import java.util.*;
import java.io.*;

class BufferQueue {
    public Vector buffers = new Vector();

    public synchronized void enqueueBuffer(Buffer b) {
        if (buffers.size() == 0)
            notify();
        buffers.addElement(b);
    }

    public synchronized Buffer dequeueBuffer()
      throws InterruptedException {
        while (buffers.size() == 0)
            wait();
        Buffer firstBuffer = (Buffer) buffers.elementAt(0);
        buffers.removeElementAt(0);
        return firstBuffer;
    }
}
```

key class responsible for providing flow control between the reader and the writer. It is *also* the place where condition variables are used. There are two key methods:

- **void enqueueBuffer(Buffer b)**: This method puts b on the FIFO. If there is a thread waiting for a buffer to appear (because the FIFO is empty), this method notifies the thread.

- **Buffer dequeueBuffer()**: If the FIFO is empty, this method waits for the FIFO to become nonempty and removes the first buffer from the FIFO.

The `FileCopyReader1` and `FileCopyWriter1` classes (shown in Example 3-11 and Example 3-12, respectively, hereafter the "reader" and the "writer") represent the rest of the story; the file copying is actually done by this pair of classes. Both of these classes work similarly. We will focus the remaining discussion on understanding the `run()` methods of both classes. The constructor code should be self-explanatory.

Example 3-11 FileCopyReader1

```java
import java.io.*;
import java.util.*;

class FileCopyReader1 extends Thread {
    private Pool pool;
    private BufferQueue copyBuffers;
    private String filename;
    FileReader fr;

    public FileCopyReader1(String filename, Pool pool,
      BufferQueue copyBuffers) throws IOException {
        this.filename = filename;
        this.pool = pool;
        this.copyBuffers = copyBuffers;
        fr = new FileReader(filename);
    }
    public void run() {
        Buffer buffer;
        int bytesRead = 0;
        do {
            try {
                buffer = pool.use();
                bytesRead = fr.read(buffer.getBuffer());
            } catch(Exception e) {
                buffer = new Buffer(0);
                bytesRead = 0;
            }
            if (bytesRead < 0) {
                buffer.setSize(0);
            } else {
                buffer.setSize(bytesRead);
            }
            copyBuffers.enqueueBuffer(buffer);
        } while (bytesRead > 0);
        try { fr.close(); }
        catch(Exception e) { return; }
    }
}
```

Example 3-12 FileCopyWriter1

```java
import java.io.*;
import java.util.*;

class FileCopyWriter1 extends Thread {
    private Pool pool;
    private BufferQueue copyBuffers;
    private String filename;
    FileWriter fw;

    public FileCopyWriter1(String filename, Pool pool,
      BufferQueue copyBuffers) throws IOException {
        this.filename = filename;
        this.pool = pool;
        this.copyBuffers = copyBuffers;
        fw = new FileWriter(filename);
    }

    public void run() {
        Buffer buffer;
        while (true) {
            try {
                buffer = copyBuffers.dequeueBuffer();
            } catch(Exception e) { return; }
            if (buffer.getSize() > 0) {
                try {
                    char[] buffer = buffer.getBuffer();
                    int size = buffer.getSize();
                    fw.write(buffer, 0, size);
                } catch(Exception e) {
                    break;
                }
                pool.release(buffer);
            } else break;
        }
        try { fw.close(); }
        catch(Exception e) { return; }
    }
}
```

The `run()` method of the reader works as follows:

- It obtains a `Buffer` instance, `buffer`, from the `Pool of Buffers`.

- It reads up to `buffer.getBuffer().length` bytes from the source file (stream). Note that `getBuffer()` is returning a reference to the contained array (`char[]`) object and that the `read()` call works with arrays. (In Java, unlike C, this operation can be performed safely, since the length of an array is always known and cannot be violated.)

- If, for any reason, an exception occurs [I/O is most likely at the point of the `read()` call], `run()` creates a buffer of size 0.

- If EOF occurs (which is not an exception in Java), sets the size of `buffer` to zero. This will allow the writer to know that EOF has been encountered and terminated gracefully.

- Otherwise, `run()` sets the size of `buffer` to `bytesRead`, the number of bytes actually read. This number is always guaranteed to be less than `buffer.getSize()`.

- It enqueues `buffer` onto `copyButters`.

The `run()` method of the writer is very similar to the reader code and works as follows:

- It dequeues a `buffer` from `copyBuffers`. This is the next block of data to be copied.

- If `buffer.getSize() > 0`, we have not yet reached the end of file. `run()` then writes the block to the file. If end of file has been reached, the program exits the thread.

- It returns `buffer` to `pool`. This is very important to do, as the reader could be waiting for the pool to be nonempty.

Locks–Binary Semaphores: An Example of Using Conditions

Other multithreading systems do not have implicit locks built into the syntax, but instead require you to create and call methods of explicit *lock* objects. A lock object is also called a mutex or a binary semaphore. A given lock may only be in one of two states: locked or unlocked. Initially, a lock is normally in the *unlocked* state. Example 3-13 presents the code for an explicit lock object, written in pure Java.

The following relatively intuitive operations are defined on locks:

- `lock()`—This operation locks the lock. The lock is first tested (atomically) to see whether it is locked. If it is locked, the current thread must wait until it becomes unlocked before proceeding.

Example 3-13 Lock: A Class to Support Binary Semaphores

```java
// Lock.java - a class to simulate binary semaphores

class Lock {
    protected boolean locked;

    public Lock() {
        locked=false;
    }

    public synchronized void lock()
        throws InterruptedException {
        while (locked) wait();
        locked=true;
    }

    public synchronized void unlock() {
        locked=false;
        notify();
    }
}
```

- `unlock()`—This operation unlocks the lock. If the lock is currently in the locked state, `unlock` notifies any thread that may be waiting and the state of the lock is then set to unlocked.

Example 3-13 shows the code for a Java implementation of the concept of a lock, which makes use of conditions.

Notice that the code follows almost exactly from the above definitions. The state of the lock is represented by a boolean variable. This variable is set true if the lock is presently locked and false otherwise. The constructor for class `Lock` initializes locked to false. It is perfectly acceptable to have a constructor that initializes locked to true; however, this is not commonly practiced in real-world applications. (For another kind of lock, called a semaphore—which maintains a count—such an initialization is meaningful. We will discuss this possibility a bit later.)

The `lock()` method checks to see whether the state of the lock is currently locked. Notice that, as described earlier, a `while` loop is used to test this condition. This loop will not terminate unless the state of the lock becomes unlocked. The unlock method explicitly sets the state of the lock to false (without checking its current state) and subsequently notifies any waiting thread that the condition has changed.

Typically, a thread that performs the lock operation is going to perform a matching unlock operation (on the same lock) after executing its critical section; however, it is not an absolute requirement that a lock be used in this manner. (In fact, to impose this restriction would complicate the lock implementation considerably!) Therefore, it is possible that a group of threads could all have references to a common lock and use it in a rather undisciplined way. For instance, one thread could just perform an unlock while another thread "thought" it held the lock. Locks are intended to be used in a disciplined way (i.e., following the prescribed steps). Java enforces lock discipline by not allowing the possibility of a user ever locking an object without eventually unlocking it in a given block of code (short of intentionally setting up an infinite loop).

The `throws InterruptedException` declaration deserves a brief explanation. Because the `lock()` method calls `wait()`, it can result in an `InterruptedException`. It simply lets that exception pass through to its caller, so `InterruptedException` must be declared in the `throws` clause. This is a very common programming practice in Java. When working with exceptions in Java, you must either handle the exception right away or pass the exception to an outer context.

Because the `Lock` class defined here is intended to be useful to those in need of an explicit lock similar to those found in other threads packages (usually used by C and C++ programmers), the latter approach has been taken. Users will expect the behavior of `lock()` to be similar to that of `wait()`, since both have the potential of blocking and being subsequently interrupted.

Locks: Where else can you find them?

Locks are found in both the `pthreads` and `Win32` threads libraries. In `pthreads`, you find `pthreads_mutex_t`, which is the type used to declare a lock variable.

A number of methods exist to actually manipulate this variable:

`pthread_mutex_init()`—This method is used to initialize the `mutex` with a set of attributes. These attributes can be specified using a variable of type `pthread_mutexattr_t`.

`pthread_mutex_lock()`—This method is used to perform the `lock` operation on the mutex.

`pthread_mutex_unlock()`—This method is used to perform the `unlock` operation.

The `Win32` library works similarly:

`HANDLE`—This method is used to refer to the lock.

`HANDLE CreateMutex()`—This method is used to create a `mutex` and return a `HANDLE`.

`WaitForSingleObject()`—This method is used to perform the `lock` operation on the mutex.

`ReleaseMutex`—This method is used to perform the `unlock` operation on the `mutex`.

Race2: *Reworked* **Race1** *Using Locks*

Example 3-14 shows the code used to eliminate the race condition found in Shared0. The code employs the Lock class we just developed. As before, with the examples of Race1 and Shared1, significant changes are required only for the Shared class—the class that represents the shared data to be protected with synchronization. A member variable, mutex, refers to an instance of the lock used to protect the other variables x and y whenever dif() and bump() are called.

Note that, in this example, dif() and bump() are not synchronized, because the synchronization will be done entirely in mutex lock() and unlock() calls. These calls are both themselves declared to be *synchronized*. They are now also declared to throw an InterruptedException, since they both call lock() on mutex, which can throw the exception, and then they simply pass it back to their caller.

An interesting difference between the implementation of dif() in class Shared2 and dif() in Shared0 or Shared1 is that dif() in Shared2 needs to declare a temporary variable, compute the difference, and then return the temporary variable. This might appear awkward, but it is easily understood by considering that the synchronized version of dif() (as presented in Shared1) does not need to worry about locking and unlocking because both are done implicitly. Thus, when the return x-y; command is encountered in a synchronized block, the return statement causes the object's lock to be

Example 3-14 Shared2: Eliminating Race Conditions Using Lock Class

```
class Shared2{
    protected int x=0,y=0;
    protected Lock mutex=new Lock();
    public int dif() throws InterruptedException {
        int tmp;
        mutex.lock();
        tmp=x-y;
        mutex.unlock();
        return tmp;
    }
    public void bump() throws InterruptedException {
        mutex.lock();
        x++;
        Thread.sleep(9);
        y++;
        mutex.unlock();
    }
}
```

released. The same is not true of the dif() method provided in Shared2, because the method is not declared synchronized. Thus, there is no applicable lock for the Shared2 instance itself.

It is possible to simulate what is normally done in Java by making use of the try statement. This statement is usually used to execute one or more statements that may result in an exception. Additionally, the statement can be used to guarantee that something is done, regardless of the outcome of the statements, by using the finally clause. The dif() code can be modified as shown in Example 3-15. It is probably best to put the unlocking code in finally clauses. That is what the Java compiler generates for synchronized statements and methods.

In general, explicit locks (such as the Lock class) should not be used as an alternative to the Java synchronized keyword. The Lock class has been illustrated here because many programmers who have worked with concurrency in other languages (such as C and C++) will undoubtedly be familiar with it. The Lock class is also an excellent (minimal)

Example 3-15 Reworking **Shared2** to Guarantee Proper Release of the Explicit **Lock.**

```java
class Shared2{
    protected int x=0,y=0;
    protected Lock mutex=new Lock();
    public int dif() throws InterruptedException {
        mutex.lock();
        try {
            return x-y;
        } finally {
            mutex.unlock();
        }
    }
    public void bump() throws InterruptedException {
        mutex.lock();
        try {
            x++;
            Thread.sleep(9);
            y++;
        } finally {
            mutex.unlock();
        }
    }
}
```

example of how to use conditions. Should you ever forget how a condition in Java works, feel free to revisit the `Lock` class as a refresher example.

Is the `Lock` Class Useful?

The answer to this question depends on your point of view. Java objects only provide you with a single lock. Thus, if you need multiple locks to protect variables separately, you would need to have separate objects. This is fairly easy to do: Simply declare a variable of type `Object`, and make sure that it really refers to an object:

```
Object xLock = new Object();
```

Then use a synchronized block to protect the critical section:

```
synchronized (xLock) {

}
```

Of course, the cost of creating an instance of class `Lock` is the same and is perhaps easier to use.

It's up to you!

Classic Synchronization Mechanisms

The `Lock` class illustrated how conditions can be useful to evolve a familiar synchronization mechanism using the intrinsic lock and condition mechanisms supported by every Java object. The remainder of this chapter is dedicated to other high-level synchronization mechanisms: counting semaphores, barriers, and simple futures. Counting semaphores are addressed in numerous textbooks on operating systems and systems programming. Barriers are discussed in textbooks on parallel processing and are used extensively in scientific computation. Futures have their roots in functional programming and have been discussed in numerous textbooks on programming languages.

Counting Semaphore

A counting semaphore is very similar to a lock. Recall that a lock is sometimes called a binary semaphore. This is because it is either in a locked (1) or an unlocked (0) state. In the counting semaphore, an integer count is maintained. Usually, the semaphore is initialized to a count N. There are two operations that are defined on the semaphore:

- **up()**: This operation adds one to the count and then notifies any thread that may be waiting for the count to become positive.

- **down()**: This operation waits for the count to become positive and then decrements the count.

Example 3-16 shows the code for a counting semaphore.

The implementation of a counting semaphore is very similar to that of a lock. The first noticeable difference between the two is that the methods are named `down()` and `up()` instead of `lock()` and `unlock()`. The reason for this difference is that semaphores are

Are Counting Semaphores Useful?

Counting semaphores are very useful. They can be used to allow at most N resources to be utilized at the same time. A resource can be anything you want it to be. Operating-systems textbooks usually give examples of resources that are managed by an OS, such as disk drives, tape drives, etc. Other examples of resources (in the context of this book) are open network connections, worker pools, etc.

Sometimes, it is easy to overlook the obvious. The semaphore can easily be used to maintain a safe atomic counter between a group of threads. Of course, this could be construed as a case of overkill, since atomic counters are supported by the Java standard using volatile variables. Any variable marked volatile cannot be cached and therefore has a write-through update policy, used when any operation is performed on it. An example of the code is

```
volatile int x = 0;
x++;
```

Example 3-16 Class `Semaphore`: An Implementation of a Counting Semaphore

```
public class Semaphore {
    protected int count;

    public Semaphore(int initCount)
        throws NegativeSemaphoreException{
        if (initCount<0)
            throw new NegativeSemaphoreException();
        count=initCount;
    }
    public Semaphore() { count=0; }

    public synchronized void down()
        throws InterruptedException {
        while (count==0) wait();
        count--;
    }
    public synchronized void up() {
        count++;
        notify();
    }
}
```

---

usually defined in the former terms in typical operating systems textbooks. (The original paper on the subject, written by Dijkstra, actually used `P()` and `V()`, the first letters of the Dutch words for "signal" and "notify," respectively.)

The `down()` method implementation resembles that of the `lock()` method. It waits indefinitely for the semaphore count to be positive. When the count becomes positive, the count will be decremented. As done in the `lock()` method (class `Lock`), the `InterruptedException` is passed to an outer context by declaring `throws Interrupted-Exception` in the method header. The `up()` method is very similar to the `unlock()` method (class `Lock`). The counter is incremented and notifies any waiting thread that the count has a positive value.

Barrier

In parallel and distributed computing applications, there is often a need to synchronize a group of threads (parallel tasks), usually inside a loop. A later chapter will address loop parallelism in greater detail. A barrier is an abstraction for performing this synchronization and is fairly straightforward. It is similar to the notion of a semaphore, but works somewhat backwards. The barrier, much like the counting semaphore, is initialized to a count N. The `barrier()` method, when called by a thread, decrements the count atomically. Then the caller waits (is blocked) until the barrier count reaches 0. If any call to `barrier()` results in the count reaching 0, all threads awaiting the count of 0 are notified, and the count is reset to N.

Thus, the `barrier()` is a great deal different than a semaphore in two ways:

- Most threads (N-1) reach the barrier and are forced to wait until the count is correct. When calling `down()` on a semaphore, a thread waits only when the count is 0.

- All threads are notified when the count reaches 0. In a semaphore, only a *single* thread is notified each time the `up()` operation is called.

Example 3-17 shows the code for the implementation of class `Barrier`.

The `Barrier` class has two instance variables:

- **count**: This variable is the current value of the barrier. When `count` becomes 0, it is reset to the value of variable `initCount`.

- **initCount**: This variable is the initial value of the barrier. It is a cached copy of the value passed in the constructor.

The constructor initializes `Barrier` to a positive count. An initial value that is negative or 0 results in a `BarrierException` code being thrown. (For conciseness, the code for `BarrierException` is not shown here, but it can be found on the accompanying CD. Its details are not essential to understand the `Barrier` class.) The `count` and `initCount` fields are initialized to the specified count.

The `barrier` method atomically decrements the count. If the count has not yet reached 0, the caller blocks indefinitely; otherwise, the count is reset to the value specified origi-

Example 3-17 Barrier Synchronization

```java
// Barrier.java

public class Barrier {
    protected int count, initCount;

    public Barrier(int n) throws BarrierException{
        if (n <= 0)
            throw new BarrierException(n)
        initCount = count = n;
    }

    public synchronized void barrier()
        throws InterruptedException {
        if (--count > 0)
            wait();
        else {
            count = initCount;
            notifyAll();
        }
    }
}
```

nally in the `Barrier` constructor, and all waiting threads are notified and, hence, unblocked.

An interesting question now arises: Earlier in the chapter, we mentioned that the proper way to wait for a condition is to first use a `while` loop to test the condition and then wait. In the `barrier()` method, this has not been done. The reason is that we are not waiting for the barrier to reach any particular value; we are simply waiting for it to be reset. Once it has been reset, every single thread that posted a `wait()` should be awakened and allowed to proceed. Effectively, the last thread to make a call to the `barrier()` method does not wait. Only the first `N-1` threads to arrive at the `barrier()` wait.

Futures

A future is an assign-once variable that can be read any number of times once it is set. Futures have their origins in functional programming languages. A typical use for a future is to support the familiar notion of a procedure call, in which the arguments being passed to the call may not yet have been evaluated. This is often acceptable, since very often a parameter is not used right away in a procedure call. (It is very difficult to use all of the parameters simultaneously. This fact can be verified by inspecting a substantial piece of code with a few parameters.) Futures also make sense in a multiprocessor system, in which there may be many processors to evaluate a set of futures.

A future is implemented in Java using a "wrapper." The code for the class `Future` is shown in Example 3-18. The wrapper is used to maintain a protected reference to a value. If the future has not yet been set, the value is set to the future instance itself. (This is a sensible value, since a future cannot have itself as a value, but must be able to have the value `null`. Alternatively, a boolean flag could be maintained; however, as Example 3-18

Example 3-18 The Future

```
public class SimpleFuture {
 protected Object value;

 public SimpleFuture() {value=this;}

 public SimpleFuture(Object val) {
    value=val;
 }

 public synchronized Object getValue()
    throws InterruptedException{
    while (value == this)
      wait();
    return value;
 }

 public synchronized boolean isSet(){
    return (value!=this);
 }

 public synchronized void setValue(Object val){
    if (value == this) {
      value = val;
      notifyAll();
    }
 }
}
```

points out, some of the ugliness that is inherent in the Java object model happens to be useful!) There are two key methods for working with a future:

- **getValue()**: This method is used to wait until the future has been set, then return a reference to the value of the future.

- **setValue()**: This method is used to set the value of the future, if it has not already been set. It also notifies all threads that might be awaiting the value of the future. If the future is already set, its value cannot be changed, and no further notifications are to be done.

Futures will be addressed again in greater detail later in this book. For now, think of a future as a clever trick used to wait for something to be produced—once. The concept of a future could be used, for example, to implement the concurrent-Web-page example, discussed in Chapter 1. For each Web page to be read, a thread can be created. Once the page has been read, it can be "written" to a future. Then, another waiting thread (usually, the main one) can wait for all of the futures, one at a time. The interesting aspect of this is that one can write concurrent applications that are fairly sophisticated without having to know all of the details of how threads and synchronization really work. Of course, we will discourage you from not knowing the details, since we want you to know them.

Deadlock

What is Deadlock?

Deadlock occurs when each thread in a group of threads is waiting for a condition that can only be caused by another member of the the group. For example, given threads T1 and T2, it is possible that T1 is holding a resource X while waiting for resource Y to become available. Meanwhile, T2 is holding resource Y and is waiting for resource X to become available. This condition is known, in the computing literature, as deadlock.

How to Know When Deadlock Has Hit You?

Aside from having to debug a distributed program (i.e., one that runs on many machines—something we will discuss later in this book), deadlock is perhaps one of the most difficult programming errors to correct. At times, deadlock appears to behave almost like an infinite loop. Sometimes, the program will appear to run normally by not "locking up." Often, the program will need to be run multiple times to even notice the problem. The tragedy of it all is that the results are usually not reproducible nor consistent.

Four Conditions of Deadlock

Four conditions enable the possibility for deadlock:

- Mutual exclusion: It must not be possible for more than one thread to use a resource at the same time.

- Hold and wait: Threads must hold resources and wait for others to become available. Deadlock is not possible if no thread ever holds more than one resource at a time. Nor is it possible if a thread can acquire more than one resource, but acquires all its resources at one instant.

- No preemption: It must not be possible to remove a resource from a thread that holds it. Only the thread that holds a resource can give it up.

- Circular wait: There must be a cycle of threads, each holding at least one resource and waiting to acquire one of the resources that the next thread in the cycle holds.

If any of the foregoing conditions is enforced, deadlock simply cannot occur. This idea comes from operating systems literature (textbooks). We will show how to put it into practice, focusing on eliminating circular waits.

A Classic Example: Dining Philosophers

Synchronization problems have been the subject of study for many decades. One of the classic problems, known as the Dining Philosophers problem, was presented by Dijkstra, who is also credited with the invention of the semaphore (which was presented earlier).

The Dining Philosophers problem is stated as follows. There are five philosophers sitting around a circular dinner table eating spaghetti. (You can substitute your favorite pasta here, without affecting your overall understanding of the problem.) Each philosopher is in one of two states: thinking or eating. Each philosopher has his own plate. There are five forks, one located between each plate. To eat, a philosopher needs two forks.

After thinking for a while, the philosopher will stop thinking, pick up one fork at a time, one from each side of his plate, and eat for a while. Then he will put down the forks, again one at each side of his plate, and return to thinking.

If each philosopher starts to eat at the same time, each might pick up the fork from the left side of his plate and wait for the one to the right to become available, resulting in deadlock. To solve the problem, a Java program that avoids such deadlocks needs to be written.

The code is organized in three classes:

- `Fork`: This class is an object that is shared between a pair of diners (instances of `Diner0`; see next).

- `Diner0`: This class is a threaded object that implements the moves of a typical diner in its `run()` method.

- `Diners0`: This class is a driver code that simply creates instances of `Fork` and `Diner0` and then sets the simulation in motion.

A `Fork` (shown in Example 3-19) is implemented using the `Lock` class described in Example 3-13. For output purposes, an `id` is maintained for each `Fork`. Aside from this difference, a fork, for all intents and purposes, is a lock. In keeping with our desire to be

Example 3-19 `Fork`

```
class Fork {
  public char id;
  private Lock lock=new Lock();

  public void pickup() throws InterruptedException {
    lock.lock();
  }

  public void putdown() throws InterruptedException {
    lock.unlock();
  }

  public Fork(int i) {
    Integer i = new Integer(i);
    id = i.toString().charAt(0);
  }
}
```

object oriented, the methods are named `pickup()` and `putdown()`, which are the actual operations that can be performed on a fork (*responsibilities,* in object jargon).

Each diner is represented by `Diner0` (shown in Example 3-20). A diner has a state (which again exists for the purpose of output) and references to two forks (L and R in the code). The `run()` method of the diner is where the diner actually does his work. He thinks (which blocks him for a specified time), then picks up the left fork L, blocks himself, then picks up his right fork R, then eats (again, blocking himself), and then puts both forks L and R down to take a break from eating. This process is repeated 1,000 times for each diner.

The driver code (shown in Example 3-21) is responsible for setting the table, metaphorically speaking. This is done in the `main()` method. Two arrays are initialized:

- **fork**: This is an array of `Fork` instances.

- **diner**: This is an array of `Diner` instances.

The assignment of forks to diners is relatively straightforward. `Diner` 0 is assigned forks 0 and 1; `diner` 1 is assigned forks 1 and 2, and so on. The last diner, 4, is assigned forks 4 and 0. It will be apparent that this last numbering, although it makes the coding somewhat easier by not having to encode a special case, is precisely what causes the possibility of a deadlock.

Once all of the forks and diners have been created, the simulation of dining is commenced. The `main()` method, being effectively the main thread, establishes itself as a "watcher"

Example 3-20 `Diner0`

```java
class Diner0 extends Thread {
    private char state='t';
    private Fork L,R;

    public Diner0(Fork left, Fork right){
        super();
        L=left;
        R=right;
    }

    protected void think() throws InterruptedException {
        sleep((long)(Math.random()*7.0));
    }

    protected void eat() throws InterruptedException {
        sleep((long)(Math.random()*7.0));
    }

    public void run() {
        int i;
        try {
            for (i=0;i<1000;i++) {
                state = 't';
                think();
                state=L.id;
                sleep(1);
                L.pickup();
                state=R.id;
                sleep(1);
                R.pickup();
                state='e';
                eat();
                L.putdown();
                R.putdown();
            }
            state='d';
        } catch (InterruptedException e) {}
    }
}
```

or "monitor" of the other threads. Its priority is set to be slightly higher than any of the other running threads.

Example 3-21 `Diners0`: **The Driver**

```java
class Diners0 {
    static Fork[] fork=new Fork[5];
    static Diner0[] diner=new Diner0[5];

    public static void main(String[] args) {
        int i,j=0;
        boolean goOn;

        for (i=0;i<5;i++) {
            fork[i]=new Fork(i);
        }
        for (i=0;i<5;i++) {
            diner[i]=new Diner0(fork[i],fork[(i+1)%5]);
        }
        for (i=0;i<5;i++) {
            diner[i].start();
        }
        int newPrio = Thread.currentThread().getPriority()+1;
        Thread.currentThread().setPriority(newPrio);
        goOn=true;
        while (goOn) {
            for (i=0;i<5;i++) {
                System.out.print(diner[i].state);
            }
            if (++j%5==0)
                System.out.println();
            else
                System.out.print(' ');
            goOn=false;
            for (i=0;i<5;i++) {
                goOn |= diner[i].state != 'd';
            }
            try {
                Thread.sleep(51);
            } catch (InterruptedException e) {return;}
        }
    }
}
```

The main thread then goes into an indefinite (not infinite) loop, which will terminate only when all of the diners are in the "done" state. The only way this can happen is if a given diner thread terminates (i.e., executes its loop 1,000 times). The way thread termination is determined is by examining the *state* of each particular diner to see whether or not it is d (done). The only way goOn (the condition by which the monitor thread's loop is terminated) becomes false is when all of the diners are in the d state.

Taking a step back, we now want to know what is the point of setting the priority? Java uses a priority scheduler that will run the highest priority thread available to run, or one of the highest priority threads available if there is more than one at the highest priority level. The reason we set the priority level of the main thread higher than that of the diners is so that any running diner can be preempted to examine (and print) its state.

There are only a few priority levels available to a thread (12), which are represented as an integer. The higher the integer, the higher the priority. You can examine a thread's priority using method getPriority(), and assign a thread a new priority using setPriority(). As mentioned in the previous chapter, there are also a number of constant values available in the Thread class to make use of normal priority values: Thread.MAX_PRIORITY, Thread.NORMAL_PRIORITY, and Thread.MIN_PRIORITY. You must be careful to ensure that a higher priority thread does not prevent other threads from running. This is always a possibility, especially when you use MAX_PRIORITY. Until the thread does something to block itself (I/O or synchronization—two examples of a blocking primitive), the thread will be allowed to run to completion, preventing any other threads from running in the process. In this example, the watcher thread is explicitly putting itself to sleep for so many milliseconds—hence the Thread.sleep(51). This is intended not as a kludge, but to explicitly guarantee that the main thread does block for a reasonable amount of time. Remember this: The main thread's purpose for existence is to show you the states of the various diners so you will know how much progress they are making as a whole (and so you will see what happens when they get into a deadlock situation).

The following box shows output from a particular run. As discussed for the example Race0, the output is likely to be different between different runs, due to different serializations of events.

A brief explanation of the output is in order. The output represents the states of the five diners in order (0 through 4). The output is grouped by iteration in the main thread, separated by either a space or a new line, the intent being to make the output as neat as possible without using too many lines. Of course, because the program occasionally deadlocks, this causes an infinite loop to occur—the last line of output clearly shows that a circular wait has occurred. That is, each diner is waiting for a fork that he will never be able to acquire. (i.e., never be able to *pick up*).

As mentioned earlier, there are four ways in which deadlock can occur. To eliminate deadlock, all you need to do is find a way to eliminate one of the conditions that can cause it. It is not always desirable to eliminate a given condition. We will return to a discussion of this point shortly; however, we consider here the possibility of eliminating a *circular wait* condition.

```
1133t 0e24e 02t30 023et 0t24e
0e24e t2230 02t30 t234e et240
12et4 t134e t134e 1et30 023et
023e4 et240 1et34 023et t134e
e1240 12et4 t134e 1et30 02e30
023et t124t 0tt4e 12e30 t134e
1et30 12et4 113et t134e 1et30
1tt34 02et0 t13et e1240 1e230
12et4 t234e tt230 1et34 02e34
t134e 1e230 02e30 t23e4 t2ett
e1340 1et30 023et t134e 1et30
023et t134e 1et30 12e34 12et4
t134e ttt3e et230 1et34 023et
et240 12et4 123e4 0234e t1240
1et30 023et 023et et340 12e34
02t44 0134e et240 12e34 013tt
et240 01240 12340 12340 12340
12340 12340 12340 12340 12340
12340 12340 12340 12340 12340
12340 12340 12340 12340 12340
12340 12340 12340 12340 12340
12340 12340 12340 12340 12340
```

In the above run, it is clear where the deadlock occurs. The simulation gets stuck in a pattern "12340," which indicates that a circular wait condition has occurred that will never terminate. In this simulation, execution was halted explicitly by typing *control-C*.

One way to prevent circular waiting is to do *resource enumeration* and only allow individual threads to acquire resources in ascending order.

When you acquire resources (such as the Fork object) in ascending order, circular wait is impossible: for a circular wait to occur, some thread must be holding a higher numbered resource waiting for a lower numbered resource, but that is forbidden. Here is how we can use resource enumeration in the Dining Philosophers problem to eliminate deadlock.

The following loop excerpt from Example 3-21 to define a Diner is where the problem occurs:

```
for (i=0;i<5;i++) {
    diner[i]=new Diner0(fork[i],fork[(i+1)%5]);
}
```

A simple fix, which reorders the Fork objects such that a lower-numbered instance is always picked up first is to do the following:

```
for (i=0;i<4;i++) {
    diner[i]=new Diner0(fork[i],fork[(i+1)%5]);
}
diner[4] = new Diner0(fork[0], fork[4]);
```

It should be obvious how this code fixes the problem. The problem is caused by the last iteration of the loop, which is equivalent to the following long-winded code (an expansion of the first version of the loop):

```
diner[0] = new Diner0(fork[0], fork[1]);
diner[1] = new Diner0(fork[1], fork[2]);
diner[2] = new Diner0(fork[2], fork[3]);
diner[3] = new Diner0(fork[3], fork[4]);
diner[4] = new Diner0(fork[4], fork[0]);
```

The second version of the loop stops one short of the last iteration and simply does an explicit ordering of the final two forks. Instead of fork[4] being diner 4's left fork and fork[0] being diner 4's right fork, the forks are swapped. The notion of left and right is purely a matter of convention: one of the philosophers can always be considered to be left handed.

In summary, the diners are programmed to pick up their left fork before their right fork. So `diner j`, for j ranging from 0 through 3, will pick up `fork j` and then `fork j+1`.We explicitly tell diner 4 to pick up fork 0 before fork 4. The reworked code with the above changes appears in Example 3-22. The c hanges to support resource enumeration are shown in bold.

Chapter Wrap-up

This chapter has focused on race conditions, which represent one of your biggest enemies when it comes to programming concurrent applications. Java helps you to address the problem of race conditions using object locking, which is supported by each and every Java object created using the `new` operator. Java is one of the first modern (and popular) languages to support object locking. In languages such as C and C++, programmers are forced to make use of platform-specific libraries, such as `pthreads` (the UNIX standard) and `Win32` threads (the Microsoft de facto standard). This by no means implies that a great amount of work has not been done to bring similar features to C and C++; however, in all cases and at some level, the solution is predominantly driven by libraries, not by the language itself.

While Java makes it considerably easier to support concurrency by providing support directly in the language, its features, in many respects, are not radically different from those found in `pthreads` or `Win32` threads. Often, programmers find the need for more elaborate synchronization than that provided by merely locking objects. Java conditions were discussed as a way of providing more elaborate synchronization—a lock can be held for a while, but released "temporarily" while awaiting a certain condition. This can lead to better performance, since repeatedly acquiring and releasing locks does have a cost. As will be discussed in the next chapter, the word "wait" introduces the possibility of an encounter with another common enemy: deadlock.

Example 3-22 `Diners1`**: The Driver**

```
class Diners1 {
    static Fork[] fork=new Fork[5];
    static Diner0[] diner=new Diner0[5];

    public static void main(String[] args) {
        int i,j=0;
        boolean goOn;

        for (i=0;i<5;i++) {
            fork[i]=new Fork(i);
        }
        for (i=0;i<4;i++) {
            diner[i]=new Diner0(fork[i],fork[(i+1)%5]);
        }
        diner[4]=new Diner0(fork[4],fork[0]);

        for (i=0;i<5;i++) {
            diner[i].start();
        }
        int newPrio = Thread.currentThread().getPriority()+1;
        Thread.currentThread().setPriority(newPrio);
        goOn=true;
        while (goOn) {
            for (i=0;i<5;i++) {
                System.out.print(diner[i].state);
            }
            if (++j%5==0)
                System.out.println();
            else
                System.out.print(' ');
            goOn=false;
            for (i=0;i<5;i++) {
                goOn |= diner[i].state != 'd';
            }
            try {
                Thread.sleep(51);
            } catch (InterruptedException e) {return;}
        }
    }
}
```

The chapter concluded with a discussion of some other mutual-exclusion and synchronization mechanisms that are widely familiar to programmers—locks, semaphores, and barri-

ers—and one that perhaps is less familiar: the future. These classes are all built rather easily from the concurrency framework provided by Java and are very useful for developing concurrent applications. (One could argue that these classes belong in the `java.lang` package because they are foundational, but this is an argument for another day and time.)

Exercises

1. (Easy) Explain what the following code from Example 3-2 is doing:

   ```
   System.out.print(".X".charAt(s.dif()));
   ```

   In particular, explain why it is permissible for a string "constant" to appear on the left-hand side of the dot operator. Is there ever the possibility that this string is not indexed properly with the `s.dif()` call?

2. (Easy) In the same example as the preceding problem, what are all of the valid results of `s.dif()`? Sketch a proof of why it is impossible for a value other than one of these results to be produced.

3. (Easy) Using the Java documentation, see if you can find classes that make use of synchronized methods. What classes can be used in a thread-safe manner? Can you find a Java class that might not work reliably in a multithreaded context?

4. (Intermediate) Sketch or implement a program that will compute the length of a time slice in milliseconds. If it is not possible to develop such a program, provide an explanation.

5. (Intermediate) Study the Java library source code to better understand the classes you discovered in Part 3.

6. (Intermediate) In Example 3-1, why is it necessary for the `q.setDaemon(true)` method call to be inserted in the main method? Is there another way to gracefully prevent the main method from exiting prematurely?

7. (Intermediate) Explain why it is possible for two (or more) threads to enter a synchronized method (or methods) when one (or more) threads is waiting for a condition. As a more advanced problem, explain what is happening from the operating system's point of view.

8. (Easy) `FileCopy0` and `FileCopy1` are both working versions of a concurrent file-copying algorithm. Using the `System` class (which provides support for "timing" using the `currentTimeMillis()` method), compare the performance of the two programs. Use a sufficiently large file (at least one megabyte) with a block size of 4,096 to do the comparison.

9. (Easy) If a `RuntimeException` occurs in the `run()` method (e.g., something like a `NullPointerException`), does the method terminate?

10. (Intermediate) Example 3-2 shows a version of shared data that does not make use of synchronized methods. Is synchronization necessary in this case? Why or why not?

11. (Easy) The Semaphore class shown in Example 3-16 is an example of how to implement a counter that can be incremented or decremented atomically, provided its value never becomes negative. Show how to implement a class called Counter that can be incremented or decremented at will by a particular value.

12. (Intermediate) Compare the locking framework of Java (the synchronized statement) with the Lock and Semaphore classes shown in this chapter. Does Lock do anything that synchronized does not? What about Semaphore? How do Lock and Semaphore compare with one another?

13. (Hard) Using the URL class of Java, write a program that fetches three Web pages in a loop. Use the timing function (see problem 5) of the System class to determine the time. Write a second version of this program that creates separate threads to fetch each page and uses an array of Future instances. The main thread should wait for each Future instance. Again, use the timing function to determine the total execution time.

Chapter 4

Monitors

Monitors, at their most general, are classes that control threads' access to resources. Java synchronization is based on the variety of monitors that were developed in the early 1970s by Per Brinch-Hansen and C. A. R. Hoare, but Java synchronization is not as well developed as Brinch-Hansen and Hoare monitors are.

In this chapter, we will compare Java's synchronization to monitors. We will present our Monitor class. This class will allow you to use full-monitor facilities in Java, although it will not allow the compiler to check your program for correctness, as Brinch-Hansen's and Hoare's do. The implementation of the Monitor class will itself be instructive on how to use Semaphores.

Real Monitors and Java Monitors

When Brinch-Hansen and Hoare did their work, they were faced with the following problems: Concurrent programs were unreliable and hard to write. Semaphores were already understood; Dijkstra had developed them half a decade earlier, but semaphores were often used incorrectly, and a compiler could provide no help on using them.

What Brinch-Hansen was after was a facility for synchronizing concurrent programs that would be easy to use and could also be checked by a compiler.

The first requirement for this facility is that while they are concurrently executing, threads (processes) must be accessing different sets of variables. When they have to access the same variables, they must be granted mutually exclusive access. Moreover, one thread must be able to wait for a condition that another thread can cause.

Brinch-Hansen and Hoare called their solution *monitors*. They gave this definition of a monitor:

> *A monitor is essentially a shared class with explicit queues.*

Thus, it has two components: *a shared class* and *explicit queues*. We will consider them one at a time.

Shared Classes. The effect of a shared class can occur in Java by creating a class in which all fields are private and all methods are synchronized.

In a monitor, the only variables that can be accessed by more than one thread are the fields of a monitor. Since the fields are private, they cannot be accessed outside the monitor. Since the methods of the monitor are synchronized, the accesses inside the monitor are mutually exclusive. This meets the requirement that threads have mutually exclusive access to shared variables.

Explicit Queues. Threads must be able to wait for other threads to cause conditions. In a monitor, the conditions are represented by *condition variables*. These variables contain queues of threads waiting for the conditions to hold.

In the bounded-buffer example, there are two conditions that a thread could be waiting for. If a thread wishes to read a value from the buffer, the buffer must first contain a value. If a thread wishes to place a value in the buffer, the buffer must not be full.

Java has only one queue for threads waiting at an object, so in our bounded-buffer code, we must notify *all* waiting threads when we put a value into the buffer (making it non-empty) or remove a value (making it nonfull). We must wake up all of the threads in order to see if the buffer permits their execution. This is inefficient.

Using true monitors, we would use two condition variables. When we put a value in the queue, we would only wake up one thread waiting for the queue to be nonempty. When we remove a value, we would only wake up one thread waiting for the queue to be nonfull. The code to do this in a dialect of Pascal might be

```
shared class BoundedBuffer (size: integer)
var
        notEmpty, notFull: Condition;
```

```
        hd, tl: integer;
        buffer: array 0 .. size-1 of Object;
procedure put(v: Object)
        begin
                if tl - hd >= buffer.length then
                        await notFull;
                buffer[tl mod buffer.length] := v;
                tl:=tl+1;
                signal notEmpty;
        end
function get(): Object
        begin
                var v: Object;
                if tl=hd then await notEmpty;
                v := buffer[hd mod buffer.length];
                hd:=hd+1;
                signal notFull;
                return v;
        end
begin
                hd:=0;
                tl:=0;
end.
```

Notice that not only is there more than one queue that a thread can wait on, but also that the threads do not wait in loops. In Java, a thread waits in a `while` loop testing the condition, for example,

```
while (!condition) wait();
```

In Java, the thread awakened by `notify()` or `notifyAll()` does not get immediate control of the lock. By the time the thread runs, the condition may no longer be true, so it must check the condition again. With a monitor, however, the shared object is immediately handed off to the thread that has been awakened, so that when the thread starts running, the condition is guaranteed to still be true.

Overall. Monitors provide greater security from system breakdown than Java does. Compilers for languages that support monitors can assure that all fields that can be accessed by more than one thread are protected by monitors. They can also assure mutual exclusion to those fields. They can check for the possibility of deadlock due to cycles in the graph of monitor calls. The implementation of these compilers can guarantee that a thread waiting for a condition will gain access to the monitor immediately, so the condition will still be true.

Despite Java's goal of reliability and catching as many errors at compile time as possible, it provides nowhere near the same level of support for writing reliable concurrent programs that monitors provide.

This led Brinch-Hansen to express a great disappointment with Java's synchronization.

He writes:

> *Java's most serious mistake was the decision to use the sequential part of the language to implement the run-time support for the parallel features.*
>
> *In 1975, Concurrent Pascal demonstrated that platform-independent parallel programs (even small operating systems) can be written as a secure programming language with monitors. It is astounding to me that Java's insecure parallelism is taken seriously by the programming language community a quarter of a century after the invention of monitors and Concurrent Pascal. It has no merit.*[1]

Class **Monitor** in the **Thread** Package

The thread package provides the Monitor class with condition variables similar to those defined by Hoare and Brinch-Hansen. The condition variables are provided by the inner class Condition. Of course, the syntax is not the same, and the compile-time checking provided by monitors is not possible.

To use a monitor to protect your class, you can have your class extend Monitor, as in the following bounded-buffer example:

```
class BoundedBuffer3 extends Monitor{
  Condition notEmpty=new Condition();
  Condition notFull=new Condition();
  volatile int hd=0,tl=0;
  Object[] buffer;
  public BoundedBuffer3(int size) {
     buffer=new Object[size];
  }
  public void put(Object v)
        throws InterruptedException {
     enter();
     if(tl - hd >= buffer.length) notFull.await();
     buffer[tl++ % buffer.length] = v;
     notEmpty.signal();
     leave();
  }
  public Object get()
        throws InterruptedException {
     enter();
     Object v;
     if (tl==hd) notEmpty.await();
     v = buffer[hd++ % buffer.length];
     notFull.signal();
     leave();
     return v;
  }
}
```

[1] Brinch-Hansen, Per, "Java's Insecure Parallelism," *ACM SIGPLAN Notices*, 34(4) April 1999.

Or, you can use a separate `Monitor` object:

```
class BoundedBuffer4 {
  Monitor mon = new Monitor();
  Monitor.Condition notEmpty = mon.new Condition();
  Monitor.Condition notFull = mon.new Condition();
  volatile int hd=0,tl=0;
  Object[] buffer;
  public BoundedBuffer4(int size) {
      buffer=new Object[size];
  }
  public void put(Object v)
          throws InterruptedException {
      mon.enter();
      if(tl - hd >= buffer.length) notFull.await();
      buffer[tl++ % buffer.length] = v;
      notEmpty.signal();
      mon.leave();
  }
  public Object get()
          throws InterruptedException {
      mon.enter();
      Object v;
      if (tl==hd) notEmpty.await();
      v = buffer[hd++ % buffer.length];
      notFull.leaveWithSignal();
      return v;
  }
}
```

A Monitor must be entered with a call to the method `enter()` and exited with a call to the method `leave()`. You may enter the same monitor more than once, for example, calling one monitor-protected method from another. Of course, you must eventually leave as many times as you enter.

`Condition` is an inner class. It must be created within a monitor object. It represents a condition that a thread may wish to wait on.

To wait for condition `C` to hold, a thread calls
```
C.await();
```
To signal that the condition holds, a thread calls
```
C.signal();
```
If one or more threads are awaiting the condition at the time of a signal, one of the threads will be given immediate control of the monitor. The thread executing the `signal()` will wait to reacquire the monitor.

To simultaneously signal a condition and leave the monitor, you can call `leaveWithSignal()`. It is more efficient than a `signal()` followed by a `leave()`, since the executing thread does not have to wait to reacquire the monitor before executing the `leave()`. The method is called with

```
C.leaveWithSignal();
```

Be sure that you declare the fields of the monitor-protected class to be `volatile`. A Java compiler is permitted to cache fields in registers. This causes problems for concurrency, since one thread could change its cached copy of a shared field without storing it into memory. Then another thread would not see the change in its own cached copy or in memory. A thread, however, *is* forced to synchronize shared fields with their copies in memory when entering or leaving synchronized sections of code or when executing `wait,` `notify`, or `notifyAll`. This permits concurrent threads to communicate. Unfortunately, when trying to use other facilities to provide synchronization, such as the `Monitor` class, the compiler doesn't know to synchronize its cache with memory, so two threads trying to communicate through a monitor-protected class may not be able to see each other's changes. But if the fields are declared `volatile`, the compiler will store into memory on assignment and fetch from memory on access. This may slow down execution, but it will permit threads to communicate.

Monitor's Methods

A thread enters a monitor by calling the `enter()` method. It must call this before

```
public void enter()
```

accessing the fields of the protected object. The fields must be declared `volatile` for reasons already given.

A thread leaves the monitor by calling the method `leave()`. A thread must not access

```
public void leave()
          throws MonitorException
```

fields of the protected object after calling `leave()`. Leave throws `MonitorException` if the thread executing this does not have the monitor locked.

To leave the monitor temporarily, a thread may call `release()`. Release returns a `MonitorLock` object that can be used to reenter later. Note that if the thread has entered several monitors, it can release and reacquire any or all of them, no matter where it is in the program.

```
public MonitorLock release()
      throws MonitorException
```

`MonitorLock` contains the entry count, the number of times the monitor has been entered, but not yet left, and the identification of the monitor and the thread that had it locked. `MonitorLock`'s `reacquire()` method is called reentered the monitor later.

`Release` throws `MonitorException` if the thread executing this does not own the monitor.

Interface **MonitorCondition**'s *Methods*

Interface `MonitorCondition` is implemented by class `Monitor.Condition` (i.e., the local class `Condition` within class `Monitor`). To create a `MonitorCondition` in monitor M, call `M.new Condition()`. The purpose of `MonitorCondition` is to allow threads to wait for conditions to hold and to signal that the conditions hold.

To wait for the condition to hold, a thread calls the method `await()`. This method throws

```
public void await()
            throws java.lang.InterruptedException,
                   MonitorException
```

`InterruptedException` if interrupted while waiting, and `MonitorException` if the executing thread does not own this `Monitor`.

A thread calls the method `signal()` to signal that the condition has occurred. If there

```
public void signal()
            throws MonitorException
```

are any waiting threads, it will wake up one of them to resume execution, hand over the monitor to it, and itself wait to reenter the monitor. `Signal` throws `MonitorException` if the executing thread does not own the `Monitor`.

The method `leaveWithSignal()` simultaneously signals a condition and leaves the monitor. It is equivalent to

```
          cond.signal(); mon.leave();
```

```
public void leaveWithSignal()
            throws MonitorException
```

If there are any waiting threads, it signals one of them to resume execution and hands over the monitor to it.

If the current thread has entered the monitor only once, `leaveWithSignal()` is faster than a call to `signal()` followed by a call to `leave()`. The executing thread does not have to enter the monitor again just to leave it. However, if this thread has entered the monitor more than once, `leaveWithSignal()` behaves like `signal()` followed by `leave()`. After the signaled thread has run, the signaling thread will reenter the monitor to complete its execution.

The method `leaveWithSignal()` throws `InterruptedException` if the thread is interrupted while trying to reenter the monitor. It throws `MonitorException` if the thread executing this is not inside the `Monitor`.

Interface `MonitorLock`

The Lock class within Monitor (`Monitor.Lock`) has only one method: `reacquire()`. It is used to enter the monitor again after an earlier `release()`. It

```
public void reacquire()
      throws MonitorException
```

throws `InterruptedException` if the thread is interrupted while waiting to enter. It throws `MonitorException` if the thread that called `reacquire()` wasn't the thread that released the monitor.

A `Monitor.Lock` object contains a reference to the thread that executed `release()`, the monitor it released, and the count of the number of locks it held on the monitor. The `reacquire()` method reestablishes all the locks the thread had on the monitor.

`MonitorLocks` and the methods `release()` and `reacquire()` are not part of the original specification of monitors. Almost certainly, the designers of the monitors concept would not approve of them. They were added as a possibility for avoiding deadlock. They allow a thread to release several monitors if it must wait for a condition.

Examples using `Monitor` Objects

You've already seen two implementations of a bounded buffer implemented using monitors. We'll show `Monitor` objects being used for implementations of `SimpleFuture` (see Example 3-18) and a subset of `SharedTableOfQueues` (whose full implementation is described in the chapter entitled "Shared Tables of Queues").

SimpleFuture

The code for our implementation of `SimpleFuture` using a `Monitor` object is shown in Example 4–1. Its fields are

- `value`: This is the value stored in the future. To indicate that there is currently no value present, the `value` field points to the future object itself. (The theory is that one value that the user will never wish to put in the future is the future itself.)

- `is_set`: This is a condition variable. Threads that try to get the value before it is set wait on this condition.

Recall that a future is a variable that can be assigned only once. When threads attempt to fetch a value from the future, they are delayed until the value has been assigned. In the Java implementation, we could release all threads with a `notifyAll()` method call. With monitors, we cannot awaken all at the same time.

Let's examine the implementation of methods `isSet`, `getValue`, and `setValue`.

`isSet()`. The way we determine whether a value has been set is by examining the `value` field. If it references this `SimpleFuture` itself, then there is no value present.

The other conspicuous trick in `isSet()` is using `try...return...finally...leave` to leave the monitor after returning the value. This may not be as obvious as saving the value to be returned in a variable, leaving the monitor, and then executing a return statement.

`setValue()`. The `if` statement at the top of the code tests to see if the future has already been assigned a value and, if so, to refuse to reassign it. If the value hasn't been set yet, `setValue()` does the assignment and hands off the monitor to one of the waiting threads (if there are any). It does *not* loop and wake them all up. Each thread that is awakened hands off the monitor to the next waiting thread.

`getValue()`. Method `getValue()` is forced to wait if the value hasn't been assigned yet, but can return immediately if the value has been. It will throw an `InterruptedException` if it is interrupted while waiting. The `try...catch` handles leaving the monitor while interrupted.

As explained for `setValue()`, the call to `leaveWithSignal()` hands off the monitor to another waiting thread. Each of the waiting threads hands off the monitor to the next

Example 4–1 Class `SimpleFuture`

```
public class SimpleFuture extends Monitor {
 private volatile Object value;
 private Condition is_set=new Condition();
 public SimpleFuture() {value=this;}
 public SimpleFuture(Object val) {value=val;}
 public Object getValue()
    throws InterruptedException {
        enter();
      try {
        if (value==this) is_set.await();
        is_set.leaveWithSignal();
        return value;
      } catch (InterruptedException ie) {
        leave();
        throw ie;
      }
 }
 public boolean isSet() {
        enter();
        try {
            return (value!=this);
        } finally {leave();}
 }
 public void setValue(Object val) {
        enter();
        if (value!=this) {
                leave();
                return;
        }
        value=val;
        is_set.leaveWithSignal();
 }
}
```

as it exits. Since `leaveWithSignal()` is equivalent to `leave()` when no threads are waiting, it is okay to call it even if there are no threads waiting.

SharedTableOfQueues

This implementation of a subset of `SharedTableOfQueues` is a subclass of `Monitor`. Its overall structure is shown in Example 4–2. It uses a hash table to look up the queues. The queues themselves are represented by the local class `Folder`. (The name was chosen for historical reasons: It was used in the `Memo` system, which provides a distributed memory communication system based on a shared table of queues.)

Example 4–2 Class `SharedTableOfQueues`

```
class SharedTableOfQueues extends Monitor {
  Hashtable tbl=new Hashtable();
   private class Folder {
        volatile QueueComponent q=new QueueComponent();
        volatile Condition notEmpty=new Condition();
        volatile int numWaiting=0;
        }
  public void put(Object key, Object value) { ... }
  public Object get(Object key)
       throws InterruptedException {... }
  public Object getSkip(Object key) {... }
  }
```

The class `Folder` is used strictly as a data structure. It has no methods. Its fields are

*   q: This is the actual queue. It is an object of class `QueueComponent` which is used in other classes in the thread package as well as well.

*   notEmpty: This is the `Condition` that the queue, q, is not empty. Threads calling `get()` wait for this condition. This condition is bound to the surrounding `SharedTableOfQueue`'s Monitor.

*   numWaiting: This field counts the number of waiting threads. It is used to decide when to remove folders. If there are no values in the queue and no threads waiting, the folder may be removed; it will be created in exactly the same state if it is referenced again.

The methods are implemented as follows:

put(). The `put(key, value)` method (see Example 4–3), puts a `value` into the queue associated with a `key`. It uses a hash table to look up the queue, represented by a `Folder` object. The queue has to be created if one doesn't already exist. The `put()` method leaves the monitor signaling the folder's `notEmpty` condition.

get(). The `get(key)` method has to accomplish several things:

*   If the `key` does not already have a folder, one is created.

*   Field `numWaiting` is incremented before this thread waits for the queue to have something in it and is decremented afterwards.

Example 4–3 The `SharedTableOfQueues` method `put()`

```java
public void put(Object key, Object value) {
        enter();
        Folder f = (Folder)tbl.get(key);
        if (f==null) tbl.put(key,f=new Folder());
        f.q.put(value);
        f.notEmpty.leaveWithSignal();
}
```

Example 4–4 The `SharedTableOfQueues` method `get()`

```java
public Object get(Object key)
            throws InterruptedException {
   Folder f=null;
   enter();
   try {
        f=(Folder)tbl.get(key);
        if (f==null) tbl.put(key,f=new Folder());
        f.numWaiting++;
        if (f.q.isEmpty()) f.notEmpty.await();
        f.numWaiting--;
        return f.q.get();
   } finally {
        if (    f!=null &&
                f.q.isEmpty() &&
                f.numWaiting==0   )
                        tbl.remove(key);
        leave();
   }
}
```

- After getting a value from the queue, if the queue is empty and there are no threads waiting to remove something from it, `get()` removes the queue.

getSkip(). Method getSkip(key) returns immediately, whether or not the queue contained a value. If there is no folder associated with the key or if the queue is empty, it simply returns null. Its code is shown in Example 4–5.

Example 4–5 SharedTableOfQueues method getSkip()

```
public Object getSkip(Object key) {
    Folder f=null;
    enter();
    try {
        f=(Folder)tbl.get(key);
        if (f==null || f.q.isEmpty()) {
            return null;
        }
        return f.q.get();
    } finally {
        if (     f!=null &&
                 f.q.isEmpty() &&
                 f.numWaiting==0   )
                       tbl.remove(key);
        leave();
    }
}
```

As with get(), getSkip() removes the queue if it is empty and no other threads are waiting to get a value from it.

Implementation of Monitor, Condition, and MonitorLock

The overall structure of class Monitor is shown in Example 4–6.

The Monitor class has three fields. The Semaphore, monitorEntry, gives exclusive access to the monitor:

- monitorEntry.down(): locks the monitor on entry,

- monitorEntry.up(): unlocks the monitor on exit.

The current field references the thread that currently possesses the monitor. It is null if the monitor isn't currently owned by any thread. The monitorEntryCount field

Example 4–6 Structure of class `Monitor`.

```
public class Monitor{
 Semaphore monitorEntry=new Semaphore(1);
 volatile Thread current=null;
 volatile int monitorEntryCount=0;
 public class Condition implements MonitorCondition {
    volatile int waiting=0;
    Semaphore waitCond=new Semaphore(0);
     public void await()
       throws InterruptedException, MonitorException {...}
     public void signal()
        throws MonitorException {...}
     public void leaveWithSignal()
       throws MonitorException {...}
 }
 public void enter() {...}
 public void leave() throws MonitorException {...}
 private class Lock implements MonitorLock{
 int n = monitorEntryCount;
 Thread owner = current;
 public void reacquire() throws
        MonitorException {...}
 }
 public MonitorLock release() throws MonitorException {...}
 }
```

`Monitor` fields

`java.lang.Thread current`; The current thread.

`Semaphore monitorEntry`; Semaphore to lock the `Monitor`

`int monitorEntryCount`; The number of times the monitor's current owner
has entered it minus the number of times it has exited it.

counts the number of times the thread that currently owns the monitor has entered it minus the number of times it has left. Upon leaving the monitor, if `monitorEntryCount` becomes zero, the monitor is unlocked.

Monitor Entry and Exit

Method `enter()` checks to see if the current thread already owns the monitor. If so, it merely increments the `monitorEntryCount`. If not, it must seize the monitor by downing the `monitorEntry` semaphore. Once it owns the monitor, it assigns itself (a reference to its `Thread` object) to the `current` field and places an initial count of unity in the `monitorEntryCount` field.

Example 4–7 The `Monitor` method `entry()`

```
public void enter() {
        if (current == Thread.currentThread())
                monitorEntryCount++;
        else {
                boolean interrupted=Thread.interrupted();
                for(;;) try {
                        monitorEntry.down(); break;
                } catch (InterruptedException ie) {
                        interrupted=true;
                }
                current = Thread.currentThread();
                monitorEntryCount=1;
                if (interrupted) current.interrupt();
        }
}
```

However, a question concerning many of these methods is, "How should they work with `InterruptedException`?" Our underlying implementation waits to acquire the monitor by downing semaphores. The `down()` method can throw an `InterruptedException`. If we just pass that through, we could throw `InterruptedExceptions` on `enter()`, `await()`, `signal()`, `leaveWithSignal()`, and `reacquire()`. Having to put in `try–catch` statements around all these calls would make `Monitors` inconvenient to use.

We follow the lead of Java's monitors. `InterruptedException` will not be thrown upon entering or leaving a monitor, but can be thrown upon waiting for a condition to be signalled. Thus, `enter()`, `signal()`, `leaveWithSignal()`, and `reacquire()` should not be able to throw `InterruptedException`. They should, however, preserve the state of the thread. If the thread was interrupted when it called the method, it should still be interrupted when it returns.

This explains the boolean variable `interrupted`. This variable is set if the thread enters the method in an interrupted state, or if it is interrupted while waiting on a semaphore within the method. At the end of the method, the thread is again interrupted if the `interrupted` flag is set.

Thus, we have the following code:

```
for(;;) try {
        monitorEntry.down(); break;
} catch (InterruptedException ie) {
        interrupted=true;
}
```

The infinite loop will keep catching interrupts while the thread is trying to enter the monitor. When there is an interrupt, the `interrupted` flag is set to allow the thread to be interrupted again when it leaves the method. If the method successfully downs the `monitorEntry` semaphore, it breaks out of the loop.

Method `leave()` first checks that the thread that called it actually owns the monitor. If the thread doesn't own the monitor, it throws an exception. If it does own the monitor, it decrements `monitorEntryCount`. If the count is still greater than zero, this thread still owns the monitor. If the count goes to zero, the monitor is free, so `leave()` sets the current reference to null and ups the `monitorEntry` semaphore to allow some other thread to seize the monitor.

Example 4–8 The `Monitor` method `leave()`

```
public void leave() throws MonitorException{
        if (current!=Thread.currentThread())
            throw new MonitorException("leave()");
        monitorEntryCount--;
        if(monitorEntryCount==0) {
                current = null;
                monitorEntry.up();
        }
}
```

Method `release()` allows a thread to temporarily give up all locks the thread has on a monitor. First, it checks that the thread executing it owns the monitor. If the thread does not own the monitor, `release()` throws an exception. If it does own the monitor, `release()` creates a `Monitor.Lock` object to return. The initialization for the `Lock` object grabs copies of the `Monitor` objects fields `current` and `monitorEntryCount`. Then, `release()` releases the monitor.

Example 4–9 The **Monitor** method **release()**

```
public MonitorLock release() throws MonitorException {
        if (current!=Thread.currentThread())
            throw new MonitorException("release()");
        Lock L=new Lock();
        current = null;
        monitorEntryCount=0;
        monitorEntry.up();
        return L;
}
```

Monitor.Condition

The local class `Condition` within `Monitor` implements interface
`MonitorCondition`. It is used to represent conditions (also known as *events*) in the
Brinch-Hansen and Hoare monitors.

Monitor.Condition fields

`Semaphore waitCond;` The semaphore upon which the waiting threads wait.

`int waiting;` The number of threads waiting on this condition.

`Condition` has two fields. The `waitCond` field is a semaphore used to delay threads
that are waiting on the condition. The `waiting` field is a count of the number of threads
waiting on the semaphore. This count is important, as semaphores maintain the count of
the number of up operations performed, whereas conditon variables are memoryless. As
we will see in `signal()`, a signal operation can only be translated into upping the semaphore if there are threads waiting.

In the code for the methods in `Condition`, fields `current, monitorEntry,` and
`monitorEntryCount` are fields of the surrounding `Monitor` object.

Method `await()` first checks that the executing thread owns the surrounding monitor. If
the thread does not own the monitor, it throws an exception. If it does own the monitor, it
releases the monitor and waits as follows:

- It saves the `monitorEntryCount` in the local variable `count` so it can restore it
  later.

- It marks the monitor as free by setting `current` to `null` and
  `monitorEntryCount` to zero.

- It increments the `waiting` field of the condition.

- It ups the `monitorEntry` semaphore to allow another thread to enter the monitor.

- It waits on the `Condition`'s `waitCond` semaphore.

- Once it's been awakened, it restores its own reference to `current` and the proper count to `monitorEntryCount`.

Example 4–10 The `Monitor.Condition` method `await()`

```
public void await()
  throws InterruptedException, MonitorException {
    if (current!=Thread.currentThread())
        throw new MonitorException("await()");
    int count = monitorEntryCount;
    monitorEntryCount = 0;
    current = null;
    waiting++;
    monitorEntry.up();
    waitCond.down();
    current=Thread.currentThread();
    monitorEntryCount=count;
}
```

Notice that `await()` increments the `waiting` field before waiting on the `waitCond` semaphore, but does not decrement it after being awakened. Methods `signal()` and `leaveWithSignal()` handle that. They decrement the count, because, as soon as they up the semaphore, they awaken the thread, even if it hasn't started running yet.

Decrementing the waiting count in `signal()` would be especially important if we were implementing Javalike monitors, where the currently executing thread continues running inside the monitor or another thread can seize the monitor before the awakened thread gets to run. Here's what could happen: Thread X is the only thread awaiting a condition. The condition count is one. Thread Y signals the condition, so X is made runnable. But if Y doesn't decrement the count, the count will stay one. Now, thread Y leaves the monitor, and thread Z seizes it. Z signals the same condition, and since the count is one, it ups the semaphore again. Since there is no waiting thead, the semaphore remembers the up in its internal counter. Z leaves, and X runs. But the next thread, W, that tries to await the condition will not wait at all, because the semaphore's counter was greater than zero.

Decrementing `waiting` in `signal()` is not as important here, because the monitor is handed off from one thread to another, and thus the monitor remains locked, the awakened thread begins running in it, and the thread that called `signal()` queues up on the `monitorEntry` semaphore to reenter the monitor.

Example 4–11 The `Monitor.Condition` method `signal()`

```
public void signal()
    throws MonitorException {
     if (current!=Thread.currentThread())
         throw new MonitorException("signal()");
     if (waiting>0) {
             waiting--;
             int count = monitorEntryCount;
             monitorEntryCount = 0;
             current = null;
             waitCond.up();
             boolean interrupted=Thread.interrupted();
             for(;;) try {
                     monitorEntry.down(); break;
             } catch (InterruptedException ie) {
                     interrupted=true;
             }
             current=Thread.currentThread();
             monitorEntryCount=count;
             if (interrupted) current.interrupt();
     }
}
```

Method `signal()` begins with the usual check that the thread executing it actually owns the monitor, throwing an exception if it doesn't.

If the `waiting` count is zero, signal performs no operation. Otherwise, it must hand off the monitor to one of the threads waiting for the condition. It does this as follows:

- It decrements the condition's `waiting` count, for the reasons just explained.

- It saves its `monitorEntryCount` to restore later.

- It clears fields `current` and `monitorEntryCount` to denote that it has no ownership of the Monitor. This is actually unnecessary.

- It wakes up one waiting thread by upping `waitCond`.

- It waits to enter the monitor again by downing `monitorEntry`. Here, in a way described by `enter()`, it preserves but ignores the fact of the thread being interrupted.

- Once it gets past monitorEntry, it reestablishes fields current and monitorEntryCount to denote that it owns the monitor again.

Example 4–12 The `Monitor.Condition` method `leaveWithSignal()`

```
public void leaveWithSignal()
  throws MonitorException {
    if (current!=Thread.currentThread())
        throw new MonitorException("leaveWithSignal()");
    monitorEntryCount--;
    if (waiting>0) {
        waiting--;
        if (monitorEntryCount>0) {
            int count = monitorEntryCount;
            monitorEntryCount = 0;
            current = null;
            waitCond.up();
            boolean interrupted=
                    Thread.interrupted();
            for(;;) try {
                monitorEntry.down(); break;
            } catch (InterruptedException ie) {
                interrupted=true;
            }
            monitorEntryCount = count;
            current=Thread.currentThread();
            if (interrupted) current.interrupt();
        } else {
            current = null;
            waitCond.up();
        }
    } else {
        if (monitorEntryCount==0) {
            current = null;
            monitorEntry.up();
        }
    }
}
```

Method leaveWithSignal() begins simply enough with checking that the current thread owns the monitor and then decrementing its monitorEntryCount. Then, alas, there are four cases to consider:

1. There is a thread waiting at the condition, and `monitorEntryCount` is not zero. The `leaveWithSignal()` must behave like a `signal()`, since the current thread must continue executing in the monitor after the awakened thread has had its chance. This code was explained for method `signal()`.

2. There is a thread waiting at the condition, and `monitorEntryCount` *is* zero. The current thread can hand off the monitor and continue executing. This only requires three things:

    a. decrementing the `Condition`'s waiting count,

    b. setting `current` to `null` so the current thread can't try to enter the monitor again and think it already owns it, and

    c. upping the `Condition`'s `waitCond` semaphore to wake up one waiting thread.

3. There are no threads waiting at the condition, and `monitorEntryCount` is zero. The current thread must leave the monitor. This code was explained in the method `leave()` from class `Monitor`.

4. There are no threads waiting at the condition and `monitorEntryCount` is not zero. The current thread goes on executing in the monitor. This doesn't require any code.

Monitor.Lock

`Lock` is a class defined in `Monitor`. You cannot create an instance of it directly, but only by calling `Monitor`'s `release()` method.

Monitor.Lock fields
```
int n = monitorEntryCount;
Thread owner = current;
```

Method `release()` will give up your lock on the monitor, but will save enough information in the `Monitor.Lock` object it retuns to allow you to reacquire the monitor. It must remember the following:

1. Who you are, so somebody else cannot reacquire the monitor pretending to be you, and

2. How many times you have entered the monitor so that it can reestablish the proper number of locks.

There is only one method for a `MonitorLock`. Calling `reacquire()` will relock the monitor for you. If a different thread tries to reacquire the monitor, `reacquire()` will

Example 4–13 The `Monitor.Lock` method `reacquire()`

```
public void reacquire() throws
              MonitorException {
      if (owner != Thread.currentThread())
         throw new MonitorException(
            "attempt to reacquire Monitor"+
                     " by a different thread");
      boolean interrupted=Thread.interrupted();
      for(;;) try {
             monitorEntry.down(); break;
      } catch (InterruptedException ie) {
             interrupted=true;
      }
      current = owner;
      monitorEntryCount=n;
      owner = null;
      if (interrupted) current.interrupt();
}
```

throw a `MonitorException`. Since `Monitor.Lock` class is declared within `Monitor`, `reacquire()` can access the fields of the surrounding `Monitor` object directly. Here's what it does:

- It checks that the monitor is being reacquired by the same thread that released it.

- It locks the monitor by downing the `monitorEntry` semaphore. Again, the `interrupted` flag is used to preserve the fact that the thread has been interrupted while ignoring it in this method.

- It records that it is the current owner of the monitor.

- It reestablishes the monitor entry count.

- It clears the owner of the `Monitor.Lock` object so that it cannot be used again to enter the monitor.

The Multiple Reader–Writer Monitors

Threads that share data structures can run into problems if one of the threads is writing into the structure while another thread is reading from it or if two threads try to write into it at the same time. This is because several values must typically be stored to move the data structure from one consistent state to another. If only some of the stores have been made when it is read, the reader will get confused. If more than one thread is writing into it, some of the fields may end up changed by one of the threads and other fields changed by the other. Thereafter, anything reading from it will be confused.

The easiest solution is to lock the data structure whenever accessing it. Any other thread trying to access the structure will have to wait until it is unlocked before being able to lock the structure itself.

The problem with locking the data structure is that although it is essential to prevent any thread from writing to the data structure while another thread is writing to or reading from it, there is no reason to prevent several threads from simultaneously reading. If many threads are permitted to read at the same time, we would expect better performance.

Policies

We present five policies for synchronizing threads trying to read from or write to a shared data structure:

1. The **single reader–writer monitor** locks the data structure so that only one thread can access the data structure at a time, whether the thread is a reader or a writer. It is equivalent to a semaphore.

2. The **writers-preferred monitor** gives the shared structure to a waiting writer (if there is one) and only if there is no writer waiting will it be given to readers. All waiting readers will be allowed to access the structure at the same time.

3. The **readers-preferred monitor** gives the shared structure to all waiting readers (if there are any) and gives it to a writer only if there is no reader waiting.

4. The **alternating readers–writers monitor** gives the shared structure to a waiting writer when readers have finished with it and to readers when a writer has finished with it.

5. The **take-a-number monitor** gives the shared resource to the threads in order of arrival. It requires a kind of busy waiting. The threads must check to see whether the number they've taken is now being served.

These algorithms are animated in: `http://www.toolsofcomputing.com`.

The **queued reader–writer monitor**, presented later in Chapter 8, "Shared Tables of Queues," gives the shared resource to the threads in order of arrival. It uses a `FutureQueue` from the thread package to give the resource to the threads in a first-come, first-served order. Unlike the **take-a-number monitor**, which also gives the shared resource to the threads in order of arrival, the **queued reader–writer monitor** doesn't require busy waiting.

The writers-preferred, readers-preferred, and alternating reader–writer monitors all have complexities in design that are discussed in their individual sections.

Entering and Leaving the Critical Sections

Readers and writers must explicitly lock and unlock the shared resource. The locking is done via method calls to a monitor object that implements the desired policy, as in the following:

Reader

```
monitor.startReading();
try {
        ...read...
} finally {monitor.stopReading();}
```

Writer

```
monitor.startWriting();
try {
        ...write...
} finally {monitor.stopWriting();}
```

The reason for the `try...finally` statements is that the thread could throw an exception within the code to read or write. It is important to unlock shared resources upon abnormal exit.

The Single-Reader–Writer Monitor

This demonstration shows a simple lock on the data structure. Only a single reader or writer can access the shared resource at one time.

With a fair scheduling algorithm, each thread, in turn, should get a chance to run, cycling through the threads over and over. We've tried this out on a number of Java implementations. They are not fair. A small subset of the threads run while all the others wait.

The Single-Reader–Writer Monitor is equivalent to a lock or binary semaphore. Methods `startReading()` and `startWriting()` are identical, as are `stopReading()` and `stopWriting()`.

Example 4–14 Class `SingleReaderWriter`

```
class SingleReaderWriter extends
            MultipleReadersWritersMonitor{
int n=0; /* number readers reading and writers writing,
                    0 or 1*/
public void reset(){
    n=0;
}
public synchronized void startReading()
        throws InterruptedException{
    while (n!=0) wait();
    n=1;
}
public synchronized void stopReading(){
    n=0;
    notify();
}
public synchronized void startWriting()
        throws InterruptedException{
    while (n!=0) wait();
    n=1;
}
public synchronized void stopWriting(){
    n=0;
    notify();
}
public String getMonitorInfo(){
    return "Single Reader Writer Monitor";
}
}
```

The Readers-Preferred Monitor

The Readers-Preferred Monitor gives the resource to a reader (if there are any available). Only if there are no readers present will the resource be given to a writer.

> If you run this animation with threads choosing randomly whether to read or write, you will notice that most threads end up waiting to write for a long time. If you run it with a fixed number of readers, you will observe the animation alternately giving the resource to a batch of readers and then to a writer while the readers are inactive.

State of the monitor. The state of the readers-preferred monitor is contained in four variables:

> nr: The number of threads currently reading nr $> = 0$.
>
> nw: The number of threads currently writing (zero or one).
>
> nrtotal: The number of threads either reading or waiting to read
>> nrtotal $> = $ nr.
>
> nwtotal: The number of threads either writing or waiting to write.

Example 4–15 The **ReadersPreferredMonitor** method **startReading()**

```
public synchronized void startReading()
throws InterruptedException{
        nrtotal++;
        while (nw!=0) wait();
        nr++;
}
```

startReading(). If a thread tries to start reading, it must wait until there are no threads currently writing; in other words, it must wait until nw is zero.

Example 4–16 The **ReadersPreferredMonitor** method **startWriting()**

```
public synchronized void startWriting()
throws InterruptedException{
        nwtotal++;
        while (nrtotal+nw != 0) wait();
        nw=1;
}
```

startWriting(). To start writing, a thread must wait until there are no other threads reading, waiting to read, or writing (i.e., nrtotal = nw = zero).

Example 4–17 The **ReadersPreferredMonitor** method **stopReading()**

```
public synchronized void stopReading(){
        nr--; nrtotal--;
        if (nrtotal==0) notify();
}
```

stopReading(). When the last present reader finishes reading, it wakes up a waiting writer (if there are any present), which will seize the monitor and start writing.

Example 4–18 The **ReadersPreferredMonitor** method **startWriting()**

```
public synchronized void stopWriting(){
        nw=0; nwtotal--;
        notifyAll();
}
```

stopWriting(). When a writer finishes writing, it wakes up all waiting readers and writers to let them compete for the monitor.

The Writers-Preferred Monitor

A Writers-Preferred Monitor gives the resource to a writer if any is waiting. Only if there is no writer available will it be given to readers.

> If you run this animation with threads choosing randomly whether to read or write, you will observe that more and more threads accumulate waiting to read until there are no writers left. Then, all the waiting readers will run.
>
> If you run it with a fixed set of readers, a batch of readers may run before the first writer enters the monitor, but thereafter, typically, all the writers will run to completion before any readers run again. (You can set the number of readers and rest time to give the readers a better chance.)

State of the monitor. The state of the monitor is contained in four variables:

> nr: The number of threads currently reading.
>
> nw: The number of threads currently writing (zero or one).
>
> nrtotal: The number of threads either reading or waiting to read. (nrtotal ≥ nr).
>
> nwtotal: The number of threads either writing or waiting to write.

startReading(). If a thread tries to start reading, it must wait until there are no threads either writing or waiting to write; in other words, it must wait until nwtotal is zero.

startWriting(). To start writing, a thread must wait until there are no other threads reading or writing, indicated by nr and nw both equaling zero.

Example 4–19 The `WritersPreferredMonitor` method `startReading`

```
public synchronized void startReading()
      throws InterruptedException{
   nrtotal++;
   while (nwtotal!=0) wait();
   nr++;
}
```

Example 4–20 The `WritersPreferredMonitor` method `startWriting`

```
public synchronized void startWriting()
      throws InterruptedException{
   nwtotal++;
   while (nr+nw != 0) wait();
   nw=1;
}
```

Example 4–21 The `WritersPreferredMonitor` method `stopReading()`

```
public synchronized void stopReading(){
   nr--; nrtotal--;
   if (nr==0) notifyAll();
}
```

`stopReading().` When the last reader of a group finishes reading, it wakes up all waiting readers and writers. If there are any waiting writers, no reader will be able to start reading, but will wait again. Eventually, a writer will seize the monitor and start writing.

Example 4–22 The `WritersPreferredMonitor` method `stopWriting()`

```
public synchronized void stopWriting(){
   nw=0; nwtotal--;
   notifyAll();
}
```

`stopWriting().` When a writer finishes writing, it wakes up all waiting readers and writers to let them compete for the monitor.

The Alternating Readers–Writers Monitor

The idea of the Alternating Readers–Writers Monitor is that readers and writers should take turns. Trying to specify this a bit more carefully, we come up with the following elements:

- General alternation. A batch of readers run, followed by a single writer, followed by another batch of readers, etc.

- Immediate access. If a reader arrives and there are no writers present, it is given access to the resource immediately. If a writer arrives and neither readers nor writers own the resource, it is allocated the resource immediately.

State of the monitor. The state of an Alternating Readers–Writers Monitor is contained in four variables:

> `nr[2]`: The number of threads currently reading.
>
> `thisBatch`: Index in `nr` of the batch of readers currently reading (zero or one).
>
> `nextBatch`: Index in `nr` of the batch of readers waiting to read (always `1-thisBatch`).
>
> `nw`: The number of threads currently writing (zero or one).
>
> `nwtotal`: The number of threads either writing or waiting to write.

Example 4–23 The `AlternatingReadersWritersMonitor` method `startReading()`

```
public synchronized void startReading()
       throws InterruptedException{
    if (nwtotal==0) nr[thisBatch]++;
    else {
        nr[nextBatch]++;
        int myBatch=nextBatch;
        while (thisBatch!=myBatch) wait();
    }
}
```

`startReading().` When a thread tries to start reading, it checks first to see if there are any writers present. If there are none, it starts reading immediately, recording its presence in `nr[thisBatch]`.

If there are writers present, it must wait until one writer has run, so it adds itself to the number of readers in the next batch by incrementing `nr[nextBatch]`. It saves the value of `nextBatch` in the variable `myBatch` and waits until `thisBatch` equals `myBatch`, which will indicate that a writer has finished running.

Example 4–24 The `AlternatingReadersWritersMonitor` method `stopReading()`

```
public synchronized void stopReading(){
    nr[thisBatch]--;
    if (nr[thisBatch]==0) {
        notifyAll();
    }
}
```

`stopReading().`   When a thread stops reading, it subtracts itself from
`nr[thisBatch]`. It then notifies all waiting threads to try accessing the resources.
Readers will wait again, since `thisBatch` has not been set to the value they are waiting
for, but one of the writers will be able to start writing.

Example 4–25 The `AlternatingReadersWritersMonitor` method
`startWriting()`

```
public synchronized void startWriting()
            throws InterruptedException{
    nwtotal++;
    while (nr[thisBatch]+nw != 0) wait();
    nw=1;
}
```

`startWriting().`   When a writer attempts to start writing, it adds itself to the
total number of writers present. Then, it waits until no threads are reading or writing. Once
that condition is true, it sets nw to one to indicate that it is writing and begins writing.

Example 4–26 The `AlternatingReadersWritersMonitor` method `stopWriting()`

```
public synchronized void stopWriting(){
    nw=0; nwtotal--;
    int tmp=thisBatch;
    thisBatch=nextBatch;
    nextBatch=tmp;
    notifyAll();
}
```

`stopWriting().`   When a thread stops writing, it sets nw back to zero to indicate
that no thread is writing, and it subtracts itself from the total number of writers present. It

then swaps the values of `thisBatch` and `nextBatch` to release the next batch of readers, and it notifies all waiting threads, which wakes up the readers.

The Take-a-Number Monitor

As each reader or writer arrives, it takes the next number, and threads are served in order by their number. However, all readers with consecutive numbers are served at the same time.

State of the monitor. The state of this monitor is contained in three variables:

> `nr`: The number of threads currently reading.
>
> `nextNumber`: The number to be taken by the next thread to arrive.
>
> `nowServing`: The number of the thread to be served next.

Example 4–27 The `TakeANumberMonitor` method `startReading()`

```
public synchronized void startReading()
    throws InterruptedException{
      int myNumber = nextNumber++;
      while (nowServing!=myNumber) wait();
      nr++;
      nowServing++;
      notifyAll();
}
```

`startReading()`. If a thread tries to start reading, it takes a number and waits until its number comes up. Then, it increments the number of readers and the number currently being served. By incrementing `nowServing`, a reader allows the reader with the next sequential number to start. If the thread with the next number is a writer, it will wait until the readers are done before starting.

Example 4–28 The `TakeANumberMonitor` method `startWriting()`

```
public synchronized void startWriting()
throws InterruptedException{
      int myNumber = nextNumber++;
      while (nowServing!=myNumber) wait();
      while(nr>0) wait();
}
```

startWriting().   To start writing, a thread takes a number, waits until its number comes up, and then waits until any preceding readers are finished. It will not increment `nowServing` until it is finished writing, since no subsequent thread should run until this writer is done.

Example 4–29 The `TakeANumberMonitor` method `stopReading()`

```
public synchronized void stopReading(){
        nr--;
        if (nr==0) notifyAll();
}
```

stopReading(). When the last present reader finishes reading, it wakes up a waiting writer (if there is one present). Unfortunately, it has to wake up all threads just for one of them to start writing.

Example 4–30 The `TakeANumberMonitor` method `stopWriting()`

```
public synchronized void stopWriting(){
        nowServing++;
        notifyAll();
}
```

stopWriting(). When a writer finishes writing, it increments `nowServing` and wakes up all waiting readers and writers to let them see if they are next.

Chapter Wrap-up

We discussed what monitors are supposed to be and observed that Java's synchronized methods provide degenerate forms of monitors. We then studied the thread package's `Monitor` class, which provides more of the facilities of monitors, but without any of the syntactic support. The implementation of `Monitor` and related classes shows sophisticated uses of semaphores.

We then considered multiple reader–writer monitors, which provide shared access to resources for readers, but mutual exclusion for writers. The different implementations provide different scheduling policies. The readers-preferred monitor gives readers priority over writers. The writers-preferred monitors do exactly the opposite. The alternating readers–writers monitor alternates between giving access to a single writer and a batch of readers. The take-a-number monitor gives access to threads in first-come, first-served order while alternating between single writers and batches of readers. A tricky problem in implementing these monitors is properly allocating a monitor to a newly arriving thread when no thread is currently using it and no threads are queued for it when the new thread arrives.

Exercises

1. The language Python provides lock objects similar to binary semaphores (i.e., semaphores for which the count is either zero or one). Here are the facilities of a Java version of Python locks:

The constructor

```
Lock L=new Lock();
```

creates a `Lock` object, which is initially unlocked. The method

```
L.acquire();
```

which locks the `Lock` object (similarly to `down()` for a semaphore). It blocks the thread's execution until the `Lock` object is available. The call

```
boolean a=L.acquire(false);
```

will immediately return, saying whether it acquired the lock. It assigns `true` to a if the lock was acquired. If the lock wasn't acquired, it assigns `false`. The call `L.acquire(true)` is equivalent to `L.acquire()`. The method

```
L.release();
```

releases a lock, allowing another thread to acquire it. A blocked thread waiting for the lock is given the chance to acquire it.

If a thread tries to lock the same `Lock` object more than once, it is deadlocked with itself.

Implement `Lock` objects in Java that provide the facilities of Python locks.

2. Python provides reentrant locks similar to the monitors in Java that allow the same thread to synchronize more than once on the same object. For that matter, they are like the monitors described in this chapter, which allow a thread to enter the same monitor more than once before leaving it. The Java version is as follows:

The constructor call

```
RLock L=new RLock();
```

creates a reentrant lock. The operations on an `RLock` object are the same as on a `Lock` object, except that a thread will not block itself if it tries to acquire the same lock more than once before releasing it. The `RLock` object is not released for other threads until the thread that owns it has released it as many times as it has acquired it.

Implement `RLock` objects in Java that provide the facilities of Python `RLocks`.

3. The language Python provides `Condition` objects similar to the `Monitor.Condition` objects in the thread package. The following is a Java syntax for them:

The constructor call

```
Condition C=new Condition(L);
```

creates a `Condition` object that uses underlying `Lock` or `RLock` object L. If L is omitted, as in

```
Condition C=new Condition();
```

a new `RLock` object is created for the `Condition`. The call

```
C.acquire();
```

locks the underlying `Lock` object. It blocks until the lock object is available. Call

```
boolean a=C.acquire(false);
```

will return immediately, saying whether it acquired the lock or not. It assigns `true` to a if the lock was acquired. If the lock wasn't acquired, it assigns `false`. The call `C.acquire(true)` is equivalent to `C.acquire()`, and

```
C.release();
```

releases the underlying lock. The method

```
C.wait();
```

must only be called by the thread that has acquired the lock. It releases the lock and waits until some other thread calls `C.notify()` or `C.notifyAll()`. The method

```
C.wait(timeout);
```

will wait until awakened by `notify()` or `notifyAll()` or until `timeout` seconds have elapsed. The parameter `timeout` is a floating-point number, so fractions of a second may be specified. Calling

```
C.notify();
```

will awaken at most one thread waiting on a `Condition`. If no threads are waiting, `notify()` performs no operation. Method `notify()` may only be called by the thread that has acquired the condition's lock. As in Java, a thread being awakened must reacquire the lock before returning from `wait()`. The thread executing the `notify()` does not simultaneously release the lock, so the awakened thread will be delayed. Other threads may acquire the lock before the waiting thread does. The method

```
C.notifyAll();
```

will awaken all waiting threads. The same caveats apply to it as for `notify()`.

Implement a `Condition` class whose objects behave in the fashion just described.

## Chapter 5

Parallel Execution of Subroutines in Shared Memory

U sing parallelism solves problems more quickly than using a single-processor machine, as is the case where groups of people solve problems larger than one person can solve. But just as with groups of people, there are additional costs and problems involved in coordinating parallel processors:

• We need to have more than one processor work on the problem at the same time. Our machine must have more than one processor, and the operating system must be able to give more than one processor to our program at the same time. Kernel threads allow this in Java. An alternative approach is to have several networked computers work on parts of the problem; this is discussed in Chapters 11 and 12, "Networking" and "Coordination."

• We need to assign parts of the problem to threads. This at least requires rewriting a sequential program. It usually requires rethinking the algorithm as well.

- We need to coordinate the threads so they perform their operations in the proper order, as well as avoid race conditions and deadlocks. A number of useful facilities are not provided by the standard Java language package. We provide a good collection for your use in our thread package.

- We need to maintain a reasonable grain size. Grain size refers to the amount of work a thread does between communications or synchronizations. Fine grain uses very few instructions between synchronizations; coarse grain uses a large amount of work. Too fine a grain wastes too much overhead creating and synchronizing threads. Too coarse a grain results in load imbalance and the underutilization of processors.

Two easy, practical approaches to dividing the work among several processors are executing subroutines in parallel and executing iterations of loops in parallel. Parallelizing loops will be presented in the next chapter. In this chapter we will discuss running subroutines in parallel.

Executing subroutines in parallel is an easy way to speed up computation. The chunks of code are already packaged for you in methods; you merely need to wrap runnable classes around them. Of course, there are certain requirements:

- The subroutines must be able to run in parallel with some other computation. This usually means that there are several subroutine calls that can run independently.

- The subroutines must have a reasonable grain size. It costs a lot to get a thread running, and it doesn't pay off for only a few instructions.

Two kinds of algorithms particularly adaptable to parallel execution of subroutines are the divide-and-conquer and branch-and-bound algorithms. Divide-and-conquer algorithms break large problems into parts and solve the parts independently. Parts that are small enough are solved simply as special cases. You must know how to break a large problem into parts that can be solved independently and whose solutions can be reassembled into a solution of the overall problem. The algorithm may undergo some cost in breaking the problem into subparts or in assembling the solutions.

Branch-and-bound algorithms use is a search technique that we will look at later in this chapter.

Creating and Joining

The obvious way to run subroutines in parallel is to create a thread to run the subroutine, run the thread, and later wait for it to terminate via `join()`.

If the subroutine doesn't return a value, `join()` alone is adequate, but if it is to return a value, there is the question, "How should a thread return a result?" One easy option is to assign it to a public field of the thread object. After the call to `join()`, the caller just extracts the result from the subthread object.

Example: Trapezoidal Numeric Integration

Sometimes, a program needs to integrate a function (i.e., calculate the area under a curve). It might be able to use a formula for the integral, but doing so isn't always convenient, or even possible. An easy alternative approach is to approximate the curve with straight line segments and calculate an estimate of the area from them.

Principles. Figure 5–1 shows the situation. We wish to find the area under the curve from a to b. We approximate the function by dividing the domain from a to b into g equally sized segments. Each segment is $(b - a)/g$ long. Let the boundaries of these segments be $x_0 = a, x_1, x_2, \ldots, x_g = b$. The polyline approximating the curve will have coordinates $(x_0, f(x_0)), (x_1, f(x_1)), (x_2, f(x_2)), \ldots, (x_g, f(x_g))$.

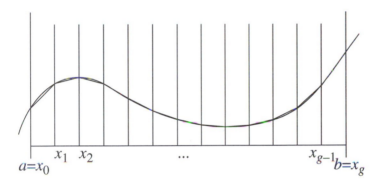

Figure 5–1 Approximating an integral with trapezoids.

This allows us to approximate the area under the curve as the sum of g trapezoids. The ith trapezoid ($i=1,\ldots,g$) has corners $(x_{i-1},0)$, $(x_{i-1}, f(x_{i-1}))$, $(x_i, f(x_i))$, and $(x_i,0)$. The area of each trapezoid is given by the formula $(1/2) \cdot (x_i - x_{i-1}) \cdot (f(x_i) + f(x_{i-1}))$.

The area under the curve is approximated by the sum of all the trapezoids:

$$A = \sum_{i=1}^{g} \frac{1}{2} \cdot \frac{(b-a)}{g} \cdot (f(x_{i-1}) + f(x_i))$$

If we apply that formula unthinkingly, we will evaluate the function twice for each value of *x*, except the first and the last values. A little manipulation gives us

$$A = \frac{b-a}{g} \cdot \left(\frac{f(a)}{2} + \frac{f(b)}{2} + \sum_{i=1}^{g-1} f(x_i) \right)$$

Interface. We allow the integrand to be passed in as a parameter. Since Java doesn't have function closures, we use an object that implements the `F_of_x` interface shown in Example 5-1.

Example 5-1 `F_of_x` interface

```
public interface F_of_x {
    public double f( double x );
}
```

To perform a numeric integration, you first create an instance of class `IntegTrap1`, shown in Example 5-2, passing its constructor `numThreads`, the number of threads you wish to use, and `granularity`, the granularity for each thread. Each thread will be given an equal part of the region over which to integrate the curve. This granularity is the number of trapezoids each thread is to use in its region. The total number of trapezoids is, therefore, `numThreads × granularity`. The reason we refer to the number of trapezoids as granularity is that it determines the computational granularity: The number of computations a thread performs before synchronizing with the calling thread is a linear function of the number of trapezoids it calculates.

Example 5-2 Interface of class `IntegTrap1`

```
public IntegTrap1( int numThreads, int granularity )
public double integrate(double a,double b,  F_of_x fn)
```

To perform the integration of a function from *a* to *b*, call the method `integrate()` of the `IntegTrap1` object. Any number of integrations can be performed, one at a time or concurrently, using the same `IntegTrap1` object to specify the number of threads and the granularity. Each of these integrations will create the number of threads specified.

Code. The actual work of integration is done in the class `IntegTrap1Region`, an extension of `Thread`, shown in Example 5-3. An instance is created with a region to integrate over (`x_start` to `x_end`), a `granularity`, and a function `f` to integrate. When the `IntegTrap1Region` thread runs, it calculates the area it is responsible for using the formula previously derived and places the result in field `areaOfRegion`. The value of `areaOfRegion` can be fetched using the method `getArea()`.

Example 5-3 Class `IntegTrap1Region`

```
class IntegTrap1Region extends Thread {
    private double x_start, x_end;
    private int granularity;
    private double areaOfRegion = 0;
    private F_of_x f;
    public IntegTrap1Region( double x_start, double x_end,
                int granularity, F_of_x f ) {
        super( new String( x_start + "-" + x_end ) );
        this.x_start = x_start;
        this.x_end = x_end;
        this.granularity = granularity;
        this.f = f;
    }
    public void run() {

        double area = 0.0d;
        double range = x_end - x_start;
        double g=granularity;
        for( int i=granularity-1; i>0; i-- ) {
            area += f.f((i/g)*range+x_start);
        }
        area += (f.f(x_start)+f.f(x_end))/2.0;
        area = area*(range/g);
        areaOfRegion = area;
    }
    public double getArea() {
        return areaOfRegion;
    }
}
```

The `integrate()` method is shown in Example 5-4. Essentially, it calls `numThreads` subroutines concurrently to integrate the function over parts of the region. It creates an array of `numThreads` `IntegTrap1Region` threads and starts them. Then, it loops,

waiting for them to terminate and adding their areas to the total. When all subthreads have
been processed, it returns the area.

Example 5-4 The method `Integrate()`

```
public double integrate(double a, double b, F_of_x fn){
  int i;
  Thread [] childThreads = new IntegTrap1Region[ numThreads ];
  double totalArea = 0.0d;
  if( a > b ) throw new BadRangeException();
  if( a == b ) throw new NoRangeException();
  try {
        double range = b - a;
        double start = a;
        double end = a + ((1.0d)/numThreads * range);
        for(i=0; i < numThreads; i++ ) {
          childThreads[i] =
            new IntegTrap1Region(start,end,granularity,fn );
          childThreads[i].start();
          start = end;
          end = a + ((i + 2.0d)/numThreads * range);
        }
  } catch( Exception e ) {
     System.out.println("Exception occured in creating and"+
        " initializing thread.\n" + e.toString() );
  }
  for (i=0; i < numThreads; i++) {
    try {
      childThreads[i].join();
      totalArea+=
           ((IntegTrap1Region)childThreads[i]).getArea();
    } catch(Exception e) {
      System.out.println("Could not join with child threads!");
      System.exit( 1 );
    }
  }
  return totalArea;
}
```

Discussion. A number of changes are possible that might be improvements, including
the following:

1. The `integrate()` method could create subthreads for all but one of the regions
   and then caluclate the area of the final region itself. This saves one thread creation,
   and thread creation is expensive. The code doing the actual integration would be

removed from the `run()` method of `IntegTrap1Region` and packaged in a separate static method.

2. As an alternative to using `join()` and looking in a field for the result, the sub-thread can return its result in a `SimpleFuture` object (see Chapter 3, "Futures").

RunQueue

There is a problem with creating threads and waiting for them to terminate: It is possible to create a lot of threads. Threads are expensive to create and may pose problems for some garbage collectors.

An alternative provided by our thread package is the class `RunQueue`. The `RunQueue` class allows you to queue up `Runnable` objects for execution. It creates its own threads to run them. These threads loop, removing the `Runnable` objects and calling their `run()` methods, so the threads are reused, rather than having to be created and garbage collected for each `Runnable` object.

A `RunQueue` object may be created with a parameterless constructor. Alternatively, you

---

RunQueue *constructors*

`RunQueue()`

`RunQueue(maxCreatable)`

---

can provide the maximum number of threads that can be in existence at one time and, optionally, the maximum number of threads that will be allowed to wait for more runnables to be enqueued. Normally, the `RunQueue` object will allow as many threads to be created as necessary to run all the runnables enqueued. That is the only safe default, since restricting the number can result in deadlock if you aren't careful. However, there are circumstances where a smaller limit may be best. They occur particularly when all the runnables are guaranteed to run to completion without blocking. We will discuss this programming style later, particularly in the chapters on *chores*. (See Chapter 7, "Chores," and Chapter 8, "Thread and Chore Synchronization.")

RunQueue *Methods*

run(runnable). The primary method provided by `RunQueue` enqueues a runnable for execution. There are three names for this method depending on how the programmer thinks of `RunQueue`. Method `rq.run(r)` says to run the `Runnable r`. Method `rq.put(r)` acknowledges that `rq` is a queue and puts `r` into the queue.

RunQueue *methods*

```
public void run(runnable)
public void put(runnable)
public void runDelayed(runnable)
```

Method `rq.runDelayed(r)` is provided for convenience. It's use won't be obvious until we discuss *chores*.

Managing the created threads. The rest of RunQueue's methods are related to

---

Remaining **RunQueue** *methods*

```
public void setMaxThreadsWaiting(int n)
public void setMaxThreadsCreated(int n)
public int getMaxThreadsWaiting()
public int getMaxThreadsCreated()
public int getNumThreadsWaiting()
public int getNumThreadsCreated()
public void terminate()
public void setWaitTime(long n)
public long getWaitTime()
public void setPriority(int n)
public int getPriority()
public void setDaemon(boolean d)
public boolean getDaemon()
```

---

managing the threads it creates. These threads are implemented in the internal class `Xeq`, so we will call them `Xeq` threads. There are five controlling attributes of a `RunQueue` object:

1. **maxThreadsCreated**: The maximum number of `Xeq` threads that may be in existence at any one time. By default, this will be the maximum positive integer. You can set it to some other value by calling `setMaxThreadsCreated()`.

2. **maxThreadsWaiting**: The maximum number of threads that may wait for more runnables to be enqueued. By default, this also will be the maximum positive integer. You can set it to some other value by calling `setMaxThreadsWaiting()`.

3. **priority**: The priority of the threads that are created. If you want it to be something other than normal priority, you can call `setPriority()`.

4. **waitTime**: The number of milliseconds a thread will wait for a new runnable before terminating.

5. **makeDaemon**: If true, `Xeq` threads will be created as daemon threads; if false, they will not.

Termination. The most important of these from your point of view are `setMaxThreadsWaiting()` and `terminate()`. You will need to use one of them to get the `Xeq` threads to terminate. If you do not eliminate the threads as soon as you are done, they will stay in existence and waste system resources.

To eliminate a thread, when you are done with the object `rq`, call `rq.setMaxThreadsWaiting(0)`. Any waiting `Xeq` threads are awakened, and seeing that the number of waiting threads now allowable is zero, they will terminate. You could set the maximum number of threads allowed to wait to zero before you are done with the run queue, but if the run queue is allowed to create the maximum number of threads, a new thread will be created whenever a runnable is enqueued, and that's no advantage over just creating and starting threads yourself.

You can alternatively call `terminate()`, which will both set the allowed number of waiting threads to zero and set a flag to disable the run queue. If more runnables are enqueued, they will not be run.

A third possibility is to call `rq.setWaitTime(t)` to force waiting threads to terminate after `t` milliseconds. If you set this time too low, the run queue may not allow threads to stay around long enough to be reused when more runnables are enqueued later. However, when there will be no more runnables enqueued, it is safe to set the wait time to zero. As with `maxThreadsWaiting`, if this value is changed, all waiting threads are awakened, and if they find no runnables to execute, they will try waiting again with the new wait time. If a time out occurs and a thread wakes up to find no runnable waiting, it will terminate.

Adjusting maxThreadsCreated. The field `maxThreadsCreated` limits the number of threads that may be in existence at any one time (*not* the overall number). Normally, a runnable placed in the run queue will be given a thread to execute it immediately with no limits on the number of threads created.

If these runnables can themselves make parallel subroutine calls placing their runnables in the queue, then it is essential that there be no limits on the number created. If the limit is, say, four, the system could easily deadlock with four callers holding on to their threads waiting for their subroutines to terminate, while the subroutines can't run at all, because they are in the run queue waiting for threads to become available to run them.

So why might you ever wish to set the number lower? If you can do it safely, you may want to throttle your parallelism:

- Threads are expensive to create. They take up a lot of storage. They take a fraction of processor time while they are runnable.

- You have only a limited number of processors available. Beyond the number of available processors, more runnable threads will not give you more parallelism.

Thus, you might prefer a run queue that does not create more than a certain number of threads.

The problem, of course, is that to be safe, the runnables you place in the queue should not block the thread executing them waiting for events that can be caused by other runnables in the queue. We call runnables that do not block their threads *chores*. We will discuss chores and how to synchronize them in a later chapter.

Adjusting `maxThreadsWaiting`. The purpose of a run queue is to allow `Xeq` threads to be reused for running more than one runnable. There are two ways this can happen:

1. An `Xeq` thread can find another runnable waiting when it completes processing one. You would expect this to be common only when the maximum number of threads is limited, since, otherwise, a thread is created for each runnable enqueued, and the thread that completes another runnable must slip in after the runnable is enqueued, but before the created thread dequeues it.

2. An `Xeq` thread can already be waiting for another runnable to be enqueued. It will be awakened when the runnable is put in the queue.

Why might you want to limit the number? You have already seen one reason: You want to get rid of the threads in a run queue that you are no longer using. You can set the maximum number of waiting threads to zero after you are done with the run queue.

A good reason to set the limit before you are done with the run queue is to save space. Suppose you generally have no more than 5 runnables active at any one time, but once you may have up to 20. You could set `maxThreadsWaiting` to 5 to handle the normal case and just pay the thread-creation and garbage-collection cost for the other 15. That way, you don't have 20 threads taking up space for long periods.

Adjusting `waitTime`. You might prefer to adjust `waitTime` rather than `maxThreadsWaiting`. The parameter `waitTime` determines how many milliseconds a thread will wait for a runnable to be enqueued before terminating on its own. It has the advantage that it will automatically free storage for unneeded threads. However, to use it well, instead of having to know the normal maximum number of runnables in the system, you need to know something about the interarrival time distribution.

RunQueue *Implementation*

Implementing RunQueue requires solving some tricky problems in thread synchronization, as we will see in this section.

Fields. RunQueue has the following fields:

Fields of RunQueue Object

```
protected QueueComponent runnables=new QueueComponent();
protected volatile int numThreadsWaiting=0;
protected volatile int numNotifies=0;
protected volatile int maxThreadsWaiting=Integer.MAX_VALUE;
protected volatile int numThreadsCreated=0;
protected volatile boolean goOn=true;
protected volatile int maxThreadsCreated=Integer.MAX_VALUE;
protected volatile int priority=Thread.NORM_PRIORITY;
protected volatile long waitTime=...;
protected volatile long makeDaemon=true;
```

- runnables is the actual queue that the runnables are placed in.

- numThreadsWaiting is the number of Xeq threads waiting for runnables to execute.

- numNotifies is the number of waiting threads awakened by notify() operations, but not started running yet. As described later, this is used by a waking thread to recognize whether it has been awakened by a notify() or by a time out.

- maxThreadsWaiting is the maximum number of threads that are allowed to wait for runnables at any one time.

- numThreadsCreated is the number of Xeq threads that are currently in existence.

- goOn is set to false by method terminate() to shut down the run queue.

- maxThreadsCreated is the maximum number of threads that are allowed to be created at any one time.

- priority is the thread priority at which the Xeq threads will run.

- `waitTime` is the number of milliseconds an `Xeq` thread will wait to be awakened before timing out and terminating.

- `makeDaemon` determines whether or not a created thread will be daemon. It's default value is true.

Xeq threads. The states of an `Xeq` thread are shown in Figure 5–2. It's code is shown in Example 5-5. An `Xeq` thread just loops getting runnables from the `runnables` queue and running them. Flag `goOn` will tell it if it should continue executing or if the `RunQueue` has been terminated.

There are two kinds of exceptions that `Xeq` threads handle. An `InterruptedException` is used to indicate that the thread timed out and should terminate. Any other kind of exception causes the thread to terminate with a stack trace, the same as uncaught exceptions terminating normal threads.

Figure 5–2 States of a `RunQueue` `Xeq` thread.

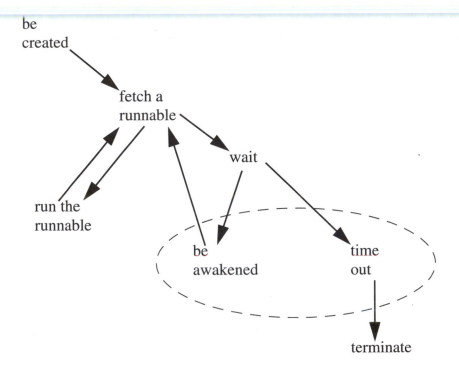

Example 5-5 Code for class Xeq

```
protected class Xeq extends Thread {
 public void run() {
       Runnable  r;
       try {
          while (goOn) {
              r = dequeue();
              r.run();
          }
       } catch (InterruptedException ie){//nothing
       } catch (Exception e){
              e.printStackTrace();
       }
       numThreadsCreated--;
 }
}
```

Enqueueing Runnables. The code to put runnables into the run queue is shown in Example 5-6.

Example 5-6 Code to put runnables into a run queue.

```
public void put(Runnable  runnable){
   boolean createThread=false;
   synchronized (this) {
       runnables.put(runnable);
       if (numThreadsWaiting>0) {
              numThreadsWaiting--; numNotifies++;
              notify();
       } else if (numThreadsCreated<maxThreadsCreated) {
              numThreadsCreated++;
              createThread=true;
       }
   }
   if (createThread) {
       Thread t=new Xeq();
       t.setPriority(priority);
       t.setDaemon(makeDaemon);
       t.start();
   }
}
```

The put() method is divided into two parts. The first puts the runnable into the runnables queue and decides whether to wake up a waiting thread, create a new thread, or do nothing. The second part actually creates the new thread. The second part isn't included in the first, because thread creation is slow, and we do not wish to leave the run queue locked during the creation of the thread.

To wake up a waiting thread, the put() method decrements the number of waiting threads and increments the number of threads being awakened (numNotifies). The reasons for this are as follows:

Why does the thread putting the runnable into the queue decrement the number of threads waiting, rather than let that thread decrement the number when it wakes up? The reason is that the notified thread does not get to lock the run queue immediately. Other threads can get in before it runs. Suppose there is one thread waiting and 10 threads enqueue runnables before the waiting thread runs. If the enqueueing thread didn't decrement the count of threads waiting, it would appear to all 10 threads that there is a waiting thread to run its runnable, so all would try to awaken it, but only the one thread would actually wake up. That would leave nine runnables without threads to execute them.

Why is it necessary to keep track of the number of threads being awakened (numNotifies)? It is used in method dequeue(), described later, to decide whether it was awakened explicitly or whether it timed out. When the Xeq thread awakens, if numNotifies is nonzero, it assumes that it was awakerned on purpose. If numNotifies is zero, it assumes it timed out.

Dequeueing Runnables. The code that Xeq threads use to dequeue runnables is shown in Example 5-7. When there are runnables in the queue, it will remove one and return it. If the queue is empty, it must either wait or terminate. It will wait if the number of threads already waiting is less than the maximum number of threads permitted to wait. Otherwise, it is not allowed to wait, so it terminates by throwing an InterruptedException, which the run() method in the Xeq class interprets as a request for termination.[1]

If the dequeue() method waits, it specifies waitTime as a timeout period. When it falls out of the wait(), it doesn't know whether it timed out or was awakened by a notify. In Figure 5–2, the two states "be awakened" and "time out" are circled to indicate that they execute the same code.

How does the thread figure out which state it's in? It checks numNotifies. When a thread putting a runnable into the queue wishes to wake up a waiting Xeq thread, it increments numNotifies. The Xeq thread sees that numNotifies is greater than zero, decides that it has been awakened by a notify rather than timing out, and then decrements

---

[1] We really should have invented our own exception class for this.

Example 5-7 **Dequeueing runnables by** **Xeq** **threads.**

```
protected synchronized Runnable dequeue()
                throws InterruptedException {
     Runnable  runnable;
     while (runnables.isEmpty() ) {
         if (numThreadsWaiting<maxThreadsWaiting) {
             numThreadsWaiting++;
             wait(waitTime);
             if (numNotifies==0) {
                     numThreadsWaiting--;
                     throw new InterruptedException();
             } else {numNotifies--;}
         } else { //terminate
             throw new InterruptedException();
         }
     }
     runnable = (Runnable ) runnables.get();
         return runnable;
 }
```

numNotifies. If a thread wakes up and finds that numNotifies is zero, it will assume that it timed out so it will decrement numThreadsWaiting—since it is no longer waiting and no one else decremented it—and will terminate by throwing an InterruptedException.

To determine whether this will always work, we consider some possible anomolies:

1. Suppose one Xeq thread is waiting, times out, and before it runs, a runnable is enqueued. The thread enqueueing the runnable will see that numThreadsWaiting is greater than zero, decrement it, increment numNotifies to one, and issue a notify(), which will have no effect. When the Xeq thread falls out of the call to wait(), it will decide that it has been awakened, which is what we need.

2. Suppose two Xeq threads are waiting, and that one times out, but before it can sieze the run queue, the other thread is awakened by a notify(). The timed-out thread may run first and, thinking that it was awakened, go off to run the runnable that was enqueued. The notified thread may run second, think that it timed out, and terminate. The overall effect is correct, even if the actual threads did the opposite of what they theoretically should have.

Note that the test `runnables.isEmpty()` is in a loop, since before a notified thread can dequeue a runnable, another `Xeq` thread could call `dequeue()` and grab the runnable for itself.

setMaxThreadsWaiting().   Changing the number of threads allowed to wait results in one having to wake up threads in excess of the new number to allow them to terminate. This is complicated by the common code for the "be awakened" and "time out" states. What we do is to treat them as threads being awakened and let them decide not to wait again, because they would exceed the maximum number of threads now allowed.

Example 5-8 The `RunQueue` method `setMaxThreadsWaiting()`

```
public synchronized void setMaxThreadsWaiting(int n){
      maxThreadsWaiting=n;
      numNotifies += numThreadsWaiting;
      numThreadsWaiting=0;
      notifyAll();
}
```

makeDaemon().   The `makeDaemon` field determines whether the created `Xeq` threads will be daemon threads or user threads. By default, they will be daemons. Why? If there are `Xeq` threads still in existence when the rest of the user program terminates, we don't want these threads to keep the program running.

Recursive Shell Sort: `RunQueue`s and `SimpleFuture`s

The Shell sort, named after its inventor Donald Shell, is an improvement on the insertion sort, which, as you recall, divides the array to be sorted into two parts: the part that has not yet been sorted and the part that has. Initially, none have been sorted. The algorithm works by taking one element at a time from the portion that has not been sorted and inserting it into its proper place in the portion that is sorted.

The insertion sort runs faster if the array is already almost ordered when the algorithm starts, since each element being inserted won't need to be moved far. Shell's innovation was to sort subsequences of the array (e.g., elements *h* positions apart) to put the array into a nearly sorted order before performing the final sort.

Using the divide-and-conquer approach, class `ShellsortDC` recursively divides the array into two interspersed subarrays, sorts them, and then sorts the overall array. The two interspersed subarrays are the even-numbered elements and the odd-numbered elements. If the subarray has few enough elements, it is sorted by the insertion sort. If it is longer, it is itself sorted recursively by a `ShellsortDC` object.

ShellsortDC. The code for ShellsortDC, except for the contained class, which actually does the sorting, is shown in Example 5-9.

Example 5-9 Divide-and-conquer Shell sort

```
class ShellsortDC {
  static int minDivisible=3;
  private static class Sort implements Runnable {
          . . . . .
  }

  static int numInSequence(int i, int k, int n){
          return (n-i+k-1)/k;
  }

  static void isort(int[] a,int m,int k) {
          int i,j;
          for (j=m+k; j<a.length; j+=k) {
              for (i=j; i>m && a[i]>a[i-k]; i-=k) {
                  int tmp=a[i];
                  a[i]=a[i-k];
                  a[i-k]=tmp;
              }
          }
  }

  public static void sort(int[] a) {
          SimpleFuture f=new SimpleFuture();
          RunQueue rq=new RunQueue();
          rq.run(new Sort(a,0,1,f,rq));
          try{ f.getValue();
          }catch(Exception ex){}
          rq.setMaxThreadsWaiting(0);
  }
}
```

Method numInSequence(i,k,n) calculates the number of elements in a subsequence starting at position i, stepping by k, and not extending up to or beyond n. It is used to decide whether to sort a sequence recursively with ShellsortDC or simply with an insertion sort. The field minDivisible is the size limit beneath which insertion sort is used.

An insertion sort is performed by method isort(). Method isort(a,m,k) sorts the subsequence of array a starting at m and stepping by k. It is not optimized. More efficient implementations would remove the element to be inserted, use a binary search to decide where the element goes, move blocks of elements over to make space, and drop it in.

Method sort(a) sorts the integer array a by deligation to the internal, runnable class Sort. When run, Sort(a, i, h, f, rq) will sort the subsequence of a starting at position i and stepping by h. It will assign a null value to future f when it is done, and it will use run queue rq for running subsorts. Method sort() has to create SimpleFuture f and RunQueue rq. It creates the Sort object, telling it to sort array a from position 0 by step 1 (i.e., all of the array). It puts the Sort into rq to be run and waits for it to complete by calling method getValue(). At the end, it sets the maximum number of Xeq threads permitted to wait in rq to zero, forcing them to terminate.

ShellsortDC Sort class. The Sort class (see Example 5-10) contains two methods: the run() method, of course, and a sort() method that does its real work.

Example 5-10 Internal **Sort** class of the divide-and-conquer Shell sort

```
private static class Sort implements Runnable {
    int[] a; int i, h; SimpleFuture f; RunQueue rq;
    Sort(int[] a, int i, int h, SimpleFuture f,RunQueue rq){
        this.a=a; this.i=i; this.h=h; this.f=f; this.rq=rq;
    }
    void sort(int i, int h) {
        if (numInSequence(i,h,a.length)<=minDivisible)
                isort(a,i,h);
        else {
                SimpleFuture nf=new SimpleFuture();
                Sort s=new Sort(a,i+h,2*h,nf,rq);
                rq.run(s);
                sort(i,2*h);
                        try{
                nf.getValue();
                        }catch(InterruptedException iex){}
                isort(a,i,h);
        }
    }
    public void run() {
        sort(i,h);
        f.setValue(null);
    }
}
```

Method `sort(i,h)` sorts the subsequence of the array starting at position `i` and stepping by `h`. It will call `isort()` to sort a small enough sequence. If the sequence is long enough, it recursively sorts both odd and even subsequences concurrently. The even subsequence consists of positions *i, i+2h, i+4h, ...* The odd subsequence consists of positions *i+h, i+3h, i+5h, ...*

Method `sort()` creates another `Sort` object to sort the odd subsequence with a future in which to signal its completion and puts it in the run queue to be executed. Then, method `sort()` calls itself recursively to sort the even subsequence. After both subsequences have been sorted, `sort()` calls `isort()` to merge them into a single sorted sequence.

All that method `run()` need do is call `sort()` and then set the simple future to null to report that it is done.

Accumulator

The code for `IntegTrap1` was a bit awkward. We had to build an array of Threads to keep track of all the subthreads we had to join with and extract return values from. It would be nice if there were only one data object to keep track of, and we could use this object to wait for the completion of a set of threads and accumulate the sum of the values the threads have computed. Accumulators were designed for this use.

An `Accumulator` has a count, a data object, and a future associated with it. Subthreads can signal the accumulator, decrementing its count. When the count becomes zero, the data value is assigned to the future by calling its `setValue()` method. The calling thread can wait for all the subthreads to signal the accumulator by getting the value from the future. If the subthreads are to return values that are, for example, to be summed, the subthreads themselves can add their results to the data object before signaling, which allows the caller to get the sum directly from the future.

Accumulators use the `Future` class, not `SimpleFuture`. `Future` is a subclass of `SimpleFuture`, so all the `SimpleFuture` methods will work. `Future` adds the method `runDelayed()` to submit runnables to a `RunQueue` object when the value is assigned (via method `setValue()`). This will be discussed in more detail later.

Accumulator *Operations*

An `Accumulator` has the following operations:

- **`Accumulator(int n)`** creates an `Accumulator` object that will wait for n completions. It will assign null to its data value, so null will also be sent to the future if method `setData()` has not been called.

Accumulator operations

Constructors

```
Accumulator(int n)
Accumulator(int n, Object data)
Accumulator(int n, Object data, Future f)
```

Methods

```
void signal()
Future getFuture()
Object getData()
void setData(Object val)
void runDelayed(Runnable r)
```

- **Accumulator(int n, Object data)** creates an Accumulator object that will wait for n completions before placing Object data in its Future variable.

- **Accumulator(int n, Object data, Future f)** creates an Accumulator object that will wait for n completions before placing data in Future f.

- **void signal()** is called by a thread to signal that it's operation on the accumulator is complete. The nth of these signals will place the contents of the Accumulator object's data field in its Future variable.

- **Future getFuture()** gets the Future object that will have its value set upon the correct number of signals.

- **Object getData()** gets the data object.

- **void setData(Object val)** sets the data object to val.

- **void runDelayed(Runnable r)** will place the runnable r in a run queue after n signals have accumulated. It delegates it to the runDelayed() method in class Future.

Patterns of Use of Accumulators

Accumulators allow several different patterns of use.

Awaiting completion. To simply await the completion of a set of subthreads, the data value may be ignored. The calling thread would do something similar to the following:

```
Accumulator a=Accumulator( n);
. . .
a.getFuture().getValue();
```

The subthreads respond with

```
a.signal();
```

***And* or *Or*.** If the subthreads are to test whether some condition is true and the caller needs to conjoin *(and)* or disjoin *(or)* their results, the calling thread can initialize the accumulator to the default value, and subthreads can conditionally assign their result to the data value.

For example, suppose the caller needs the conjunction of the results of the subthreads. The caller might do the following:

```
Accumulator a=Accumulator(n,new Boolean(true));
. . .
if (((Boolean)a.getFuture().getValue())
                .booleanValue())....
```

The subthreads may respond with

```
if (!result) a.setData(new Boolean(false));
a.signal();
```

If the caller needs the disjunction of the values, the code becomes

```
Accumulator a=Accumulator(n,new Boolean(false));
. . .
if (((Boolean)a.getFuture().getValue())
                .booleanValue())....
```

and the subthreads may respond with

```
if (result) a.setData(new Boolean(true));
a.signal();
```

Associative, commutative operations. For an associative, commutative operation on a primitive type, you must wrap the primitive type in an object. We consider one approach for summation:

To get the sum in variable v the caller does the following:

```
Accumulator a=Accumulator(n,new Double(0.0));
. . .
v = ((Numeric)a.getFuture().getValue()).doubleValue();
```

The subthreads respond with

```
synchronized(a) {
        a.setData(new Double(
          ((Double)a.getData()).doubleValue()+result));
}
a.signal();
```

It might be more efficient, and no less clear, to have the double in a mutable object. The subthreads could get a reference to the object, lock it, and update the value there. This leads to the next pattern.

Shared data structures. To update a shared data structure, the subthreads simply get a reference to the data object and update it. For example, to have the subthreads place associations in a hash table, the caller might execute the following statements:

```
Accumulator a=Accumulator(n,new Hashtable());
...
Hashtable h = (Hashtable)a.getFuture().getValue();
```

The subthreads execute the following:

```
((Hashtable)a.getData()).put(key,value);
a.signal();
```

Since the `put()` method of class `Hashtable` is synchronized, the subthreads do not have to lock the hash table themselves.

Using Accumulators

Numeric Integration

With run queues and accumulators, we can perform another, more efficient version of numeric integration, `IntegTrap3`. There are parameters to `IntegTrap3` to handle the

---

IntegTrap3 interface
```
public IntegTrap3(int numThreads, int numRegions, int granularity )
public double integrate(double a,  double b,  F_of_x fn)
```

---

number of threads and the number of regions separately. Why? You probably want to consider the number of processors when you set the number of threads. You won't get all the processors all the time assigned to your threads. There are probably more runnable threads in your program, and there are other processes running on your machine that may be using some of the processors. This would indicate that you may not want to create more threads than there are processors, indeed, maybe not more than the number of processors you can reasonably expect to get at any time. On the other hand, you might decide to try to steal processors away from other work or other users by creating more threads, increasing the likelihood that when a processor is given to the next runnable thread, the thread will be one of yours.

The many threads you create are unlikely to all run at the same rate. Some will complete sooner than the others. If you divide up the work evenly among them, you will have to wait for the slow ones to complete. It would be nice to take some of the work from the slow threads and give it to those that are done first. That is what creating a lot of regions does; the threads that are done first can grab more work.

In choosing both the number of threads and the number of regions, remember that you are aiming for a medium grain size. The fewer threads and regions there are, the more coarse grained your computation is, and the more likely your work is to be delayed by unbalanced loads. The more regions there are, the finer the grain is, and the larger the fraction of time your program will spend creating and queueing them.

The code for the `integrate()` method is shown in Example 5-11. One major difference from `IntegTrap1` is that it uses an accumulator. The subthreads to add their areas into its data field and signal their completion through it. The `integrate()` method can then just get the total area out of the accumulator's `Future` variable.

It uses `RunQueue regionQueue` in which to run the subthreads. At the end, it sets the maximum number of threads permitted to wait to zero, causing them all to terminate.

The code for `IntegTrap3Region` is shown in Example 5-12. It is a straightforward implementation of the associative, commutative operator pattern for using accumulators.

Example 5-11 `integrate` method in `IntegTrap3`, using `Accumulator` and `RunQueue`

```java
public double integrate(double a, double b, F_of_x fn){
        int i;
        double totalArea = 0.0d;
        Accumulator acc=null;
        if( a > b )
                throw new BadRangeException();
        if( a == b )
                throw new NoRangeException();
        RunQueue regionQueue = new RunQueue( numThreads );
        try {
            double range = b - a;
            double start = a;
            double end = a + ((1.0d)/numRegions * range);
            acc=new Accumulator(numRegions,new Double(0.0));
            for( i=0; i < numRegions; i++ ) {
                regionQueue.put( new IntegTrap3Region(start,
                    end,granularity, fn, acc ));
                start = end;
                end = a + ((i + 2.0d)/numRegions * range);
            }
        }
        catch( Exception e ) {
            System.out.println("Exception occured in" +
              " creating and initializing thread.\n" +
                        e.toString() );
        }
        try {
          totalArea= ((Double)acc.getFuture().getValue()).
                    doubleValue();
        } catch(Exception e) {
            System.out.println(
                "Could not retrieve value from " +
                    "Accumulator's Future." );
            System.exit( 1 );
        }
        regionQueue.setMaxThreadsWaiting(0);
        return totalArea;
    }
```

Example 5-12 `IntegTrap3Region` adding value to an `Accumulator`

```
class IntegTrap3Region implements Runnable {
    private String name;
    private double x_start, x_end;
    private int granularity;
    private F_of_x f;
    private Accumulator result;
    public IntegTrap3Region( double x_start, double x_end,
            int granularity, F_of_x f, Accumulator result ) {
        this.name = new String( x_start + "-" + x_end );
        this.x_start = x_start;
        this.x_end = x_end;
        this.granularity = granularity;
        this.f = f;
        this.result = result;
    }
    public void run() {
        double area = 0.0d;
        double range = x_end - x_start;
        double g=granularity;
        for( int i=granularity-1; i>0; i-- ) {
            area += f.f((i/g)*range+x_start);
        }
        area += (f.f(x_start)+f.f(x_end))/2.0;
        area = area*(range/g);
        synchronized (result) {
            result.setData( new Double(
                area+((Double)result.getData()).doubleValue()));
        }
        result.signal();
    }
}
```

TerminationGroup

An accumulator allows a caller to wait for a fixed number of subthreads to terminate. Sometimes, however, you won't initially know how many subthreads will be created. Sometimes, subthreads create further subthreads, which create further still, and the only synchronization required is waiting for them all to terminate.

To handle this case, we provide the interface `TerminationGroup`.

`TerminationGroup` is an interface. The class that implements the interface is `SharedTerminationGroup`. The name leaves open the ability to create a `DistributedTerminationGroup` class later. The idea of a termination group is

---

TerminationGroup methods
```
void  awaitTermination()
TerminationGroup fork()
void runDelayed(Runnable r)
void terminate()
```

---

this: There are a collection of TerminationGroup objects in a termination group. From any one of those objects, we can create other objects that will also be in the group. We get to *terminate* each object in the group precisely once. Once an object has been terminated, we are no longer allowed to create new group members from it. We can, however, reference any object in the group and call its awaitTermination() method. The awaitTermination() method will delay us until all objects in the termination group have been terminated.

Interface TerminationGroup declares the following methods:

- **void awaitTermination()** waits for all elements of a termination group to terminate.

- **TerminationGroup fork()** creates another element in the termination group and returns it. This method may not be called for an element that has already been terminated.

- **void terminate()** terminates this element of the termination group. If this is the last member of the termination group to be terminated, any threads awaiting termination will be allowed to run.

- **void runDelayed(Runnable r)** delays the Runnable r until all elements of the group have terminated and then places it in a run queue. This will be discussed Chapter 7, "Chores."

The class SharedTerminationGroup is used in a shared memory system. It has two constructors:

- **SharedTerminationGroup(Future f)**: A SharedTerminationGroup object contains a Future object and assigns null to it when termination has occurred. This constructor allows you to supply the future it uses yourself.

- **SharedTerminationGroup()**: This form allocates a future for the group. You don't need to get a reference to the future yourself, since methods awaitTermination() and runDelayed(Runnable r) do all the operations on the future that you would want.

Figure 5–3 shows a picture of forking and termination. The creation of a `SharedTerminationGroup` object must lead to a terminate. Each fork must also lead to a termination.

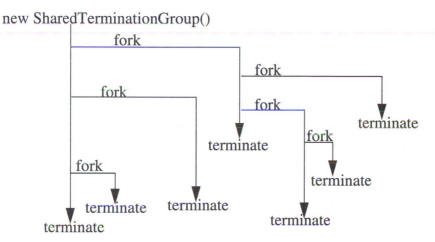

Figure 5–3 Example of use of a termination group.

Combinatorial Search

There are a number of optimization problems that involve finding the optimal combination of things (i.e., finding some combination of the items that maximizes or minimizes some function subject to some constraints).

In the worst case, these algorithms will have to try out each combination of the items, see if they meet the constraints, calculate their value, and remember the best combination. N things have 2^N combinations. Each additional item can double the number of combinations and the amount of time you may have to spend.

For many of these problems, there are ways to cut down on the number of combinations you have to search through. Quite often, the median search time for these problems will be quite modest. But it is the nature of these problems that there will be some instances that would go on until after the sun burns out or you press control-C to force the execution to quit.

The 0–1 Knapsack Problem

As an example of a combinatorial search problem, we will look at the 0–1 knapsack problem. In this metaphor, you have a knapsack that can hold only a certain weight. You have a number of items that you could put in the knapsack. Each item has a profit and a weight. You want to pack the maximum value into the knapsack without exceeding its capacity. You must include an item as a whole, or exclude it. You can't include only a part of an item.

These rules are formulated as follows:

$$Maximize \quad \sum x_i \cdot p_i$$
$$where \quad C \geq \sum x_i \cdot w_i$$
$$x_i \in \{0, 1\}$$
$$p_i > 0$$
$$w_i > 0$$

x_i indicates whether or not item i is included, so x_i can only take on a 0 or a 1, hence the name 0–1 knapsack problem. p_i is the profit from including item i, and w_i is the weight of item i. C is the capacity of the knapsack.

Suppose you have N items, numbered 0 through N–1. How do you search for a solution? Well, you could try writing N nested loops, each setting an x_i to 1 and 0 and testing the constraint and evaluating the profit in the innermost loop, remembering the best found.

That, however, is not a general-purpose program. What we can do is use a recursive depth-first search (DFS) method to assign values to the x's. Suppose when we call dfs(i,rc,P), all the variables x_j, $0 \leq j < i$, have been assigned 0s and 1s, leaving rc remaining capacity and accumulating P profit. (See Figure 5–4.) If $i=N$, we have assigned values to all the x's. Setting the x's to one value specifies the combination of the items we're including. If the remaining capacity rc≥0, we have not exceeded the capacity of the knapsack. If P is greater than the profit we got for any previous combination, we should remember this one.

If $i<N$, we haven't assigned all the x_i's yet. We should first try including the next item, assigning x_i the value one and recursively calling dfs() for position i+1. Then we assign x_i zero and recursively call the function again.

These recursive calls are said to search a state-space tree. (See Figure 5–5). Each assignment to the values of variables x_j, $0 \leq j < i$, is known as a state of the search. The state space is the set of all states. Our search treats the state space as a tree, and each state is a node of the tree. The leaves of the tree represent combinations of the items that we are considering including in the knapsack.

There is an obvious optimization we can put in. If in some recursive call of dfs() we have already exceeded the capacity of the knapsack, which we will know by rc being less than zero, we can omit searching the subtree. No leaf in it will meet the constraint. This is known as a cutoff (cutting off the search if we know it cannot lead to an optimum solution).

There's another cutoff that works well for the 0–1 knapsack problem, but it requires sorting the items before running the algorithm. The idea is that we can cut off searching a sub

Figure 5–4 Simple 0–1 algorithm (in pseudo code)

```
dfs(i,rc,P):
        if i==N and rc>=0 and P>bestP
                remember this solution
        else
                xᵢ = 1
                dfs(i+1,rc-wᵢ,P+pᵢ)
                xᵢ = 0
                dfs(i+1,rc,P)
```

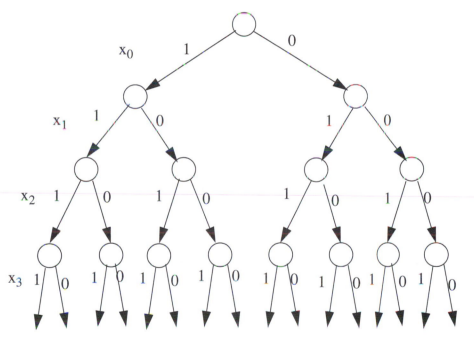

Figure 5–5 Top levels of state-space tree for 0–1 knapsack problem.

tree if, with the profit accumulated so far and with the remaining capacity, there is no way for the subtree to give us a better profit than we have found so far.

We sort the items by nonincreasing value per weight. This means that we will greedily gather up the items with the best profit for their weight first. To decide whether to continue, we multiply the remaining capacity times the profit per weight of the next item and add that to the profit we have accumulated thus far: $rc*p_i/w_i+P$. This will tell us how much profit we could get if we could exactly fill the remainder of the knapsack with items as profitable for their weight as the next item. This will give us an upper bound on how much profit we could get exploring the current subtree, since no remaining item will have a greater profit per weight than this next item. If this upper bound is less than or equal to the best profit we've found so far, we can cut off searching this subtree. (See Figure 5–6.)

Figure 5–6 Optimized 0–1 algorithm (in pseudo code)

```
dfs(i,rc,P):
            if i==N and rc>=0 and P>bestP
                    remember this solution
        else
                    if rc*pi/wi + P <= bestP then return
                    if rc>=wi then
                            xi = 1
                            dfs(i+1,rc-wi,P+pi)
                    xi = 0
                    dfs(i+1,rc,P)
```

Parallel Depth-first Search for the Knapsack Problem

A depth-first search has a huge number of procedure calls. If the procedures are independent, the program is a candidate for parallel execution.

In the algorithms sketched in Figure 5–4 and Figure 5–6, there are two ways that the procedure calls are not independent:

1. The *x*'s are global variables.

2. The best solution and it's profit are global variables.

If we can make these independent, we can parallelize the computation.

The *x*'s can be made independent by passing *x* by value (i.e., giving each procedure instance its own copy).

The global variables for the best solution found so far and its profit can be kept in a monitor, a shared object that the threads lock. Indeed, if the profit can be kept in four bytes (e.g., in an `int` or `float`), it can be declared volatile and examined directly.

Thus, we can make the subroutines independent and parallelizable. That still leaves the problems of the grain size and flooding. The procedure calls are too parallelizable. We could create a thread for each call, but that would eat up memory at a ferocious rate, and the individual calls don't do much computation, so the grain size would be tiny. We need to throttle the computation.

Here's how we can do it. We decide on our grain size by the size of a search tree we would be willing to search by a recursive DFS method. We want to pick a number of levels (k) that gives us a reasonable number of nodes to examine. If k is 10, we will search through about a thousand nodes; if k is 20, we will search through about a million. We then divide the search along level $N–k$ in the tree. (See Figure 5–7.) Beyond level $N–k$, the DFS method just searches an entire subtree out to the leaves. Above that level, we use a special version of our DFS algorithm to `generate` parallel searches. When it gets down to level $N–k$, it creates a `search runnable` to do the rest of the search. The `generate` part of the algorithm then returns to follow another branch and generate another search.

This is not the same algorithm as a simple depth-first search. The simple DFS can spend a long time searching a subtree that would have been cut off if another subtree had been searched first. The parallel solution can spend some time examining the other subtree, set a bounding value from it, and cut off the futile subtree. As a consequence, the parallel DFS can produce super-linear speedups. That is, parallel DFS with N processors can run in less

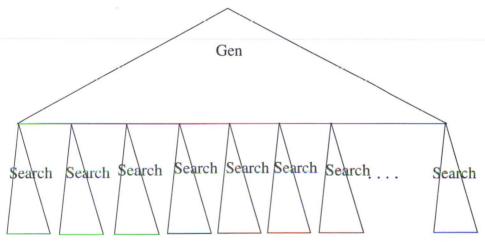

Figure 5–7 Parallel DFS tree. Gen generates searches that search k-level DFS trees.

than $\frac{1}{N}$ th the time of the sequential. The extra processors can reduce each other's work. Of course, by the rule that speedup must be computed compared to the *best* sequential algorithm, perhaps we should be comparing the parallel version to a concurrent execution of itself on a single processor, which may remove the superlinearity.

Knapsack2

Knapsack2 is a parallel DFS algorithm for the 0–1-knapsack problem. It's overall structure is shown in Example 5-13.

Example 5-13 Knapsack2: a parallel DFS algorithm for the 0–1-knapsack problem.

```java
class Knapsack2 {
 private static class Item{
        int profit,weight,pos;
        float profitPerWeight;
 }
 int LEVELS;
 BitSet selected;
 int capacity;
 volatile float bestProfit=0;
 Item[] item;
 RunQueue rq=new RunQueue();
 Future done=new Future();
 TerminationGroup tg =new SharedTerminationGroup(done) ;
 public BitSet getSelected() throws InterruptedException {
     // see Example 5-17
 }
 public int getProfit() throws InterruptedException {
        done.getValue();
        rq.setMaxThreadsWaiting(0);
        return (int)bestProfit;
 }
 void gen(int i, int rw, int p, BitSet b) {
     // see Example 5-15
 }
 public Knapsack2(int[] weights, int[] profits, int capacity,
                int LEVELS){
     // see Example 5-14
 }
 class Search implements Runnable {
     // see Example 5-16
 }
}
```

The local class `Item` and the corresponding array `item` are used to keep all the relevant information about each item that could be included in the knapsack. Fields `profit` and `weight` are self-explanatory. Field `profitPerWeight` keeps the ratio of the `profit` and `weight` fields. This value is used throughout the algorithm, so it is probably cheaper to store it than recompute it. The field `pos` indicates the original position of the item in the arrays of profits and weights provided by the user. The array `item` is sorted by nonincreasing `profitPerWeight` to facilitate cutoffs.

Field `LEVELS` is the number of levels the generator will go to before releasing separate depth-first searches. Assuming that there are no cutoffs due (e.g., the next item not fitting in the knapsack), we see that there will be 2^{LEVELS} searches that could be done in parallel. The larger the value of `LEVELS` is, the greater the cost of creating search objects and queueing them for execution. The smaller the value of `LEVELS` is, the deeper the searches will be. The grain size of the searches is inversely exponentially proportional to the value of `LEVELS`.

Field `selected` indicates the members of the item array that are selected in the best solution found so far. The field `bestProfit` is the profit obtained from the selected items.

Field `rq` is the run queue that the search runnables are placed in to be run in FIFO order.

Field `tg` is the termination group that search runnables use to indicate that they have completed their part of the search. `Future done` is assigned null by `tg` when all searches have completed. Therefore, to wait for the search to be completed, one need only call `done.getValue()`

Constructor. There are four sections to the `Knapsack2` constructor:

1. Check the arguments and throw an exception if an error is detected.

2. Initialize the item array.

3. Sort the item array by nonincreasing profit per weight. Here, we use an insertion sort. A faster sorting algorithm is not warranted for just a few items, and if there are a great many items, the exponential running time of the search itself will so dominate the running time as to make the sort trivial.

4. Do the actual search. The heart of this section is calling recursive routine `gen()` to generate the searches. There are several other things to do here as well:

    - Make sure that `LEVELS` isn't greater than the number of items, since the number of items is the full depth of the search tree.

    - Set parameters on `rq`. Here, we are not allowing more than four threads to be created.

Example 5-14 Knapsack2 constructor

```java
public Knapsack2(int[] weights, int[] profits, int capacity,
            int LEVELS){
    this.LEVELS=LEVELS;
    if (weights.length!=profits.length)
        throw new IllegalArgumentException(
            "0/1 Knapsack: differing numbers of"+
            " weights and profits");
    if (capacity<=0)
        throw new IllegalArgumentException(
            "0/1 Knapsack: capacity<=0");
    item = new Item[weights.length];
    int i;
    for (i=0; i<weights.length; i++) {
        item[i]=new Item();
        item[i].profit=profits[i];
        item[i].weight=weights[i];
        item[i].pos=i;
        item[i].profitPerWeight=
            ((float)profits[i])/weights[i];

    int j;
    for (j=1; j<item.length; j++) {
        for (i=j;
             i>0 &&
             item[i].profitPerWeight >
                 item[i-1].profitPerWeight;
             i--) {
            Item tmp=item[i];
            item[i]=item[i-1];
            item[i-1]=tmp;
        }
    }
    if (LEVELS>item.length) LEVELS=item.length;
    rq.setWaitTime(10000);
    rq.setMaxThreadsCreated(4);
    gen(0,capacity,0,new BitSet(item.length));
    tg.terminate();
}
```

- After generating the searches, we call terminate() to terminate object tg. This terminate() will terminate the original instance of the termination group that was constructed when this Knapsack2 object was created.

Method gen(). Method gen() searches the top levels of the state-space tree in class Knapsack2. If it has searched through LEVELS levels, it creates a DSearch object to do the rest of the depth-first search and places it in rq to be searched in parallel with other searches. For this search, we must clone the bitset b that represents the x variables and fork another element of the termination group tg for the search to use.

Example 5-15 Method gen(): top level of the tree in class **Knapsack2**

```
void gen(int i, int rw, int p, BitSet b) {
        if (i>=LEVELS) {
                rq.run(new Search(i,rw,p,
                        (BitSet)b.clone(),tg.fork()));
                return;
        }
        if (rw - item[i].weight >= 0) {
                b.set(i);
                gen(i+1,rw-item[i].weight,p+item[i].profit,b);
        }
        b.clear(i);
        gen(i+1,rw,p,b);
        return;
}
```

Method gen() walks over the state-space tree in a greedy order. It first includes the next item in the knapsack and generates all searches that include it. Then, it excludes the item and generates all searches that do not include it. Since the searches are executed by FIFO order, those trees that include a lot of the initial high profit per weight items will be searched first. It is highly likely that the best solution will be found quickly and will prevent a lot of the later, fruitless searches.

The Search class. The internal class Search handles the final depth-first search down to the leaves of the tree. Its fields are as follows:

- selected: The bits give the values of the *x* variables: set with 1 and cleared with 0. Initially, it has the bits set that gen() gets.

- from: This holds the position of the item at which the search starts. In Knapsack2, this will equal LEVELS.

- startWeight: This is the remaining capacity that this search can allocate.

- startProfit: This is the profit accumulated before this search was created, the profits for the items in the initial value of selected.

Example 5-16 Search class of `Knapsack2`

```java
class Search implements Runnable {
    BitSet selected;
    int from;
    int startWeight=0;
    int startProfit=0;
    TerminationGroup tg;
    Search(int from,
        int remainingWeight,
        int profit,
        BitSet selected,
        TerminationGroup tg) {
            this.from=from;
            startWeight=remainingWeight;
            startProfit=profit;
            this.selected=selected;
            this.tg=tg;
    }
    void dfs(int i, int rw, int p) {
        if (i>=item.length) {
            if (p>bestProfit) {
                synchronized(Knapsack2.this) {
                    if (p>bestProfit) {
                        bestProfit=p;
                        Knapsack2.this.selected=
                            (BitSet)selected.clone();
                    }
                }
            }
            return;
        }
        if (p+rw*item[i].profitPerWeight<bestProfit) return;
        if (rw-item[i].weight>=0) {
            selected.set(i);
            dfs(i+1,rw-item[i].weight,p+item[i].profit);
        }
        selected.clear(i);
        dfs(i+1,rw,p);
        return;
    }
    public void run(){
        dfs(from,startWeight,startProfit);
        tg.terminate();
    }
}
```

Search's method `run()` is trivial. All it has to do is call the DFS method `dfs()` and then terminate this search's instance of the termination group when `dfs()` returns.

Method `dfs()` does the real work and is reasonably straightforward. It's one unusual feature is the way it decides whether to record a new better solution. If it has reached a leaf, recognized by `i>=item.length`, it first checks to see if its profit is better than the best found so far (`p>bestProfit`). It can do this check relatively cheaply, since `bestProfit` is a volatile shared variable. It can just fetch and examine it. Only if `p` is greater than `bestProfit` is it worth locking the enclosing `Knapsack2` object containing the shared `selected` and `bestProfit` variables. It locks the enclosing object [by calling `synchronized(Knapsack2.this)`] and then again checks that it still has a better profit. Some other thread could have changed the shared values before this thread got the lock.

Methods `getSelected()` and `getProfit()`. Methods `getSelected()` and `getProfit()` have to wait for the search to terminate by calling `done.getValue()`. This is a good place, knowing that the search is done, to set the number of threads allowed to wait in the run queue `rq` to zero. The run queue won't be needed any more, now that the search is over.

Example 5-17 Method `getSelected()` of **Knapsack2**

```
public BitSet getSelected() throws InterruptedException {
        done.getValue();
        rq.setMaxThreadsWaiting(0);
        BitSet s=new BitSet(item.length);
        for(int i=0; i<item.length; i++) {
                if (selected.get(i)) s.set(item[i].pos);
        }
        return s;
}
```

The loop in `getSelected()` translates the `selected` bit set into the correct form for the caller. The field `selected` assigns bits in terms of positions in the `item` array, whereas the bits returned to the caller must be in terms of the positions in the input `weight` and `profit` arrays.

PriorityRunQueue

The `PriorityRunQueue` class has the same operations as `RunQueue`, except that the operations to insert runnables into the queue take a second parameter, the priority. When an

Xeq thread removes a runnable to execute it, the thread will always get the runnable with the highest priority. If several have the highest priority, it will get an arbitrary one of them.

`PriorityRunQueue` constructors and methods

```
PriorityRunQueue()
PriorityRunQueue(int maxCreatable)

public void put(Runnable runnable, double priority)
public void run(Runnable runnable, double priority)
public void setMaxThreadsWaiting(int n)
public void setMaxThreadsCreated(int n)
public int getMaxThreadsWaiting()
public int getMaxThreadsCreated()
public int getNumThreadsWaiting()
public int getNumThreadsCreated()
public void setWaitTime(long n)
public long getWaitTime()
public void terminate()
public void setPriority(int n)
public int getPriority()
public void setDaemon(boolean makeDaemon)
public boolean getDaemon()
```

This would make no real difference if the priority run queue is set up to create as many threads as needed to run all enqueued runnables. It only matters if some runnables are forced to wait.

The default value of `maxThreadsCreated` for a `PriorityRunQueue` object is one.

Although `PriorityRunQueue` has much the same methods as `RunQueue`, there is no class relationship between them. Neither is a subclass of the other, nor do they inherit from any common ancestor other than `Object`.

We now present a couple of notes on the methods:

- As in the class `RunQueue`, `put()` and `run()` are synonyms. Although they take a double-precision priority, the priority is kept internally as a `float`, so don't count on the full double-precision number of digits to make subtle distinctions between priorities.

- Methods `getPriority()` and `setPriority()` refer to the priority of the `Xeq` threads that will execute the runnables. They have nothing to do with the priorities specified in the `put()` and `run()` methods.

Branch-and-Bound with Priority Run Queues

Branch-and-bound algorithms are search algorithms. When the search has to make a choice, the branch-and-bound algorithm branches; in effect, it goes both ways. The branch-and-bound algorithm estimates which alternatives are most likely to produce better solutions, so that they can be pursued first. It also remembers the best solution it has found so far and ceases searches of alternatives that cannot produce a better solution. Finding good solutions quickly can prevent making a lot of futile computation.

Branch and Bound for 0–1 Knapsack

Using a priority run queue, threads can pursue the most promising paths first. Threads can dynamically generate searches and place them in the priority run queue. This gives a branch-and-bound algorithm.

The 0–1 knapsack branch-and-bound algorithm, `Knapsack3`, is shown in Example 5-18. It is not a pure branch-and-bound algorithm, because it switches to depth-first search to search the final subtrees, just as does `Knapsack2`.

One difference in the fields from `Knapsack2` is that the run queue `rq` has been replaced by a priority run queue `prq`. Another difference is the addition of a field `searchFactory` that references an object that allows us to recycle `Search` objects, rather than having to create a new one each time we need one.

Class `Search`. The structure of the `Search` class in `Knapsack3` is shown in Example 5-19. It combines the functions of both method `gen()` and class `Search` in `Knapsack2`. In translating `Knapsack2` to `Knapsack3`, the parameter names of `gen()` became the field names of `Search`, so if you wish to do a comparison of the code, `i` in `Knapsack3` corresponds to `from` in `Knapsack2`, `rw` to `remainingWeight`, `p` to `profit`, and `b` to `selected`. Field `tg` remains the same.

Class `SearchFactory`. `SearchFactory` is a new class in `Knapsack3`. Its purpose is to reuse `Search` objects. When a new `Search` object is needed, `SearchFactory`'s `make()` method is called. It will try to allocate a `Search` object off a local stack, or if the stack is empty, it will create a new one. When searches terminate, the objects call the `searchFactory`'s `recycle()` method to push their objects on the stack. When the entire search is done, the algorithm calls `searchFactory`'s `terminate()` method to dispose of all the `Search` objects that are no longer needed.

The method `run()` in class `Search` (see Example 5-21) performs most of the functions of method `gen()` in `Knapsack2`. It searches the levels of the state-space tree nearest the

Example 5-18 Knapsack3: Branch-and-bound algorithm

```
class Knapsack3 {
 private static class Item{
        int profit,weight,pos;
        float profitPerWeight;
 }
 int LEVELS=5;
 BitSet selected;
 int capacity;
 volatile float bestProfit=0;
 Item[] item;
 PriorityRunQueue prq=new PriorityRunQueue();
 Future done=new Future();
 TerminationGroup tg =new SharedTerminationGroup(done) ;
 public BitSet getSelected() throws InterruptedException {
     //as in Knapsack2
 }
 public int getProfit() throws InterruptedException {
     //as in Knapsack2
 }
 class SearchFactory {
     // see Example 5-20
 }
 SearchFactory searchFactory= new SearchFactory();
 class Search implements Runnable {
     // see Example 5-19
 }
 public Knapsack3(int[] weights, int[] profits, int capacity,
                 int DFSLEVELS){
     // see Example 5-22
 }
}
```

root, calling method dfs() to search the further reaches of the branches. Figure 5–8 shows this graphically, with solid lines indicating paths followed by run() and the dotted edges representing runnables created to explore other branches. It has a number of features that need to be discussed:

1.   The for loop is used to optimize tail-end recursion. If the last thing a recursive method is going to do before returning is recursively call itself, it can save on overhead by assigning new values to its parameters and jumping back to its top. That's why the for loop is here.

Example 5-19 Class **Search** in **Knapsack3**

```
class Search implements Runnable {
    int i; int rw; int p; BitSet b; TerminationGroup tg;
        Search(int i,int rw,int p,
                            BitSet b,TerminationGroup tg){
            this.i=i; this.rw=rw; this.p=p;
            this.b=b; this.tg=tg;
        }
        public void run(){
            // see Example 5-21
        }
    void dfs(int i, int rw, int p) {
            // same as in Knapsack2 with the name
            // Knapsack2 replaced with Knapsack3
    }
}
```

Example 5-20 Class **SearchFactory**

```
class SearchFactory {
    Stack prev=new Stack();
    Search make(int i, int rw, int p,
            BitSet b, TerminationGroup tg) {
        Search g=null;
        synchronized (this) {
            if (!prev.isEmpty()) g=(Search)prev.pop();
        }
            if (g==null)
            return new Search(i,rw,p,b,tg);
        else {
            g.i=i; g.rw=rw; g.p=p; g.b=b; g.tg=tg;
            return g;
        }
    }
    synchronized void recycle(Search g) {
        if (prev!=null) prev.push(g);
    }
    synchronized void terminate() {
        prev=null;
    }
}
```

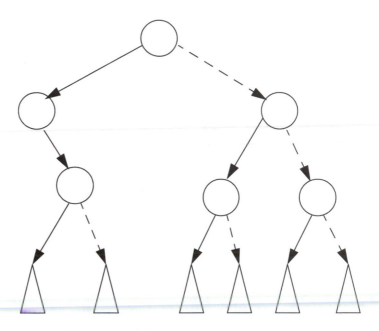

Figure 5–8 Example of paths followed by method `run()` of `Knapsack3`.

2. The first `if` statement is to cut off the search if the best profit we can hope to achieve in this search is less than or equal to the best we've found so far.

3. The second `if` statement converts to a regular DFS if we have searched down enough levels in `run()`.

4. The third `if` statement checks to see if we have enough capacity to include the next item in the knapsack. If so, we create another `Search` object to explore the consequences of *not* including it. *That* search we schedule in the priority run queue `prq` associated with the upper bound on its profit as its priority. Then, we add in the profit and subtract the weight of the next item, increment the position `i` on the item array, and loop back around to continue the search.

5. The `else` part of the third `if` statement considers the case where we are not able to include this item in the knapsack. We simply skip it and loop back to continue the search.

Example 5-21 Method `run()` in class `Search` of `Knapsack3`

```
public void run(){
    for(;;){
        if (p+rw*item[i].profitPerWeight<bestProfit)
            break;
        if (i>=LEVELS) {
            dfs(i,rw,p);
            break;
        }
        if (rw - item[i].weight >= 0) {
            // first, start zero's subtree
            b.clear(i);
            prq.run(searchFactory.make(i+1,rw,p,
                (BitSet)b.clone(),tg.fork()),
                p+rw*item[i+1].profitPerWeight);
            // then iterate to search the one's subtree
            b.set(i);
            rw-=item[i].weight;
            p+=item[i].profit;
            ++i;
        } else { //just iterate to  search zero subtree
            b.clear(i);
            ++i;
        }
    }
    tg.terminate();
    searchFactory.recycle(this);
}
```

6. The loop follows the greedy path through the tree, including the next most profitable item repeatedly until we are cut off or have reached the proper level to do a depth-first search, which we do by calling `dfs()`.

7. When we drop out of the loop, we are done with this `Search` object. We call `terminate()` on our termination group object `tg` to denote that we're done, and then we recycle our `Search` object. We only dare call `recycle` as the last action before returning, since our object could be reused immediately, which would clobber our fields.

The method `dfs()` in `Knapsack3` is the same as it is in `Knapsack2`, except that occurrences of the identifier `Knapsack2` are replaced with `Knapsack3`, of course.

Constructor. The constructor for Knapsack3 (see Example 5-22) is similar to the constructor for Knapsack2 (Example 5-14). There are two major differences:

Example 5-22 Constructor for Knapsack3

```java
public Knapsack3(int[] weights, int[] profits, int capacity,
                 int DFSLEVELS){
      if (weights.length!=profits.length)
          throw new IllegalArgumentException(
              "0/1 Knapsack: differing numbers of"+
              " weights and profits");
      if (capacity<=0)
          throw new IllegalArgumentException(
              "0/1 Knapsack: capacity<=0");
      item = new Item[weights.length];
      int i;
      for (i=0; i<weights.length; i++) {
              item[i]=new Item();
              item[i].profit=profits[i];
              item[i].weight=weights[i];
              item[i].pos=i;
              item[i].profitPerWeight=
                      ((float)profits[i])/weights[i];
      }
      int j;
      for (j=1; j<item.length; j++) {
          for (i=j;
              i>0 &&
              item[i].profitPerWeight >
                      item[i-1].profitPerWeight;
              i--) {
              Item tmp=item[i];
              item[i]=item[i-1];
              item[i-1]=tmp;
          }
      }
      LEVELS=Math.max(1,item.length-DFSLEVELS);
      prq.setWaitTime(10000);
      prq.setMaxThreadsCreated(4);
      prq.run(
              searchFactory.make(0,capacity,0,
                      new BitSet(item.length),tg),
                      0);
}
```

1. Knapsack3 takes the parameter DFSLEVELS rather than LEVELS. It indicates how many levels are desired in the final tree to be searched by method dfs(). The constructor has to compute LEVELS from that, which is simply item.lengthDFSLEVELS. If DFSLEVELS is larger than the number of items, it is set to one.

2. Rather than calling gen(), as Knapsack2 can do, Knapsack3 has to execute the run() method of a Search object. It does this by simply creating the object and dropping it into the priority run queue. It arbitrarily gives it the priority 0. Any priority would do. This is the first entry in the queue. No others will be added until it is run.

A Purer Branch-and-Bound 0–1 Knapsack

Knapsack3 is not a pure implementation of branch-and-bound principles. Although the runnables created for other branches are scheduled in a priority run queue, the path that the run() method takes through the tree is not rescheduled. According to branch-and-bound principles, it should be. It could, at some point, no longer have the highest possible profit. The branch-and-bound algorithm should always be following the most promising path.

Knapsack4 is a purer branch-and-bound algorithm. The only difference from Knapsack3 is the run() method in class Search, shown in Example 5-23. The for loop is no longer present. Instead of looping back to follow a path, it simply resubmits itself to the priority run queue. If it is still following the most promising path, it will be immediately removed from the run queue and executed. If some other path is more promising, that path will get the processor.

It is still an impure branch-and-bound algorithm, however, since it switches to a depth-first search part of the way down the tree. The smaller a value of DFSLEVELS you supply when you create the Knapsack4 object, the closer it is to a pure branch-and-bound algorithm.

Example 5-23 The method `run()` of `Knapsack4`.

```java
public void run(){
        if (p+rw*item[i].profitPerWeight<bestProfit) {
                tg.terminate();
                searchFactory.recycle(this);
                return;
        }
        if (i>=LEVELS) {
                dfs(i,rw,p);
                tg.terminate();
                searchFactory.recycle(this);
                return;
        }
        if (rw - item[i].weight >= 0) {
                // first, start zero's subtree
                b.clear(i);
                prq.run(searchFactory.make(i+1,rw,p,
                        (BitSet)b.clone(),tg.fork()),
                                p+rw*item[i+1].profitPerWeight);
                // then search the one's subtree
                b.set(i);
                rw-=item[i].weight;
                p+=item[i].profit;
                ++i;
        } else { //just search zero subtree
                b.clear(i);
                ++i; //gen(i+1,rw,p,b,tg);
        }
        prq.run(this,p+rw*item[i].profitPerWeight);
        return;
}
```

Figure 5–9 depicts the execution of `Knapsack4`. The dotted lines in the figure indicate that the computation at the head of the line is submitted to the priority run queue for later execution.

Chapter Wrap-up

In this chapter, we explored executing subroutines in parallel to gain parallelism. Throughout the chapter, we had to consider such issues as how to design or reorganize the algorithms for parallel execution, how to maintain a good grain size, and how to synchronize threads performing the calculations.

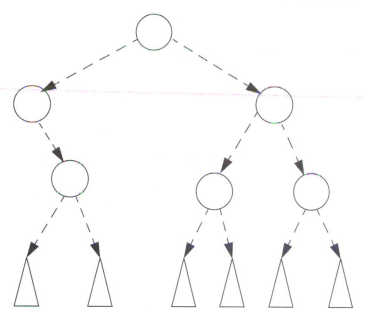

Figure 5–9 Example of paths followed by `run()` method of `Knapsack4`.

Although we could have created a new thread for each subroutine, we used the `RunQueue` class to allocate threads. Instead of creating a new thread for each subroutine, a `Runnable` object for the subroutine is placed in the run queue. When threads are finished running one runnable from the run queue, they recycle themselves and wait at the run queue for another runnable to be enqueued, which they remove and run.

`RunQueue` objects have parameters that control how many threads can be created to handle the runnables placed in the queue. This allows throttling the computation. Embarrassingly parallel computations that create a flood of subcomputations will not swamp the system with threads if the run queue restricts the number of threads that can be created. However, we must take care not to create a deadlock, which could happen if some of the runnables wait on calculations that later runnables in the run queue perform. Then later runnables would not be able to run, because the earlier runnables would be holding all the threads.

We presented the `Accumulator` and `SharedTerminationGroup` classes to detect the termination of the subcalculations. The `Accumulator` class allows the results of the subcalculations to be combined by associative, commutative operators (e.g., be added up). The `SharedTerminationGroup` does not help the subcalculations combine their results, but neither does it restrict the number of subcalculations to a fixed number. New members can be added to the group while it is running. Other threads can wait for the all the computations in the group to terminate.

We looked at two techniques for designing algorithms with parallel subroutines: divide and conquer and branch and bound. Branch and bound is used for combinatorial search. It gives precedence to the most promising search paths. For branch-and-bound algorithms, we introduced the `PriorityRunQueue` class which gives the highest priority runnables to threads before the lower priority runnables. For this to be useful, the number of threads that the priority run queue can create must be limited.

Although we do not make much use of it in this book, factories with recycling, such as the `SearchFactory` class, can significantly improve performance of systems that place runnables in run queues. It is clear when the runnables are about to terminate, they will no longer be needed, so it is safe to recycle them. Just as run queues save us the expense of creating threads, factories with recycling can further save us the expense of allocating and garbage collecting runnables.

Exercises

1. Try using a parallel depth-first search and a branch-and-bound search for the following two-processor scheduling problem:

There are *N* jobs that are to be scheduled. The jobs can run on either of two unique processors, so the time a job takes on processor 1 will not necessarily be the same as on processor 2. Indeed, one job may take longer on processor 1; another may take longer on processor 2. Jobs may not be preempted or moved to another processor before completion. Once started on a processor, a job will run to completion.

You are given the times that each job will take on each processor (t_{ij}, where $i=1,2$ is the processor number and $j=1,...,N$ is the job number).

A schedule for the jobs will assign each job to one of the processors. The completion time on a processor is the sum of the times for all the jobs scheduled on it. The completion time for the entire schedule is the maximum of the completion times for both processors.

Do a parallel depth-first search or a branch-and-bound algorithm to find the schedule that achieves the minimum completion time for the entire schedule.

2. Implement a mergesort. A mergesort works by partitioning the array to be sorted into two subarrays, recursively sorting them and merging the results into a single sorted array. A merge of two sorted arrays *A* and *B*, where *A* is of length *M* and *B* is of length *N*, copies the contents of *A* and *B* into the *M+N* element array *C*. The merge repeatedly moves the smallest remaining element in either array *A* or array *B* into the next position of array *C*. While elements remain in both *A* and *B*, the merge will have to compare two elements, the next elements in each, to see which is the smallest. As soon as one of the arrays is exhausted, all the remaining elements of the other may be copied without examination.

3. Write a parallel directory-search method. Given a directory `File` object and a `String` object, it will search that directory and all subdirectories recursively for all files whose names contain the specified string. Have it search the subdirectories concurrently.

Chapter 6

Parallelizing Loops

▼ CHORE GRAPHS

▼ EXAMPLE: WARSHALL'S ALGORITHM

▼ EXAMPLE: LONGEST COMMON SUBSEQUENCE (LCS)

▼ EXAMPLE: SHELL SORT

Loops are probably the best place to look for parallelism; they account for most of the computing time in most programs, and they have a small amount of code that can be packaged into runnables. When converting loops to parallel threads, there are a number of things to consider:

Some loops are trivially parallel: Each iteration is independent of the others. Some loops are serial; their iterations must be completed in order. Some nestings of serial loops can be parallelized by staggering (or skewing) the executions of the inner loops into pipelines.

The grain size is always a consideration. If the body of the loop is too short, it is not worth executing separately. It is faster to run several iterations of the loop in each thread. Several iterations take longer than one, but they require fewer initializations of threads or runnables, and that saves time.

Alternatively, inner serial loops can provide a natural grain size for the computation. Suppose every element of a two-dimensional array can be updated independently. A single element update is probably not worth creating a thread, but an entire row or an entire column might be.

As with parallel executions of subroutines, the number of processors available is another consideration. Creating too few threads won't use all the parallelism available. Creating too many will waste the overhead required to create them.

Chore Graphs

Chore graphs (usually called *task graphs*) provide a way of describing the dependencies among parts of a computation. We will not be formalizing them. We will be using them for sketching a computation and describing how it might be parallelized.

A *chore* is a piece of computation executed sequentially. A chore graph is a directed graph that represents a computation. The chores are represented by nodes. The directed edges represent the dependencies. The chore at the source of the edge must be completed before the chore at the destination of the edge can be started. There are various sorts of dependencies. *Control dependencies* are exemplified by if statements, where some chore is only to be done if some test yields true. *Data dependencies* refer to one chore reading data that another writes or two chores writing data that must be written in the correct order. On a multiprocessor machine, it should be possible to execute chores in parallel if there are no dependencies between them.

It is the intention that chores do not communicate with other chores while they are executing. We want all other chores that chore x depends on to complete before x is scheduled. We do not want x to block waiting for another thread to do something. This is to make it easier to figure out how to allocate chore graphs to parallel threads.

Figure 6–1 represents a chore graph for a loop, each of whose iterations is independent. The 0, 1, 2, ...$n-1$ are the iteration numbers for the loop. They may or may not be the values of a loop index. The loop might not use an index variable.

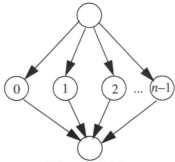

Figure 6–1 Chore graph for parallel loop.

If we want to describe an entire computation, we will have an acyclic chore graph. The nodes represent actual executions of chores.

Unfortunately, chore graphs for full executions are usually too large and too data dependent to draw in their entirety, so we will often draw cyclic graphs to represent loops and let dashed nodes represent entire subgraphs, particularly where the nodes are subroutine calls. Figure 6–2 shows chore graphs for some algorithms discussed in the previous chapter, "Parallel Execution of Subroutines in Shared Memory."

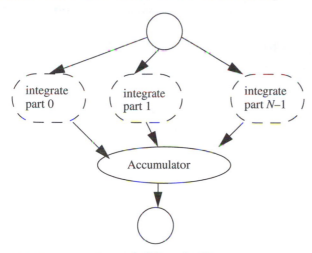

IntegTrap (see "Numeric Integration")

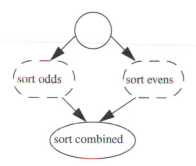

ShellsortDC, (see "Recursive Shell Sort: `RunQueues` and `SimpleFu-tures`")

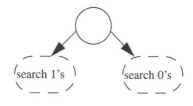

0–1 Knapsack (see "Branch and Bound for 0–1 Knapsack")

Figure 6–2 Chore graphs for algorithms in Chapter 5, "Parallel Execution of Subroutines in Shared Memory."

Gathering Chores into Threads

Paths of chores in a chore graph can be assigned to a thread. Each path has its own class with its code in a `run()` method. There is no synchronization problem between chores in the path assigned to an individual thread, since these are done in the proper order by the flow of control. There is a problem synchronizing chores in different threads. Crossthread synchronization can be done by having the source *up* a semaphore that the destination *downs*, by setting a `Future` object that the destination awaits with `getValue()`, by putting a value into a queue that the destination reads from, or by some other mechanism.

Example: Warshall's Algorithm

We will use Warshall's algorithm as an example in describing a number of techniques. Warshall's algorithm solves a number of similar problems:

- Given a directed graph, find which nodes are connected by paths.

- Given a relation R, find the transitive closure of the relationship, R^*. That is, if there are elements $x_1, x_2,...,x_n$ such that $x_1 R x_2, x_2 R x_3,..., x_{n-1} R x_n$, then $x_1 R^* x_n$.

- Given a network (i.e., a graph with distances associated with edges), find the shortest path between each pair of nodes.[1]

Warshall's algorithm expresses a graph or relationship as a boolean matrix. Let A be the matrix. For graphs, A is an adjacency matrix. A_{ij} is true if and only if there is an edge between the nodes numbered i and j in the graph. Similarly, for relationships, A_{ij} is true if and only if the elements numbered i and j are related in R. For the shortest-path problem, we use an array of numbers where A_{ij} is infinity if nodes i and j are not adjacent and contains the distance between them otherwise.

Warshall's algorithm transforms the matrix in place. The description of the result varies with the problem being solved. The graph represented by the adjacency matrix is converted into another graph where there is an edge for every path in the original graph. The relationship represented by the input matrix is converted into its transitive closure. The matrix representing the network is converted into a matrix showing the minimum distances between nodes.

Warshall's algorithm is shown in Example 6-1. It consists of three nested loops, the inner two of which can be executed in parallel. The best way to understand it is to think of it in terms of graphs. Figure 6–3 shows the operation of Warshall's algorithm. Suppose this figure represents a shortest path from node a to node z. We will ignore the trivial case

---

[1] This modification of Warshall's algorithm is due to Robert Floyd.

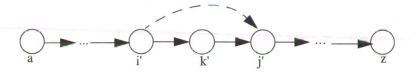

Figure 6–3 Warshall's algorithm operation: bypassing k^th node.

Example 6-1 Warshall's algorithm.

```
for (k=0; k<N;k++)
    for (i=0; i<N; i++)
        for (j=0; j<N; j++)
            A[i][j] = A[i][j] || (A[i][k] && A[k][j]) ;
```

where the path has only one edge and no internal nodes. Let k' be the lowest numbered internal node. When the outer loop executes for index $k = k'$, at some point the middle loop will set i to i', and the inner loop will set j to j'. At that point, $A[i][k]$ will be true, since there is an edge from i' to k', and $A[k][j]$ will be true since there is an edge from k' to j'. Therefore $A[i][k]$ && $A[k][j]$ is true, which sets $A[i][j]$ true. This draws an edge from i' to j', bypassing k'. There is now a shorter path from a to z. If this new path has more than one edge, it has a lowest numbered internal node with a number higher than k'. The process of bypassing internal nodes will continue until all internal nodes have been bypassed and there is an edge directly from a to z.

The algorithm works on all paths at the same time, bypassing all paths by adding direct edges from source to destination. The graph representing the resulting matrix will have an edge in the resulting graph for every path in the original graph.

The outer loop must execute one iteration to completion before beginning the next. Each node must be bypassed entirely, so that the new edges can be seen when processing the next node. The inner loops, however, can be executed completely in parallel. Figure 6–4 shows the chore graph for Warshall's algorithm.

The Floyd variant for solving the shortest-path problem is shown in Example 6-2.

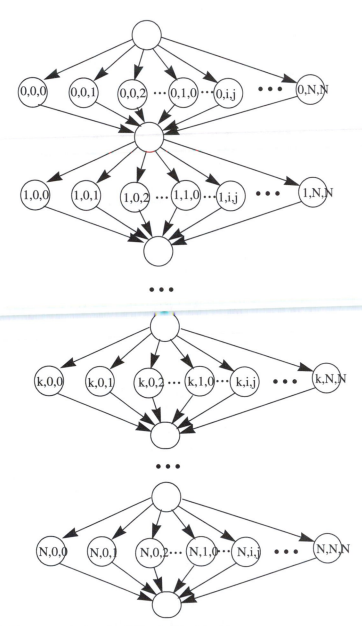

Figure 6–4 Chore-graph sketch of Warshall's algorithm.

Example 6-2 **Warshall/Floyd shortest path algorithm.**

```
for (k=0; k<N;k++)
    for (i=0; i<N; i++)
        for (j=0; j<N; j++)
            A[i][j] = Math.min(A[i][j], A[i][k] + A[k][j]);
```

Static Scheduling

Our first implementation of Warshall's algorithm, `Warshall1`, is shown in Example 6-3. An instance of a `Warshall1` object, x, is created specifying the number of threads to use in computing the transitive closure. A transitive closure can then be performed on a boolean matrix A by passing it to `Warshall1`'s `closure` method, `x.closure(A)`.

Several threads run the inner loops in parallel. Each of them is an instance of class `Close`. The closure method creates one `Close` object for each thread and passes it the following four things:

1.   The boolean array.

2.   The thread's number: 0, 1,...,(`numThreads-1`).

3.   A `SimpleBarrier` object for the threads to use to synchronize on between processing iterations of the outer k loop.

4.   An `Accumulator` object to use to signal when the threads are finished running the algorithm.

There are n^2 inner computations that could be done in parallel. They are too small to assign each to a separate thread. Each of the n rows could be done separately, but that's again too many. The solution we use is to give each of the t threads n/t of the rows. We number the threads from 0 to $t-1$. Thread i takes rows $i, i + t, t + 2t, \ldots$. This is an instance of *static scheduling*, since the division of labor is determined before the threads are run. Alternative partitionings would put contiguous sequences of rows together. Several methods for static allocation of rows are shown in the sidebar entitled "Static allocation" on page 179.

The performance of Warshall's algorithm with static scheduling is shown in Example 6-5. The horizontal axis shows the number of rows and columns. The number of elements is the square of that, and the number of operations is the cube. It was run on a dual-processor system running Solaris. The Java system used kernel threads. Two threads, matching the number of processors, performed best.

Dynamic Scheduling

A risk of static scheduling is that, having divided up the work evenly among t threads, there might not be t processors available to execute them. Several threads may run in parallel, but the completion of an iteration of the k loop will be delayed until other threads can be given processors. If, for example, we created four threads, but only three processors

Example 6-3 Warshall's algorithm, version 1

```java
class Warshall1{
 int numThreads;

 public Warshall1(int numThreads){
        this.numThreads=numThreads;
 }
 private class Close extends Thread{
    boolean[][] a; int t; SimpleBarrier b; Accumulator done;
    Close(boolean[][] a, int t, SimpleBarrier b,
             Accumulator done){
        this.a=a;this.t=t;this.b=b;this.done=done;
    }
    public void run() {
      try {
        int i,j,k;
        for (k=0;k<a.length;k++) {
            for (i=t;i<a.length;i+=numThreads) {
                if (a[i][k])
                    for(j=0;j<a.length;j++) {
                        a[i][j] = a[i][j] | a[k][j];
                    }
            }
            b.gather();
        }
        done.signal();
      } catch (InterruptedException ex){}
    }
 }
 public void closure(boolean[][] a) {
        int i;
        Accumulator done=new Accumulator(numThreads);
        SimpleBarrier b=new SimpleBarrier(numThreads);
        for (i=0;i<numThreads;i++) {
                new Close(a,i,b,done).start();
        }
        try {
            done.getFuture().getValue();
        } catch (InterruptedException ex){}
 }
}
```

were available, then three threads might run to completion, and then two of the processors would have to wait while the remaining thread runs.

Static allocation

Suppose we have N rows of an array that must be processed. How can we divide them evenly among P threads?

1. We could give $\lfloor N/P \rfloor$ rows to each of the first $P-1$ threads and the remaining rows to the last thread.[a] If $N = 15$ and $P = 4$, threads 0, 1, and 2 get 3 rows, and thread 3 gets 6. The load is unbalanced, and the completion time will be dominated by the last thread.

2. We could give $\lceil N/P \rceil$ rows to each of the first $P-1$ threads and the remaining rows to the last.[b] If $N = 21$ and $P = 5$, we would assign 5 rows to each of the first 4 threads and 1 to the last. The last is underutilized, but it's not as severe as case (1) where the last thread was the bottleneck.

3. We could try to assign the rows so that no thread has more than one row more than any other thread. An easy way to do this is to assign thread i all rows j such that j modulus $P = i$, assuming that rows are numbered 0 through $N-1$ and that threads are numbered 0 through $P-1$. Thread i will contain rows i, $i+P$, $i+2P$, $i+3P$,....

4. We can assign blocks of rows to threads as in (1) and (2), but guarantee that no thread have more than one more row than any other as in (3). Assign thread i the rows in the range L_i to U_i inclusive, where

$$L_i = i \cdot \left\lfloor \frac{N}{P} \right\rfloor + \min(i, \mathrm{mod}(N, P))$$

$$U_i = L_{i+1} - 1$$

---

[a] ($\lfloor x \rfloor$ means the largest integer less than or equal to x.)

[b] ($\lceil x \rceil$ means the smallest integer greater than or equal to x.)

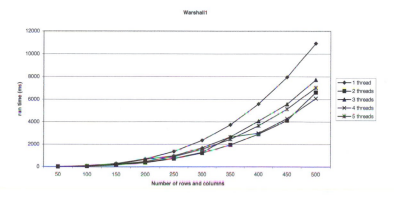

Figure 6–5 Performance of Warshall's algorithm with static scheduling.

This would be ameliorated somewhat by time slicing. The three processors could be swapped among the four threads by the operating system. But even swapping processors is a bit expensive compared with just leaving the processor allocated to a single thread.

Dynamic scheduling doesn't allocate all the work to the threads in even chunks, but allows threads to allocate more work when they are done with one chunk. It allows threads that have a processor to continue running.

Our second implementation of Warshall's algorithm, `Warshall2`, uses dynamic allocation. Each thread requests a sequence of rows to process from a *dynamic allocation object*. Abstract class `DynAlloc` (see Example 6-4) shows the public interface of our dynamic allocation objects. A call to method `alloc()` will fill in a `Range` object with the bounds

Example 6-4 DynAlloc class

```
public abstract class DynAlloc {
  public static class Range{int start,end,num;}
  public abstract boolean alloc(Range r);
}
```

of a range of values (e.g., row numbers) to process. It will return a boolean to indicate whether any rows were allocated (`true`) or whether the iteration is complete (`false`).

The fields of `DynAlloc.Range` are as follows:

- `start` and `end`: The allocated range of values is from `start` up to, but not including, `end`, the semiopen interval [`start, end`).

- `num`: This is the number of values in the interval. It is redundant, since it equals `end-start`.

An implementation of `DynAlloc` is `DynAllocShare`, which is shown in Example 6-5. `DynAlloc` and `DynAllocShare` are best discussed together.

A `DynAllocShare` object has the policy of allocating on each call $\left\lceil \dfrac{1}{n} \right\rceil$ of the remaining numbers in the range, where n is the number of threads. It allocates large blocks of numbers to the first calls and smaller blocks on subsequent calls. The idea is that the larger blocks can be processed without delays for synchronization. The smaller blocks later fill in the schedule to even up the processing time. However, to avoid allocating blocks that are too small for efficient processing, `DynAllocShare` takes a minimum size of block to allocate and will not allocate any block smaller than that until the very last allocation.

Example 6-5 `DynAllocShare` class

```
public class DynAllocShare extends DynAlloc{
  int range;int nt;int min;
  int zc; int current;
  public DynAllocShare(int range,int nt,int min){
        this.range=range;
        this.nt=nt;
        this.min=min;
        zc=0;
        current=0;
  }
  public synchronized boolean alloc(Range r){
        if (current>=range){
                zc++;
                if (zc>=nt) {
                        current=0;
                        zc=0;
                }
                r.start=r.end=range;
                r.num=0;
                return false;
        }
        r.start=current;
        int rem=range-current;
        int num=(rem+nt-1)/nt; //ceiling(rem/nt)
        if (num<min) num=min;
        if (num>rem) num=rem;
        current+=num;
        r.end=current;
        r.num=num;
        return true;
  }
}
```

The `DynAllocShare` objects are self-resetting. They keep track of the number of calls in a row that have returned false and given empty ranges. Once that number is equal to the number of threads, the object is reset and will start allocating over again. This allows the `DynAllocShare` objects to be reused in inner loops, rather than requiring new ones be allocated for each iteration.

The parameters and local fields of `DynAllocShare` are as follows:

- `range`: This is the upper bound on the range of integers to return. The `DynAllocShare` object will allocate contiguous blocks of integers in the range [0,range) (i.e., from zero up to, but not including, `range`).

- `nt`: This is the number of threads. It used both to compute the next block size to allocate (1/nt of the remaining range) and to determine when to reset the object (after allocating nt zero-length ranges).

- `min`: This is the minimum size block to allocate until there are fewer than that left.

- `zc`: This is the zero count, the number of zero-sized ranges allocated. When zc equals nt, the object will reset.

- `current`: This stores the beginning number of the next block to allocate. When `current` equals `range`, there are no more values to allocate.

`Warshall2`, shown in Figure 6–6, is Warshall's algorithm with dynamic scheduling. The major difference from `Warshall1` is that the `Close` threads are given a `DynAlloc` object d as one of their parameters. A `Close` thread has an extra loop, `while(d.alloc(r))`, around its outer `for` loop, allocating ranges of rows to process. When `alloc` returns `false`, there are no more rows to process, so the thread drops down to the `gather` call at the end of its outer `for` loop.

The performance of Warshall's algorithm with dynamic scheduling is shown in Figure 6–6. As with Figure 6–9, the horizontal axis shows the number of rows and columns. The number of elements is the square of that, and the number of operations is the cube. The program was run on a dual-processor system running Solaris. The Java system used kernel threads. Two threads, matching the number of processors, performed best.

A comparison of the two implementations of Warshall's algorithm is shown in Figure 6–7. The runs using two threads are compared. The two algorithms perform much alike.

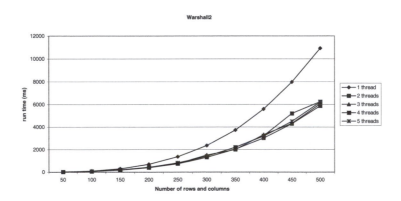

Figure 6–6 Performance of Warshall's algorithm with dynamic scheduling.

Example 6-6 `Warshall2`: **Warshall's algorithm with dynamic allocation.**

```
class Warshall2{
 int numThreads;
 public Warshall2(int numThreads){
        this.numThreads=numThreads;
 }
 private class Close extends Thread{
    boolean[][] a;
    DynAlloc d; SimpleBarrier b; Accumulator done;
    Close(boolean[][] a, DynAlloc d,
           SimpleBarrier b, Accumulator done){
           this.a=a;
           this.d=d; this.b=b; this.done=done;
    }
    public void run() {
      try {
        int i,j,k;
        DynAlloc.Range r=new DynAlloc.Range();
        for (k=0;k<a.length;k++) {
            while(d.alloc(r)){
              for (i=r.start;i<r.end;i++) {
                if (a[i][k])
                    for(j=0;j<a.length;j++) {
                        a[i][j] = a[i][j] | a[k][j];
                    }
                }
              }
              b.gather();
            }
            done.signal();
        } catch (InterruptedException ex){}
    }
 }
 public void closure(boolean[][] a) {
    int i;
    Accumulator done=new Accumulator(numThreads);
    SimpleBarrier b=new SimpleBarrier(numThreads);
    DynAllocShare d=new DynAllocShare(a.length,numThreads,2);
    for (i=0;i<numThreads;i++) {
            new Close(a,d,b,done).start();
    }
    try {
        done.getFuture().getValue();
    } catch (InterruptedException ex){}
 }
}
```

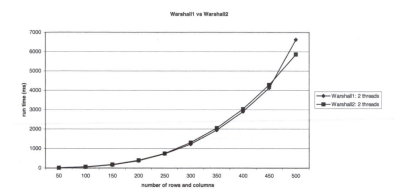

Figure 6–7 Comparison of static and dynamic scheduling in Warshall's algorithm.

Example: Longest Common Subsequence

A *longest common subsequence* (LCS) of two strings is a longest sequence of characters that occurs in order in the two strings. It differs from the *longest common substring* in that the characters in the longest common subsequence need not be contiguous. There may, of course, be more than one LCS, since there may be several subsequences with the same length.

There is a folk algorithm to find the length of the LCS of two strings.[2] The algorithm uses a form of dynamic programming. In divide-and-conquer algorithms, recall that the overall problem is broken into parts, the parts are solved individually, and the solutions are assembled into a solution to the overall problem. Dynamic programming is similar, except that the best way to divide the overall problem into parts is not known before the subproblems are solved, so dynamic programming solves all subproblems and then finds the best way to assemble them.

The algorithm works as follows: Let the two strings be `c0` and `c1`. Create a two-dimensional array `a`

```
int [][] a=new int[c0.length()+1] [c1.length()+1]
```

We will fill in the array so that a[i][j] is the length of the LCS of `c0.substring(0,i)` and `c1.substring(0,j)`. Recall that `s.substring(m,n)` is the substring of `s` from position m up to, but not including, position n.

---

[2] By "folk algorithm," we mean that the algorithm is widely known, but no single inventor is known.

Initialize `a[i][0]` to 0 for all `i` and `a[0][j]` to 0 for all `j`, since there are no characters in an empty substring. The other elements, `a[i][j]`, are filled in as follows:

```
if (c0.charAt(i-1) == c1.charAt(j-1)) a[i][j]=a[i-1][j-1]+1;
else a[i][j]=Math.max(a[i][j-1],a[i-1][j]);
```

Why? Element `a[i-1][j-1]` has the length of the LCS of string
`c0.substring(0,i-1)` and `c1.substring(0,j-1)`. If elements
`c0.charAt(i-1)` and `c1.charAt(j-1)` are equal, that LCS can be extended by one to
length `a[i-1]  [j-1]+1`. If these characters don't match, then what? In that case, we
ignore the last character in one or the other of the strings. The LCS is either `a[i][j-1]`
or `a[i-1][j]`, representing the maximum length of the LCS for all but the last character
of `c1.substring(0,j-1)` or `c0.substring(0,i-1)`, respectively.

The chore graph for calculation of the LCS is shown in Figure 6–8. Any order of calculation that is consistent with the dependencies is permissible. Two are fairly obvious: (1) by
rows, top to bottom, and (2) by columns, left to right.

Another possibility is along diagonals. All `a[i][j]`, where `i+j==m` can be calculated
at the same time, for `m` stepping from 2 to `c0.length()+c1.length()`. This order
of calculation is pictured in Figure 6–9. Visualizing waves of computation passing across
arrays is a good technique for designing parallel array algorithms. It has been researched
under the names *systolic arrays* and *wavefront arrays*.

Our implementation of the LCS algorithm divides the array into vertical bands and is pictured in Figure 6–10. Each band is filled in row by row from top to bottom. Each band
(except the leftmost) must wait for the band to its left to fill in the last element of a row

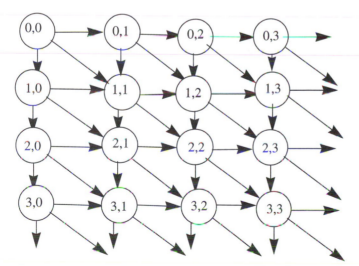

Figure 6–8 Chore graph for LCS.

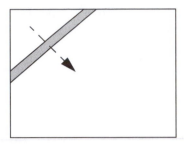

Figure 6–9 Wavefront calculation of LCS.
Shading represents elements being calculated.

before it can start can start filling in that row. This is an instance of the producer–consumer releationship.

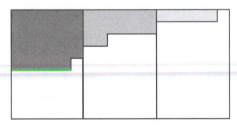

Figure 6–10 LCS calculated in vertical bands. Shading represents elements that have been calculated.

The code for class LCS is shown in Example 6-7. It has the following fields:

- numThreads: This is the number of threads to run in parallel, hence the number of bands.

- c0 and c1: These are character arrays to find the LCSs.

- a: This is the two-dimensional array used as previously described.

- done: This is an accumulator used to detect when the threads have terminated.

Class LCS has two constructors. Both take three parameters: the two strings and the number of threads to use. In one of the constructors, the strings are represented as character arrays and in the other, as String objects.

The constructor that takes character arrays is the one that does the actual work. It allocates the Accumulator done to detect when the threads have terminated. It allocates the array a. The array's top and left edges are automatically initialized to zero when it is cre-

Example 6-7 Class `LCS`

```
class LCS {
 int numThreads;
 char [] c0; char [] c1;
 int[][] a;
 Accumulator done;
 public LCS ( char [] c0, char [] c1, int numThreads){
        this.numThreads=numThreads;
        this.c0=c0;
        this.c1=c1;
        int i;
        done=new Accumulator(numThreads);
        a=new int[c0.length+1][c1.length+1];
        Semaphore left=new Semaphore(c0.length),right;
        for (i=0;i<numThreads;i++) {
                right=new Semaphore();
                new Band(
                    startOfBand(i,numThreads,c1.length),
                    startOfBand(i+1,numThreads,c1.length)-1,
                    left,right).start();
                left=right;
        }
 }
 public LCS ( String s0, String s1, int numThreads){
        this(s0.toCharArray(),s1.toCharArray(),numThreads);
 }
 private class Band extends Thread{
        // see Example 6-8
 }
 int startOfBand(int i,int nb,int N) {
        return 1+i*(N/nb)+Math.min(i,N%nb);
 }
 public int getLength() {
        try {
            done.getFuture().getValue();
        } catch (InterruptedException ex){}
        return a[c0.length][c1.length];
 }
 public int[][] getArray() {
        try {
            done.getFuture().getValue();
        } catch (InterruptedException ex){}
        return a;
 }
}
```

ated. It finishes by creating one Band thread (see Example 6-8) for each vertical band. These Band threads are told the first and last column numbers they are to fill in and are given two semaphores. They down their left semaphore before starting a row and up their right semaphore after finishing a row. This is the extent of the producer–consumer synchronization they use.

The calculation of the bounds for a band are performed by method startOfBand(i,nt,N), which gives the starting column position of band number i, for nt threads and N columns. Band i, $0 \le i < nt$, extends from column startOfBand(i,nt,N) to startOfBand(i+1,nt,N)-1. The calculation is designed to guarantee that no band has more than one more column in it than another.

Method getLength() will return the length of the LCS, and getArray() will return the array that the algorithm has filled in. Both of them must wait for the bands to finish computing before they can return.

Example 6-8 LCS class Band

```
private class Band extends Thread{
        int low; int high; Semaphore left,right;
        Band(int low, int high,
            Semaphore left,Semaphore right){
                this.low=low;this.high=high;
                this.left=left;this.right=right;
        }
        public void run() {
          try {
            int i,j,k;
            for (i=1;i<a.length;i++) {
                left.down();
                for (j=low;j<=high;j++) {
                    if(c0[i-1]==c1[j-1])
                        a[i][j]=a[i-1][j-1]+1;
                    else
                        a[i][j]=Math.max(a[i-1][j],a[i][j-1]);
                }
                right.up();
            }
            done.signal();
          } catch (InterruptedException ex){}
        }
}
```

Example: Shell Sort

Shell sort works by sorting all sequences of elements *h* positions apart with insertion sort, then those elements a smaller number of positions apart, and so on with diminishing increments, until finally sorting the overall array with insertion sort. Since insertion sort on an already nearly sorted array runs quickly, the shell sort can be much faster than the insertion sort alone.

`ShellsortDC`, presented in the section entitled "Recursive Shell Sort: `RunQueues` and `SimpleFutures`," uses powers of two as the increments. This is not the best method possible, since it is not until the last pass that elements in even-numbered positions are compared with elements in odd-numbered positions. If all the largest elements are in, say, the even-numbered positions, and the smallest are in, say, the odd-numbered positions, the last pass will itself be of order $O(N^2)$, moving odd-numbered elements past increasingly long sequences of larger elements.

The shell sort works best if the array is sorted in several stages. Each stage sorts a number of nonoverlapping subsequences, but the subsequences from different stages do overlap. For example, one stage could sort all five sequences of elements five spaces apart, and then the next could sort all elements three spaces apart. This avoids the problem of whole sets of elements not being compared until the last step.

One wonders, though, whether a new pass with a smaller increment may undo the work of a previous pass. The answer is no. Suppose that the array is first *h* sorted (i.e., that all elements *h* positions apart are sorted) and then it is *k* sorted. After the end of the *k* sort, it will still be *h* sorted. Rather than do a formal proof, let's consider an example. Suppose a high school girls' athletic team of 12 members is being posed for a photograph. The photographer poses them in two rows of six. She wants them arranged from the shortest girl in the first row to her left up to the tallest girl on the second row to her right. This will be the girls' right and left, respectively. She wants a taller girl standing behind a shorter in each column and the rows ordered by ascending height. The well-known method is to have the girls get into the two rows and then (1) ask the girls in the second row to change places with the girl in front of her if the girl in front is taller, and then (2) ask the girls in the rows to repeatedly change places along the rows while the girl on the right is taller than the girl on her left. After these two passes, the girls are in proper order.

Why doesn't pass (2) spoil the order from pass (1)? Consider a girl, Pat, fourth place from the right (her right) on the second row at the end of this sorting. Is it possible for the girl in front of her to be taller than she is? Pat has three girls to her right who are shorter than she is. Each of those girls had a girl in front of her in the first row at the end of step (1) who was shorter than she, and hence shorter than Pat. Pat had a girl in front of her who was shorter. That means that there are at least four girls in the front row who are shorter than Pat, so after step (2), at least the rightmost four positions in the first row must be occupied by girls shorter than Pat, so the girl in front of Pat must be shorter.

The same principle applies to the passes in the shell sort.

It is usual to give the shell sort an ascending series of increments h_i that will be the distance apart of the elements to be sorted. The shell sort can start with the largest h_i smaller than the size of the array and go down the series sorting with each. Of course, h_0 is 1.

When you are sorting elements h_i apart, there are h_i series of those elements. The lowest-numbered element in series j is element number j, $0 \le j < h_i$. The chore graph for the shell sort is shown in Figure 6–11.

So what are good step sizes for a shell sort? Let's consider several sequences for h_0, h_1, h_2,..., h_i, ...:[3]

- What about $h_i = (i + 1)$? This is a bad idea. There will be N passes, and each pass (at least from $h_{N/2}$ down) will need to look at all N elements. That gives an order of $O(N^2)$ before considering how long the insertion sorts themselves take.

- As previously mentioned, powers of two are not a good sequence, since the last pass must compare entire sequences of elements never compared before. The last pass alone is in the worst case of order $O(N^2)$.

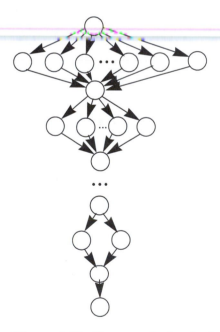

Figure 6–11 Chore graph sketch of `Shellsort`.

[3] I am relying of an abstract of a survey talk by Robert Sedgewick of Princeton University, *Analysis of Shellsort and Related Algorithms*, that he published on his Web site at `http://www.cs.princeton.edu/~rs/shell/index.htm`.

- The sequence 1, 3, 7, ..., $2^{i+1}-1$,..., will give an order of $O(N^{3/2})$. For a long time, the shell sort was thought to be of order $O(N^{3/2})$.

- Knuth recommended the sequence 1, 4, 13, 40, 121, ... ,where

$$h_0 = 1$$
$$h_i = 3h_{i-1} + 1$$

It has been shown empirically to do reasonably well.

- Sedgewick found that the series 1, 8, 23, 77, ..., $4^{i-1} + 3 \cdot 2^{i-1} + 1$ gives the shell sort a running time of order $O(N^{4/3})$.

- A series that gives an order of $O(N \cdot (\log N)^2)$ behavior is obtained from the accompanying table, where the upper left corner is 1, each row is three times the preceding row, and each column is twice the column to its left. Choose the elements of the table smaller than N, sort them, and go down the list.

1	2	4	8	...
3	6	12	24	...
9	18	36	72	...
27	54	108	216	...
...	...	...	...	...

The reason for the $(\log N)^2$ is that there will be $\log_2 N$ columns and $\log_3 N$ rows with relevant entries, giving $O((\log N)^2)$ passes. Each sorting pass will require only N comparison, since an element will move at most one position. Why? Consider sorting an array that is already 2 and 3 sorted. An element is already in order with all elements an even number of positions away. It is in order with elements three positions away and then because of the 2 sorting, 5, 7, 9, ..., away. Indeed, the only elements it may be out of position with are those one position away. This translates to elements k positions apart. If the array is $2k$ sorted and $3k$ sorted, then it can be k sorted with elements moving at most one step and hence requiring only $O(N)$ comparisons.

The problem with this is that the number of steps is too large, so the constant factor is too large for practical use.

- A geometric series with a ratio of 2.2 does well. You can start off with, say, h=N/5, to sort series of length 5 and then repeatedly decrease h to next h = ⌊h/2.2⌋ for the rest of the series, being careful to use an increment of one the last time through. This is the series in general use.

ShellsortBarrier class. ShellsortBarrier.java in Example 6-9 uses a fixed number of threads to sort an array. In early stages, there are more subse-

quences than threads, so the threads take several subsequences. In later stages, there may
be more threads than subsequences, so some of the threads have no work to do.

Example 6-9 ShellsortBarrier overall structure.

```
class ShellsortBarrier {
  static int minDivisible=3;
  int numThreads;

 public ShellsortBarrier(int numThreads){
        this.numThreads=numThreads;
 }
 private class Sort implements Runnable {
        //see Example 6-10
 }

 static void isort(int[] a,int m,int h) {
        int i,j;
        for (j=m+h; j<a.length; j+=h) {
            for (i=j; i>m && a[i]>a[i-h]; i-=h) {
                int tmp=a[i];
                a[i]=a[i-h];
                a[i-h]=tmp;
            }
        }
 }
 public void sort(int[] a) {
        if (a.length<minDivisible) {
                isort(a,0,1);
                return;
        }
        SimpleBarrier b=new SimpleBarrier(numThreads);
        for (int i=numThreads-1;i>0;i--)
            new Thread(
                new Sort(a,i,a.length/minDivisible,b)).start();
        new Sort(a,0,a.length/minDivisible,b).run();
 }
}
```

ShellsortBarrier has this interface to the user:

- ShellsortBarrier(int n): This is the constructor; it creates a
  ShellsortBarrier object that will sort arrays of integers using n threads. It
  saves n in field numThreads.

- `sort(int[] a)`: This method sorts the integer array a. It uses `numThreads` threads to do the sorting unless the array is too short to justify creating the threads.

Method `sort(a)` first checks the length of a to see if it is short enough to sort directly. If so, the method calls the static method `isort()` that performs the actual sorts.

If there are enough elements in the array to justify creating threads, `numThreads Sort` objects are created. Of these, `numThreads-1` are run as separate threads, and one is executed by the thread that called `sort()`. Method `sort()` gives these threads a `SimpleBarrier` object to synchronize with.

Class Sort. `ShellsortBarrier`'s internal class `Sort`, shown in Example 6-10, handles the concurrent threads. Sort has the following constructor:

```
Sort(int[]a, int i, int h, SimpleBarrier b)
```

Example 6-10 ShellsortBarrier class Sort

```
private class Sort implements Runnable {
   int[] a; int i, h; SimpleBarrier b;
   Sort(int[] a, int i, int h, SimpleBarrier b){
       this.a=a; this.i=i; this.h=h; this.b=b;
   }
   public void run() {
       try{
         while (h>0) {
           if (h==2) h=1;
           for (int m=i; m<h; m+=numThreads) {
               isort(a,i,h);
           }
           h=(int)(h/2.2);
           b.gather();
         }
       }catch(Exception ex){}
   }
}
```

The parameters to the constructor are the following:

- a: This is the array to sort.

- i: This is the number of this thread.

- h: This is the initial increment between elements in a sequence being sorted.

- b: This is the barrier with which to synchronize.

If the increment between elements in a sequence is h, then there are h such sequences beginning at array indices 0, 1, 2,..., h−1. If there are n threads, thread number i handles the sequences i, i+n, i+2n, ...

All the Sort threads sort their sequences of elements for the initial value of h. Then, they all set their copy of the value of h to next h = $\lfloor h/2.2 \rfloor$ and repeat until the array is entirely sorted. Since they are all doing the same updates on h, they all get the same values. There is one trick in the calculations of h. They detect that they are done when h takes on the value zero, which it will after sorting for an increment of one. They check to see if they have gotten an increment of two, and if they have, they set it to one. If they didn't, after dividing 2/2.2, they would get h=0, skipping the last pass, h=1.

Performance. The performance of the shell sort with barriers is shown in Figure 6–12. Again, this was run on a dual-processor system, but unlike the implementations of Warshall's algorithm, the performance got better as more threads were used. In Warshall's algorithm, two threads, the same as the number of processors, was best.

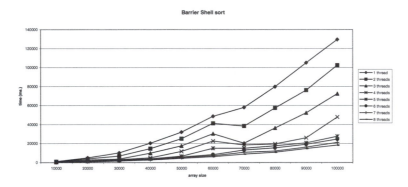

Figure 6–12 Performance of the shell sort with barriers.

Chapter Wrap-up

In this chapter, we explored how to execute loop iterations in parallel. Since, typically, most of a program's processing time is spent in a few, innermost loops, executing loops in parallel will often vastly speed up a program.

Parallel loop execution is sometimes impossible; some loops must be executed sequentially. Sometimes, it is trivial, and every iteration is independent of the others, as are the two inner loops in Warshall's algorithm. Sometimes, it is in between, such as the iterations in the LCS algorithm, which need to be executed skewed.

We presented an informal way of describing computational dependencies: chore graphs. Sketching chore graphs allows us to look for ways to organize the computation into parallel threads, while still maintaining dependencies.

One of the most useful objects for coordinating loops is the barrier. Our `SimpleBarrier` class allows a number of threads to synchronize at the bottom of a sequential outer loop, as in Warshall's algorithm, or between stages of the computation, as in the shell sort.

Exercises

1. How would trapezoidal integration (see the Example: Trapezoidal Numeric Integration) change if rephrased in terms of parallel loops?

2. Could you use `termination groups` or `accumulators` instead of `simple barriers`?

3. Redo the LCS algorithm using a `BoundedBuffer` object to pass values along rows between bands. This provides a model for distributed execution: The bands could be on different machines, and the values could be sent between the machines through sockets, as will be discussed later in Chapter 11 "Networking."

4. A two-dimensional version of the Laplace equation works as follows: It updates the elements of a two-dimensional array (except for the border elements) by repeatedly assigning each element the average value of its orthogonal neighbors. (The orthogonal neighbors are the up, down, left, and right neighbors.) The border elements are set at constant values. The top, bottom, right, and left borders may have different values, but the elements along a border have the same value. The corners are irrelevant, since they aren't used to calculate any average. The process of updating elements continues until no element in the array changes by more than a small amount. (The "small amount" must be a large enough fraction of the magnitude of the border elements so that floating-point arithmetic can detect termination.)

Different versions of the algorithm update the elements in different orders. One way updates the elements in two nested loops, processing them row-wise, left to right, and top to bottom. It updates an element using newer values for the up and the left neighbors than for the down and right neighbors, but that is okay. It makes it terminate more quickly.

Implement this version using parallel threads similarly to the LCS algorithm. Divide the array into bands. Assign the bands to threads. Use semaphores to synchronize the threads. You will need two semaphores to communicate between adjacent bands: one to prevent the right thread from using the left neighbor along a row before it has been computed and the other to prevent the left thread from updating a right border element a second time before the right thread has used it. These semaphores should prevent threads from accessing the same array element at the same time.

5. Another way to solve the Laplace equation (described in Exercise 4) is to imagine the array as a chessboard. Each element is either red or black, as are the squares on a chessboard. The algorithm alternately updates all the red squares and then all the black ones. All the red squares may be updated in parallel, and all the black squares may be updated in parallel.

Implement this version.

6. Write a method that when given an array of URL's of Web pages and a string, will search the Web pages in parallel for an occurrence of the string and return an array of the URL's that contained the string.

Chapter **7**

Chores

▼ THE `RunDelayed` INTERFACE

▼ `Futures`

▼ `FutureFactory`

▼ CHORE-PROGRAMMING TECHNIQUES

▼ MACRO DATAFLOW EXAMPLES: VECTOR ADDITION

▼ CHORE EXAMPLES: WARSHALL'S ALGORITHM

We gain two large advantages from the use of threads:

- We can make use of multiple processors (assuming that we have native threads and several processors available).

- We can continue running parts of our computation when other parts are blocked waiting for data to become available. This is particularly the case when running distributed computations on computer networks, as we will discuss in later chapters.

Threads come with a cost, however. They take time to create, and they occupy a large amount of storage.

We use `RunQueue` objects to reuse threads, saving us the expense of creating them over and over. But the cost of creating threads repeatedly is only part of the problem. A danger of parallel computation is having too much parallelism—in our case, too many threads. We also want to avoid filling our memory with threads.

197

RunQueue objects have the ability to limit the number of threads that can be created, which can help us throttle the computation and avoid the danger of flooding memory with threads, but that leads to another danger, deadlock. All the threads created by the run queue may be waiting for conditions that only runnables still on the run queue can cause, but those runnables cannot execute because the run queue will not allow any more threads to be created.

We will try to overcome this problem by breaking our computation into chores that we put in their own runnables. Recall in the last chapter we defined the concept of a chore as a small amount of computation which communicates with other chores only at its beginning and its end. A thread running a chore does not wait in the middle of its computation for another thread to cause a condition.

Rather than assigning paths of chores to threads, we use a different approach in which we make each chore a separate Runnable object and drop it into a run queue when its predecessors have completed. These chores can run to completion and then give up the thread they are running on. The threads then remove and run other chores from the run queue. Since threads are not suspended awaiting completion of chores in other threads, fewer threads are needed overall.

Here's how we intend to use chores to throttle our computation:

- We will pack chores in runnables. Conceptually, we would like a single kind of chore to have a single runnable class, but later, again for efficiency, we will consider how to reuse runnable objects for more than one chore.

- We will provide facilities for chores to be delayed on various kinds of synchronization objects (e.g., Future, Barrier, and TerminationGroup objects).

- While delayed, the chore gives up not only the processor, but the thread that is running it.

- Chores are placed in a run queue to be allocated a thread to execute them. Chores can wait for multiple conditions before they start their main computation, but they can't hold on to the thread while waiting. We'll see how to program this. A chore will run to completion once its main computation has begun.

- Because chores will not hold onto threads, chores can be scheduled in run queues with a limit on the number of threads that can be created. This will effectively throttle the computation.

Naturally, there are problems with using chores in this way. Chores can be quite small. A multitude of small chores can be expensive to create and schedule. Grain size should always be taken into account when breaking a computation into chores. It might be more efficient just to use straight threads for parts of the computation. Also, a proliferation of chores can result in a proliferation of class definitions with obscure interactions.

The `RunDelayed` Interface

Scheduling chores is based in the `RunDelayed` interface. The interface `RunDelayed` defines the single method `void runDelayed(Runnable)`. It is implemented by all classes that provide a `runDelayed()` method.

```
interface RunDelayed {
  public void runDelayed(Runnable)
}
```

Method `runDelayed(r)` will cause runnable `r` to be placed in a run queue when some condition is satisfied.

Futures

The class `Future` is an extension of `SimpleFuture` that implements `RunDelayed`. All the operations on `SimpleFuture` will also work on `Futures`.

A chore can be scheduled for execution upon a value being assigned to a `Future`. The call `future.runDelayed(chore)` will schedule the chore for execution when the future's value is set. If `runDelayed` is called after the `Future` has had a value assigned, the chore is immediately placed in a run queue.

Each `Future` object contains a reference to the `RunQueue` object that run-delayed chores will be placed in.

The constructor call `new Future()` creates a `Future` with no value yet assigned, while `new Future(val)` creates a `Future` with `val` assigned to its value. It may not be immediately obvious why one might want to create a `Future` with a value assigned from the beginning. It is useful when writing subroutines that arrange for a value to be computed. The subroutine sometimes can perform the computation immediately and sometimes will create threads or chores to perform the calculation. In either case, it can return a `Future` object that the caller can look in when the value is actually needed. It is a small programming convenience for the subroutine to be able to supply the value when it creates the `Future` if it already has it computed.

Method `getValue()` waits until a value has been assigned to the `Future` and then returns it. It is the same as in `SimpleFuture`. Similarly, method `isSet()` checks to see if a value has been assigned to the `Future` yet.

Method `setValue(val)` assigns the object `val` to the `Future`, notifies all waiting threads, and places all run-delayed runnables in a run queue.

Future constructors and methods

Future() creates a Future object with no value yet assigned.

Future(java.lang.Object val) creates a Future object with a value initially assigned.

java.lang.Object getValue() waits until a value has been assigned to the Future object and then returns it.

boolean isSet() checks to see if a value has been assigned to the Future object yet.

void setValue(java.lang.Object val) assigns a value to the Future object, notifies all waiting threads, and schedules all run-delayed runnables.

static RunQueue getClassRunQueue() gets the RunQueue object for the Future class. This is the run queue that will be used for chores that are run delayed on a Future object unless setRunQueue() has been called to assign a different run queue.

void runDelayed(java.lang.Runnable r) schedules a Runnable object to execute when the Future object has its value set. When the Future has been assigned a value, the runnable is placed on the run queue associated with the Future object.

void setRunQueue(RunQueue rq) sets the run queue associated with a Future object.

RunQueue getRunQueue() gets the run queue associated with a Future object.

Each Future object has an associated run queue in which it will place the run-delayed runnables. There is a run queue associated with class Future that will be used if no other run queue is specified. Static method getClassRunQueue() returns the run queue associated with the Future class. This run queue starts off placing no limit on the number of threads that can be created to run the runnables placed on it. You can assign other limits to it.

Method call f.setRunQueue(rq) sets the run queue for a Future object f to rq, and method f.getRunQueue() returns f's run queue. You would use f.setRunQueue to override the default use of the Future class's run queue.

Method `f.runDelayed(r)` schedules the `Runnable` object r to execute when `Future` f has its value set. If it is called when the value has already been set, r is immediately placed in f's run queue. If the value is not yet set, r is stored in f and will be placed in the run queue by `f.setValue()`.

FutureFactory

When creating chore graphs, we will often need to create futures that use a particular run queue. Rather than pass the run queue around and assign it to every future we create, we can use a `FutureFactory` object. A `FutureFactory` object will generate futures that reference a particular run queue.

Class FutureFactory

FutureFactory(RunQueue runQueue) creates a `FutureFactory` object. All the futures created by the future factory will place run-delayed objects in the run queue (i.e., unless their run queue is changed by `setRunQueue()`).

Future make() creates a future.

RunQueue getRunQueue() gets the run queue for a `FutureFactory` object. This can be used to set the parameters of the run queue.

void setRunQueue(RunQueue rq) sets the run queue for a `FutureFactory` object to rq.

The constructor call `ff=new FutureFactory(rq)` creates a future factory that will create futures that place their run-delayed chores in `RunQueue rq`. The call `f=ff.make()` has `FutureFactory ff` make a new future f. Calling `f.runDelayed(r)` will place `Runnable r` in `RunQueue rq` when a value has been assigned to f. Calls to `ff.setRunQueue(rq)` and `ff.getRunQueue()` set and get, respectively, the run queue that `FutureFactory ff` will place in futures.

Chore-programming Techniques

There are a number of programming techniques for chores and ways to think about chore programming. We will present them in this section and then show them in use in later examples.

There are two algorithms whose variants form many of our examples: vector addition and Warshall's algorithm for transitive closure of boolean matrices (first presented in "Example: Warshall's Algorithm" on page 174). By vector addition, we mean mathematical vectors, represented by arrays of double-precision numbers, not `Vector` objects from the `java.util` package.

Job Jars

Job jars are one way to think of programming with chores. A job jar is a queue of chores—a run queue. As a thread finishes one chore, it can pick another chore from the job jar and execute it.

The term *job jar* comes from home economics: It is a jar full of slips of paper naming chores to be done. When another chore is discovered, it is written on a slip of paper and dropped in the job jar. When a member of the household has some free time, he or she takes a slip of paper from the jar and does the chore.

Some chores may require that other chores be done, so part of a chore may be the creation of more chores to put into the job jar. There may be dependencies among chores that require that, at the completion of a chore, members of the household decide whether it is now time to place another chore in the job jar or whether the chore has some dependencies that are not yet fulfilled.

Chore Graphs

In the previous chapter, we discussed chore graphs as a design tool for laying out parallel computations in threads. If we are programming using chores directly, the chore graphs are more than just a conceptual tool. We have to create the chores in the chore graph as actual objects and coordinate them.

What we will often do is write methods that, instead of directly computing the actual result, will generate chore graphs to compute the result.

If the chore graph is not data dependent, we can write methods that generate the entire graph. For example, a shell sort will execute passes that depend on the size of the array to sort, but not on the contents. Given an array, we can immediately generate chores to do the sorting. We will see this in the section entitled "Shell sort" on page 248.

On the other hand, if the chore graph is data dependent, we may have to have the chores themselves generate more of the chore graph. For example, `quicksort` creates subsorts whose bounds depend on the position that the pivot element ends up in. That is data dependent. Therefore, a chore-based approach to `quicksort` would have the chore that partitions a part of the array then create chores to sort the subarrays. We will see this in the section entitled "Parallel `Quicksort`" on page 244.

Macro Dataflow

Dataflow is a processor organization that can be extended into a software design. The principle of dataflow is that operations should be scheduled for execution when their operands become available. It is the availability of the operands that triggers computation. Moreover, there is no limit on how long the computation may wait before executing. This is unlike the common von Neumann computer, where an instruction not only must not execute before its operands are defined, but must not delay in executing past when an operand has been reassigned. Moreover, in a von Neumann computer, instructions are not scheduled according to the availability of their operands, but by control flow. The control flow must be constructed with awareness of operand availability.

There are two important concepts related to dataflow:

1. **Pure values**. Unlike the conventional computer memory that may be continually modified, dataflow values are assumed to be unchanging. This is what allows the arbitrary delay in executing dataflow instructions.

2. **Single assignment**. An instance of a variable in a dataflow program may be assigned a value only once. If it could be reassigned, there would be a window in which the instructions using it could execute, rather than simply having to wait for it to be assigned once. This means that each iteration of a loop and each procedure call creates new instances of the variables that are assigned values in it.

Dataflow processors use the dataflow principle at the individual-instruction level. Scalar operands such as integers, floats, and booleans trigger individual instructions that compute scalar results.

Some early dataflow hardware designs were *static dataflow*. The machines instructions themselves had space in them for the operands. The instructions indicated where to store their results. When the second operand of a two-operand instruction was stored, for example, the instruction with its operands was sent to an execution unit. The code for such machines is not naturally reentrant: It requires special hardware or software to allow code to be reused in loops.

Some dataflow hardware was designed as a distributed-memory parallel processor. When instructions execute, they do not store their results directly in the destination instructions, but send them out in tokens over a network that will deliver them to the correct destination processor, instruction address, and operand position (left or right).

A tagged-token dataflow hardware design got around the problem of providing reentrant code by tagging the tokens not only with the destination processor, instruction address, and operand position, but also with a subroutine activation number and loop iteration count. Instead of operands being stored in the instruction itself, a processor has a matching store, a kind of cache, where one operand waits until the other operand arrives. When all the operands for an instruction are present, the instruction is fetched, packed with its operands, and sent off to an instruction execution unit.

Dataflow has obvious application to parallelism. When the operands become available, an instruction can execute. The instruction needn't wait for flow of control to come to it. The design principle works as well on a network or distributed-memory machine as on a multiprocessor. And dataflow can be implemented in software, as well as in hardware.

An obvious approach to software dataflow is to put operands in futures. Instructions can get their operands from futures, being delayed until the future has its value set. Then the instructions place their results in futures.

The problem is that this works poorly at the scalar level. The overhead would be dozens or hundreds of machine instructions executed in synchronization and thread dispatching for each instruction that does actual work.

Macro dataflow is a software dataflow implementation that tries to operate, to the highest extent possible, on blocks of data, rather than individual scalars. For example, a vector–matrix package could operate on entire vectors and rows of matrices at a time. The cost of dispatching an operation would be amortized over all the length of the vector, rather than a single scalar.

Macro dataflow chore graphs. Macro dataflow executions can be represented by chore graphs where the nodes are blocks of code and the edges represent the data dependencies. You may imagine data flowing along the edges from the tail of the edge where the data are produced to the head that uses them. That means the edges will typically represent futures that are assigned values by the chore at the tail of the edge and whose value is required by the chore at the head.

It is probably aesthetically more pleasing to change the chore graph into a bipartite graph where futures are also represented by nodes. (See Figure 7–1.) A single edge will typically enter each node, from the chore that assigns it a value. More than one edge entering a future would indicate that, for example, the future is being set by both branches of an if statement, and we are picturing both sides.

Figure 7–1 Chore graph vs. macro dataflow with explicit future.

Chore constructors. For our macro dataflow operations, we will typically use classes whose constructors have the pattern

```
ChoreClass(inputs, otherParameters, outputs)
```

The inputs and outputs will typically be `Future` objects for macro dataflow, but the same pattern can be used for other chore graphs.

Fetching operands. The first problem we face in trying to implement macro dataflow with chores is how to implement instructions that require more than one operand. The idea behind chores is that chores will not block holding onto a thread. What if a two-operand chore (a binary operator) fetches its left operand and then is forced to wait for its right operand to become available? We would expect the code to add two float arrays to be something like Example 7-1.

Example 7-1 Example of blocking binary dataflow operation.

```
class BinAddFloatArray implements Runnable {
   Future lopnd; Future ropnd;  Future result;
   public BinAddFloatArray(Future lopnd,
      Future ropnd, Future result){
      this.lopnd = lopnd; this.ropnd = ropnd;
      this.result = result;
   }
   public void run() {
     try{
      float[] left=(float[])lopnd.getValue();
      float[] right=(float[])ropnd.getValue();
      float[] sum=new float[left.length];
      for (int i=0;i<sum.length;i++)
         sum[i]=left[i]+right[i];
      result.setValue(sum);
     } catch (InterruptedException ex){}
   }
}
```

Won't the attempt to fetch the right operand block its thread? Well, this code would. What we have to do is check that the operands are available and give up the thread we are using if we have to wait. We would code it something like Example 7-2.

The first lines of the `run()` method now check to see if the operands are assigned yet. If an operand is not yet assigned a value, they make this chore wait for it to be assigned by calling `runDelayed(this)` and give up the chore's thread by returning. If the right operand isn't available and the left one is, then the next time the chore is started, it performs a redundant test, but that should be a relatively minor overhead.

Example 7-2 **Nonblocking binary dataflow operation.**

```java
class BinAddFloatArray implements Runnable {
    Future lopnd; Future ropnd;  Future result;
    public BinAddFloatArray(
            Future lopnd, Future ropnd,
            Future result){
        this.lopnd= lopnd; this.ropnd= ropnd;
        this.result= result;
    }
    public void run() {
      try {
        if (!lopnd.isSet()){
            lopnd.runDelayed(this);return;
        }
        if (!ropnd.isSet()){
            ropnd.runDelayed(this);return;
        }
        float[] left=(float[])lopnd.getValue();
        float[] right=(float[])ropnd.getValue();
        float[] sum=new float[left.length];
        for (int i=0;i<sum.length;i++)
            sum[i]=left[i]+right[i];
        result.setValue(sum);
      } catch (InterruptedException ex){}
    }
}
```

Flow of Control

Even though our approach is to break computation into independent chores, we will no doubt be thinking in terms of flow of control. We will especially miss flow of control when there are a lot of small operations to perform in sequence. Here are some techniques to implement flow of control in chore graphs, including reusing the same class for more than one chore.

Changing run queues. One easy way to allow flow of control is to use a thread instead of a chore. A thread is allowed to block between the chores it is composed of, whereas a chore should run its body to completion. Since either a chore or a thread may be packaged in a runnable and either may be placed in a run queue, why not just run delay code for a thread on a future? The major reason why not is that futures for chores will have run queues that limit the maximum number of threads they can create at a time, and as remarked before, this can lead to deadlock. After being run delayed on a future, a runnable is associated with whatever run queue the future used to schedule it. This run queue might have a limit on the number of threads it will create. If the runnable actually is not a chore but a full thread, needing to block, for example on `getValue()` from a future or a `down()` on a semaphore, then it would reduce the number of threads for executing other runnables on that run queue. If all the runnables holding threads created by that run queue are blocked waiting for some actions that can only be performed by runnables still enqueued on that queue and the queue is not allowed to create any more threads, the system is deadlocked.

Therefore, a runnable may need change the run queue of the thread that is executing it. It may need to use a thread from a run queue that has no limit on the number of threads that can be created.

This can be accomplished with the code shown in Example 7-3. The intention is to change the run queue of the runnable to one with an unlimited number of threads. The first time the runnable is scheduled, it assigns itself to the unlimited run queue, handing itself over to a different thread. When that thread starts running it, it will skip the hand-over and just run.

Example 7-3 Runnable changing run queues

```
class ...{
boolean firstEntry=true;
...
  public void run() {
    if (firstEntry) {
      firstEntry=false;
      unlimitedRunQueue.run(this);
      return;
    }
    ...
  }
}
```

Switch statement. Another approach to simulating flow of control is to put the code for several chores in a flow of control in the same run method as cases in a `switch` statement. The pattern is shown in Example 7-4. Keep a program counter, `pc`, field in the class.

Example 7-4 Chores in a switch statement

```
class ...{
int pc=0;
...
  public void run() {
     for (;;) try {switch (pc){
case 0:
        ...
case 1:
        ...//body of chore 1
        pc=2;
        if (!f.isSet()) {
            f.runDelayed(this);
            return;
        }
case 2: v=f.getValue();
        ...
     } } catch (InterruptedException e){...}
  }
}
```

Use the program counter in the `switch` statement to jump to the proper code. Naturally, each section of code will assign the number of its successor to `pc`. This example shows the handoff from the chore at `case 1` to the next chore at `case 2`. At the end of the first chore's processing, chore number two should run. However, it needs to get the Object `v` out of `Future f`, but it may not be assigned yet. So the last thing chore one does is to set `pc` to 2, so that if it gives up the thread, chore two will execute next. Then it tests to see if `f` has already had its value assigned. If not, it runs itself delayed on the future, so when it runs again, `f` will have been defined, and chore two will not block on the `getValue()` call. If however, `f` does already have a value, chore one just falls through into chore two.

The reason for the try statement is to placate the Java compiler. Calling `getValue()` can theoretically throw an `InterruptedException`, and the compiler will issue warnings if we don't make provision for them.

Create a continuation object. The method truest to the spirit of chores is to have each chore schedule another chore object to execute the next chore in sequence. This successor object can be dropped in a run queue or be run delayed on a `Future` object. This approach has a lot in common with *continuation-passing style*.

A continuation is a function that represents the rest of a program execution. The idea behind it has been around since the early days of computing when people were figuring out how to implement the language Algol 60. There was a question over what features are really essential and what can be implemented in terms of others. One researcher realized that you could get away with sequential execution, `if` statements, procedures and procedure calls, but you didn't need loops or procedure return. Suppose procedure A calls procedure B. You would take the rest of the code in procedure A following a call of procedure B and make it into a procedure of its own, a continuation procedure. The continuation procedure says what you would do after the return from B. Then, the continuation is passed to procedure B as an additional parameter. Now instead of returning, procedure B ends by calling the continuation procedure it has been passed, which will do what A was going to do after the return. You do this for all procedures and all calls.

What about loops? A loop can be translated into a procedure that calls itself recursively at the end.

Is this ever used? Yes. The language Scheme requires it. It is a common implementation technique for functional languages. Tail-end calls, such as the calls of continuations, can be efficiently implemented by loading parameters in registers and jumping. Passing a continuation only requires creating a functional object composed of an entry address and an environment.

Our use of this concept is to create an object for each chore. Each chore in the sequence will schedule its successor. Sometimes, a chore will create an instance of its continuation. Sometimes, we will create a chain of such objects before starting the first of them running.

Create a local continuation object. A convenient form of continuation object is a local object, declared using a nested class. The contained, local object can access all the fields of the containing object. Therefore, all the data fields the continuations need can be placed in the surrounding object, and the continuation objects can just provide code in their `run()` methods.

Macro Dataflow Examples: Vector Addition

We will demonstrate a number of macro dataflow techniques in this section using examples of vector addition. By vector addition, we mean mathematical vectors, not `java.util.`Vector objects. Vectors in n-dimensional space are n-tuples of real numbers, which we represent by arrays of length n of double-precision floating-point numbers. Vector addition is performed by adding the corresponding elements of the two vectors.

We have already shown two versions of vector addition in Examples 7-1 and 7-2. A picture of our data structure is shown in Figure 7–2. In those examples, the operations of

Future   array

Figure 7–2 Vector addition data structure.

waiting for and fetching operands, performing the addition, and storing the results are all combined in one object and one `run()` method. Here we will divide the operations into more than one class so that we will have components that plug together. We have components to fetch operands, to perform the operations, and to store the results. Using components makes it easier to increase the functionality by adding additional, simple components later.

The plugs we use to connect components are the interfaces Op1 and Op2 shown in Example 7-5. Both of them define a method op(). For Op1, op() takes a single argument; for Op2, it takes two. An object that implements either Op1 or Op2 is a continuation object. It exists to continue some computation. It says what is to be done next.

Example 7-5 Op1 and Op2 interfaces

```
interface Op1{
    public void op(Object opnd);
}
interface Op2{
    public void op(Object lopnd,Object ropnd);
}
```

Continuations to Separate Operand Fetch from Operation

Our first example using Op1 and Op2 continuations will fetch the two operands, add them, and store the result in separate objects. This resembles the operand fetch, execute, and store stages of a computer processor.

The operand fetch is performed by class `Binop1` (binary operation, version 1), pictured in Figure 7–3 and shown in Example 7-6. A `Binop1` object is created with references to two futures for its left and right operands and an Op2 continuation to which to pass the operands once it has fetched them. As shown before, it first tests the operand futures to see if the operands are present. If they both are present, it fetches them and passes them to its

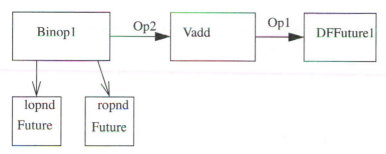

Figure 7–3 Vector addition by fetching the operands in the same class.

Example 7-6 class `Binop1`

```
import com.toolsofcomputing.thread.*;
class Binop1 implements Runnable{
    Future lopnd,ropnd;
    Op2 continuation;
    public Binop1(
        Future lopnd,
        Future ropnd,
        Op2 continuation){
    this.lopnd=lopnd;
    this.ropnd=ropnd;
    this.continuation=continuation;
    }
    public void run() {
    try {
        if (!lopnd.isSet()) {lopnd.runDelayed(this); return;}
        if (!ropnd.isSet()) {ropnd.runDelayed(this); return;}
        continuation.op(lopnd.getValue(),ropnd.getValue());
    } catch (InterruptedException e){
        continuation.op(e,e);
    }
    }
}
```

continuation. If either operand isn't present, `Binop1` run delays itself on that operand's future. This will wait for the operand to become available without holding on to a thread. When it is reawakened, it will start again testing whether the operands are present. There is the extra cost of a redundant test if it was waiting for the right operand to be available.

The actual vector addition is done by class Vadd, shown in Example 7-7. Vadd implements the Op2 interface, so it has an op() method that is called with the two vector operands. It is given a Op1 continuation when it is created. The continuation will be given the result of the vector addition. It is up to the continuation to store the result or perhaps perform more operations on it.

Example 7-7 class Vadd

```
class Vadd implements Op2{
    Op1 continuation;
    Vadd(Op1 contin){continuation=contin;}
    public void op(Object lopnd,Object ropnd){
        double [] x,y,z;
        if (lopnd instanceof Exception)
            continuation.op(lopnd);
        if (ropnd instanceof Exception)
            continuation.op(ropnd);
        try {
            x=(double[])lopnd;
            y=(double[])ropnd;
            z=new double[x.length];
            for (int i=0;i<z.length;++i)
                z[i]=x[i]+y[i];
            continuation.op(z);
        } catch (Exception e){continuation.op(e);}
    }
}
```

Because the Op1 and Op2 interfaces are used for a variety of operations, they cannot be specific about what kinds of operands are being passed. They declare their parameters of type Object and leave it up to the object implementing the interface to cast objects to the specific type required. Thus, Vadd has to cast its left and right operands into arrays of doubles.

The result of the vector addition needs to be stored in a future for other uses later. Clearly there has to be some operation implementing the Op1 interface that can store its operand in a future. We allow a future to do this itself. Class DFFuture1 (dataflow future, version 1), shown in Example 7-8, extends Future and implements Op1. Its op() method simply stores its operand.

Class TestVadd1, shown in Example 7-9, shows Binop1, Vadd, and DFFuture1 in action. The significant line is

```
f1.runDelayed(new Binop1(f1,f2,new Vadd(f3)));
```

Example 7-8 class `DFFuture1`

```
import com.toolsofcomputing.thread.*;
class DFFuture1 extends Future implements Op1{
    public void op(Object opnd){
        setValue(opnd);
    }
}
```

Example 7-9 `TestVadd1`

```
import com.toolsofcomputing.thread.*;
class TestVadd1 {
    public static void main(String[] args)
        throws InterruptedException{
        double [] x={1.0,2.0,3.0};
        double [] y={4.0,5.0,6.0};
        DFFuture1 f1=new DFFuture1();
        DFFuture1 f2=new DFFuture1();
        DFFuture1 f3=new DFFuture1();
        f1.runDelayed(new Binop1(f1,f2,new Vadd(f3)));
        f1.setValue(x);
        f2.setValue(y);
        double [] z=(double[])f3.getValue();
        for (int i=0;i<z.length;++i)
            System.out.print(z[i]+" ");
        System.out.println();
        Future.getClassRunQueue().setMaxThreadsWaiting(0);
    }
}
```

The operands will be found in futures $f1$ and $f2$. The result will be placed in DFFuture1 $f3$. The Vadd object is given $f3$ as its continuation. The operands are fetched by Binop1 and passed to the Vadd object. The Binop1 object could have been placed on a run queue, but for efficiency, it was run delayed on its left operand. It won't be able to run until both operands are present anyway, so it might as well be delayed until at least one of them is present.

Static Dataflow Style and Storing Operands in Instructions

Our second version of vector addition will use a static dataflow style. We will store operands in the dataflow instructions themselves, and when all the operands are present, we will execute the instruction.

For the static dataflow, we introduce the interface StoreOp, shown in Example 7-10.

Example 7-10 interface **StoreOp**

```
interface StoreOp{
    public void store(int i,Object value);
}
```

Interface StoreOp declares a single method store(int i, Object value). Method store() will place the value at the position i in the object implementing the interface.

We now can create a static-dataflow version of Binop, class Binop2, shown in Example 7-11. Binop2 (binary operation, version 2) implements the StoreOp interface. It does

Example 7-11 class **Binop2**

```
import com.toolsofcomputing.thread.*;
class Binop2 implements StoreOp{
    Object lopnd,ropnd;
    Op2 continuation;
    int needed=2;
    public Binop2(Op2 continuation){
          this.continuation=continuation;
    }
    public void store(int i,Object value){
          if (i==0) lopnd=value;
          else ropnd=value;
          if (--needed==0) continuation.op(lopnd,ropnd);
    }
}
```

not implement the Runnable interface, since it is no longer responsible for fetching its own operands. When a Binop2 object is created, it is given an Op2 continuation object, which it is to call with the two operands stored in it—lopnd and ropnd. Initially, these operands have no value. Conceptually, the left operand, lopnd, has position zero, and ropnd has position one. Method store(int i,Object value) will place the value in lopnd if i is zero and the ropnd field if i is one (actually, anything other than zero). The Binop2 object keeps track of how many operands it still needs in its needed field.

Example 7-12 class **Fetch**

```
import com.toolsofcomputing.thread.*;
class Fetch implements Runnable {
    Future src;
    Op1 continuation;
    public Fetch(Future src, Op1 continuation){
        this.src=src;
        this.continuation=continuation;
    }
    public void run() {
    try {
        if (!src.isSet()) src.runDelayed(this);
        continuation.op(src.getValue());
    } catch(InterruptedException e) {
        continuation.op(e);
    }
    }
}
```

Example 7-13 class **Store**

```
import com.toolsofcomputing.thread.*;
class Store implements Op1{
    StoreOp dst;
    int pos;
    public Store(StoreOp dst,int pos){
        this.dst=dst;
        this.pos=pos;
    }
    public void op(Object value){
        dst.store(pos,value);
    }
}
```

Class Fetch, shown in Example 7-12, fetches operands from futures. It will pass the value it fetches to an Op1 object. Class Store, shown in Example 7-13, is used to store the operands in Binop2 binary dataflow instructions. It implements the Op1 interface. It is created with a StoreOp destination dst and an index pos. When it's op() method is called, it stores the operand at the specified index in the destination.

TestVadd2, shown in Example 7-14, shows Binop2, Fetch, and Store in action.

Example 7-14 class TestVadd2

```
import com.toolsofcomputing.thread.*;
class TestVadd2 {
    public static void main(String[] args)
        throws InterruptedException{
        double [] x={1.0,2.0,3.0};
        double [] y={4.0,5.0,6.0};
        DFFuture1 f1=new DFFuture1();
        DFFuture1 f2=new DFFuture1();
        DFFuture1 f3=new DFFuture1();
        Binop2 bop=new Binop2(new Vadd(f3));
        f1.runDelayed(new Fetch(f1,new Store(bop,0)));
        f2.runDelayed(new Fetch(f2,new Store(bop,1)));
        f1.setValue(x);
        f2.setValue(y);
        double [] z=(double[])f3.getValue();
        for (int i=0;i<z.length;++i)
            System.out.print(z[i]+" ");
        System.out.println();
        Future.getClassRunQueue().setMaxThreadsWaiting(0);
    }
}
```

The most significant lines are

```
Binop2 bop=new Binop2(new Vadd(f3));
f1.runDelayed(new Fetch(f1,new Store(bop,0)));
f2.runDelayed(new Fetch(f2,new Store(bop,1)));
```

The first line creates

1.   a vector add that will store its result in future f3 and

2.   a binary operation that will pass two operands to the vector addition when the operands become available.

The second line creates a Fetch–Store pipe to fetch the left operand and store it in the binary operation. The third line fetches the right operand. Both lines are run delayed on the futures from which they fetch their operands.

Fetching in continuations

The third version of vector addition fetches the right operand in a continuation. Class `TestVadd3`, shown in Example 7-15, shows the code to test out the idea. The significant code is as follows:

```
Fetch operation=
    new Fetch(f1,
        new Fetch2nd(f2,
            new Vadd(f3)));
```

The Fetch operation fetches the left operand and passes it to the `Fetch2nd` operation, which fetches the right operand and passes the pair of them to the `Vadd` instruction.

Example 7-15 class `TestVadd3`

```
import com.toolsofcomputing.thread.*;
class TestVadd3 {
    public static void main(String[] args)
        throws InterruptedException{
        double [] x={1.0,2.0,3.0};
        double [] y={4.0,5.0,6.0};
        DFFuture1 f1=new DFFuture1();
        DFFuture1 f2=new DFFuture1();
        DFFuture1 f3=new DFFuture1();
        Fetch operation=
            new Fetch(f1,
                new Fetch2nd(f2,
                    new Vadd(f3)));
        f1.runDelayed(operation);
        f1.setValue(x);
        f2.setValue(y);
        double [] z=(double[])f3.getValue();
        for (int i=0;i<z.length;++i)
            System.out.print(z[i]+" ");
        System.out.println();
        Future.getClassRunQueue().setMaxThreadsWaiting(0);
    }
}
```

Class `Fetch2nd`, shown in Example 7-16, implements both `Op1` and `Runnable`. It is created with `Future src` and an `Op2 continuation`. When its `op()` method is called with the left operand, it saves it in field `lopnd` and then executes its `run()` method. The `run()` method tries to fetch the right operand from `src`. If the `src` future doesn't have a value yet, it run delays itself on `src` to try again when `src` has been given a value. When `src` does have a value, `Fetch2nd` passes the left operand it

Example 7-16 class `Fetch2nd`

```java
import com.toolsofcomputing.thread.*;
class Fetch2nd implements Runnable, Op1{
    Object lopnd;
    Future src;
    Op2 continuation;
    public Fetch2nd(Future src,Op2 continuation){
        this.src=src;
        this.continuation=continuation;
    }
    public void op(Object value){
        lopnd=value;
        run();
    }
    public void run() {
        try {
            if (!src.isSet()) src.runDelayed(this);
            continuation.op(lopnd,src.getValue());
        } catch(InterruptedException e) {
            continuation.op(lopnd,e);
        }
    }
}
```

got from its `op()` method and the right operand it got from `src` to its continuation's `op()` method.

Version 3 has a bit of cleanliness compared with the two other versions. Unlike the first version's `Binop1` object, it doesn't have to check the left operand more than once. `Binop1` will check it's left operand again, even if it was run delayed on its right operand. Unlike `Binop2`, version 3 doesn't have to have the extra four objects to fetch the two operands and store them in the `Binop2` object. The cost is simply one object per operand, one for the operation, and one more to dispose of the result.

Chore Examples: Warshall's Algorithm

We presented Warshall's algorithm for transitive closure in Example 6-1 on page 175. Even there, we used an optimization of it, as shown in Example 7-17. In the original, the code within the three loops is

```java
A[i][j] = A[i][j] || (A[i][k] && A[k][j]);
```

where we conjoin the `j`th position of row `k` into the `j`th position of row `i` if `A[i][k]` is true. Since `A[i][k]` will be the same for all values of `j`, we remove the test to outside

Example 7-17 Warshall's algorithm

```
for (k=0; k<N; k++)
    for (i=0; i<N; i++)
        if (A[i][k])
            for (j=0; j<N; j++)
                A[i][j] = A[i][j] || A[k][j] ;
```

the inner j loop. We test to see if row i has a true value in the kth position, A[i][k]. If so, we conjoin into it the kth row. Otherwise, we leave the ith row unaltered.

In our code in this section, the middle i loop has vanished. We operate in parallel on the rows. Each row, in fact, is processed by a separate object, each of which has its own copy of index i. The i loop has vanished into parallel chains of chores.

We will show four versions of Warshall's algorithm using chores. The first, WarshallDF1, uses dataflow techniques. The other three, WarshallC1 through WarshallC3, use chores, but they modify the rows in place, which violates the dataflow spirit by making the computations timing dependent.

WarshallDF1 *and Warshall's Algorithm in Dataflow*

Class WarshallDF1 is a dataflow approach to Warshall's algorithm. Example 7-18

Example 7-18 WarshallDF1 structure

```
class WarshallDF1{
  int numThreads;
  public WarshallDF1(int numThreads){
     this.numThreads=numThreads;
  }
  private class RowUpdate implements Runnable {
...
}
  public boolean[][] closure(boolean[][] a) {
...
  }
}
```

shows the global structure of WarshallDF1. When we create a copy of WarshallDF1, we specify the number of threads it is to use in computing the transitive closure of a boolean matrix.

When we wish to compute the transitive closure of a matrix, we pass the matrix to method `closure()`, which will return a new matrix that is the transitive closure of the input matrix. Method `closure()` builds a dataflow graph to compute the transitive closure. It does the updates in stages, as pictured in Figure 7–4. For an $N \times N$ boolean matrix, there are N stages in the dataflow graph. A row is updated as a unit by a chore. The chores are instances of the `RowUpdate` class.

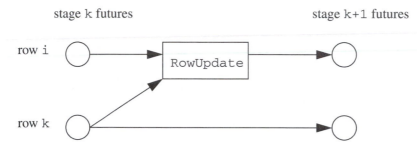

Figure 7–4 `WarshallDF1 RowUpdate`. Updating the values in rows at step `k` to yield their values at step `k+1`.

Method `closure()`, shown in Example 7-19, builds the stages using two arrays of futures, the source array `src`, and the destination array, `dst`. The futures in these arrays will have rows assigned to them. To create the futures, `closure()` creates a future factory `ff` that uses a run queue that is restricted to create no more than the desired number of threads at a time. The original `src` array is initialized to futures, which are themselves initialized to the values of the rows of the input array.

The stages are generated by a loop that creates an array of destination futures. This loop is the translation of the outer `k` loop of Warshall's algorithm. Except for the kth row, all rows `i` from the stage `k` to stage `k+1` are updated by creating

1. a destination `future` and

2. a `RowUpdate` operation that will conditionally disjoin it with the kth source row.

The kth row would not be changed by a `RowUpdate`, so we omit any operation by simply reusing the kth source future as the kth destination future, and not creating any update operation.

`RowUpdate`, shown in Example 7-20, is created with four parameters:

1. **myRow:** The future from which it will read the row it is updating.

2. **kthRow:** The future from which it will read the kth row, if necessary.

3. **k:** The step number.

4. **resultRow:** The future into which it will place the row it is updating.

Example 7-19 Method `closure()` of `WarshallDF1`

```
public boolean[][] closure(boolean[][] a) {
    int i,j,k;
    RunQueue rq=new RunQueue(numThreads);
    FutureFactory ff=new FutureFactory(rq);
    Future[] srcRows=new Future[a.length];
    for (i=0;i<srcRows.length;++i) {
        srcRows[i]=ff.make();
        srcRows[i].setValue(a[i]);
    }
    for (k=0;k<a.length;k++) {
        Future[] dstRows=new Future[a.length];
        for (i=0;i<a.length;i++) {
            if (i==k) dstRows[i]=srcRows[i];
            else {
                dstRows[i]=ff.make();
                srcRows[i].runDelayed(
                    new RowUpdate(
                        srcRows[i],
                        srcRows[k],
                        k,
                        dstRows[i]) );
            }
        }
        srcRows = dstRows;
    }
    boolean[][] result=new boolean[a.length][];
    try {
        for (i=0;i<a.length;i++)
        result[i]=(boolean[])srcRows[i].getValue();
    } catch (InterruptedException ex){}
    rq.setMaxThreadsWaiting(0);
    return result;
}
```

If `row[k]` is true, `RowUpdate` must fetch `kthRow` and disjoin it with `row`. If `row[k]` is false, it can ignore the kth row. Therefore, `RowUpdate`'s `run()` method first fetches `row`, the contents of future `myRow`, run delaying itself on `myRow` if necessary. Then, it checks `row[k]` to see if it must also fetch `kthRow`'s contents. If it doesn't need to fetch `kthRow`'s contents, it just stores `row` into the `resultRow` future.

If it must fetch the kth row, it checks to see if the `kthRow` future is already set. If it is set, `RowUpdate` can fetch its contents and compute the result immediately; otherwise, it must

Example 7-20 Class `RowUpdate` of `WarshallDF1`

```
private class RowUpdate implements Runnable {
  boolean[] row=null;
  Future myRow;
  int k;
  Future kthRow;
  Future resultRow;
  int j;

  RowUpdate( Future myRow,
      Future kthRow,
      int k,
      Future resultRow){
    this.myRow=myRow;
    this.k=k;
    this.kthRow=kthRow;
    this.resultRow=resultRow;
  }

  public void run() {
    try {
      if (row==null) {
        if (!myRow.isSet()){
          myRow.runDelayed(this);
          return;
        }
        row = (boolean[])myRow.getValue();
        if (!row[k]) {
          resultRow.setValue(row);
          return;
        }
      }
      if (!kthRow.isSet()) {
        kthRow.runDelayed(this);
        return;
      }
      boolean[] row_k = (boolean[])kthRow.getValue();
      boolean[] result=new boolean[row.length];
      for(j=0;j<row.length;j++) {
        result[j] = row[j] | row_k[j];
      }
      resultRow.setValue(result);
    } catch (InterruptedException ex){}
  }
}
```

run delay itself on the `future`. When it is reawakened, it checks to see if it already has the row from the `Future myRow`, and discovering it has, it doesn't fetch it again.

The performance of `WarshallDF1` is shown in Figure 7–5. It was run on a dual-processor machine having a Java implementation with kernel threads. In this experiment, more threads performed better than fewer threads, at least up to five threads.

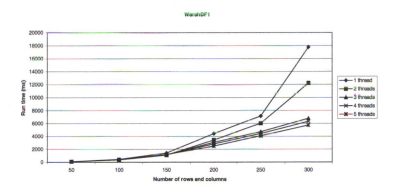

Figure 7–5 Performance of `WarshallDF1`.

`WarshallC1` *through* `WarshallC3`: *Chores, But not Dataflow*

The principle behind examples `WarshallC1` through `WarshallC3` is to use runnable objects for the calculation, but not dataflow. An `instance` of a class is created for calculating each row of the result. These update their rows communicating only when necessary.

Warshall's algorithm has three nested loops. The outer `k` loop takes the algorithm through *N* steps. The middle `i` loop selects a row, and the inner `j` loop updates the row. The inner loops can be run in parallel.

In these versions of Warshall's algorithm, the `i` loops are removed. Each row is processed by its own runnable object. Each object keeps track of its copy of variable `k` and has an inner `j` loop.

A runnable object only has to communicate when either

1.   It has the `k`th row and the step number is `k`. It has to provide its row to all other runnables that need it.

2.   In `step k`, this object's `row[k]` is true. This object must read the value of the `k`th row at `step k` to disjoin into its own row.

The communication is accomplished as follows: There is a shared array of *N* futures, `row_k_step_k`. Each of the runnables keeps track of the step number it is processing.

(That is, each of them keeps its own copy of the k value.) On step k, the runnable with the kth row stores a copy of its row in the kth element of the shared array row_k_step_k. Similarly, on the kth step, any runnable with row[k] true will get the value of the kth row at row_k_step_k[k].

The runnables do not have to run lock stepped. They can have their own separate, unequal values of k. They are only synchronized when they need to fetch values out of row_k_step_k.

Here is a quick preview of the variants of Warshall's algorithm:

- **WarshallC1** is the baseline Warshall's algorithm. It uses a thread for each row, so it is not chore based. The other versions can be considered variants of this algorithm. The problem in translating to chores is that the thread can be blocked in the middle while waiting at a getValue() to fetch the value out of a future. This getValue() call marks a chore boundry in the thread.

- **WarshallC2** uses one runnable object to handle each row. The run() method consists of several chores. It uses the trick of having a switch and a pc field to allow each entry of run() to execute the correct chore.

- **WarshallC3** uses several objects to handle each row. All the data for handling a row are kept in one object. The code for different chores is kept in subobjects declared in inner classes. Each of these inner classes provides code for a continuation chore.

WarshallC1.

The overall structure of WarshallC1 is given in Example 7-21. To

Example 7-21 WarshallC1 overall structure

```
class WarshallC1{
  private class Row extends Thread{...}
  public boolean[][] closure(boolean[][] a) {...}
}
```

perform transitive closures, you create an instance of a WarshallC1 object and call its closure method.

The closure() method, shown in Example 7-22, manages the computation of the transitive closure. The actual work is performed by the thread class Row. There will be one thread for each row of the matrix. Method closure() performs the following operations:

1. Since the algorithm operates in *N* steps and during each step *k*, the rows of the matrix are updated by disjoining them with the kth row, closure() creates an

Example 7-22 Method `closure()` of `WarshallC1`

```java
public boolean[][] closure(boolean[][] a) {
    int i;
    Future[] kthRows=new Future[a.length];
    for (i=0;i<kthRows.length;++i)
        kthRows[i]=new Future();
    Accumulator done=new Accumulator(a.length,
        new boolean[a.length][]);
    for (i=0;i<a.length;i++) {
        new
        Row((boolean[])a[i].clone(),i,kthRows,done).start();
    }
    boolean[][] result=null;
    try {
        result=(boolean[][])done.getFuture().getValue();
    } catch (InterruptedException ex){}
    return result;
}
```

array of `Future` objects, `kthRows`, to hold each of the kth rows to be used during the kth step of computing the other rows.

2. To be consistent with `WarshallDF1`, `closure()` will return a boolean matrix as its value. Each of the `Row` threads will produce one row of the result. The `Row` threads will place their rows in an array. The `closure` method creates an accumulator, `done`, for the `row` threads to use in producing their parts of the result. The data in the accumulator contains a boolean matrix with the rows empty. The `row` threads will place their rows in the matrix and signal their completion. Method `closure()` will wait for the completion of the computation by waiting for the `accumulator` to yield its value.

3. Method `closure()` starts the threads to calculate the rows. Each `Row` thread is given its row to work on. These rows are cloned from the input array to be consistent with `WarshallDF1`. Normally, transitive closure operations are done in place, modifying the input array. Each row object is also told its row number, the array of futures `kthRows` that will hold the rows needed during the kth step, and the `done` accumulator that it will place its row into and signal when it completes.

Local class Row, shown in Example 7-23, performs the actual computation of the rows of the transitive closure. The class is created with the following parameters:

- **row[]**: The contents of the row it is to work on, a boolean array.

Example 7-23 Row class of `Warshall1C1`

```
private class Row extends Thread{
    boolean[] row; int myRowNumber; Future[] row_k_step_k;
Accumulator done;
    Row( boolean[] row,
         int myRowNumber,
         Future[] row_k_step_k,
         Accumulator done){
       this.row=row;
       this.myRowNumber=myRowNumber;
       this.row_k_step_k=row_k_step_k;
       this.done=done;
    }
    public void run() {
      try {
        int j,k;
        boolean[] row_k;
        for (k=0;k<row_k_step_k.length;k++) {
            if (k==myRowNumber)
                row_k_step_k[k].setValue(row.clone());
            else if (row[k]) {
                row_k = (boolean[])row_k_step_k[k].getValue();
                for(j=0;j<row.length;j++) {
                    row[j] |= row_k[j];
                }
            }
        }
        boolean[][] result=(boolean[][])done.getData();
        result[myRowNumber]=row;
        done.signal();
      } catch (InterruptedException ex){}
    }
}
```

- **myRowNumber**: The number of its row, an integer.

- **row_k_step_k**: The array of futures that will contain the kth rows to be used during the kth steps.

- **done**: The accumulator into which to place its result.

The Row class's `run()` method does most of its work in the k loop. This loop goes through the *N* steps of the algorithm. If step k of the algorithm is equal to the number of the row that this thread is processing, it stores a copy of its row in the kth element of the array of futures, `row_k_step_k`. Otherwise, it checks to see if it needs the kth row. It will only need it if the kth element of its row, `row[k]`, is true. If it needs it, it waits for it to be computed and fetches the value

```
row_k_step_k[k].getValue()
```

and disjoins it into its own row in the `for (j...)` loop.

When the loop is done, it gets a reference to the array of rows in the accumulator `done`, puts its row into the result matrix, and signals its completion.

One thing to notice about this code is that the `Row` threads do not run lock stepped. There is no barrier to synchronize them. They can be running with different values of `k`. The only synchronization in their main loops is that when one thread needs the kth row, it fetches it from a future. This will delay it if the row hasn't been computed yet.

This code provides a baseline implementation for us. We want to do the same thing with chores, rather than threads. The problem we will face is that the threads block in the middle. They block trying to get the value out of a future inside an `if` statement inside a loop. It is not trivial to rearrange this code so that calling a `run()` method will execute the next chore.

WarshallC2. The first technique we use to convert `WarshallC1` to chores makes the body of the `Row`'s `run()` method a loop containing a `switch` statement. A program counter variable `pc` will select which code to execute next. This means the control structures of `WarshallC1`'s `Row` thread will have to be hand translated to blocks of code that can jump to each other by assigning to the `pc` field. This converts a structured program into one containing the equivalent of `goto` statements, which damages the clarity of the code.

The overall structure of `WarshallC2` is shown in Example 7-24. `WarshallC2` is cre-

Example 7-24 Overall structure of `WarshallC2`

```
class WarshallC2{
  int numThreads;
  public WarshallC2(int numThreads){
    this.numThreads=numThreads;
  }
  private class Row implements Runnable{ ... }
  public boolean[][] closure(boolean[][] a) { ... }
}
```

ated with a `numThreads` parameter to control the number of threads that will be created to compute the transitive closure. Private class `Row` will be responsible for computing a particular row. This version of `Row` implements `Runnable`, rather than extending

Thread; it will be placed in a runqueue to execute chores, rather than running as a thread. Method `closure()` has the same interface as in `WarshallDF1` and `WarshallC1`; it is given a boolean matrix, and it computes a transitive closure matrix without modifying its input.

`WarshallC2`'s `closure()` method is shown in Example 7-25. Its major differences

Example 7-25 `closure()` method of `WarshallC2`

```
public boolean[][] closure(boolean[][] a) {
    int i;
    RunQueue rq=new RunQueue(numThreads);
    FutureFactory ff=new FutureFactory(rq);
    Future[] kthRows=new Future[a.length];
    for (i=0;i<kthRows.length;++i)
        kthRows[i]=ff.make();
    Accumulator done=new Accumulator(a.length,
        new boolean[a.length][]);
    for (i=0;i<a.length;i++) {
        rq.run(new
            Row((boolean[])a[i].clone(),i,kthRows,done));
    }
    boolean[][] result=null;
    try {
        result=(boolean[][])done.getFuture().getValue();
        rq.setMaxThreadsWaiting(0);
    } catch (InterruptedException ex){}
    return result;
}
```

from the `closure()` method of `WarshallC1` is that it uses a run queue to limit the number of threads that will be used in the transitive closure.

The `closure()` method begins by creating a run queue `rq` that will create no more than `numThreads` threads for a single transitive closure. It uses this run queue in the future factory `ff` that it uses to initialize the `kthRows` futures. Now all the chores that are dispatched when these futures are assigned will be placed in `rq` and will be restricted to run in no more than `numThreads` threads at a time.

When `closure()` creates the `Row` objects, the objects are set running by being placed in `rq`. Again, no more than `numThreads` threads can process them at a time.

At the end, the `closure()` method sets the maximum number of threads that may be waiting in the run queue to zero. This will force the waiting threads to terminate. If this weren't done, the threads would wait around until they timed out.

The overall structure of the Row class is shown in Example 7-26. The major addition is the

Example 7-26 Row class of Warshall C2

```
private class Row implements Runnable{
    boolean[] row;
    int myRowNumber;
    Future[] row_k_step_k;
    Accumulator done;
    int pc=0;
    int j,k;

    Row( boolean[] row,
         int myRowNumber,
         Future[] row_k_step_k,
         Accumulator done){
        this.row=row;
        this.myRowNumber=myRowNumber;
        this.row_k_step_k=row_k_step_k;
        this.done=done;
    }

    public void run() { ... }
}
```

int field pc (initially zero), which controls which chore will execute when run() is called.

Row's run() method is shown in Example 7-27. It contains code for three chores, indicated by case 0:, case 1:, and case 2:. The body is a loop around a switch, for(;;) try{ switch(pc). The loop allows one chore to jump directly to another by pc=i; continue without having to go through a run queue. The functions of the chores are as follows:

case 0:

Chore 0 starts the implicit k loop by initializing k to zero, sets pc to one to select the next chore and falls through to execute it immediately. Yes, this could have been done a bit more simply by just having an initializer for k in the class declaration, but we wanted to show that there is usually some initialization code executed only at the beginning.

Example 7-27 Method `run()` from `Row` of `Warshall1C2`

```java
  public void run() {
    boolean[] row_k;
    for(;;) try { switch (pc) {
case 0:
      k=0; pc=1;
case 1:
      if (k>=row_k_step_k.length){
          boolean[][] result=(boolean[][])done.getData();
          result[myRowNumber]=row;
          done.signal();
          return;
      }
      if (k==myRowNumber) {
          row_k_step_k[k].setValue(row.clone());
          k++;
          continue;
      }
      if (!row[k]) {
          k++;
          continue;
      }
      pc=2;
      if (!row_k_step_k[k].isSet()) {
          row_k_step_k[k].runDelayed(this);
          return;
      }
case 2:
      row_k = (boolean[])row_k_step_k[k].getValue();
      for(j=0;j<row.length;j++) {
          row[j] |= row_k[j];
      }
      pc=1;
      k++;
      continue;
    }//switch
  } catch (InterruptedException ex){}
  }
```

case 1:

Chore 1 is the top of the k loop. First, it checks to see if k is greater than the number of steps in the algorithm. If so, we are done. In `WarshallC1`, the code to finish the computation is at the bottom, following the k loop, but here we have moved the code into the loop.

Next, chore 1 checks to see whether it has the kth row. If so, it puts it in the proper future in the array `row_k_step_k`, increments k, and loops back to immediately execute chore 1 again for the next value of k.

Similarly, if we don't need the kth row (i.e., our `row[k]` is false), we increment k and loop back to immediately execute chore 1 again.

If we do need the kth row, we set `pc=2` to choose chore 2 to run next. We check to see if the future containing the kth row has been set yet. If it has, we just fall through into chore 2. If not, we run ourselves delayed on the future, which will wake us up to run chore 2 when the value is present.

case 2:

Chore 2 fetches and uses the kth row during step k of the algorithm. We only enter chore 2 when we know that the future in `row_k_step_k[k]` has a value in it. Thus, the `getValue` will not block.

We end by disjoining the kth row with our row, incrementing k, assigning `pc=1` to go back to the top of the loop, and then starting chore 1 immediately by going on to the next iteration. The `continue` here is for consistency. It isn't needed.

The performance of `WarshallC2` on a dual-processor kernel-thread Java system is shown in Figure 7–6. The number of threads barely made a difference.

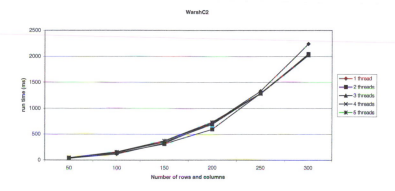

Figure 7–6 Performance of `WarshallC2`.

WarshallC3. By representing continuations as cases in a `switch` statement, `WarshallC2` obscures the code. There is no mnemonic meaning associated with these de facto numeric statement labels. Just using the same class for several different chores may obscure the meaning.

WarshallC3 tries to be clearer by putting different chores in different classes. The names of the classes try to make the intention of the code clearer.

The overall structure of WarshallC3 is shown in Example 7-28. Here, class Row itself

Example 7-28 Overall structure of **WarshallC3**

```
class WarshallC3{
  int numThreads;
  public WarshallC3(int numThreads){
    this.numThreads=numThreads;
  }
  private class Row implements Runnable{
      Row( boolean[] row,
        int myRowNumber,
        Future[] row_k_step_k,
        Accumulator done,
        RunQueue rq){ ...
      }
    class Loop implements Runnable {
      public void run() {
    }
    Loop loop=new Loop();

    class UpdateRow implements Runnable {
      public void run() {...}
     }
    UpdateRow updateRow=new UpdateRow();

    public void run() {// for Row class
        k=0;
        rq.run(loop);
    }
  }
  public boolean[][] closure(boolean[][] a) { ...}
  }
```

has two inner classes. Row.Loop is the top of the k loop in Warshall's algorithm, corresponding to case 1 in WarshallC1. Class Row.UpdateRow corresponds to case 2. It handles fetching the kth row and disjoining it with row.

Method `closure()`, shown in Example 7-29, is fundamentally the same as in

Example 7-29 `closure()` method of `WarshallC3`

```
public boolean[][] closure(boolean[][] a) {
    int i;
    RunQueue rq=new RunQueue(numThreads);
    FutureFactory ff=new FutureFactory(rq);
    Future[] kthRows=new Future[a.length];
    for (i=0;i<kthRows.length;++i)
        kthRows[i]=ff.make();
    Accumulator done=new Accumulator(a.length,
        new boolean[a.length][]);
    for (i=0;i<a.length;i++) {
        rq.run(
            new Row((boolean[])a[i].clone(),i,kthRows,done,rq));
    }
    boolean[][] result=null;
    try {
        result=(boolean[][])done.getFuture().getValue();
        rq.setMaxThreadsWaiting(0);
    } catch (InterruptedException ex){}
    return result;
}
```

`WarshallC2`. The only change other than renaming is having to provide Row with a run queue to use. The chores in Row objects will need this to schedule their successors.

The structure of class Row is shown in Example 7-30. The major function of Row is to hold the data shared by the local classes Loop and UpdateRow. When a Row is created, it creates a single instance of each of the local classes. The run() method for Row has the same functionality as case 0 in `WarshallC2`. It initializes k and runs the chore contained in local class Loop.

Row's Loop class is shown in Example 7-31. The body of Loop's run() method is contained in a for(;;) loop, so that it can keep on executing as long as possible, increasing the grain size.

Loop first checks to see if it is done with its part of the algorithm (i.e., if k >= row_k_step_k.length), and if so, it stores its part of the result and terminates. Next, it checks to see if k is equal to its row number, and if so, it stores a copy of its row in the kth future in row_k_step_k for the other chores to access and goes on to the next iteration.

Example 7-30 Row class of `WarshallC3`

```
private class Row implements Runnable{
    boolean[] row;
    int myRowNumber;
    Future[] row_k_step_k;
    Accumulator done;
    RunQueue rq;
    int j,k;

    Row( boolean[] row,
         int myRowNumber,
         Future[] row_k_step_k,
         Accumulator done,
         RunQueue rq){
        this.row=row;
        this.myRowNumber=myRowNumber;
        this.row_k_step_k=row_k_step_k;
        this.done=done;
        this.rq=rq;
    }
    class Loop implements Runnable {
        public void run() { ... }
    }
    Loop loop=new Loop();

    class UpdateRow implements Runnable {
        public void run() {...}
    }
    UpdateRow updateRow=new UpdateRow();

    public void run() {// for Row class
        k=0;
        rq.run(loop);
    }
}
```

Then, `Loop` checks to see if it needs the kth row to update its own. It will need it if the kth element of its row is true. If it doesn't need the kth row, it increments k and loops back to the top of its code. If it does need the kth row, it run delays its `updateRow` on `row_k_step_k[k]` and returns to give up the thread it is running on. When the kth row is available, this row's `UpdateRow` chore will be scheduled.

Example 7-31 Loop from Row of Warshall C3

```
class Loop implements Runnable {
  public void run() {

    for(;;) {
      if (k>=row_k_step_k.length){
          boolean[][] result=(boolean[][])done.getData();
          result[myRowNumber]=row;
          done.signal();
          return;
      }
      if (k==myRowNumber) {
          row_k_step_k[k].setValue(row.clone());
          k++;
          continue;
      }
      if (!row[k]) {
          k++;
          continue;
      }
      row_k_step_k[k].runDelayed(updateRow);
      return;
    }
  }
}
```

The UpdateRow chore will get the kth row out of the future in row_k_step_k[k] and disjoins it with its own row. Then, it increments k and schedules chore Loop to execute.

In comparison to WarshallC2, WarshallC3 has a couple of notable differences. WarshallC3's chores are named and individually packaged, which is probably more intuitive than the numbers in WarshallC2. Of course, WarshallC2 could name its chores by use of some final int declarations. An efficiency problem for WarshallC3 is that it schedules other chores by placing objects on a run queue, rather than just falling through or jumping to them. This can take a lot more instruction executions. It can be ameliorated somewhat by having one chore immediately execute the next by calling the other's run() method. For example, the run() method of Row could end by calling

```
loop.run();
```

rather than

```
rq.run(loop);
```

Example 7-32 **UpdateRow** from **Row** of **WarshallC3**

```
class UpdateRow implements Runnable {
  public void run() {
    boolean[] row_k;
    try {
      row_k = (boolean[])
          row_k_step_k[k].getValue();
      for(j=0;j<row.length;j++) {
        row[j] |= row_k[j];
      }
      k++;
      rq.run(loop);
    } catch (InterruptedException ex){}
  }
}
```

Class UpdateRow could do the same thing. One might go further and have Loop check whether the future row_k_step_k[k] is set and call updateRow.run(), rather than runDelayed(). The problem here is that Java is not required to optimize tail-end recursion. Each call can grow the thread's stack deeper, and if one is not careful, the thread could run out of stack space.

The performance of WarshallC3 on a dual-processor, kernel-threads Java implementation is shown in Figure 7–7. Any number of threads greater than one ran faster than one thread, but other than that, there was not much difference in run times among the different numbers of threads.

Chapter Wrap-up

This chapter is devoted to programming with chores. A chore is a small amount of computation that communicates with other chores only at its beginning and end. The advantage of using chores is that they needn't be handed to threads until the chores they depend upon have completed; hence, they do not block while holding threads. This allows run queues to limit the number of threads created without fear of deadlock. This can save the expense of creating a multitude of threads.

The use of chores requires two things:

- Synchronization objects that support chore scheduling and
- A collection of chore-programming techniques.

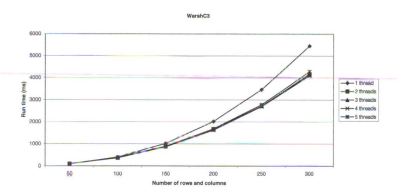

Figure 7–7 Performance of `WarshallC3`.

Most of the thread package synchronization classes have versions that allow chore scheduling. All of them implement the `RunDelayed` interface. They implement method `runDelayed(Runnable r)`, which puts `r` into a run queue when some event occurs.

The class `Future`, a subclass of `SimpleFuture`, will wake up the delayed runnables, placing them into a run queue when the future has its value set. The runnables are thus delayed on the future the same as are threads that call `getValue()`. A `FutureFactory` object generates futures that all place runnables on the same run queue.

The chore programming techniques include the use of job jars, macro dataflow, chore graphs, and continuations.

Exercises

1. For each example of vector addition, add a third vector (7.0,8.0,9.0) to the sum of the other two, and store the result in `f3`.

For `TestVadd2`, have the `add` of the first two vectors store its result directly in the `Binop` object for the second addition.

For `TestVadd3`, have the `add` method of the first two vectors pass its result directly to the fetch of the third operand.

2. Change `WarshallC1`, `WarshallC2`, and `WarshallC3` to update the input array in place, rather than returning a new array.

3. Rewrite `WarshallDF1` to use a class `RowUpdateFactory`, a factory with recycling, to make `RowUpdate` objects. Compare the running times with and without the factory. This should be instructive, even on a single-processor machine.

4. Continue Exercise 3 by adding a semaphore to RowUpdateFactory to limit the number of RowUpdate objects that can be created. This will force the thread generating the RowUpdate objects to wait for recycling. It is the equivalent of using a bounded buffer as a run queue. It will prevent the program from being flooded with RowUpdate objects. Experiment with different limits on the initial semaphore count, and see if it improves or worsens performance.

5. It is possible that updating individual rows gives too small a grain size for Warshall's algorithm. Rewrite WarshallDF1, WarshallC2, or WarshallC3 to update blocks of several consecutive rows in each chore, rather than just one row. Does it make a difference?

Chapter **8**

Thread and Chore Synchronization

▼ TerminationGroup

▼ Barrier

▼ BarrierFactory

▼ AccumulatorFactory

▼ PARALLEL Quicksort

▼ SHELL SORT

$\mathbf{C}$hores have the same need for synchronization as threads. We therefore provide versions of synchronization primitives that allow both chores and threads to be synchronized. Here we will look at termination groups, barriers, and accumulators to see how they interact with chores. We will examine two parallel sorting algorithms as examples of their use.

TerminationGroup

We discussed most of the methods of the TerminationGroup interface in the section entitled "TerminationGroup" in Chapter 5. We left the discussion of its runDelayed() method until now.

Recall that we create an initial, single member of a termination group. Then, by calling the fork() method for any member, we create other members. Eventually, we call terminate() for a member. After a member has been terminated, no more members can be forked from it. When all members of a termination group have terminated, the termination group terminates.

TerminationGroup methods

```
void awaitTermination()
TerminationGroup fork()
void runDelayed(Runnable r)
void terminate()
```

The TerminationGroup interface extends RunDelayed(), so chores can be run-delayed on a termination group. Naturally, such chores are stored with the termination group until all members of the termination group have been terminated, whereupon they are placed in a run queue.

We use a SharedTerminationGroup for shared-memory systems. A SharedTerminationGroup contains a Future. It assigns null to the future when termination has occurred. Naturally, SharedTerminationGroup delegates runDelayed() calls to the future.

The SharedTeminationGroup has two constructors:
SharedTerminationGroup(Future f) and SharedTerminationGroup().
You can either supply the future yourself, or you can have the SharedTermination-Group allocate one. If you supply one, you can decide what run queue the chores will be placed in when the group terminates. If you don't supply one, you will be choosing, by default, the run queue associated with the Future class.

If you wish to create several shared termination groups that will place chores in the same run queue, you can use a SharedTerminationGroupFactory. Naturally, a

---

SharedTerminationGroupFactory

SharedTerminationGroupFactory(FutureFactory futureFactory): Creates a SharedTerminationGroupFactory object.

SharedTerminationGroup make(): Creates a SharedTerminationGroup object.

FutureFactory getFutureFactory(): Gets the FutureFactory object for a SharedTerminationGroupFactory object.

void setFutureFactory(FutureFactory futureFactory): Sets the FutureFactory object for a SharedTerminationGroupFactory object.

`SharedTerminationGroupFactory` generates `SharedTerminationGroup` objects. Its constructor takes a `FutureFactory` object to generate the futures it places in the termination groups.

Barrier

`Barrier` extends `SimpleBarrier` and implements `RunDelayed`, so chores can wait at barriers, as well as can threads. When a chore is run delayed at a barrier, it counts as a member of the group being synchronized. Method `runDelayed()` counts as a `gather()`.

Barrier constructor and methods

```
Barrier(int n)
void gather()
void runDelayed(Runnable r)
void signal()
RunQueue getRunQueue()
void setRunQueue(RunQueue rq)
static RunQueue getClassRunQueue()
```

Being able to run delay runnables, as well as gathering threads, makes barriers *lightweight*. If you do not have to pay the cost of creating threads to execute a loop, you can more easily justify using barriers and parallel loops in other parallel structures. For example, you could have a reentrant server that uses a parallel loop. Normally, each call would create a new set of threads, but with `runDelay()`, you can implement it so that the runnables will share a run queue and not create more threads than the run queue allows.

Of the group of objects gathering at a barrier, all can be threads calling `gather()`, all can be chores placed at the barrier by calls to `runDelayed()`, or there can be some of each.

A further difference between `Barier` and `SimpleBarrier` is the method `signal()`. You may signal a barrier, which has the same effect on the barrier as a call to `gather()`, but the thread that calls `signal()` is not blocked.

Why use `signal()`? It appeared to be useful in some loops. Consider the loop represented by the chore graph in Figure 8–1. Chores A, B, C, D, and E execute in the loop. Chores A and B execute at the start of the loop; D must execute after A; E, after B; and C after both A and B. The edges leading upwards represent dependencies between iterations.

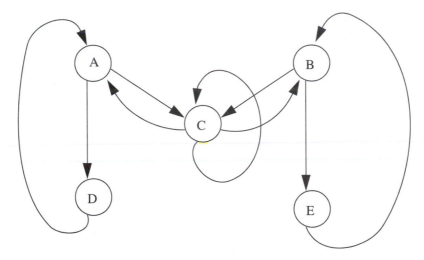

Figure 8–1 Chore graph for a hypothetical loop.

Before beginning the second loop, A must wait for C and D to be done with the previous iteration; B must wait for C and E.

We can synchronize this loop with barriers, as shown in Figure 8–2. We will group A and D into one thread, B and E into another, and put C into a thread of its own. Although AD and BE are not required to be synchronized with each other, we will gather them at a barrier at the top of the loop. C, however, represents a bit of a problem. It needs to complete one iteration before AD and BE can continue with the next, but C must wait for chores A and B to complete each time around the loop, so whatever synchronization object C waits on, it must reset each iteration.

One option would have AD, BE, and C gather at a barrier at the top of the loop, and then C could *down* a semaphore twice. As A and B complete, they *up* the semaphore. This would cause C to potentially block three times in rapid succession without doing any useful work in between.

The solution we show uses two barriers, both requiring three threads. Both AD and BE gather at barrier B1. C signals B1, without blocking there. C gathers at barrier B2. When chore A completes, before starting chore D, thread AD signals B2. Similarly, BE signals B2 when chore B completes.

So this design allows C to only block once. The `signal()` operation allows barriers to be used for internal synchronization within loop iterations without unnecessary blocking.

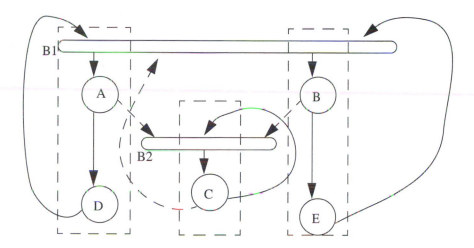

Figure 8–2 Chore graph for the hypothetical loop with Barriers.

BarrierFactory

If you want to synchronize runnables at barriers with `runDelayed()`, you may want to

---

BarrierFactory constructor and methods

```
public BarrierFactory(RunQueue rq)

public RunQueue getRunQueue()

public void setRunQueue(RunQueue rq)

public Barrier make(int n)
```

---

use a `BarrierFactory` object to create the barriers. The `BarrierFactory` object is given a run queue when it is created. Each barrier it constructs will use that run queue for the run-delayed objects. You can set the parameters of the run queue to limit the number of threads that will run them.

A `BarrierFactory` object allows you to get and set the `RunQueue` object after it is created.

You call `make(n)` to get a new barrier that will gather n threads.

AccumulatorFactory

Accumulators have already been discussed in the section entitled "Accumulator" in Chapter 5. Accumulators, recall, assign a value to a future when enough signals have accumulated. Class `Accumulator` implements `RunDelayed` by simply delegating it to the future.

`AccumulatorFactory` constructor and methods

```
public AccumulatorFactory(FutureFactory futureFactory)

public FutureFactory getFutureFactory()

public void setFutureFactory(FutureFactory futureFactory)

public Accumulator make(int n)

public Accumulator make(int n, Object data)
```

An `AccumulatorFactory` object can be used to allocate accumulators. It uses a `FutureFactory` object to create the futures they contain. The `FutureFactory` object, in turn, allows you to set the parameters on the run queues the futures place their run-delayed runnables on. You can get and set the future factory in an already existing accumulator factory by the obvious calls.

You make a new `Accumulator` object by calling one of the `make()` methods:

```
Accumulator make( n)
Accumulator make( n, data)
```

In the call, you must specify the number of signals the accumulator is waiting on. You may also specify the initial data value the accumulator contains. If you don't specify another data value, the value will be null.

Parallel `Quicksort`

Quicksort is easy to run in parallel. Quicksort works by picking an arbitrary element in an array to be the *pivot element*. The algorithm partitions the array around the pivot, moving the elements so that all elements to the left of the pivot element are less than or equal to it, and all the elements to the right are greater than or equal to it. Then, each side of the array can be sorted independently in the same manner. In the conventional implementation, each side is sorted recursively. In a parallel implementation, both sides can be sorted by parallel threads.

Example 8-1 Overall structure of `ParQuickSort2`

```
public class ParQuickSort2 {
 int numThreads;
 int minDivisible=8;

  class QuickSortThread2 implements Runnable{
    int ary[],m,n; TerminationGroup tg; RunQueue rq;
    public QuickSortThread2(int ary[],int mm, int nn,
          TerminationGroup t, RunQueue rq) {
      this.ary=ary; m=mm; n=nn; tg=t; this.rq=rq;
    }
    public void run() {
        quicksort(m,n);
        tg.terminate();
    }
    void quicksort(int m, int n) {...}
  }

  public ParQuickSort2(int numThreads){
    this.numThreads=numThreads;}
  public void sort(int[] ary) {...}
}
```

Example 8-2 Method `sort()` of `ParQuicksort2`

```
public void sort(int[] ary) {
    int N=ary.length;
    TerminationGroup terminationGroup;
    RunQueue rq=new RunQueue();
    FutureFactory ff=new FutureFactory(rq);
    TerminationGroupFactory tgf=
          new SharedTerminationGroupFactory(ff);
    Runnable subsort;
    rq.setMaxThreadsCreated(numThreads);
    terminationGroup=tgf.make();
    subsort=new QuickSortThread2(ary,0,N,terminationGroup,rq);
    rq.run(subsort);
    try {
    terminationGroup.awaitTermination();
    }catch(InterruptedException e){}
     rq.setMaxThreadsWaiting(0);
}
```

Example 8-3 Method `quicksort()` of `QuickSortThread2`

```java
void quicksort(int m, int n) {
 //System.out.println("quicksort("+m+","+n+")");
 int i,j,pivot,tmp;
 if (n-m<minDivisible) {
     for (j=m+1;j<n;j++) {
         for (i=j;i>m && ary[i]<ary[i-1];i--) {
             tmp=ary[i];
             ary[i]=ary[i-1];
             ary[i-1]=tmp;
         }
     }
     return;
 }
 i=m;
 j=n;
 pivot=ary[i];
 while(i<j) {
     j--;
     while (pivot<ary[j]) j--;
     if (j<=i) break;
         tmp=ary[i];
         ary[i]=ary[j];
         ary[j]=tmp;
     i++;
     while (pivot>ary[i]) i++;
         tmp=ary[i];
         ary[i]=ary[j];
         ary[j]=tmp;
 }
 Runnable subsort;
   if (i-m > n-i) {
     subsort=new QuickSortThread2(ary,m,i,tg.fork(),rq);
     rq.run(subsort);
     quicksort(i+1,n);
   } else {
     subsort=new QuickSortThread2(ary,i+1,n,tg.fork(),rq);
     rq.run(subsort);
     quicksort(m,i);
   }
 }
}
```

How fast can a parallel implementation of quicksort run? A sequential version of quicksort runs on the average in $O(N \log N)$ time, where N is the size of the array.[1] The parallel version can never be better than $O(N)$ time. The first partition of the array will look at every element and therefore take N time. (If you can think of some way to partition the array in parallel, you could make it run faster.)

Our implementation of quicksort, `ParQuickSort2`,[2] uses chores for subsorts. These chores partition the array and then create other chores for the recursive calls. The chores use a `TerminationGroup` object to report when the sort is done.

The overall structure of `ParQuickSort2` is shown in Example 8-1. An instance of `ParQuickSort2` is created with a maximum number of threads that may be used in a sort. The method `sort()` is called in this object to sort an array. The internal class `QuickSortThread2` contains the chore that actually perform the sorts.

Method `sort()`. Method `sort()`, shown in Example 8-2, begins with a number of statements just to set up the sort. It has to create a run queue for the sorting chores to be placed on. It needs a termination group for the chores to use to report when they are done. It is a bit of overkill, since we don't need to create the termination group factory or the future factory. The actual sorting is done by the following two lines:

```
subsort=new QuickSortThread2(ary,0,N,terminationGroup,rq);
rq.run(subsort);
```

The `QuickSortThread2` object is told the array to sort, the bounds within which it is to sort, the termination group to signal when it is done, and the run queue to run subsorts on.

We run the subsort by placing it in the run queue `rq`. We could have run it ourselves by calling `subsort.run()`. Anyway, we wait for the sort to finish by calling `terminationGroup.awaitTermination()`, which we had to put in a try statement, since it could, theoretically, throw an `InterruptedException`.

`QuickSortThread2`. As can be seen from Example 8-1, the real work in `QuickSortThread2` is done in method `quicksort()`. `QuickSortThread2`'s constructor places its parameters in fields of the object. The `run()` method calls `quicksort()`, signals termination, and returns.

Method `quicksort()`. Method `quicksort()` has three major parts.

1. If the portion of the array is small enough, it sorts it with insertion sort, which is faster for small arrays than quicksort.

---

[1] $O(N \log N)$ is read as order of $N \log N$. It means that the running time of the algorithm will be no worse than some constant times $N \log N$ as N grows large enough.

[2] The numeral 2 is for historic reasons. It uses the second partitioning method for quicksort shown in the sorting algorithm animations at http://www.toolsofcomputing.com/.

2.   If the portion of the array isn't small enough for the insertion sort, quicksort partitions it. It selects the first element in the subarray as the pivot element. It moves `j` downwards from the top of the subarray past elements larger than the pivot and `i` upwards from the bottom past elements smaller. The pivot element is bounced back and forth between `ary[i]` and `ary[j]`.

3.   After partitioning, it creates a runnable to sort one side of the array, and it recursively sorts the other side. It chooses to sort the smaller side itself. This is an attempt to control the grain size by creating fewer runnables, but with larger subarrays to sort.

Shell Sort

We discussed the shell sort in the section entitled "Recursive Shell Sort: `RunQueues` and `SimpleFutures`" in Chapter 5 and "Example: Shell Sort" in Chapter 6. Remember that the Shell sort is an improvement on the insertion sort. The insertion sort runs much faster if the array is already in nearly sorted order. Shell sort uses a series of increasing increments h_i. It goes down the series from larger increments to smaller ones, sorting the elements in the array that are h_i apart, sorting those h_{i-1} apart, and so on. Increment h_0 is one, so the last pass is a straight insertion sort. The idea is that sorting with the larger increments first quickly puts the elements close to the ultimate positions and limits how far they will have to move in subsequent sorts.

When the increment is h_i, there are h_i sequences of elements, the sequences whose lowest positions are 0, 1, ..., h_i-1. When h_i is large, the parallelism is good. There are plenty of sequences, and they have a small enough grain size; that is, they are not so long as to keep threads waiting for one or two long computations to complete.

As h_i gets smaller, however, the number of sequences decreases, and their length increases. This can do bad things to the amount of parallelism available. We want more parallelism late in the sort. Here's how we get it:

We can break down a long sequence of elements into two halves and sort them separately in parallel. Then, we merge the two sequences into one sorted sequence. How?

We merge the two halves by a small variant of insertion sort itself. We take the bottom element of the upper half and move it down to its proper place in the lower half; then, we take the next element from the upper half and do the same. We continue until the next element from the upper half doesn't move.

If the array wasn't almost sorted, there wouldn't be any advantage to this method, but since the array is in close-to-correct order already, the merge will not have to move many elements and will not have to move them very far.

Naturally, we can apply this recursively. A long sequence can be broken into two parts to be sorted separately and then merged, each of those two parts can be broken into two parts, and so on. Consider the effect on the last pass with an increment of one. Suppose that the array is

Example 8-4 ShellSort6

```java
public class ShellSort6{
  int numThreads=8;
  int minDivisible=16;
  class SortPass implements Runnable {
      int ary[],i,k,n; Accumulator finish;
      SortPass(int ary[],int i,int k, int n,
          RunDelayed start,Accumulator finish){...}
      public void run(){
          isort(ary,i,k,n);
          finish.signal();
      }
  }
  class IMerge implements Runnable {
      int ary[], i,k,m,n; Accumulator finish;
      IMerge(int ary[],int i,int k, int m, int n,
          RunDelayed start,Accumulator finish){ ... }
      public void run(){
          imerge(ary,i,k,m,n);
          finish.signal();
      }
  }
  int numInSequence(int i, int k, int n){
      return (n-i+k-1)/k;
  }
  int midpoint(int i, int k, int n){
      return i+numInSequence(i,k,n)/2*k;
  }
  void setupSequence(int ary[],int i, int k, int n,
          RunDelayed start,Accumulator finish,
          AccumulatorFactory af) {...}
  Accumulator setupPass(int ary[],RunDelayed start, int k,
          AccumulatorFactory af) {...}

  public ShellSort6 (int numThreads){
          this.numThreads=numThreads;}
  public void sort(int a[]){...}
  void isort(int[] a,int m,int k, int n) {...}
  void imerge(int[] a,int m, int k, int mid, int n) {...}
}
```

large and that you have four processors. Since the array is large, it can be broken into a large number of parts. These parts can be sorted in parallel. Then, there will be merges that can be done in parallel, and after that, more merges. Instead of having to wait for a single processor

Example 8-5 `isort` and `imerge`

```
void isort(int[] a,int m,int k, int n) {
    int i,j;
    for (j=m+k;j<n;j+=k) {
        for (i=j;i>=m+k && a[i]<a[i-k];i-=k) {
            int tmp=a[i];
            a[i]=a[i-k];
            a[i-k]=tmp;
        }
    }
}
void imerge(int[] a,int m, int k, int mid, int n) {
    int i,j;
    for (j=mid;j<n;j+=k) {
        if (a[j]>=a[j-k]) return;
        for (i=j;i>=m+k && a[i]<a[i-k];i-=k) {
            int tmp=a[i];
            a[i]=a[i-k];
            a[i-k]=tmp;
        }
    }
}
```

to examine each element in the array, the other processors can be busy working on parts of it until very near the end. Finally, the number of merges will fall beneath the number of processors, but the amount of work they have left to do will be small.

The overall structure and some of the detail of this parallel implementation, Shellsort6, is shown in Example 8-4. It contains two runnable subclasses, SortPass and IMerge, to handle sorting and merging sequences in parallel.

The purposes of methods numInSequence and midpoint are obvious from their names. Method numInSequence() computes the number of elements in a sequence from i up to, but not including, n, with an increment of k. Method midpoint() gives the index of an element near the center of that sequence.

Method setupPass() starts a parallel pass over the array. For the step size k, it will arrange to sort the k subsequences in parallel. It uses method setupSequence() to arrange to sort the sequence recursively. Method setupSequence() breaks the sequence into fragments to sort and builds a tree to merge them.

The real work of the algorithm is done by methods isort() and imerge(), shown in Example 8-5. The parameters to both have the same names: They work on array a from

Example 8-6 `SortPass` **and** `IMerge`

```
class SortPass implements Runnable {
    int ary[],i,k,n; Accumulator finish;
    SortPass(int ary[],int i,int k, int n,
        RunDelayed start,Accumulator finish){
        this.ary=ary;
        this.i=i;
        this.k=k;
        this.n=n;
        this.finish=finish;
        start.runDelayed(this);
    }
    public void run(){
        isort(ary,i,k,n);
        finish.signal();
    }
}
class IMerge implements Runnable {
    int ary[],  i,k,m,n; Accumulator finish;
    IMerge(int ary[],int i,int k, int m, int n,
        RunDelayed start,Accumulator finish){
        this.ary=ary;
        this.i=i;
        this.k=k;
        this.m=m;
        this.n=n;
        this.finish=finish;
        start.runDelayed(this);
    }
    public void run(){
        imerge(ary,i,k,m,n);
        finish.signal();
    }
}
```

position m up to, but not including, position n with an increment k between elements. In `imerge`, parameter `mid` is the position of the lowest element in the upper side of the sequence. Method `isort()` is an insertion sort, and `imerge()` is based on insertion sort, so they should be clear in themselves.[3]

---

[3] True, they are not the most efficient implementation of insertion sort. They use exchanges, rather than just rotating an element to its final position.

Example 8-7 Methods `setupPass()` and `setupSequence()`

```
void setupSequence(int ary[],int i, int k, int n,
      RunDelayed start,Accumulator finish,
      AccumulatorFactory af) {
   if (numInSequence(i,k,n)<=minDivisible)
      new SortPass(ary,i,k,n,start,finish);
   else {
      Accumulator a=af.make(2);
      int m=midpoint(i,k,n);
      setupSequence(ary,i,k,m,start,a,af);
      setupSequence(ary,m,k,n,start,a,af);
      new IMerge(ary,i,k,m,n,a,finish);
   }
}
Accumulator setupPass(int ary[],RunDelayed start, int k,
      AccumulatorFactory af) {
   Accumulator finish=af.make(k);
   for (int i=0;i<k;i++){
      setupSequence(ary,i,k,ary.length,start,finish,af);
   }
   return finish;
}
```

Class `SortPass`, shown in Example 8-6, is an encapsulation of method `isort()`. Its job is to call `isort()` and then signal an accumulator when it is done. It is created with the parameters it is to pass to `isort()` and with two extra parameters it uses for scheduling, `start` and `finish`. Parameter `start` indicates a condition the `SortPass` object is to wait for before running. Parameter `finish` is the accumulator it needs to signal when it is done. The constructor for `SortPass` itself calls `start.runDelay(this)` to schedule itself to run when `start` indicates it should. What will the start condition be? `SortPass` objects are given accumulators as their start objects. When they execute `runDelayed()` on the accumulator, they will be delayed until the accumulator has received the correct number of signals. These accumulators will indicate the previous pass of the sorting algorithm is complete.

Class `IMerge` is to `imerge()` what `SortPass` is to `isort()`. It will wait until a start condition is met, then run, and finally signal its completion. The start condition that it waits for by calling `runDelayed()` will actually be an accumulator. The accumulator will indicate that sorting of the two subsequences is complete and they now may be merged.

Example 8-8 `sort()`

```
public void sort(int a[]){
    int N=a.length;
    if (N<minDivisible) {
        isort(a,0,1,N);
        return;
    }
    RunQueue rq=new RunQueue();
    rq.setMaxThreadsCreated(numThreads);
    FutureFactory ff=new FutureFactory(rq);
    AccumulatorFactory af=new AccumulatorFactory(ff);
    Accumulator waitFor=af.make(1);
    waitFor.signal();
    int k,m;
    k=N/5;
    waitFor=setupPass(a,waitFor,k,af);
    k=N/7;
    waitFor=setupPass(a,waitFor,k,af);
    for (k=(int)(k/2.2);k>0;k=(int)(k/2.2)) {
        if (k==2) k=1;
        waitFor=setupPass(a,waitFor,k,af);
    }
    try{
      waitFor.getFuture().getValue();
    } catch(InterruptedException ie){}
      ff.getRunQueue().setMaxThreadsWaiting(0);
}
```

Method `setupPass()`, shown in Example 8-7, sets up a pass of the shell sort. By *pass*, we mean a sort of all the h_i subsequences with increments h_i. The parameter k is used to indicate the increment to be used. Parameter `start` indicates what the chores in the pass must wait on before starting. It will be an accumulator that will count the completion of chores in the previous pass and indicate when they are done. Method `setupPass()` creates an accumulator of its own to count the completion of its subsorts and returns it to the caller.

Method `setupSequence()`, shown in Example 8-7, sets up the sort of a subsequence of the array. If the subsequence is short enough, it simply creates a `SortPass` object to handle it. Otherwise, it breaks the sequence down into two parts, calls itself recursively to set up chore graphs to sort both sides, and creates an `IMerge` object to merge them. It creates an accumulator with a count of two, which it passes to itself to indicate when the sides are done. It passes this accumulator to the `IMerge` as its start condition, so the `IMerge` object will be scheduled when both sides are sorted.

Method `sort()`, shown in Example 8-8, in a `Shellsort6` object sorts an array. Method `sort()` starts by creating a run queue with a restriction on how many threads it can create, a future factory using the run queue, and an accumulator factory using the future factory.

Method `sort()` uses variable `waitFor` to hold the accumulators that signal the completion of passes. Initially, it creates an accumulator and triggers it itself. It passes this to `setupPass()` to allow the first pass to begin immediately. Each call to `setupPass()` returns the next value for `waitFor`, the accumulator that will signal the completion of the pass.

The first two passes use sequences of approximately five and seven elements, respectively. This was chosen at the whim of the implementer without any research supporting it as a good decision. Subsequent passes use increments approximately 1/2.2 as large as the previous. The last increment is one, of course. The loop skips the increment i.e., two and goes directly to one because 2/2.2 would go directly to zero, skipping an increment of one.

After setting up the computation, `sort()` simply waits for the accumulator `waitFor` to be triggered, indicating that the computation is over.

Notice that `sort()`, `setupPass()`, and `setupSequence()` do not do any of the actual computation themselves. They set up the chore graph, and the chores do the computation. Moreover, the chore graph starts executing before it is completely set up.

The performance of `Shellsort6` is shown in Figure 8–3. As with the other charts, the results are for a Java system with kernel threads on a dual-processor system. In this case, two threads, the same as the number of processors, performed best.

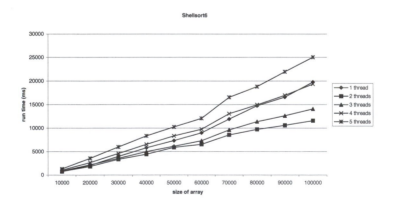

Figure 8–3 Performance of `ShellSort 6`.

One high cost paid by `Shellsort6` is the large number of `SortPass` and `IMerge` objects it creates. Just as we have been reusing threads by the use of run queues, we can reuse these `SortPass` and `IMerge` objects. We implemented `ShellSort6F`, a version of `ShellSort6` that uses factories to create `SortPass` and `IMerge` objects. These factories provide recycling. When a `SortPass` or `IMerge` object comes to the end of its `run()` method, it passes itself to the `recycle()` method of its factory. The factory saves the object on a stack. When called to allocate an object, the factory reuses an object from the stack, or if the stack is empty, it allocates a new object. Recycling is much like explicit deallocation of storage in C or C++. You might worry that a recycled object may still be in use, just as explicitly freed objects may be, introducing obscure bugs when the same storage is being reused as two different objects. It is not a problem in this case, since when `SortPass` and `IMerge` objects come to the end of their `run()` methods, they will be abandoned.

The performance of `ShellSort6F` is shown in Figure 8–4. Again, two threads performed best. In Figure 8–5, we compare the best series for the shell sort using a barrier (see Figure 6–12 on page 194), `ShellSort6` and `ShellSort6F`. `ShellsortBarrier` is comparable to `ShellSort6`, although at larger array sizes, `ShellSort6` appears to be gaining the advantage. `ShellSort6F`'s speed is about five times the speed of `ShellSort6`. (That is, it runs in about 1/5 the time.) It's clear that recycling pays.

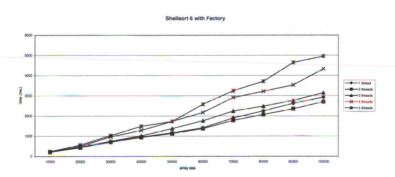

Figure 8–4 Performance of `ShellSort6F`, a version of `ShellSort6` using factories and recycling.

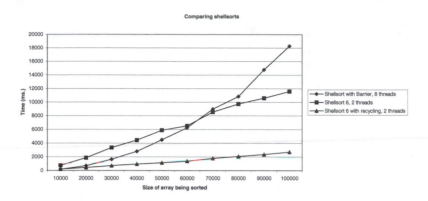

Figure 8–5 Comparison of three versions of the shell sort.

Chapter Wrap-up

In this chapter, we continued to explore programming with chores. We looked at some more synchronization classes in the thread package that implements `RunDelayed`: barriers, accumulators, and shared termination groups. All have corresponding factories that can create synchronization objects that use specified run queues for the delayed runnables.

Shared Tables of Queues

The `SharedTableOfQueues` class provides an associative data structure that facilitates coordination and communication among a group of threads and chores. It was inspired by the Linda project, whose *tuple space* is used to provide shared directories and queues. JavaSpaces is another knock-off of Linda.

Shared tables of queues are a shared-memory data structure. When we show how to encode other synchronization operations using them, you may wonder why we bother, since we have other, more specialized and more efficient classes for the same purposes. One reason is that we will show a distributed-memory system based on shared table of queues. (See the section entitled "Memo: A Remote Interface to `SharedTableOfQueues`.") Many of the algorithms we show will work the same way in the distributed memory version.

Shared Tables of Queues

The class `SharedTableOfQueues` combines directories and queues. Since both directories and queues are long known to be useful, it is no wonder that the combined data structure is versatile and convenient.

Methods

A shared table of queues is like a hash table, but values put into the table are queued, rather than replacing the previous value.

```
SharedTableOfQueues
public SharedTableOfQueues()
public void put(Object key,  Object value)
public Object get(Object key)
            throws InterruptedException
public Object look(Object key)
            throws InterruptedException
public boolean isEmpty(Object key)
public Object getFuture(Object key)
public Object lookFuture(Object key)
public Object getSkip(Object key)
public Object lookSkip(Object key)
public void runDelayed(Object key, Runnable r)
```

Queues are automatically created in the table when a value is put in. The names of the queues can be any object, just as in hash tables. The queues are also automatically created when a thread or chore waits for a value to be placed in it. Only objects, or null, can be placed in the queue, not primitive types. Placing null in the queue can cause some confusion, as we describe for methods `getSkip()` and `lookSkip()`.

When there are no more items in the queue and no threads or chores are waiting for a value to be placed in the queue, the queue is removed, since if it is needed later, it will be created in exactly the state it was in when it was removed.

The `get(key)` and `look(key)` methods are used to look up values in the queues. The `get()` method removes and returns the first value in the queue. The `look()` method returns a reference to the first value without removing it. Both `look()` and `get()` are blocking: They will wait for the queue to be nonempty before returning.

Methods `getSkip()` and `lookSkip()` are versions of `look` and `get` that return immediately, yielding the value they found if they were successful or null if the queue was empty.

Methods `getFuture()` and `lookFuture()` do not return the values in the queue, but rather futures containing those values. If the value is already present, the future will be returned with the value already assigned to it. If the value is not already present, the future will initially be unassigned, but will be assigned the value when it is put in the queue later.

Finally, there is a `runDelayed()` method that leaves a runnable object to be scheduled when the queue becomes nonempty.

Here are the methods in more detail:

Constructor. There is a single parameterless constructor, `SharedTableOfQueues()`.

put(). Method `put(Object key, Object value)` puts an object or null `value` into the queue with name `key`. It creates a queue with name `key` if one is not already present.

get(). Method `get(Object key)` removes and returns a reference from the queue named `key`. If the queue is empty, `get()` waits for something to be put into the queue. It throws `InterruptedException` if the thread was interrupted while waiting.

look(). Method `look(Object key)` returns a reference to the first object in the queue named `key`. If the first item in the queue is null, of course, look returns that. If the queue is empty, `look()` waits for something to be put into the queue. The object is not removed from the queue. It throws `InterruptedException` if the thread was interrupted while waiting.

isEmpty(). Method `isEmpty(Object key)` returns true if there is no queue in the shared table of queues with the name `key`, or if there is, the queue has no items queued in it.

getFuture(). Method `getFuture(Object key)` immediately returns a future. The future will contain the first object (or null) in the queue. If the queue is empty, `getFuture()` will return the future anyway, and the value will be assigned to that future when some value is enqueued later. Because this is a *get* method, the value in the future is removed from the queue.

lookFuture(). Method `lookFuture(Object key)` returns the future that is to contain the first value in the queue. The future is returned immediately. If the queue isn't empty, the future will have the value already in it. If the queue is empty, the future will be assigned when some value is placed in the queue later.

getSkip(). Method getSkip(Object key) removes and returns the first value from the queue named key. If the queue is empty, it returns null. In any event, it returns immediately.

lookSkip(). Method lookSkip(Object key) returns the first value in the queue named key. If the queue is empty, it returns null immediately. The value is not removed from the queue.

runDelayed(). Method runDelayed(Object key, Runnable r) places the runnable object r in a run queue as soon as the queue named key is nonempty. Method runDelayed() returns immediately.

Implementing Synchronizations Using a Shared Table of Queues

We will show in this section how shared tables of queues can be used to implement a wide variety of concurrent programming patterns: locked objects, semaphores, queues, bounded buffers, reactive objects, barriers, and *I*-structures. The number of uses is not surprising; both directories (tables) and queues are widely used in programming systems.

Named Futures. A shared table of queues allows you to create named futures. The important instruction to use is

```
Future f=stoq.lookFuture(name)
```

where name can be any object. All threads that look up the future with the same name will get a reference to the same future. The future can be assigned a value v directly, by calling its setValue() method, as in

```
f.setValue(v)
```

or indirectly by calling

```
stoq.put(name,v)
```

There are three major dangers in using a shared table of queues to get named futures:

1. Be sure that you call lookFuture() rather than getFuture(). Method getFuture() returns a different future each call.

2. Be sure, of course, that you are not using the same name in the table for any other purpose.

3. If the futures are not removed from the table and if the whole table is not discarded, the futures will not be garbage collected.

As an alternative, you could just use the queue itself as a future with the following equivalences:

`f.getValue()`	`stoq.look(n)`
`f.setValue(v)`	`stoq.put(n,v)`
`f.isSet()`	`!stoq.isEmpty(n)`

Here, `f` is a future and `n` is the name of the simulated future.

If all you want are named futures, you may prefer to use the `FutureTable` class, rather than using a shared table of queues. `FutureTable` is presented in the section entitled "Future Tables."

Named, Locked Records.
There are several ways to used a shared table of queues to share named, locked records among threads.

Technique 1. The easiest way is to use the shared table of queues as a directory. Simply place the shared record in the table with

```
stoq.put(name,record)
```

When threads need to use it, they call

```
Record rec=(Record)stoq.look(name);
synchronized (rec){/*operate on record*/}
```

Technique 2. A way to lock records that is more in the spirit of the shared table of queues is

```
Record rec=(Record)stoq.get(name);
{/*operate on record*/}
stoq.put(name,rec);
```

This second form removes the record from the table while it is being operated on. Other threads have to wait at their `get()` calls until the record is replaced before they can access it.

Named Locks.
Technique 2 for implementing locked records can also be used for named locks. Simply keep one object in the shared table under the name. As long as the object is in the table, the lock is unlocked. To lock the name, get the object from the table. To unlock it, put an object back in.

To initialize the lock, use

```
stoq.put(name,"X");
```

To lock the name, use

```
stoq.get(name);
```

To unlock the name, use

```
stoq.put(name,"X");
```

Named Semaphores. Named semaphores can work the same way as locks, which are simply binary semaphores. Initialization and the down and up operations are simply coded.

To initialize the semaphore to a count *n,* use

```
for(int initCount=n;initCount>0;initCount--)
        stoq.put(name,"X");
```

To down the semaphore, use

```
stoq.get(name);
```

To up the semaphore, use

```
stoq.put(name,"X");
```

Named Queues. It is almost too obvious to state, but the following are queue operations and their equivalents.

`q.get()`	`stoq.get(n)`
`q.put(v)`	`stoq.put(n,v)`
`q.isEmpty()`	`stoq.isEmpty(n)`

Here, `q` is a queue and `n` is the name of a simulated queue.

On a concurrent system, queues of this sort are dangerous. The producer can run arbitrarily far ahead of the consumer, exhausting the memory. It is better to use bounded buffers, which we will show below.

Indexed Keys

Although any object can be used as a key in a shared table of queues, the `IndexedKey` class provides convenient keys for some of our purposes. An indexed key has two fields: `id` and `x`. Field `id` is in effect a name, and `x` is an index. Keys with the same `id` can be considered parts of the same data object, the parts of that object differing in their x field.

The methods of `IndexedKey` are shown in the box. `IndexedKey` has no public constructors, but it does provide a number of factory methods. Static method `make(id,x)` creates an indexed key with the specified `id` and `x` fields.

```
IndexedKey
  private int id;  private long x;
  public static IndexedKey make(int id,long x)
  public static IndexedKey unique(long x)
  public int getId()
  public long getX()
  public IndexedKey at(long x)
  public IndexedKey add(long x)
  public boolean equals(Object o)
  public int hashCode()
  public String toString()
```

Static method `unique(x)` creates an indexed key with a unique `id` field and the specified `x` field. The `id` fields are generated by a random-number generator and will not repeat unless you rapidly generate unique indexed keys for a long time. Moreover, the `id` fields generated will not lie in the range of values for short integers. If you restrict the `id` fields you pass to `make()` to shorts, unique keys will not collide with them either.

Calling `k.at(x)` creates another `IndexedKey` object with the same `id` as `k`, but with its `x` field replaced. It is equivalent to `IndexedKey.make(k.getId(),x)`. Calling `k.add(x)` adds to the `x` field. It is equivalent to `IndexedKey.make(k.getId(), k.getX() + x)`.

There is no way to change the contents of an indexed key. Since indexed keys are designed to be used as keys in tables, the ability to change them would not be safe. The `id` and `x` fields are hashed to place the key in the hash table. If the fields change, the key couldn't be found again.

Two indexed keys with equal `id` and `x` fields are reported equal by `equals()`. Method `hashCode()`, of course, is needed to look up the indexed keys in the hash table that a shared table of queues uses.

The code shown in Example 9-1, has several points of interest.

The implementation of `IndexedKey` uses two random-number generators from class `java.util.Random`. The generator `rand` is used to generate the unique symbols. The generator `hasher` is used to generate hash codes for indexed keys. Since these are static and must be shared among all indexed keys, they must be locked while in use. `Hasher` is used to hash the `id` and `x` fields as follows: The sum of the `id` and `x` fields is fed into `hasher` as a new seed; then, the second random integer from the series is used as the hash value. Actually, the first random number from the series ought to be sufficiently random, but visual inspection led us to suspect that it was not.

Example 9-1 Class `IndexedKey`

```java
import java.util.Random;
class IndexedKey {
 private static Random rand=new Random();
 private static Random hasher=new Random();
 private int id;  private long x;
 private IndexedKey(long x){
    synchronized (rand) {
        for (id=rand.nextInt();
            id < Short.MIN_VALUE && Short.MAX_VALUE < id;
            id=rand.nextInt());
    }
    this.x=x;
 }
 private IndexedKey(int id, long x){this.id=id; this.x=x;}
 public static IndexedKey unique(long x){
    return new IndexedKey(x);
 }
 public static IndexedKey make(int id,long x){
    return new IndexedKey(id,x);
 }
 public int getId(){return id;}
 public long getX(){return x;}
 public IndexedKey at(long x){
    return new IndexedKey(id,x);
 }
 public IndexedKey add(long x){
    return new IndexedKey(id,this.x+x);
 }
 public boolean equals(Object o){
    if (o instanceof IndexedKey) {
        IndexedKey k=(IndexedKey)o;
        return id == k.id && x == k.x;
    } else return false;
 }
 public int hashCode(){
    synchronized(hasher) {
        hasher.setSeed(id+x);
        hasher.nextInt();
        return hasher.nextInt();
    }
 }
 public String toString(){
    return "IndexedKey("+id+","+x+")";
 }
}
```

Implementing More Synchronizations and Shared Structures

Now we will consider some more shared data structures and synchronization objects built on a shared table of queues that use `IndexedKey` in their implementation.

Bounded buffers. Since a shared table of queues contains queues, half of a bounded buffer is already provided. The only problem is to restrict the number of items that can be placed in a queue. For this, we can use another queue containing arbitrary tokens that represent available slots in the queue of items. The code is shown in Example 9-2. We use two indexed keys as names of the queues. These keys were generated by `IndexedKey.unique()`. They differ from each other in the x field. The name `fulls` is used to access the queue of values. The queue named `empties` holds arbitrary tokens—actually, it holds string objects "X". To put something into the queue, a thread must first remove a token from the `empties` queue, which indicates that it has acquired an empty slot in the queue. When a thread gets a value out of the queue, it puts a token back into `empties`, allowing another item to be placed in the queue.

You might consider this to be a combination of a queue and a semaphore.

Example 9-2 Bounded buffer using a shared table of queues

```java
class BBuffer {
 private IndexedKey fulls=IndexedKey.unique(0);
 private IndexedKey empties=fulls.at(1);
 private SharedTableOfQueues stoq=new SharedTableOfQueues();

 public BBuffer(int num){
    for (int i=num;i>0;i--)stoq.put(empties,"X");
 }
 public void put(Object x){
    try {
       stoq.get(empties);
       stoq.put(fulls,x);
    } catch (InterruptedException e){}
 }
 public Object get(){
    Object x=null;
    try {
       x=stoq.get(fulls);
       stoq.put(empties,"X");
    } catch (InterruptedException e){}
    return x;
 }
}
```

I-structures. One of the big conceptual problems in dataflow is dealing with structured objects—arrays and records. One conceives of objects flowing among instructions in tokens, but arrays are too large to move around. Dataflow machines have had to resort to *structure stores* to hold structured objects, but these must be made compatible with the dataflow single-assignment principle.

The researcher Arvind named these structures in dataflow machines *I-structures*, or incremental structures. The structures are not present all at once. The components are assigned values over time, and each component is assigned at most once. The structure grows incrementally. Attempts to fetch a component of an *I*-structure must wait until that component has been assigned a value.

For macrodataflow, an *I*-structure can be composed of futures. With shared tables of queues and indexed keys, an *I*-structure can be an associative array of futures.

Barriers. An implementation of a barrier is shown in Example 9-3. The idea is that a barrier has to keep track of both how many threads still have to gather at it and the total number of threads that will be gathering at it. As threads gather, they decrement the count of remaining threads. When the count goes to zero, it is reset to the total number of synchronizing threads. The threads must have mutual exclusion when manipulating the remaining count. All threads except the last to gather at a barrier must wait for the last thread to arrive.

We have implemented this barrier so that threads have to register with it. When they call `register()`, they get handles on the barrier, which are of class `BarrierTQ.Handle`. The intent of this is to show how the threads can synchronize without using any shared object, but the shared table of queues and the data it contains. This is a model for how distributed programs can communicate through a shared table of queues on a remote machine. We will show such an implementation, `Memo`, later in: "Memo: A Remote Interface to `SharedTableOfQueues`."

We use a shared, named, locked record to keep the total count of threads and the remaining count. We remove it to examine and change the remaining count. All threads except the last replace it in the shared table of queues.

The threads that must delay until the last one gathers delay by calling `look()`. The value they are looking for will be placed in the table by the last thread to arrive at the `gather()`.

The tricky part of the implementation is to use the record holding the count and remaining fields as the item that the waiting threads look for to continue after a gather. This record will be moved through a series of queues. The x field of this key constitutes a step number. The record is placed in a queue at the beginning of a step. At the end of a step, it is removed from one queue and placed in the next.

Example 9-3 **Barrier using a shared table of queues**

```
class BarrierTQ {
 private IndexedKey initialKey=IndexedKey.unique(0);
 private SharedTableOfQueues stoq=new SharedTableOfQueues();
 private int stillToRegister;
 private class X{
    public int remaining,count;
    X(int c){remaining=count=c;}
 }
 public BarrierTQ(int num){
    stillToRegister = num;
    stoq.put(initialKey,new X(num));
 }
 public class Handle{
    private IndexedKey current=initialKey;
  public void gather(){
    try {
    X x=(X)stoq.get(current);
    x.remaining--;
    if (x.remaining==0) {
       x.remaining=x.count;
       current=current.add(1);
       stoq.put(current,x);
    } else {
       stoq.put(current,x);
       current=current.add(1);
       stoq.look(current);
    }
    } catch (InterruptedException e){}
  }
 }
 public Handle register() {
    if (stillToRegister-- > 0) return new Handle();
    else throw new IllegalStateException();
 }
 public String toString(){
    return "BarrierTQ("+initialKey.getId()+")";
 }
}
```

All the threads will use one value of their indexed key when they gather. They remove the record there, decrement the remaining count, and if the count isn't zero, they replace the record in the queue from which they retrieved it. Then, they look for a record to show up in the queue whose name is one larger in the index field. There is no record there already, so they wait. When the last thread gathers, it resets the remaining count, but does not replace the thread in the queue it got it from. Instead, it places it in the queue named with an x field one larger than before. When the other threads see this record, they know that all threads have gathered, so they can proceed.

Reactive Objects

Reactive objects, or Actors, provide a way of thinking about massively parallel computation. The idea is that each component of a data structure is an active, programmed entity. These objects can run in parallel, communicating by message passing. They can be used to implement data-parallel algorithms (i.e., algorithms that operate on all the components of data structures in parallel).

A reactive object is an object that receives messages and responds to them. It is only active when it has messages to process; it reacts to messages. In several of the reactive object programming systems, the code for a reactive resembles the code for a chore; it is entered at the beginning for each message it receives, like a chore being reentered at the beginning of its `run()` method.

One of the inspirations for reactive objects was to program massively parallel computers composed of hundreds of thousands of tiny computers. Dozens of the tiny computers could be placed on the same chip. Although each of the tiny computers would have a slow processor and little memory, each of them could be running in parallel, and the very number of them would make computations run blitzingly fast. It was envisioned that the programs on the tiny computers could be reactive objects.

It turned out that the idea didn't work for a number of reasons, but as is the case with dataflow, building massive systems of reactive objects is a programming technique that can sometimes be useful.

Each object in a reactive-object system has a mailbox for receiving messages and a program there that receives the messages and does the computing. The address, or name, of the object is the address of its mailbox as far as the system is concerned.

In a pure reactive object system, the objects only communicate by sending messages. There is no direct way to call a method in another object. Rather, the caller sends a message and then receives a reply message.

There are a number of ways to implement reactive-object systems using a shared table of queues. In all of them, the mailboxes are queues in the shared table. We will call the shared table `mailboxes` in the following examples. The name of the reactive object is the key that maps to its mailbox queue.

1. Each reactive object can be a thread. The object itself is the key that maps to its mailbox.

A reactive object waits for mail by executing

```
Object msg = mailboxes.get(this)
```

That is, it looks itself up in the mailboxes to find its message queue.

To send a reactive object `ro` and a message, simply call

```
mailboxes.put(ro,message)
```

2. Reactive objects may easily be decoupled from their names. You can use a `String` object to give a descriptive name to an object, or use an indexed key, which allows you to create unique new names whenever you wish. The object now needs to know its name explicitly, changing the message reception to

```
Object msg = mailboxes.get(myName)
```

There is an advantage to using indexed keys for names. Reactive objects have been proposed for array processing, with each array element, row, or block, being a reactive object. In theory, you should be able to get large amounts of parallelism. All the components of an array could be sent messages telling them to negate themselves, take their absolute values, or send themselves to the corresponding blocks of another array to be added.

But many reactive-object systems have referenced objects by pointer only. Each element of an array has its individual name, and knowing the name of one array element will not tell you the name of any other. That tends to mean that arrays have to be implemented as linked structures. A two-dimensional array could be implemented as a binary search tree with the two indices as the key. The nodes of the trees would themselves be reactive objects, so to send a message to one array element, you would send the message to the root of the tree, which would pass it to its left or right child, which would do the same until the message got to the correct node in the tree and the correct array element.

Alternatively, a two-dimensional array could be implemented as doubly-linked lists of the elements in its rows and columns, with the array's address being the address of its upper left element. Again, to get a message to a particular array element, you would first send the message to a single element, the upper left element.

It was very difficult to write array algorithms without flooding the entry node of one array or another with messages, causing a bottleneck. Actually, it is worse than a bottleneck for those machines with a massive number of small processors, as the nodes would run out of queue space and crash.

With indexed keys, the elements of the array can be addressed directly, so there is less likelihood of flooding single reactive objects with messages.

3. Reactive-object systems are often designed with the idea that there will be huge numbers of objects. It would be overly expensive if all of these objects were threads. It is desirable to implement them as chores.

With chores, the code for receiving a message becomes something more like the following:

```
public void run() {
  Object msg = mailboxes.getSkip(myName)
  if (msg==null) {
    mailboxes.runDelayed(myName,this);
    return;
  }
  . . .
```

Here it is assumed that messages are never null. As is usual with chores, and with reactive objects for that matter, the object receives a message at the start of its run() method.

If we are going to write code in the style of reactive-object systems that only are dispatched when there is a message present, our code could be as follows:

```
public void run() {
  Object msg = mailboxes.get(myName)
  . . .
  mailboxes.runDelayed(myName,this);
}
```

If the reactive object is run delayed on its message queue when it is first created, this code should work fine.

4. An advantage of implementing reactive objects as chores communicating through shared tables of queues over traditional reactive-object designs is that our objects can have more than one message queue. Traditionally, reactive objects have only one queue, and they must process the messages in the queue in first-come, first-served order. However, object A may wish to use object B as a subroutine. So, suppose A is receiving requests for service and calls object B as a subroutine by sending B a message. Object B can only return by sending messages back to A. So object A receives a request, sends a subroutine call message to object B, and must receive the response from B before it can respond to the request. But, suppose the first object receives another request for service before it receives the response to its first subroutine call. It can't respond to its first call until it receives a later message, but it must handle messages FIFO, so it must start processing another request before responding to the previous one. This is typically handled by enqueueing the service requests in an external queue. The external queue is itself a linked list of reactive objects. This certainly complicates the coding.

With multiple queues, object A can request a response from object B in a second message queue. It waits for the response in that queue before going back to the first queue to handle more requests.

Communicating through a Shared Table of Queues

A shared table of queues makes it easy to set up communications between threads. Both threads can compute names individually and then communicate through the objects at those named slots in the table.

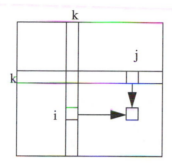

Figure 9–1 Dataflow in Warshall's algorithm.

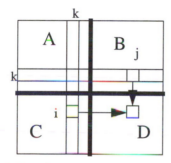

Figure 9–2 Dataflow among blocks in Warshall's algorithm.

Warshall's Algorithm.

```
for (k=0; k<N; k++)
    for (i=0; i<N; i++)
        for (j=0; j<N; j++)
            A[i][j] = A[i][j] || (A[i][k] && A[k][j]) ;
```

As an example of this, we will implement Warshall's algorithm yet again.

The overall structure of our implementation is shown in Example 9-4. As you did with the other implementations, you first create a `WarshallTQ` object and then call its

Example 9-4 Structure of Warshall's algorithm using a shared table of queues

```
class WarshallTQ{
  int blkSize;
  public WarshallTQ(int blkSize){
    this.blkSize=blkSize;
  }
  private class Block extends Thread {
    Block(...){...}
    public void run(){...}
  public void closure(boolean[][] a) {...}
}
```

Example 9-5 Method `closure()`

```
public void closure(boolean[][] a) {
    int i,j,NR,NC;
    SharedTableOfQueues tbl=new SharedTableOfQueues();
    IndexedKey kthRows=IndexedKey.unique(0);
    IndexedKey kthCols=IndexedKey.unique(0);
    NR=a.length;
    NC=a[0].length;
    int nt=((NR+blkSize-1)/blkSize)*((NC+blkSize-1)/blkSize);
    Accumulator done=new Accumulator(nt);
    for (i=0;i<NR;i+=blkSize)
        for (j=0;j<NC;j+=blkSize){
            new Block(a,i,j,tbl,
                kthRows,kthCols,done).start();
        }
    try {
        done.getFuture().getValue();
    } catch (InterruptedException ex){}
}
```

`closure()` method passing it the array to compute the transitive closure of. In this case, the parameter you pass to the constructor is not the number of threads to use. This implementation of Warshall's algorithm divides the array into rectangular blocks. Mostly, they will be square, but the last blocks along a side of the array can have unequal sides. The parameter passed, `blkSize`, is the length of the side of a square block, so the blocks will be $blkSize \times blkSize$ squares where possible.

Example 9-6 Class `Block`

```
private class Block extends Thread {
    boolean[][] a;
    boolean[][] block;
    int r,c; //upperleft
    int nr,nc;
    int N;
    SharedTableOfQueues tbl;
    IndexedKey rows, cols;
    Accumulator done;

    Block( boolean[][] a,
        int r, int c,
        SharedTableOfQueues tbl,
        IndexedKey rows,
        IndexedKey cols,
        Accumulator done){
      this.a=a;
      this.r=r;
      this.c=c;
      N = a.length;
      this.tbl=tbl;
      this.rows=rows;
      this.cols=cols;
      this.done=done;
    }
    public void run(){ ... }
}
```

Each block is given its own thread, so the number of threads created for an $N \times N$ array will be $\lceil N/(\texttt{blksize}) \rceil \times \lceil N/(\texttt{blksize}) \rceil$.

We have repeated the code for Warshall's algorithm in the box. The outer k loop iterates over the steps of the algorithm. The inner two, i and j, loops choose all elements of the array to be updated. Each `A[i,j]` has `A[i][k] && A[k][j]` disjoined with it. `A[i][k]` is the element at row i in the kth column, and `A[k][j]` is the element in the jth column of the kth row. The flow of information to `A[i,j]` is shown in Figure 9–1.

In versions of Warshall's algorithm shown before in the section entitled, "Chore Examples: Warshall's Algorithm," a chore was responsible for processing an entire row. If the chore had the kth row on the kth step of the algorithm, it had to communicate that row to the other chores.

Example 9-7   **Method** `run()` **from class** `Block`

```java
public void run(){
  int i,j;
  int k;
  boolean IHaveRow, IHaveColumn;
  boolean[] row=null, col=null;
  nr=Math.min(blkSize,a.length-r);
  nc=Math.min(blkSize,a[0].length-c);
  this.block=new boolean[nr][nc];
  for (i=0;i<nr;i++)
    for (j=0;j<nc;j++)
       block[i][j]=a[r+i][c+j];
  try {
   for (k=0;k<N;k++) {
     IHaveRow = k-r>=0 && k-r < nr;
     IHaveColumn = k-c>=0 && k-c < nc;
     if (IHaveRow) {
      tbl.put(rows.at(k+c*N),block[k-r].clone());
      row = block[k-r];
     }
     if (IHaveColumn) {
      col=new boolean[nr];
      for (j=0;j<nr;j++) col[j]=block[j][k-c];
      tbl.put(cols.at(k+r*N),col);
     }
     if (!IHaveRow) {
      row = (boolean[])tbl.look(rows.at(k+c*N));
     }
     if (!IHaveColumn) {
      col=(boolean[])tbl.look(cols.at(k+r*N));
     }
     for (i=0;i<nr;i++)
       if (col[i])
         for (j=0;j<nc;j++)
             block[i][j] |= row[j];
   }//end for k

   for (i=0;i<nr;i++)
     for (j=0;j<nc;j++)
       a[r+i][c+j]=block[i][j];
   done.signal();
  }catch (InterruptedException iex){}
}
```

Since we now divide the array into rectangular blocks and give them to threads, no thread has an entire row or an entire column that it can pass to other threads. In Figure 9–2, we draw in the edges of blocks. The element that is to be updated is in block D. Block D needs values of the kth row, stored in block B, and the kth column, stored in Block C. The block that holds a portion of the kth row during the kth step of the algorithm must pass it to all the other blocks in its column, and the block holding a portion of the kth column must pass it to all the blocks in its row.

The way a block will pass a portion of a row or column to the other interested threads is by putting it in a shared table of queues with the key indicating the step of the algorithm, k, and the position of the block in its column or row.

closure. The `closure()` method, shown in Example 9-5, sets up the computation. It is passed the array to be processed. It proceeds as follows:

- It creates a shared table of queues to use and two **IndexedKey** objects to be used in naming the data being passed.

- It calculates the number of threads `nt` it will create and creates an `Accumulator` object for those threads to signal their completion in.

- It loops to create `Block` threads to do the actual processing. Each `Block` is told the original array to process and the indices of the upper left corner element in its block.

- It awaits completion of the threads.

Block. The structure of the `Block` class is shown in Example 9-6. The constructor copies its parameters into the corresponding fields of the instance. The fields have the following meanings:

- `a` is the entire array passed to `closure`.

- `block` is an array containing the block this thread is to work on. The `run()` method copies block from a portion of `a` at the beginning of its execution and copies the updated block back at the end.

- `r` and `c` are the indices of the upper left corner element of the block.

- `N` is the number of rows in the array `a`. It is used the upper bound for the loop incrementing `k`; that is, `N` is the number of steps in the algorithm.

- `nr` and `nc` are the number of rows and columns, respectively, in block.

- `tbl` is the shared table of queues used for communication.

- `rows` and `cols` are the `IndexedKey` objects used to construct the keys used to insert and lookup the portions of rows and columns being communicated.

`Block`'s `run()` method is shown in Example 9-7. It begins by calculating the number of rows and columns in its block; `blkSize` is used unless fewer rows or columns than that remain. Then it creates its `block` array and copies a portion of array a into it.

The main loop of the algorithm cycles through all k steps. Index k is an actual row and column index in the full array. However, indices i and j are indices into the local array `block`.

The loop first figures out whether this block contains a portion of the kth row or kth column. If so, it makes them available by placing them in the shared table of queues. We'll look at the computation of the table index later.

If the block doesn't contain a section of the kth row, it reads it from the table, waiting for the row to be placed there by the block that has it. Similarly, if the block doesn't contain the kth column, it looks it up in the table. Both rows and columns are stored as boolean arrays.

To understand the construction of indices, consider the line

```
row = (boolean[])tbl.look(rows.at(k+c*N));
```

We look up the kth row for our column by looking in the shared table of queues at an index we construct. We start off with `IndexedKey` rows. The id field of `rows` will be in all the keys that name rows. We substitute a computed value for the x field of `rows`. This x field must indicate the step of the algorithm k and which column this piece of row k is in. If two blocks are in the same column, their upper left elements have the same column index. We use the value of c. Since we multiply c by N and k will always be less than N, we will have unique names for each portion of a row placed in the table.

Performance. The performance of `WarshallTQ` is shown in Figure 9–3. Unlike the other versions of Warshall's algorithm, the series does not directly correspond to the number of threads used. Rather, the series corresponds to the size of the blocks the array is divided into. The number of threads will be the number of blocks, $\left\lceil \frac{N}{B} \right\rceil^2$, where N is the number of rows and columns in the array and B is the number of rows and columns in a block. The ceiling operator is used, of course, because we allocate threads to any remaining partial blocks at the ends of rows and columns. The number of threads thus varies with the array size along the series for any given block size.

The series with block size 300×300 allocates only one thread for all the array sizes shown here. The 25×25 block size allocates from four to 144 threads.

In this case, a 100×100 block size worked best. It provided parallelism without flooding the program with threads.

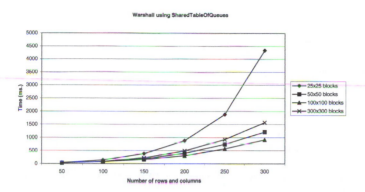

Figure 9–3 Performance of `WarshallTQ`.

Having introduced all the versions of Warshall's algorithm, we are now in a position to compare the best series of each. These results are shown in Figure 9–4. The winners are `Warshall1` with 2 threads and `WarshallTQ` with a 100×100 block size.

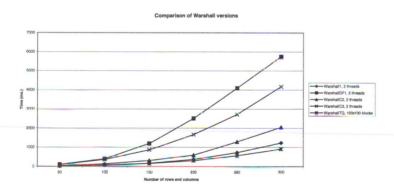

Figure 9–4 Comparison of versions of Warshall's algorithm.

Future Queues

The queues in a `SharedTableOfQueues` object are instances of the `FutureQueue` class. Although designed to facilitate the implementation of `SharedTableOfQueues`, `FutureQueue` objects have uses of their own.

FutureQueue

```
FutureQueue()
FutureQueue(FutureFactory f)
FutureQueue(RunQueue r)
Future get()
Object getSkip()
boolean isEmpty()
boolean isVacant()
Future look()
Object lookSkip()
void put(Object obj)
void runDelayed(Runnable r)
```

The idea behind future queues is this: In a normal FIFO queue, items are placed in the queue by calls to put() and removed from the queue by calls to get(). If a thread tries to get an item from the queue and there are no items present, the thread is delayed until there is an item to return to it. In a FutureQueue object, get() immediately returns a Future object. The futures are filled in with the items put in the queue as they become available. If a thread calls get().getValue(), it will wait until the time an item is enqueued, the same as it would if it tried to get a value out of a normal FIFO queue.

So why not use a normal queue? There are a couple of reasons for this. First, a future queue provides FIFO service whereas Java schedulers do not. Second, a future queue allows a thread to put in a reservation without blocking, which may be useful.

Methods

A FutureQueue object uses a FutureFactory object to generate the futures it uses. You can create a future queue specifying the future factory or a run queue to use in creating its own future factory. Or you can just let it use the Future class's run queue. If you are not using runDelayed(), you might as well use the default.

A FutureQueue is a first-in first-out queue. Items are added to the queue by its put() method. Items are removed and returned by get(), but get() has two differences from conventional FIFO queues:

1. Method get() immediately returns a future that contains the item removed from the queue rather than the item itself.

2. The future returned by get() may have its value filled in later, when the item is enqueued.

So, it is not the thread calling `get()` that is enqueued to wait for an item to return, but the future returned to that thread that waits.

It may help to understand a bit of the internal states of a `FutureQueue` object.

A `FutureQueue` object is essentially a pair of queues. One contains objects (and null references), and the other contains futures. At most, one of those queues will have something in it at a time. When you get an item out of the future queue, you will be given a future that the next item in the queue of objects will be placed in.

If you try to get an item out of the queue and there are items already waiting, you will be given the first in a future. If you try to get an item and there are no items there, you will be given a future, and the future will be placed in the queue of futures.

When you put an item into the future queue, the `put()` method checks whether there are futures enqueued. If there are, the first future is removed, and the item is placed in it. If there are no futures waiting, the item is enqueued in the normal way.

The following explains this in more detail:

get(). The `get()` method returns a future. If there are items enqueued, the first enqueued item is removed and placed in the future. If there are no items enqueued, the future will be placed FIFO on the queue of futures.

put(). The `put(obj)` method puts the value of `obj` into the future queue. If there are futures waiting in the queue of futures, the first one is removed, and `obj` is placed in it. That future has already been given to some thread that executed `get()` or `look()`. If, on the other hand, there are no futures enqueued, `obj` is placed in a FIFO queue to wait for a `get()`.

isEmpty(). Method `isEmpty()` returns true if there are no objects or nulls queued up. It would still return true if there are futures queued up waiting for puts.

isVacant(). Method `isVacant()` returns true if `isEmpty()` returns true, there are no futures enqueued, and there are no runnables rundelayed on the queue. Method `isVacant()` is used by the shared table of queues to determine that the future queue can be removed from the table. The future queue is vacant if it is in the state it would initially be created in, so if it is detected to be vacant and is removed from the table, and is ever referred to again, it will be created in exactly the same state it currently has.

getSkip(). Method `getSkip()` returns the first object from the queue of objects, not a future. It removes the object it returns. If `isEmpty()` would return true, `getSkip()` immediately returns null, which means that you should not enqueue nulls if you intend to use `getSkip()`—you won't be able to distinguish the value null from the empty indication.

look(). Method look() returns a future. It's implementation is a bit ticklish. If there are objects enqueued, it returns the first object in the object queue in the future, without of course removing the object. If the queue of objects is empty, then the future must be saved for subsequent look() calls to return and for a put() to place a value in.

lookSkip(). Method lookSkip() will return the first object in the object queue without removing it if that queue isn't empty. If isEmpty() would return true, lookSkip() immediately returns null. This can, of course, cause trouble if you wish to enqueue nulls.

runDelayed(). Method runDelayed(r) places r in a run queue if and when the future queue isn't empty. It is equivalent to fq.look().runDelayed(r).

Implementation of FutureQueue

The implementation of FutureQueue is intricate. The goal is to have it behave the same as a normal FIFO queue, except that get() and look() return immediately, and they return values in futures, rather than directly.

Desired behavior. It will help to consider two cases.

Suppose you have three puts

```
theQueue.put("a"); theQueue.put("b"); theQueue.put("c");
```

and three gets

```
x=theQueue.get(); y=theQueue.get(); z=theQueue.get();
```

It does not matter how the puts and gets are interspersed. At the end, future x will have a future containing string "a"; y, "b"; and z, "c". All the puts could be done first, last, or interspersed among the gets.

Secondly, calls to look() and calls to get() form groups that we will call look–get groups. If there are several looks in succession, they will return futures containing the same value. A get following those looks will also return that value, but after a get, looks will return a different value. This is clear if the queue already has an item in it. The looks return futures containing the first item in the queue without removing it. A get also returns it, but get removes it. We want looks and gets to have exactly the same behavior, even if the items haven't been enqueued yet.

We will define a look–get group as the longest string of zero or more look() calls terminated by a get() call. These look–get groups may have other calls (e.g. put()) interspersed among them. Remember also that a look–get group may contain no looks and one get. All the operations in the look–get group return a future that will contain the same value.

Example 9-8 shows three sequences of code that will fill array f with the same values.

Example 9-8 Equivalent series of looks, gets, and puts.

```
int i=0;              i=0;                  i=0;
q.put("a");           f[i++]=q.look();      f[i++]=q.look();
q.put("b");           q.put("a");           f[i++]=q.look();
f[i++]=q.look();      f[i++]=q.look();      f[i++]=q.look();
f[i++]=q.look();      q.put("b");           f[i++]=q.get();
f[i++]=q.look();      f[i++]=q.look();      f[i++]=q.look();
f[i++]=q.get();       f[i++]=q.get();       f[i++]=q.get();
f[i++]=q.look();      f[i++]=q.look();      q.put("a");
f[i++]=q.get();       f[i++]=q.get();       q.put("b");
```

States of the future queue. A `FutureQueue` object has three major components:

1. `q`: a queue of items (objects and null values),

2. `qf`: a queue of futures

3. `lf`: a "look future," which may be null.

The future queue may be modeled as an infinite-state machine, since the internal queues are theoretically unbounded. The states of the future queue will change as methods are called. The calls may be considered inputs to the machine. There are two particular rules that the states of the future queue will abide by:

1. Within a look–get group, `lf` will not be null. It will have a reference to the future that all the looks and the get in that group will return. Outside of a look–get group, `lf` will be null.

2. The length of `q` minus the length of `qf` will equal the number of `put`s minus the number of look–get groups that have begun. A look–get group of course begins with its initial `look`, if any, and ends with its terminal `get`.

Fourteen of the states of a future queue are shown in Figure 9–5 along with state transitions. The three major components of the state are written as *(q, qf, lf)*. At most, one of the queues, `q` or `qf`, can be nonempty at a time. When a queue is empty, we write it *[ ]*. When it is nonempty, we write it *[a,...]* or *[f,...]*. The state of `lf` is either *null* or *F*, indicating that it contains a future.

We will discuss the behavior of `get()` and `put()` alone first, and then their behavior in the presence of `look()` calls.

Let's first consider the usual queue transitions, shown in the lower left of the figure. The queue of items can be empty or nonempty. The queue of futures is empty. A `put()` will put an item into the queue of items. A `get()` will remove and return an item. After the

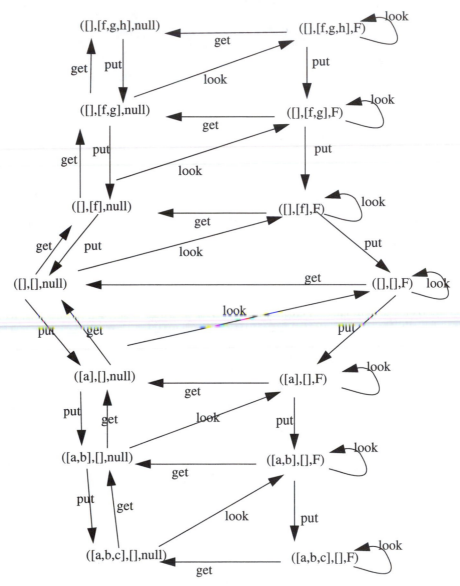

Figure 9–5 States of a future queue.

`put`, the length of `q` will be one greater than before. After a `get()`, it will be one less. Calling `put()` moves us down the column. Calling `get()` moves us up.

Now suppose `get`s run ahead of `put`s. Suppose both queues are empty and `get()` is called. The `get()` method creates a future and places it in the queue of futures and returns the future immediately. Now qf is nonempty, and q is empty. More calls to get() will lengthen the queue of futures.

When the queue of futures qf is nonempty, a put() will remove the first future from the queue and place the item in it. The queue of futures will shrink by one. Again, calling put() moves us down the column. Calling get() moves us up.

These are all the transitions on the left side of the figure.

Now consider what happens when you call look(). Suppose the call is the first look in a look–get group and the queue of items q is empty. When look is called, lf is null. The look() performs the first action of get() by placing a future in the qf. It also saves a reference to that future in lf for subsequent look() calls and the final get() of the look–get group to use. Those two actions take us up (adding to the future queue) and right (setting lf).

It's the same when the initial look() of a look–get group is called when the item queue q is nonempty. The look() will create a future and assign it to lf, moving right. Then it will remove the first item from q and assign it to the future in lf, moving up.

If a look() is called in the midst of a look–get group, it simply returns the future in lf. These are the self-loops on the right side.

When the terminal get() is called in a look–get group that has at least one look in it; that is, when get is called from one of the states on the right-hand side, it returns the future in lf and then clears lf to null. It does not remove an item from q nor enqueue a future in qf, since that has already been done by the initial look() in the group. This moves straight right to left across the figure.

A call to put() on the right side behaves the same as on the left side. If there are waiting futures in qf, it removes the first and places the item in it. If there are no waiting futures, it places the item in q. It moves down the right side.

The overall structure of FutureQueue is shown in Example 9-9. The QueueComponent objects are simple queues that have methods get(), put(), and isEmpty(). They are used as components of several other thread package classes. They are not synchronized, since they are only used within other objects that do synchronize access.

Code for the put() method is shown in Example 9-10. It will dequeue and assign a value to a waiting future if there is one or enqueue the value if there is none.

Method get() has two cases to consider. First, if lf is not null, then this is the end of a series of one or more looks in a look–get group. In this case, the get() merely needs to return the same future the looks returned (i.e., the contents of lf) and to set lf to null so later looks will find a different value. If there weren't any preceding looks, then this get() is both the beginning and the end of a look–get group. It must either remove an

Example 9-9 Overall structure of `FutureQueue`

```
public class FutureQueue {
QueueComponent q=new QueueComponent();
QueueComponent qf=new QueueComponent();
Future lf=null;
FutureFactory ff=null;
public FutureQueue(){...}
public FutureQueue(RunQueue r){...}
public FutureQueue(FutureFactory f){ff=f;}
public synchronized void put(Object obj) {...}
public synchronized boolean isVacant() {...}
public synchronized boolean isEmpty() {...}
public synchronized Future get() {...}
public synchronized Future look() {...}
public void runDelayed(Runnable r){...}
public synchronized Object getSkip() {...}
public synchronized Object lookSkip() {...}
}
```

Example 9-10 Method `put()` of `FutureQueue`

```
public synchronized void put(Object obj) {
    Future f;
    if (!qf.isEmpty()){
        f=(Future)qf.get();
        f.setValue(obj);
    } else {
        q.put(obj);
    }
}
```

item from the queue of items q and return it in a future, or it must enqueue a future in qf if q is empty.

The look() method's behavior is trivial if it is not the first look in a look–get group. It merely returns the future referenced by lf. If it is the first look in the group, it has to create the future used by the group. Then, it must either get the first item from q and put it in the future, or it must enqueue the future in qf, depending on whether there is anything in q to get.

Example 9-11 Method `get()` of `FutureQueue`

```
public synchronized Future get() {
    Object obj;
    Future f;
    if (lf!=null) {
        f=lf;
        lf=null;
        return f;
    }
    if (!q.isEmpty()) {
        obj = q.get();
        lf=null;
        return ff.make(obj);
    }
    f=ff.make();
    qf.put(f);
    return f;
}
```

Example 9-12 Method `look()` of `FutureQueue`

```
public synchronized Future look() {
    Object obj;
    if (lf!=null) return lf;
    lf = ff.make();
    if (!q.isEmpty()) {
        obj=q.get();
        lf.setValue(obj);
    } else {
        qf.put(lf);
    }
    return lf;
}
```

Example of `FutureQueue`: *The Queued Readers–Writers Monitor*

The `QueuedReadersWritersMonitor` is implemented using the `FutureQueue` class. As each reader or writer arrives, it takes the next future from a future queue and waits for a value to be assigned to that future, giving it permission to read or to attempt to write.

State of the monitor. The state of this monitor is contained in two variables:

nr: the number of threads currently reading (>=0).

fq: the FutureQueue object that queues up the threads awaiting permission to read or write.

Example 9-13 Method `startReading()` of `QueuedReadersWritersMonitor`

```
public void startReading()
  throws InterruptedException{
      Future f=fq.get();
      f.getValue();
      synchronized (this) {nr++;}
      fq.put(null);
  }
```

startReading(). If a thread tries to start reading, it takes the token from fq. This token allows it to start reading. It immediately places the token back in the queue, allowing the next thread, if present and if a reader, to start reading too. The readers also increment the count of the number of readers present. If a writer gets the token after a series of readers, it will wait until all the readers are done before proceeding.

Example 9-14 Method `startWriting()` of `QueuedReadersWritersMonitor`

```
public void startWriting()
   throws InterruptedException{
       Future f=fq.get();
       f.getValue();
       synchronized (this) {while(nr>0) wait();}
   }
```

startWriting(). To start writing, a thread not only must get the token, but must wait for the number of readers to go to zero. A writer does not immediately place the token back in the queue because no subsequent reader or writer may proceed until it is done. It waits until it stops writing to place the token into fq.

stopReading(). When a reader finishes reading, it decrements the count of readers. There may be a writer waiting for the count to become zero, so the last reader to finish calls notify() to allow the writer (if there is any) to proceed.

stopWriting(). When a writer finishes writing, it puts the token (null) into the future queue, allowing the next reader or writer to proceed.

Example 9-15 Method `stopReading()` of `QueuedReadersWritersMonitor`

```
public synchronized void stopReading(){
        synchronized(this)nr--;
        if (nr==0) notify();
}
```

Example 9-16 Method `stopWriting()` of `QueuedReadersWritersMonitor`

```
public synchronized void stopWriting(){
        fq.put(null);
}
```

Future Tables

If all you want to use from the shared table of queues is futures, a simpler data structure to

---

FutureTable

`FutureTable()`: This is the constructor. It creates an empty `FutureTable` object.

`Future get(Object key)`: This method looks up the future in the table associated with the key. It creates a future if it is not already there.

`void remove(Object key)`: This method removes the future from the table associated with key, if there is any.

---

use is `FutureTable`. A future table contains futures that you can look up with any object as key. The futures are created in the table when they are first looked up. For dataflow purposes, either the producer or the consumer can look up a variable's future first—it doesn't matter, since it is created on first access.

Futures can be removed from the table when they are no longer needed. When encoding dataflow, this is dangerous, since it's often difficult to know when the last access has been made. It's probably easier and safer to create a new future table for each scope and to simply discard it when it's no longer needed.

Chapter Wrap-up

There are two major data structures discussed in this chapter: `SharedTableOfQueues` and `FutureQueue`.

The SharedTableOfQueues class is a versatile facility for synchronization and communication. We saw how to implement a variety of parallel programming patterns using it: futures, locks, semaphores, queues, locked records, bounded buffers, barriers, *I*-structures, and reactive objects.

The class IndexedKey can be used to create a collection of related keys, which helps in coding some of the SharedTableOfQueues patterns.

Class FutureQueue is used in the implementation of SharedTableOfQueues. In turn, FutureQueue's implementation presents a number of problems. We examined it in detail as an example of advanced thread programming.

Future queues themselves can be used to get strictly first-in/first-out queueing of threads. As an example, we examined the QueuedReadersWritersMonitor class, a more efficient implementation of the same scheduling policy as the TakeANumberMonitor. (See "The Take-a-Number Monitor" in Chapter 4).

If, as is often the case, only a table of named futures is required, FutureTable provides a more efficient implementation.

Exercises

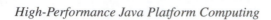

1. Implement a semaphore with first-come, first-served queueing using a FutureQueue object.

2. Implement a bounded buffer using FutureQueue objects.

3. Implement a modified version of WarshallTQ that uses FutureTable rather than SharedTableOfQueues for communicating the sections of the rows and columns. Does the simpler, presumably more efficient, data structure make a significant difference in performance?

Chapter 10

Streams Essentials

▼ THE STREAMS ABSTRACTION

▼ BUILDING YOUR OWN STREAM

▼ ADD: THE RELATIONSHIP TO NETWORKING CLASSES

S treams are Java's way of supporting I/O. A basic understanding of it is imperative in order to do parallel and distributed network programming in Java. You can find the streams classes in the java.io package.

In this chapter, we provide an overview of the streams classes that are provided in Java. This overview is intended to give the reader a sufficient idea of the workings and philosophy of streams to facilitate understanding of the networking chapter (Chapter 11). The overview begins with an explanation of the difference between the streams classes found in Java 1.0.2 (the InputStream and OutputStream classes) and those found in Java 1.1 and beyond (the Reader and Writer classes). Following this overview, we present an example that shows how to use the stream classes by creating a stream to perform an operation familiar to Unix users: Character Translation (the "tr" utility). We then show how you can extend this class to implement the Caesar Cipher, which is one of the first examples taught in courses on computer security and encryption.

The two examples will prove helpful to understand the notion of stream layering and composition, which is fundamental to working with Input/Output in Java as well as computer networking, which makes use of streams extensively for communication via network sockets. If you are already familiar with streams (in depth), you can safely skip to the networking chapter.

The Streams Abstraction

As mentioned in the chapter introduction, streams represent one of the most powerful packages in the Java programming language. To use streams, you must import the java.io package, which is indigenous to JDK 1.0.2, 1.1.x, and beyond. The streams classes of Java were extended significantly between versions 1.0.2 and 1.1 and since then have been one of the most stable, predictable, and reliable frameworks of the Java language

Before proceeding with a number of example codes, it is important to understand that there are two different sets of stream classes in Java:

- Byte streams: `InputStream` and `OutputStream` are the base classes. Byte streams are intended for use primarily in applications that only need to use the Latin character set, which is an 8-bit character (of type **byte** in Java).

- Character streams. `Reader` and `Writer` are the base classes. Character streams are intended for use in applications that are intended for worldwide use. The character encoding scheme used is known as UNICODE, which is the international standard (actually, still a de facto standard, but everyone is using it, including Microsoft).

In short, you should use the character streams classes for all application development. This is not to insinuate that the byte-stream classes are slated for removal anytime soon. In fact, it may be virtually impossible to move them. Most Java programmers come to know the `InputStream` and `OutputStream` classes via a number of standard streams found in the System package: **in**, **out**, and **err**, all of which are byte streams. Fortunately for all of us, byte streams can be freely converted to character streams. Two bridging classes exist for this purpose:

- `InputStreamReader`: This allows an input byte stream (`InputStream`) to be used as a character input stream. We will actually make use of this bridging class in a number of examples.

- `OutputStreamWriter`: This allows an output byte stream (`OutputStream`) to be used as a character output stream. Again, we will be making use of this bridging class in a number of examples.

Streams support a number of important principles that we discuss next. Throughout the examples, we will occasionally refer to these principles and assume that you have a high-level understanding of what is meant:

- Composability and layering: To do anything interesting with Java I/O, streams must be composed (or layered), usually from an existing stream. The use of composition allows you to augment the capabilities of an underlying stream with more powerful (and often more flexible) capabilities. For example, an `InputStream` (or `Reader`) by default, only allows you to perform very low-level I/O operations, such as `read()` to read a single byte or `read(byte[], offset, length)` to read multiple bytes. Neither of these functions provides the interface wanted by most users. It is usually desired (in the case of text files) to be able to read a line at a time, which can only be done by making use of a stream class layered atop an `InputStream`.

- Extensibility and filtering: One of the biggest challenges in I/O is in being able to support new I/O functionality. For example, suppose you want the ability to work with an "encrypted" stream for input. An encrypted `InputStream` is much like an Input-Stream, except that a decryption key must be specified when using it. As well, a cipher alphabet must be generated to map the cipher text (hopefully) to plaintext. This example appears shortly and demonstrates the power of Java's I/O. You can create this class and make use of the same `read()` functions without having to invent an entire new naming scheme and figure out what interfaces are appropriate.

Building Your Own Stream

In this section, we present a complete example of how to create your own Java stream that will be well behaved when used with existing (or new) stream classes. This example is inspired by a useful utility in Unix named **tr** (translate), which translates a file by replacing characters from an input alphabet, **in**, with the corresponding character in the output alphabet, **out**. The **tr** utility actually has a number of bells and whistles besides being able to perform this translation. Nevertheless, the simple character translation problem represents an interesting example of how to extend Java I/O streams to perform a similar task.

Before we begin, we will make some assumptions:

- The **tr** utility works with an input file and an output file. Files, as mentioned earlier, are supported via streams as a special case. Our **tr** utility will be designed so that any kind of stream can be used to perform the translation.

- In general, we do not know what characters actually appear in any given stream. The design here assumes that an input character, if not in the input alphabet, will be left untranslated.

The following shows the concept of character translation at a basic level.

Suppose we have the following input text:

    The quick, lazy fox jumped over the scary cat.

And suppose we have the following input alphabet:

ABCDEFGHIJKLMNOPQRSTUVWXYZ

And the following output alphabet:

abcdefghijklmnopqrstuvwxyz

If we translate the input text above according to the input and output alphabets, we would get the following:

the quick, lazy fox jumped over the scary cat.

The spaces, comma, and period are all left untranslated, because none of these characters appear in the input alphabet. This translation demonstrates how to build a simple case translator for English letters, wherein every uppercase letter is translated to lower case and vice versa.

A problem arises when the input and output alphabets are not the same length and, in particular, when the input alphabet has more characters than the output alphabet. We address this problem when *constructing* the translator stream by ensuring the input and output alphabets have the same length.

Example 10-1 and Example 10-2 present the code for `TranslateReader` and `TranslateWriter`, respectively. Let us consider this code at a high level before diving into the details:

- In general, when defining a stream in Java, you are defining something called a filter. Think of a filter as being much like the filters encountered in real life. There is an inflow of characters. The filter is applied to this inflow, yielding an outflow. Some filters in fact do not change what is read from (or written to) underlying stream. (This is particularly true of many built-in Java classes.) Our classes perform a translation in the process of reading or writing. Java provides two classes for defining your own input and output character streams: `FilterReader` and `FilterWriter`.

- The subclassing of filters is a bit tricky. You must take special care to override two methods. `FilterReader` provides two distinct read methods (overloaded names). One of the read methods is intended for reading a single character at a time; the other read method is intended for reading a block of characters at a time. Failing to define both methods in the subclass will cause your input filter to fail. The same issue applies to subclasses of `FilterWriter`. There are three write methods. You need to define all three to be assured of getting correct results.

- When defining input and output filters, it is very often the case that you are working with two different classes that work somewhat similarly. Some input and output filters work *symmetrically*. It may be important that the two classes rely on identical information to perform the input or output translation. An example of this is shown a bit later with a Caesar cipher, which was an early device used for encryption. The translator we have discussed here is not symmetric. You can convince yourself of this by studying the clarifying example just presented. When you translate out the uppercase characters, there is no information in the translated text that would allow you to know what letters were capitalized in the original text.

We will now study both classes in somewhat greater detail. Let us first consider the `TranslateReader` class shown in Example 10-1. The class contains two instance variables:

- `from`: The input character set.

- `to`: The output character set.

The term "set" may be a bit of a misnomer. Here we are referring to an ordered set of characters, where each character in the set has an ordinal position.

`TranslateReader(Reader r, String from, String to).` The constructor initializes a `TranslateReader` instance by passing a reference to an existing `Reader r`, the input character set `from`, and the output character set `to`. Passing a reference to a `Reader` allows any reference to a subclass of `Reader` to also be passed. Recall that streams are intended to be composable, and this is why you would pass a reference to `Reader` (which is the superclass of all character input streams) than a specific subclass, which would limit your options.

`int read() throws IOException.` This method is overridden to allow a single character to be read. Note that this method is actually implemented in terms of the other read method (discussed next), which reads a block of characters. Notice that great care is taken to ensure that the correct value is returned. The single character `read()` method of Java works very similarly to the `read()` function in the C language. This function must return the value of the character as an integer, or it must return the end of file flag, which is -1 in Java. The variable `oneChar` is declared as a static array of one character, so that it can be reused between successive calls to this function. It is needed to call the block `read()` function, which actually handles the details of performing the translation after reading a block of characters from the underlying stream. This eliminates code duplication between the two read calls to perform the translation in-line.

`int read(char[] cbuf, int off, int len).` This method is overridden to allow a block of characters to be read. The code for this method first calls the same `read()` function in the superclass. (`Super.read()` assures us that the superclass's method will be called, not this method's); if you study the Java source code for `FilterReader`, you'll discover that this causes the originally specified `Reader`'s (`r`) `read()` method to be called. Once the block of characters has been read into an array of characters, the translation is performed one character at a time in place on the user-specified buffer. At the end of the call, this buffer will contain the translated characters and not the original characters from the underlying stream. Again, note the special care to ensure that the block `read()` function returns what is expected: either the number of characters read (which usually matches the number of characters read from the underlying stream though not required) or an end-of-file indication (-1). You must always take special care to ensure that the end-of-file condition is handled appropriately (i.e., returned correctly) and that any exceptions, if handled locally, are propagated to the calling context. In the code here, both `read()` methods will only cause exceptions when the underlying (or superclass) `read()` method is called. Hence, it is expected that the exception is simply being rethrown.

Example 10-1 TranslateReader.java

```java
package com.toolsofcomputing.streams;

import java.io.*;

public class TranslateReader extends FilterReader {
    private String from;
    private String to;
    private static char[] oneChar;

    static {
        oneChar = new char[1];
    }

    public TranslateReader(Reader r, String from, String to) {
        super(r);
        this.from = from;
        this.to = to;
    }

    public TranslateReader(Reader r) {
        super(r);
        String upper = "ABCDEFGHIJKLMNOPQRSTUVWXYZ";
        String lower = "abcdefghijklmnopqrstuvwxyz";

        this.from = upper + lower;
        this.to = lower + upper;
    }

    public int read() throws IOException {
        int result =  read(oneChar,0,1)
        if (result < 0) return result;
        else return oneChar[0];
    }
```

Example 10-1 (Continued)

```java
public int read(char[] cbuf, int off, int len)
        throws IOException {
        int n = super.read(cbuf, off, len);
        int i;
        for (i=0; i < n; i++) {
            int mapIndex = from.indexOf(cbuf[i]);
            if (mapIndex >= 0)
                cbuf[i] = to.charAt(mapIndex);
        }
        return n;
    }

    public static void main(String[] args) {
        StringReader sr = new StringReader("Java is Great");
        TranslateReader translateReader = new TranslateReader(sr);
        LineNumberReader lnr =
          new LineNumberReader(translateReader);

        try {
            String line = lnr.readLine();
            System.out.println(line);
        } catch (Exception e) {
        }
    }

}
```

The `main()` method shown in Example 10-1 provides a quick demonstration of a simple translator. For the purpose of this demonstration, there is a second constructor that hard codes a simple alphabet, where the input alphabet `from` is the set of uppercase English letters followed by lowercase English letters, and the `to` alphabet is the opposite. The main method makes use of a couple of built-in `Reader` classes:

StringReader. This takes input from a character string. C programmers may recall the `sscanf` function, which allowed a string to be used for input.

LineNumberReader. This supports input one line at a time, instead of requiring the use of low-level `read()` functions. `LineNumberReader` supports a method, `readLine()`, that will keep calling `read()` in the underlying stream until a newline is seen (usually LF, or CR-LF, depending on your religious persuasion of Windows or Unix). The `BufferedReader` class also has this capability and could well have been used.

LineNumberReader will also keep count of the number of lines read. This feature is not used in the present example.

StringReader sr is created to allow input to be read from a hard-coded string "Java is Great." Then the newly created TranslateReader class is created, using the special constructor just described. The LineNumberReader is constructed so we can read one line of input at a time from the TranslateReader. (There will only be one line, since all of the input is contained in a string with no embedded newlines. There are no limits, however, and this has been done to keep the driver code as simple as possible.

The TranslateWriter class bears many similarities to the TranslateReader class. We will not go into the same detail here but will summarize. The constructor is very similar to the TranslateReader with the notable difference of using a Writer reference w instead of a Reader reference. Again, we provide a second constructor that will be used to hard code the translation from uppercase to lowercase and vice versa in the main driver code.

There are total of three write() methods to be subclassed. The first two are very similar to the read() methods presented in the TranslateReader. One is used to work with a single character, while the other is used to work with a block (an array) of characters. The key difference between these methods and the corresponding read() methods is that the write operation is performed after the translation here. This makes sense, because translation is happening before the data are actually written to the underlying stream. In the read() methods, translation clearly must be performed after reading from the underlying stream; otherwise, there is nothing to translate. There is a third write method, void write(String s, int off, int len) throws IOException, which exists for the purpose of being able to write a String instance more conveniently.

If you are wondering why there is not a companion read() method, it has something to do with the fact that the concept of reading a string is somewhat more complicated (and ill defined) than writing one. When you write a string, you know precisely how many characters are in the string. This means that writing a string can actually be formulated easily enough in terms of writing a block of characters. The String class is used in this third write method (presented next) to convert itself into a character array (the toCharArray() method is used for this purpose), and then a block write is performed. There is no similar read() method because you don't know how many characters to read (i.e., when to stop reading characters using the underlying read). The input consists merely of raw characters. It could be useful to have a read method that will form a string with all characters read until a certain "delimiter" is found in the input; however, this was probably not considered in the design of the I/O library, because this would have the disadvantage of assuming something that may not be true about the underlying stream.

Example 10-2 TranslateWriter.java

```java
package com.toolsofcomputing.streams;

import java.io.*;

public class TranslateWriter extends FilterWriter {
    private String from;
    private String to;
    private static char[] oneChar;
    private static char[] charArray;

    static {
        oneChar = new char[1];
    }

    public TranslateWriter(Writer w, String from, String to) {
        super(w);
        this.from = from;
        this.to = to;
    }

    public TranslateWriter(Writer w) {
        super(w);
        String upper = "ABCDEFGHIJKLMNOPQRSTUVWXYZ";
        String lower = "abcdefghijklmnopqrstuvwxyz";

        this.from = upper + lower;
        this.to = lower + upper;
    }

    public void write(int c) throws IOException {
        oneChar[0] = (char) c;
        write(oneChar, 0, 1);
    }
    public void write(char[] cbuf, int off, int len)
        throws IOException {
        if (cbuf == null)
            throw new IOException();

        int i;
        for (i=0; i < cbuf.length; i++) {
            int mapIndex = from.indexOf(cbuf[i]);
            if (mapIndex >= 0)
                cbuf[i] = to.charAt(mapIndex);
        }
        super.write(cbuf, off, len);
    }
```

Example 10-2 (Continued)

```
public void write(String s, int off, int len)
    throws IOException {
        if (s == null)
            throw new IOException();
        charArray = s.toCharArray();
        write(charArray, off, len);
    }


    public static void main(String[] args) {
        OutputStreamWriter osw;
        TranslateWriter translateWriter;

        osw = new OutputStreamWriter(System.out);
        translateWriter = new TranslateWriter(osw);

        try {
            translateWriter.write("Java is Great");
            translateWriter.flush();
        } catch(Exception e) {
            System.err.println(e);
            System.exit(1);
        }
    }
}
```

Again, the main() method provides a quick demonstration of how the Translate-Writer is combined with built-in Java Writer classes to perform the translation. This time, the translation is performed while writing instead of reading. We again provide a quick overview of the built-in Java class being used in the main() method:

OutputStreamWriter. Recall that Java provides bridging classes to allow the byte and character I/O classes to be combined. This is particularly important when you want to take advantage of the standard streams, such as System.in, System.out, and System.err, all of which are byte I/O streams. The OutputStreamWriter is used so we can write character (instead of byte) data to System.out.

The string "Java is Great" is written to the TranslateWriter instance translate-Writer. This is the class we have been talking about that will perform the translation on the data and then write it to the underlying stream, which is an OutputStreamWriter. The OutputStreamWriter object will ultimately take responsibility for writing the translated data (without any further translation) to the underlying stream, which is System.out. You can run both of these programs to verify that the output is, indeed, what is expected.

For Further Exploration

It may be a good idea at this point to reflect on the power of what you have just seen. This framework provides you with unprecedented flexibility to define your own useful I/O classes. It may not be apparent just yet, but you could perform translations recursively.

See if you can extend either of the programs in Example 10-1 or Example 10-2 to make use of a `TranslateWriter` layered atop another `TranslateWriter` (or do the same for a `TranslateReader`). Does it work?

Caesar Cipher: Very Basic Encryption

The "translate" package built into the previous section may not be much; however, it is the basis for many interesting kinds of streams. You could use these classes to develop an entry-level encryption system. The technology of encryption, surprisingly, can be traced back several centuries and is the recent subject of a recent book studying the history of cryptography from the time of Mary, Queen of Scots, to present.[1]

At the center of encryption technology is the ability to "scramble" or "encipher" (or both) a message. Enciphering is the ability to perform a substitution, usually, but not limited to, a single character at a time. This kind of cipher is known as a monoalphabetic substitution cipher, because it works by translating one character at a time. The idea is simple. You have the following two alphabets:

- The plaintext alphabet: This is an ordered character set that is used to compose messages.

- The cipher alphabet: This is usually a permutation of the plaintext alphabet that can be used to encipher (translate) the plaintext alphabet.

So if you wanted to build your own cipher, it should be as simple as memorizing the input alphabet and the cipher alphabet, and then you can decipher any enciphered message.

Well, not quite.

First of all, there are many alphabets. In fact, if your alphabet has N letters, then there are $N!$ ways of arranging those N letters. Second, chances are that you will need to send an enciphered message to someone to be subsequently deciphered. You can send the alphabet as the first part of the message, and the recipient can be smart enough to construct an apporprite "translator" at his or her end; however, there is a disadvantage:

> Everybody will know your little secret. Bummer!

---

[1] *"The Code Book"* by Simon Singh provides an excellent (and readable) historical survey of encryption and coding techniques.

This is wherein the challenge of developing a good encryption system lies. You need an elegant way to transfer the key. It is a bit beyond the scope of a book on high-performance Java computing to address this particular topic since this chapter aims to introduce the essence of streams for an understanding of networking–the subject of the next chapter. The interested reader should study the RSA algorithm to understand how the problem of key distribution is solved, using a special class of functions called one-way functions, which are studied in modular arithmetic.

Nonetheless, it is interesting to explore a way to make a cipher that does not require us to memorize a random permutation of letters. One scheme is known as the Caesar cipher. A Caesar cipher works on the principle of a key being used for enciphering and deciphering a message. The key can be used to generate a cipher alphabet in a deterministic way using the following algorithm:

- Suppose we have a key, say, GEORGE.

- First, begin by walking through the list of characters, eliminating duplicates along the way. (We cannot have any plaintext character mapping to the same letter.)

- Now, we are left with GEOR.

- Clearly, when the key is chosen, the person specifying the key should take care not to map a letter to itself. This is because the key we are now left with is going to be used to map from the plaintext to ciphertext. (That is, 'A' goes to 'G,' 'B' goes to 'E,' 'C' goes to 'O,' and 'D' goes to 'R.')

- Now, starting from the beginning of the alphabet, try to assign letters to the rest of the cipher alphabet. (In our example, we are start on the fourth letter of the ciphertext character set, since positions zero through three are already assigned to 'G,' 'E,' 'O,' and 'R,' respectively.) Special care should be taken to ensure that letters do not map to themselves.

You can actually determine the results for any key, including GEORGE, by running the Alphabet demo program shown in Example 10-3. The algorithmic sketch previously presented is actually used in the Alphabet class of this example by the method `createCipherAlphabet()`. You can show the cipher alphabet for any key as follows:

```
String key = "your key text here";
Alphabet a = new Alphabet("ABCDEFGHIJKLMNOPQRSTUVWXYZ", key);
System.out.println(a);
```

When you run the Alphabet `main()` method, which has both a hard-coded alphabet of English letters in their natural order and the a hard-coded key "GEORGE," you get the following cipher alphabet:

A:G B:E C:O D:R E:A F:B G:C H:D I:F J:H K:I L:J M:K N:L

O:M P:N Q:P R:Q S:T T:S U:V V:U W:X X:W Y:Z Z:Y:

This output tells you what gets translated into what. 'A' is translated to 'G'; 'B' to 'E'; 'C' to 'O'; 'D' to 'R'; 'E' to 'A'; ...; and, finally, 'Z' to 'Y'.

The Alphabet class itself should be straightforward to understand, as all of the complexities of it are contained in the method just described, `createCipherAlphabet()`, which uses the foregoing algorithm to generate the cipher alphabet. For all practical purposes, you can operate with a high-level understanding of what this class is doing and proceed to study the `CaesarReader` and `CaesarWriter` filters, which both make use of the same `Alphabet` class in order to generate a common cipher alphabet, given a key.

Example 10-3 Alphabet Translation

```
package com.toolsofcomputing.streams;

public class Alphabet {

    private String in;
    private String key;
    private String out;

    public static Alphabet getAlphabet(String in, String key)
    {
        Alphabet a = new Alphabet(in, key);
        return a;
    }

    public String getCipherAlphabet() {
        return out;
    }

    public Alphabet(String in, String key) {
        this.in = in;
        this.key = key;
        createCipherAlphabet();
    }

    public void createCipherAlphabet() {
        out = "";
        for (int i=0; i < key.length(); i++)
            if (out.indexOf(key.charAt(i)) < 0)
                out += key.charAt(i);

        for (int i=out.length(); i < in.length(); i++) {
            int j;
            for (j=0; j < in.length(); j++) {
```

Example 10-3 (Continued)

```
                        if (i != j && out.indexOf(in.charAt(j)) < 0){
                            out += in.charAt(j);
                            break;
                        }
                    }
                }
            }

    public String toString() {
        String out = "";
        for (int i=0; i < out.length(); i++)
            out += (in.charAt(i) + ":" + out.charAt(i) + " ");
        return out;
    }

    public static void main(String args[]) {
        Alphabet a = new Alphabet("ABCDEFGHIJKLMNOPQRSTUVWXYZ",
                                  "GEORGE");
        System.out.println(a);
    }
}
```

The `Alphabet` class does the most important work to construct the cipher alphabet from any given key. It will be used by both the `CaesarReader` and `CaesarWriter` classes, which are presented in Example 10-4 and Example 10-5.

Because we have already gone through the pains of designing general-purpose classes that can be used to perform monoalphabetic substitution as required by the Caesar cipher, to a large extent the remainder of the story is about extending these classes and using the `Alphabet` class to generate the "to" character set. (Recall that both of our translate classes had "from" and "to" character sets to aid in performing the translation of characters from or to the underlying input or output stream.)

Consider the code in Example 10-4. Class `CaesarReader` is formed by extending `TranslateReader`. The constructor does most of the work of setting up the `TranslateReader` object to do most of the work for us. This is an example of an object-oriented principle called delegation, which, in practical terms, is a way of getting "someone else" to do the work for you, the "someone else" being another class that basically already does the work. The `Alphabet` class has a special method, called a *factory* method, that will create an instance of the `Alphabet` class for us, so we need not create the instance using the new operator explicitly. Without this capability, it would be a bit messy to initialize the superclass (i.e., call its constructor using **super**), because a call to a superclass's constructor must be among the very first statements in a constructor being defined.

Example 10-4 CaesarReader.java

```java
package com.toolsofcomputing.streams;

import java.io.*;

public class CaesarReader extends TranslateReader {

    public CaesarReader(Reader r, String inAlphabet, String key) {
        super(r,
          Alphabet.getAlphabet(inAlphabet,key).getCipherAlphabet(),
          inAlphabet);
    }

    public static void main(String[] args) {
        String key = args[0];
        InputStreamReader isr = new InputStreamReader(System.in);
        CaesarReader cr;

        // ABC...XYZ is fully expanded in the version on the Web.
        cr = new CaesarReader(isr, "ABC...XYZ",key);

        try {
            while (true) {
                int result = cr.read();
                if (result < 0)
                    break;
                System.out.write((char)result);
            }
        } catch(Exception e) {
            System.out.println(e);
        } finally {
            System.out.flush();
        }

    }

}
```

This is all there is to it! Aside from defining a constructor, no additional work is required to create the `CaesarReader` class. The `read()` functions are inherited from the superclass, `TranslateReader`, since there is no fundamental difference between a `CaesarReader` and `TranslateReader`, except in how the class is constructed.

Example 10-5 CaesarWriter.java

```
package com.toolsofcomputing.streams;

import java.io.*;

public class CaesarWriter extends TranslateWriter {

    public CaesarWriter(Writer w, String inAlphabet, String key) {
        super(w, inAlphabet,

            Alphabet.getAlphabet(inAlphabet,key).getCipherAlphabet());
    }

    public static void main(String args[]) {
        OutputStreamWriter osw;
        osw = new OutputStreamWriter(System.out);
        CaesarWriter cw;
        cw = new CaesarWriter(osw,"ABC..XYZ", "GEORGE");
        try {
            cw.write("THIS IS A TEST OF THE CAESAR WRITER\n");
            cw.flush();
        } catch(Exception e) {
            return;
        }
    }
}
```

The following box shows a sample session with the `CaesarReader` and `CaesarWriter` classes developed in the foregoing discussion.

A natural question to ask at this point is, "Does one really need to know how to create his or her own stream classes in order to do multithreaded or distributed computing with Java?" Not necessarily. On the other hand, a knowledge of the streams mechanism can be helpful when a built-in stream does not exist for what is needed. Java supports fully encrypted streams as part of the Java Cryptography Extensions, so it is unlikely that you would make specific use of the Caesar cipher.

The Session (This was run with the 'bash' shell on RedHat Linux.)

The following shows how to encipher input lines (plaintext) using the key JAVATHREADS. Note that you can enter as many lines of text as desired. The last line must be terminated by ^D on Unix (^Z on Windows/DOS).

```
$ java com.toolsofcomputing.streams.CaesarWriter JAVATHREADS
THIS IS A TEST OF THE EMERGENCY BROADCAST SYSTEM.
PDSO SO J PHOP KR PDH HGHNEHIVZ ANKJTVJOP OZOPHG.
THIS IS AN EXAMPLE OF WHAT HAPPENS WHEN YOU USE SOMETHING 123
PDSO SO JI HWJGLFH KR XDJP DJLLHIO XDHI ZKQ QOH OKGHPDSIE 123
NOT IN THE
IKP SI PDH
ALPHABET.
JFLDJAHP.
^D
```

The following shows what happens when you try to decipher the message with the wrong key. The text used has been cut and pasted from the enciphered output just shown.

```
$ java com.toolsofcomputing.streams.CaesarReader JAVA
PDSO SO J PHOP KR PDH HGHNEHIVZ ANKJTVJOP OZOPHG.
QFTP TP A QJPQ LS QFJ JIJOGJKCY BOLAUCAPQ PYPQJI.
^D
```

The following shows what happens when the proper key is supplied instead.

```
$ java com.toolsofcomputing.streams.CaesarReader JAVATHREADS
PDSO SO J PHOP KR PDH HGHNEHIVZ ANKJTVJOP OZOPHG.
THIS IS A TEST OF THE EMERGENCY BROADCAST SYSTEM.
^D
```

Chapter Wrap-Up

Streams, Java's I/O framework, are an essential part of network programming. The intention of this chapter has been to introduce the basic ideas of streams, which include the principles of extension and layering. What makes streams different in Java from the interfaces found in C and C++ is the ease of which custom streams can be built and almost immediately put to use.

What we have not covered here are the multitude of streams classes that are provided in the Java language proper. This has been done partly by design as there are already a number of references on Java that provide an introductory treatment of the many streams classes provided in Java. In the networking chapter we will employ a number of useful Java streams to implement basic network services. In the last chapter on coordination, we will demonstrate that the availability of these powerful streams can be used to build a fancy coordination system (the Memo system) that can be used to write parallel programs that are to be run on a network of computers.

Exercises

1.   The 2nd constructor in example 10-1 clearly does not belong in this class. It initializes some default "to" and "from" character sets. What translation is being performed if this constructor is used? Is this something that would normally be done in an actual translation application? (The author admits to being too lazy to move this code, which had been added for quick testing. Nevertheless, it makes for a good exercise to make you think about how the code is really working.)

2.   Based on your answer to the previous question, develop two subclasses of the TranslateReader and TranslateWriter classes that can convert a character stream to all uppercase or to all lowercase. This means that you will effectively need to write four classes, although you may be able to combine functionality.

3.   The TranslateReader and TranslateWriter classes presently are limited to one to one character translation. That is, a single character can be mapped to a single character. This can make it difficult to build a useful class of translators that operate on more than a single character, such as one that is commonly found when moving between DOS/Windows and Unix platforms: converting carriage returns to carriage return/linefeed or vice versa. Extend the TranslateReader and TranslateWriter to support such a scheme. (This may keep you busy.) Write a translator that can either remove or add the linefeed character as described.

4.   Rewrite the SMA classes to use DataInputStream and DataOutputStream to read and write messages, respectively. You will need to write the table of parameters in such a way that allows you to easily put it back together again when reading it. Note: Do not use object serialization to do this. Object serialization takes all the fun out of thinking about how to do what is being asked here in this question, and it is somewhat unnecessary, since we are just encoding a table of key, value pairs, where the keys and values are all Strings.

Chapter 11

Networking

Networking is the story of Java. After all, Java, in its infancy, was an Internet programming language. Although this book has been entirely about threads and the potential of Java as a parallel language, we could not leave you without saying a few words (or chapters) about the potential of Java threads in the context of networked and distributed applications. In this chapter, we provide a self-contained introduction to networking. This introduction will provide (we hope) a solid basis for the next chapter, which introduces the ideas of distributed coordination (an area where both authors have invested a significant number of years of time doing research and applications).

The discussion of this chapter is organized as follows. First, we introduce network programming from the client side. Here we adopt somewhat of an immersive approach (an approach often used by hackers) by first learning a bit about Internet-style services and interacting with them using widely available utilities such as telnet. Then, we present the Java API for programming the client side, followed by a discussion of the server side and its respective API. The chapter concludes with a general (and simple) class library for building client–server-socket applications, called Simple Messaging Architecture. We also show the potential for making use of material presented earlier (the `RunQueue` class) to minimize the overhead of thread creation on the server side.

Exploring the Client Side

In addition to powerful I/O abstractions, Java provides extensive support for networked computing. Of particular interest in the context of this book is the support for TCP/IP networking. It is beyond the scope of this particular textbook to define every aspect of networking here; however, there are a number of basics:

- TCP/IP, the transmission control protocol/Internet protocol, is really two protocols: TCP and IP. TCP roughly corresponds to the transport layer of the OSI protocol, which is an open international standard developed by the International Standards Organization (ISO) and consists of seven layers (two of which are named transport and network).

- The practical significance of TCP is that it provides a virtual circuit service, which for all practical purposes can be thought of as a connection-oriented service, wherein you can be assured of having end-to-end continuity in a "conversation" without fear of losing the connection, subject to your link not being completely shutdown, of course.

- The practical significance of IP is that it provides unique addresses for each device connected on the network. Each address is of the form A.B.C.D, where A, B, C, and D are called *octets*. The term octet refers to an 8-bit value. Thus, an IP address in its current form is actually a 32-bit value. IP addresses will eventually have at least 6 octets, which is being proposed as part of the IPv6 standards effort.

- To support end-to-end connectivity, *routing tables* must exist to enable messages to be forwarded from one end of the "connection" to another. This is the real magic behind how the Internet is able to work.

There is a great deal more to TCP/IP than can be covered in this book. One particularly great book on the subject is by W. Richard Stevens, whose book on Unix network programming is considered (and revered) as a classic, even outside of the Unix community.

For the remainder of this chapter, we will take an *immersive* approach to learning TCP/IP networking. For you to achieve the maximum benefits from this chapter, we recommend that you acquire access to a machine running Unix, which can be done quite inexpensively these days, since you can obtain the Linux operating system (as well as other versions of Unix) for free.[1]

---

[1] Similar utilities and files to the ones found on Unix are available for Windows NT and 2000 from Cygnus (Red Hat) at http://www.cygnus.com/win32.

Example 11-1 shows the contents of the file /etc/services found on Unix. The /etc/services file is used precisely for what its name says: to indicate what services are running on what ports. Each line in the services file contains the following information:

service name   **port number/protocol**

It is not essential to understand all details of this file, and what you see on your system will more than likely contain much more than shown in our example. The service name is a user-friendly name for the network service. For example,

- **daytime** is a widely familiar service to Unix users. It can be used to find the current date and time. The **rdate** command can be used to query the daytime service from any machine. This service can always be found on port 13. The service can be contacted by using the TCP protocol or the unreliable datagram protocol (UDP) . UDP will not be used in this book in detail. It is a protocol that can be used when you know that the underlying network is reasonably reliable (usually true on a LAN), and it has lower overhead than the TCP protocol.

- **telnet** is a widely familar service as well. It is used to open a remote terminal session to another host. Nowadays, it is used less frequently, due to security considerations; **ssh** has taken its place to support encrypted remote sessions. Telnet service is always found on port 23, although it is now usually disabled or severly restricted on most systems.

Telnet is also the name of a command that is found on Unix, and even on the Windows platform. Telnet (the command) is not restricted to connections with the telnet service. You can use telnet to connect to virtually any network service, assuming that service communicates with a plaintext protocol. We will show this in a later example.

Example 11-1 /etc/services: the Unix collection of standard TCP/IP services

```
# /etc/services:

# Each line has
# service name          port/protocol
tcpmux                  1/tcp
echo                    7/tcp
echo                    7/udp
discard                 9/tcp
discard                 9/udp
systat                  11/tcp
daytime                 13/tcp
daytime                 13/udp
netstat                 15/tcp
qotd                    17/tcp
```

```
msp                     18/tcp
msp                     18/udp
chargen                 19/tcp
chargen                 19/udp
ftp                     21/tcp
fsp                     21/udp
ssh                     22/tcp
ssh                     22/udp
telnet                  23/tcp
smtp                    25/tcp
time                    37/tcp
time                    37/udp
#
# This file contains many more lines. Consult the /etc/services
# file on your system to see ALL of what is available.

linuxconf               98/tcp
```

Services: The Internet Story

Before we proceed to the next programming example, it is a worthwhile detour to see how these network services work. The knowledge gained by doing this will be used in the two subsequent examples, so this is not exactly an *aimless* detour.

The telnet command found in both the Unix and Windows operating systems allows you to specify the following:

- host: The machine to which you wish to connect.

- service: The name of the service or port to which you wish to connect.

By default, the telnet program will connect to the telnet service (port 23), if you elect not to specify an alternative service.

Normally, when you use telnet to connect to a given host (here we will assume that the destination is Unix, which has a bona fide *remote-shell* concept, unlike Windows), you are presented with a login. You log into an account, and then you can begin executing commands on the remote computer. See the box entitled "A Typical Telnet Session" for an example of how a user would conduct a typical telnet session.

In this example, a telnet session is opened from an existing shell running on Unix (the same can be done in Windows) using the **telnet** client program and passing the name of a host (euler) as the first command-line argument. When connecting to a remote telnet service, a terminal session is opened, and a **login** program is executed. The login program exists to accept your username and password and then to subsequently authenticate you. When authenticated (which on Unix is achieved by using the password crypt utility to compare the encrypted password supplied with the encrypted password usually found in /etc/passwd or /etc/shadow), the login program (currently running as the superuser)

A Typical Telnet Session

```
[gkt@gauss gkt]$ telnet euler
Trying 140.192.38.154...
Connected to euler.jhpc.cs.depaul.edu.
Escape character is '^]'.


SunOS 5.7

login: gkt
Password:
Last login: Wed Dec 22 03:44:29 from gauss
bash-2.03$ ls
2q                              Jthreads.zip
372                             JThreadsNew.zip
420                             kaffe-1.0.5
apt                             kaffe-1.0.5.zip
axhome                          keep
beta                            letter
bootnet.img                     loyola
checkins                        luiz
christophe                      lyon
controlpanel                    lyon2
core                            mail
data                            manuals.tar.gz
Desktop                         ncftp-3.0beta21
JThreads.tar.gz
bash-2.03$ exit
logout
Connection closed by foreign host.
[gkt@gauss gkt]$
```

switches user to the authenticated user (gkt) and executes a shell *as that user.* Bear in mind that this entire process is being carried out under the auspices of the telnet service. (**telnetd** or **in.telnetd** is the name of the program executable under Unix.) The input and output are both "connected" to the terminal itself.

How exactly is this possible?

The answer is a bit involved, and we will only provide an executive summary here. The telnet connection is made possible via a TCP/IP connection called a *socket.* When a socket is created, file descriptors are available to read from and to write to the socket. When connecting via telnet to any Unix system, a socket exists at all times between the client (your telnet program) and the server (the telnet daemon). Any input you type in the telnet client session is actually sent via the output file descriptor associated with this socket. Similarly, any output generated by a remotely running program is actually taken as input by the telnet client program. There is one interesting detail: typing a character on your keyboard is not a one-way operation. Why? It has to do with the way the telnet client itself works. Telnet never displays anything that is not written explicitly to the standard output or standard error (remotely). Furthermore, the telnet service is in many respects a broker. Most of the time, the telnet service executes a shell on the user's behalf. Any input that goes to the telnet service after the shell has been created remotely is in fact going straight to the shell. It is beyond the scope of this book to cover the details of the Unix shell (many good books already exist on this topic); however, the (remotely running) shell itself takes full responsibility for handling this input. As characters are received by the shell, they are echoed. This "echoing" of characters is output, which is written to the socket connecting the telnet client and the telnet service.

Thus, whenever a character is typed in a telnet session, there is no guarantee that it will be echoed on the screen. It is only echoed from the server at will. At first, this entire process appears to be somewhat unnecessary and, certainly, not terribly efficient; however, closer examination reveals that it is a necessary evil of designing a remote terminal. You simply do not want everything to be echoed. The login program, which is actually a special form of a remote shell, needs the ability to suppress echoing of the password. If the telnet client program were to do this echoing in advance, it would effectively deny the server side the opportunity to suppress echoing. It is for this reason alone (among others) that the telnet client is kept ultra-generic in nature. It's only mission in life is to send characters and receive characters. It literally does nothing else.

That said, many telnet clients do much more than this. The Windows telnet clients perform terminal emulation. This allows the client to have a little more intelligence and ensure that certain character sequences (known as escape sequences) are interpreted and displayed properly. It is important to note, however, that this is primarily for the convenience of the user and is not in any way connected to the telnet protocol itself.

Destination Sendmail

The detour to telnet exposed one reality about the telnet client found on your computer. It can be used to connect, literally, to anything. And this is where the fun of network hacking begins. Please note that hacking by our definition does not mean breaking the law. We humbly request that you observe the security note on the following page.

Now back to the fun. The box entitled "Using Telnet to Contact sendmail: The Unix Mail Delivery Service" shows an example of a telnet session with another network service called SMTP, the Simple Mail Transport Protocol, which is a major protocol used on the Internet to send mail messages. Is is also known commonly as sendmail, or the *mail agent*. The SMTP protocol consists of a number of messages. You can learn more about this protocol by reading the so-called RFC documents (request for comments), which represent

---

Security Note

The examples shown here can get you into trouble. Before accessing any computer on your (or another) network, it is your responsbility to ensure that you have permission to do so. We (Prentice Hall and the authors) cannot assume any responsibility for illegal behavior resulting from the misuse of the information provided in this chapter.

---

proposals to the Internet Engineering Task Force (IETF) that are intended to become, to expand, or to clarify open standards specifically related to the Internet.

As mentioned, the approach to this chapter is intended to be immersive. The session shown in the box entitled "Using Telnet to Contact sendmail: The Unix Mail Delivery Service" makes use of a telnet client to access the sendmail service (on Unix), which is a widely used implementation of the SMTP protocol, especially on Unix machines (Solaris and Linux). The Microsoft Exchange Server product supports the SMTP protocol, as well, and it should be possible for you to adapt what you see here to see what is done by Microsoft's implementation of SMTP.

Let us now examine the session in greater detail. The first item of note occurs before the telnet session is even established:

```
telnet leibniz smtp
```

A connection is to be opened to the *smtp* service running on host *leibniz*. Some versions of telnet may require you to specify the port where the smtp service is running (25) instead of smtp. As we discussed earlier, telnet may connect to any desired port.

The sendmail service represents an interactive protocol. This means that it has been designed to be used interactively, say, from a terminal operated by a human (like you!) The HELP comand is the most useful command available in sendmail. When typed, a great deal of useful information is dumped to your terminal, including the version of sendmail that is running, the topics that are available, and much needed information on how to report bugs in the implementation. We will not show how to use all of the commands here, but limit our discussion to how to use this interactive session to compose a simple plain-text message using the various commands that will ultimately be sent to a given recipient.

To send a message, the following commands must be sent:

```
EHLO hostname
```

The EHLO command is used to introduce yourself (by specifying the originating domain name of the message) and to enable extended SMTP commands. This is the command used by modern mail clients, such as Netscape and Internet Explorer, which both need all of the features of the SMTP protocol in order to compose messages. The MAIL command is used to specify the originator (sender) of the e-mail message:

Using Telnet to Contact sendmail: The Unix Mail Delivery Service

```
[gkt@gauss gkt]$ telnet leibniz smtp
Trying 140.192.38.152...
Connected to leibniz.jhpc.cs.depaul.edu.
Escape character is '^]'.
220 leibniz.jhpc.cs.depaul.edu ESMTP Sendmail 8.9.3/8.9.3; Wed, 22
Dec 1999 17:59:36 -0600
HELP
214-This is Sendmail version 8.9.3
214-Topics:
214-    HELO    EHLO    MAIL    RCPT    DATA
214-    RSET    NOOP    QUIT    HELP    VRFY
214-    EXPN    VERB    ETRN    DSN
214-For more info use "HELP <topic>".
214-To report bugs in the implementation send email to
214-    sendmail-bugs@sendmail.org.
214-For local information send email to Postmaster at your site.
214 End of HELP info
HELP EHLO
214-EHLO <hostname>
214-    Introduce yourself, and request extended SMTP mode.
214 Possible replies include:
// You should run 'telnet' to see the list of possible replies.
214 End of HELP info
EHLO gauss.jhpc.cs.depaul.edu
250-leibniz.jhpc.cs.depaul.edu Hello IDENT:gkt@gauss
[140.192.38.153], pleased to meet you
250-EXPN
// Again this has been abbreviated.
250 HELP
MAIL FROM: gkt@cs.depaul.edu
250 gkt@cs.depaul.edu... Sender ok
RCPT TO: pshafae@leibniz.jhpc.cs.depaul.edu
250 pshafae@leibniz.jhpc.cs.depaul.edu... Recipient ok
DATA
354 Enter mail, end with "." on a line by itself
Hi John,
It seems like you are the only person I can send e-mail to in my
list.
George
.
250 SAA07772 Message accepted for delivery
QUIT
221 leibniz.jhpc.cs.depaul.edu closing connection
Connection closed by foreign host.
```

```
MAIL FROM: sender's e-mail address
```

This information is normally obtained (easily) from the mail client, which has total knowledge of who the sender is by inspecting the user profile (in the case of a browser-based e-mail program) or from the user-id/host-id combination, in the case of the old Unix command-line mail utilities. The RCPT command is used to specify the recipient of the e-mail message:

```
RCPT TO: recipient's e-mail address
```

There is usually some attempt made to check this address for well-formedness. This information is usualy passed on from the composition window from the mail client program. Only a single recipient is specified. We'll talk about how multiple messages can be handled. The DATA command is used to indicate that the client is about to send the body (text) of the e-mail message:

```
DATA
```

Once this command is issued, the message body must be sent in its entirety, followed by "." as a single, self-contained line of text, terminated by a newline character. You can send any kind of document using the DATA command. We'll not discuss that here in any kind of detail; however, another Internet standard, called MIME, allows you to take any kind of data and structure it in such a way that it can be encoded in a plaintext format for transfer via SMTP. The QUIT command is the polite way of bidding adieux to sendmail:

```
QUIT
```

Strictly speaking, it is not essential for delivering the message. Once the DATA command has terminated, the message is formally accepted for delivery.

This session forms the basis of our first network programming example. We will return to this example shortly. First, we need to clear some preliminaries out of the way. Then, we will present a complete implementation of an SMTP client. If you absolutely cannot wait, please feel free to examine the source code for class `SendMail`, which is presented in Example 11-2.

Java Networking: `Socket` and `InetAddress`

Java as a language is among the elite when it comes to support for networking and I/O. Those familiar with the sockets programming interfaces for the C language in Unix and Windows NT libraries are almost certain to find the Java solution to be much easier to use and comprehend. We will not discuss the C programming interfaces here. We will, however, make the observation that neither author terribly misses the complexity of the lower level interfaces all that much, and we believe that you will feel the same way after having explored Java's networking in greater detail beyond what is covered here.

As the strategy of this chapter is intended to be immersive, we will present the Java classes that are needed to address a particular example (only as needed) with the idea of gradually unveiling all of the Java networking classes by the end of the chapter.

The first set of classes we present are those needed from the client-side perspective. Consider the foregoing discussion on SMTP. This discussion centered entirely on the client. The client does the following:

- connects to the server

- sends commands to the server

- receives responses from the server

- closes the connection to the server

Let us now consider how Java supports each of these aspects, again with the focus being only on the client side. To connect to SMTP, we first need to consider exactly to what we are establishing a connection: a TCP/IP service. To connect to a TCP/IP service, a standard mechanism called a *socket* exists. The concept of a socket is widely familar. We use sockets to plug in our electrical appliances, almost on a daily basis.

The Java `Socket` class is used by clients to create a connection to a TCP/IP service. It is used in Example 11-2. (The code is a bit involved, because it makes use of the Abstract Windowing Toolkit, and we will discuss the essentials for those who are unfamiliar with it in just a bit.) A socket is created in the `sendMail()` method with the following statement:

```
smtpConnection = new Socket(smtpHost.getText(),25);
```

The `Socket` constructor requires a valid hostname or IP address to be specified along with a port, which indicates the service to which you want to connect. The service to which we are connecting is SMTP (used to send mail as discussed earlier), which is a standard Internet service for mail delivery that always runs on port 25. How did we know? Well, the answer is easy when you are working on the Unix platform. The /etc/services file (shown in Example 11-2) indicates that the "smtp" service is a "tcp" service running on port 25:

```
smtp                    25/tcp
```

There are other interesting classes that prove useful from a client-side perspective that will be introduced shortly. Let us now consider how we complete the remaining steps to send commands to the server, receive responses from the server, and close the connection.

These remaining steps all involve the use of I/O classes that we discussed in the first part of this chapter. Once a socket is created, a handle can be obtained to both the input and the output streams associated with the socket. Recall that a socket is a connection. To do anything useful with it, however, requires the capabilities only offered by Java's I/O package.

Again, let us focus only on the code in the `sendMail()` method in Example 11-2. The following excerpt from the beginning of this method illustrates how you can capture the input and output streams:

```
OutputStream os = smtpConnection.getOutputStream();
OutputStreamWriter osw = new OutputStreamWriter(os);
out = new PrintWriter(osw);

InputStream is = smtpConnection.getInputStream();
in = new InputStreamReader(is);
```

Only the two statements initialize `os` and `is` objects are actually needed. `os` is the object that can be used to write output to the server, while `is` is the object used to read input from the server. As noted earlier in the section on stream composition, one of the apparent nuisances of Java is the need to do layering in order to get the kind of stream you actually want. Thus, you need to think about what you actually want. In the case of SMTP, the commands being sent to the server are actually strings terminated by a newline character. Thus, we need a stream that supports a convenience method to facilitate writing entire lines (`PrintWriter` provides a `println()` method, which will do!) Unfortunately, to create a `PrintWriter` instance, we need a `Writer` instance as the underlying stream. An `OutputStream` reference can only be turned into a `Writer` by using the briding class, the class `OutputStreamWriter`. Ultimately, object `out` is initialized, which represents the object that will actually be used to send commands to the server.

A similar task is performed to initialize variable `in`.

The code in Example 11-2 is an implementation of a graphical client to sendmail. This code makes use of the Java framework for creating basic graphical user interfaces (GUI) known as the Abstract Windowing Toolkit (AWT). It is beyond the scope of this book to cover AWT in detail; however, we will present enough information so you can get the gist of what it does. AWT is covered in many excellent textbooks. We will now discuss the code, focusing on a few aspects:

- the use of Java packages

- the use of OOP to create a GUI

- the constructor

- the use of a "layout" container

- event handling

Java packages used. This particular example makes use of a number of Java packages, each of which appears in an import declaration: java.awt, java.awt.event, java.io, java.net, and java.util. The java.awt package provides the classes for GUI containers (`Frame` is used in our example) and components (`Button`, `Label`, `TextArea`, and `TextField` are used in the example). The java.awt.event package provides classes for handling events generated by those containers and components. We only need an event handler for the `Button` object that, when pressed, is what causes mail to be sent. java.net and java.io are both used to provide support for sockets and streams. As mentioned earlier, streams are necessary in order to actually perform I/O on the socket. The socket itself provides no direct I/O capability.

The use of OOP to create the GUI. When designing graphical interfaces in Java, it is almost never the case that you start entirely from scratch (unless you are on the development team at Sun!) Java classes can usually be extended to define a custom interface. We have chosen the `Frame` class, which you can think of as a Window that can support other fancy features, such as having a title or a menu bar or to support pop-up dialog boxes. Our approach here is thus to extend the `Frame` class and then to initialize the `Frame` object accordingly. This is done in the constructor. In addition to extending the `Frame` class, we implement an interface called the `ActionListener`. The "listener" pattern is an innovation of Java's GUI framework, which allows an object that is interested in events generated by another object to *subscribe* to the event. The subscription concept (in theory) allows a GUI implementation to be very efficient, since the scope of an event is bounded to a (usually) small number of objects. The actual subscription is done in the constructor, which is discussed in the next paragraph.

The constructor. The constructor for this class looks a bit scary; however, most of what is going on is remarkably intuitive and self-documenting. In fact, most of what is happening here is true to the responsibility of a constructor: A representation is being constructed. The call to the superclass's constructor, via the `super()` method, is used to set the frame's title. A layout manager is established and will be discussed in more detail shortly. A number of `Label` and `TextField` instances are created. A label is a fairly simple component that is merely used to place text on the GUI. We use it here to label an adjacent `TextField` instance, which is used to accept a single line of input from the user. `TextField` instances are used to fetch the **to, from, subject**, and **SMTP host** values from the user. A `TextArea` instance is used to hold the message to be sent. `TextField` is in many respects a specialization of `TextArea`, since `TextArea` is able to accept multiple lines of input. The last component added to the frame is the "send" button. It is here where something occurs that may not be widely familiar to all readers:

```
send = new Button("Send");
send.addActionListener(this);
```

The instance `send` is created. After it is created, the `addActionListener()` method is called, which enables the current object (`this`) to subscribe to events that may be generated by the `send` Button when it is pressed. The `addActionListener()` method has the following signature:

```
public void addActionListener(ActionListener)
```

The class we have defined can double as an `ActionListener`, because it *implements* the `ActionListener` interface. This one statement is an example of a contract being made between two objects (an instance of a `SendMail`, `this`, and an instance of a contained `Button`, `send`). In order for this contract to be completely fulfilled, however, the

`SendMail` class must also provide a definition of the `actionPerformed()` method, which appears in the code, as is discussed shortly.

Layouts. Most graphical-interface toolkits have some notion of how to place components (such as `Label`, `TextField`, and `Button`) within a container (such as a `Frame`). In Java, the layout concept is intentionally very abstract. This has much to do with Java's origins, wherein Java was intended to be the quintessential Web programming language. The inception of the Web brought with it the notion that the display of the Web interface should be possible on a wide variety of devices. Java would only sell in the browser if it could adhere to this policy—at least that was the hope. Of course, industry politics ultimately led to a virtually Java-free browser world, despite all of the right technical decisions having been made. Java's layout concept was the right technical decision. Using Java layouts, the programmer could describe the relative placement of components with respect to one another within a container without worrying about *exactly* where the components would be placed. Although we have not gone through the pain and suffering to make the perfect-looking interface here, it is remarkable how (with little effort) you can create a reasonably attractive interface that is fully functional in a fairly small code footprint.

Earlier, in the discussion of the constructor, we mentioned that more would be said shortly about layouts. Well, that was almost true. In any event, the constructor makes use of a layout object. This is done by calling the `setLayout()` method, which is inherited from the `Frame` class (and ultimately from the `Container` class). In the example, we use an instance of `GridBagLayout` to perform the actual layout. A `GridBagLayout` can be thought of (for practical purposes) as a partitioning of a space into a grid of variable cell sizes. The traditional notion of a grid is also supported in Java by the `GridLayout` class. `GridBagLayout` is sufficiently advanced. You don't need to know much more about it and can continue to our discussion of the `sendMail()` method; however, for completeness, the details are presented in the remainder of this section.

To use `GridBagLayout`, you do not have to indicate how many grid cells there will be. You simply have to define a constraints object for each component you wish to place in the container. We have taken the approach of laying out the components in row-major order. The `GridBagConstraints` class must be used to define how components are actually added. In our example, two instances of `GridBagConstraints`, gbc0 and gbc, are used for this purpose. gbc0 is used for the first object being placed on a row, and gbc is used for the very last object placed on a row. This scheme works perfectly well for our example and is primarily being used to support the case where we need to place an instance of a `Label` next to an instance of a `TextField`. You will need to study the `GridBagConstraints` class for more details. We only make use of the `gridwidth` field of this object, which is a public instance variable that allows us to specify the number of grid cells that are "occupied" by a component. In practice, there are two values used:

- `1`: Use a single grid cell for the component.

- `GridBagConstraints.REMAINDER`: Use however many cells are needed to fill the row. In practice, this often turns out to be one cell (the last component you are adding to the container). The practical consequence of using this value for the `gridwidth` is that it also causes the next component you add to be placed on the next row.

Event handling. The event handler, `actionPerformed(ActionEvent ae)`, is called whenever the `send` button is pressed. When this method is called, the parameter `ae` contains information that can be used to determine more information about the event. In practice, you usually know exactly what the event *should* be. This is particularly true in the case of our application, since the `send` object added the `SendMail` instance `this` as the only listener. Furthermore, there were no other objects that called `addActionListener(this)` at construction time. Nonetheless, the code here errs on the conservative side by checking that the source of the event is precisely the object that we are expecting. Since we saved a reference to the `send` button at construction time, the `getSource()` method can be called on the `ae` method to verify that the `send` object actually generated the event. The beauty of Java is that we can actually do reference comparison to check that the source of the event is the `send` button itself:

```
if (ae.getSource() == send) ...
```

One might be tempted to rush to judgment and suggest that this test is completely unnecesary and should be eliminated. After all, there is only one object that can generate an `ActionEvent` (the `send` button instance). We would respond "guilty as charged" in this case. Now consider what would happen if you add another button `cancel` to change your mind. The current code would be easy to modify to accommodate the new button. Code that did not explicitly test for the `send` button would possibly require extensive modifications. In general, you should always keep references to components that generate events and explicitly test whether the source of a given event object matches the object that is responsible for having generated the event.

Sending mail: the final frontier. In graphical applications, it is often the case that the GUI code is harder to explain than the actual business problem being solved. This will no doubt help to you appreciate your e-mail client, which undoubtedly has a significantly more involved interface than our `SendMail` program. When the `send` button is pressed, this is what triggers a call to the private `sendMail()` method, which actually uses all of the information captured by the GUI to send the mail.

The `sendMail()` method itself is fairly straightforward. As shown earlier, the first several statements in this method are dedicated to opening a socket to the SMTP service.

Then, the `InputStream` and `OutputStream` references are obtained and turned into appropriate `Reader` and `Writer` streams, respectively, to perform actual I/O on the connection. Now the session can actually begin. As shown earlier in box entitled "Using Telnet to Contact sendmail: The Unix Mail Delivery Service" the rest of the code is dedicated to mimicking what happens during the interactive session. SMTP commands are sent, one at a time, to prepare a message for delivery. Each message being sent is packed into a character string (the `command` variable) and sent using the `send()` method. The `receive()` method is called to ensure the retrieval response from the server.

The `send()` method uses the output stream object `out` to transmit the message to the SMTP service. Since the SMTP service works with line-oriented commands, we use the `println()` method provided by the `PrintWriter` class (the class of the `out` instance). Some care is required when working with a socket. Just because we actually sent characters via the output stream does not imply that the characters are actually bound for the network immediately. This is due to *buffering*, which is used to improve I/O performance in virtually all programming languages and libraries for I/O. To ensure that the data are written to the underlying stream, Java provides the method `flush()`. When called, any characters that have been buffered will be forcibly written to the underlying stream. In general, you'll need to do this to guarantee a response from a server, since you cannot know in general how many layers of streams actually exist. It could well be that there is no buffering in any of the layers in a particular situation; however, in this case, it still does no harm to call `flush()`. Java does whatever it can to keep the cost of a call to `flush()` to a minimum by caching information about whether the underlying stream is actually buffered.

The `receive()` method is a bit more involved. To some extent, this has a great deal to do with the way that the SMTP protocol works. Whenever a message is sent to the server, it is possible that more than one line of output is returned to the client. Unfortunately, the protocol itself does not give you any way of finding out how much output will be returned. You can inspect this for yourself by visiting the box where we conducted the SMTP session using telnet. When sending the EHLO command, several lines of responses are generated. A more elaborate mail client would use all of these responses to know precisely what kind of mail can be sent using the service. (There are a good number of SMTP implementations out there, and not all of them adhere to the current standard.) Because our `sendmail` client is only designed to send ASCII text messages, we are more or less guaranteed to be able to send mail using any version (even old versions) of SMTP. The consequence of not knowing how much output can be generated is somewhat problematic. If the client keeps trying to read from the underlying stream, it will eventually block. This will prevent the client from writing the next command to the server, which is necessary in order to get more responses from the server. It is almost a Catch 22 situation, but can be solved in one of two ways:

- Test the stream in to determine whether a single character can be read from the stream without blocking. All classes inherited from the Reader class have the ability to determine this using the ready() method.

- Read responses from the server in a separate thread.

The code in the present example adopts the first approach. (The second approach has also been coded and is provided in the accompanying CD and on the Web.) The receive() method is designed under the assumption that it is called only after send(). Thus, it is guaranteed that there will be at least one character returned as a response without blocking indefinitely. The only reason that this would not happen is if the socket connection died, in which case an I/O exception would occur, which is acceptable. Characters are read in a bottom-tested loop that terminates only when the next attempt to read a character would cause the next read() to block indefinitely.

Once the QUIT message has been sent and the response received, the mail message can be assumed to have been sent successfully. When the sendMail() method exits, you can assume that control returns to the actionPerformed() method, which destroys the SendMail GUI and exits with a normal (0) exit status code.

Example 11-2 SendMail.java

```java
package com.toolsofcomputing.networking;

import java.awt.*;
import java.awt.event.*;
import java.io.*;
import java.net.*;
import java.util.*;

public class SendMailSync extends Frame implements ActionListener
{

    private TextField to, from, subject, smtpHost;
    private TextArea message;
    private Button send;
    private Socket smtpConnection;

    private PrintWriter out;
    private InputStreamReader in;

    public SendMailSync() {
        super("SendMail by Tools of Computing LLC");
        setLayout(new GridBagLayout());
        GridBagConstraints gbc0 = new GridBagConstraints();
        GridBagConstraints gbc = new GridBagConstraints();
        gbc0.gridwidth = 1;
```

```java
        gbc.gridwidth = GridBagConstraints.REMAINDER;
        to = new TextField(40);
        to.setText("gkt@gauss.jhpc.cs.depaul.edu");
        to.setText("gkt@localhost");
        from = new TextField(40);
        from.setText("gkt@cs.depaul.edu");
        from.setText("gkt@localhost");
        subject = new TextField(40);
        subject.setText("GEORGE MAIL: " + new Date().toString());
        smtpHost = new TextField(40);
        smtpHost.setText("gauss.jhpc.cs.depaul.edu");
        smtpHost.setText("localhost");
        add(new Label("To:"),gbc0);
        add(to,gbc);
        add(new Label("From:"),gbc0);
        add(from,gbc);
        add(new Label("Subject:"),gbc0);
        add(subject,gbc);
        add(new Label("SMTP Agent:"),gbc0);
        add(smtpHost,gbc);
        message = new TextArea(25,40);
        add(new Label("Message"),gbc);
        add(message,gbc);
        send = new Button("Send");
        send.addActionListener(this);
        add(send,gbc);
        pack();
        show();
    }

    public void actionPerformed(ActionEvent ae) {
        if (ae.getSource() == send) {
            sendMail();
            this.dispose();
            System.exit(0);
        }
    }

    private void send(String command) throws IOException {
        out.println(command);
        System.out.println("<send> " + command);
        out.flush();
    }

    private void receive() throws IOException {
        System.out.println("<receive>");
        do {
            int chi = in.read();
```

```
            if (chi < 0) break;
            System.out.print( (char) chi);
        } while (in.ready());
        System.out.println("</receive>");
    }

    private void sendMail() {
        try {
            smtpConnection = new Socket(smtpHost.getText(),25);
            System.out.println("<general> Connected to "
              + smtpHost.getText() + "\n");
            OutputStream os = smtpConnection.getOutputStream();
            OutputStreamWriter osw = new OutputStreamWriter(os);
            out = new PrintWriter(osw);

            InputStream is = smtpConnection.getInputStream();
            InputStreamReader isr = new InputStreamReader(is);
            in = isr;

            String command;

            command = "EHLO jhpc.cs.depaul.edu";
            send(command);
            receive();

            int msgLength = subject.getText().length()
              + message.getText().length() + "Subject: ".length();
            command = "MAIL FROM: <" + from.getText()
              + "> SIZE="+msgLength;
            send(command);
            receive();

            command = "RCPT TO: <" + to.getText() + ">";
            send(command);
            receive();

            command = "DATA";
            send(command);
            receive();

            command = "Subject: " + subject.getText() + "\n"
              + message.getText() + "\n" + ".";

            send(command);
            receive();
```

```
            command = "QUIT";
            send(command);
            receive();
            smtpConnection.close();
        } catch(Exception e) {
            System.out.println("<general> " +  e.toString());
        }
    }

    public static void main(String args[]) {
        SendMailSync sm = new SendMailSync();
    }

}
```

Where are The Services?

The foregoing discussion has been about SMTP, which is just one of many network services that are provided on your computer. As introduced earlier, a service is usually known by a common name, a protocol, and a port number. In Unix, the information about services is kept in the /etc/services file; Windows usually keeps this information in the registry.

The notion of exposed services that are available on a computer lends itself nicely to another programming example, which we call `PortScan` (affectionately named after the port scanners and sniffers that are available on the market, usually used by prospective eavesdroppers). The code for this is provided in two parts, which are shown in Example 11-3 and Example 11-4. The port scanner works by reading the /etc/services file, provided on all flavors of Unix, and a range of ports (low and high values) to be scanned. By iterating from the low to high values, an attempt is made to connect to the port. If the connection is successful, the port number is displayed, as well as the name of the service, if it corresponds to a well-known service; otherwise, nothing is displayed. Thus, the port scanner itself represents a very simple program overall.

Let us now examine the code in a little more detail. The code shown in Example 11-3 is a handy class that mimics the functionality found in the Perl and Python language (and library) to split a character string, given a set of delimiters, into a list of fields. Recall that the lines of the /etc/services file have the following general structure

```
# service              port/protocol
smtp                    25/tcp
```

In Perl, it is possible to parse this information—quickly—using the intrinsic `split()` function, which even allows multiple delimiters to be specified:

```
# Fragment of Perl code to quickly parse an input line into
# multiple fields, given a set of delimiters (regular expression)

FP = open("/etc/services","r")
while (<FP>) {
    (service, port, protocol) = split(/ \/\n/)
}
```

Python also supports a similar notion, but does not permit multiple delimiters to be used to perform the split. The code is still fairly straightforward:

```
# Fragment of Python code to do the same thing:

import string
fp = open('/etc/services','r')
allLines = fp.readlines()
for line in allLines:
    (service, pp) = string.split(line, ' \n')
    (port, protocol) = string.split(pp, '/\n')
```

Although Java's capabilities are very object oriented and customizable, Python and Perl provide a great deal more language-level (and library level) support for tasks that often need to be performed on strings. Text-processing applications really demand the capabilities that are found in both of these languages.

Recognizing the need, the the `Splitter` class shown in Example 11-3 was designed to support the same flexibility provided by Perl and Python, subject to the language limitations.

A Splitter is constructed from a number of user-supplied values:

- **Text**: This is the initial string to be split. It is optional to specify the text at construction time; however, the text must be specified before any attempt to extract fields.

- **Labels**: This is a set of character strings used to name the fields. Java does not permit you to have multiple variables on the left-hand side of an expression (list *L*-values). Using the labels, we can access fields of a string by name. The labels are optional. Fields can always be accessed by position, beginning with zero.

- **Delimiters**: This is a set of characters that can be used to delimit the fields. If no delimiters are specified, whitespace delimiters (space, newline, and tab) are chosen by default.

In addition to user-specified values, the splitter maintains a couple of private data structures to aid in performing the split and maintaining good performance:

- **Tokens**: These are contained in a `Vector` object of all tokens for the input line currently being processed.

- **Tokenizer**: This is Java's built-in `StringTokenizer` class that allows us to split strings according to a set of delimiters. This class does not keep track of all of the tokens and thus prevents true random access to the various tokens, hence the existence of the `Splitter` class.

The `Splitter` class supports a number of methods. We only make use of one of these methods; however, for completeness, we discuss the key capabilities of this class, which is likely to be a useful companion in your toolbox of text-processing features:

- **public String getTokenAt(int pos)**: This returns the token a given position. Positions are numbered from zero. Thus, if you want the first field, you need to specify a parameter value of zero.

- **public String getTokenAt(String label)**: This returns the token at a given label. The label is looked up in the list of labels, if they were provided by the user, and the index position is computed. For example, in the /etc/services input file, you could use `getTokenAt("service")` to return the value at that field's position (0).

- **public void getAllTokens()**: This simply returns a `Vector` object of all tokens to you; however, you should be careful to copy the vector if you need the results permanently, because a reference to the private vector is being returned and thus has the potential to be corrupted. This can easily be done with vector cloning (i.e., calling the `clone()` method).

- **public void setTokenAt(String token, int pos)**: You can change the value of a particular field. This can be useful if you want the ability to put the string back together.

- **public String join(String before, String between, String after, boolean squash)**: A string can be formed from the tokens. This is a feature supported in Python and Perl. You can also specify some "glue" to be pasted before the first token, after the last token, and between every pair of tokens.

Thus, this class provides nearly 100% compatibility with the interfaces found in Python and Perl. We only make use of the `getTokenAt()` method in the code shown in Example 11-4, which is the subject of the rest of this section.

Example 11-3 Splitter: A Convenient Little Utility for Breaking up Input Lines
```
package com.toolsofcomputing.text;

import java.util.*;

public class Splitter {
```

```java
    private String text;
    private String delimiters;
    private Vector tokens;
    private StringTokenizer tokenizer;
    private String labels[];

    public Splitter(String[] labels, String text,
       String delimiters) {
        this.text = text;
        this.delimiters = delimiters;
        tokens = new Vector();
        tokenizer = null;
        this.labels = labels;
        performSplit();
    }

    public Splitter(String text, String delimiters) {
        this(new String[0], text, delimiters);
    }

    public Splitter(String[] labels, String delimiters) {
        String defaultText = "";
        for (int i=0; i < labels.length; i++) {
            defaultText += labels[i];
            defaultText += delimiters.charAt(0);
        }
        this.text = defaultText;
        this.delimiters = delimiters;
        tokens = new Vector();
        tokenizer = null;
        this.labels = labels;
        performSplit();
    }

    public void setText(String text) {
        this.text = text;
        performSplit();
    }

    public void setDelimiters(String delimiters) {
        this.delimiters = delimiters;
        performSplit();
    }
```

```java
public void setTextAndDelimiters(String text,
  String delimiters) {
    this.text = text;
    this.delimiters = delimiters;
    performSplit();
}

public void setLabels(String[] labels) {
    this.labels = labels;
}

public String getLabel(int index) {
    if (labels == null || index < 0 || index >= labels.length)
        return index + "";
    else
        return labels[index];
}

private void performSplit() {
    tokenizer = new StringTokenizer(text, delimiters);
    tokens.removeAllElements();
    while (tokenizer.hasMoreTokens()) {
        tokens.addElement(tokenizer.nextToken());
    }
}

public int getTokenCount() {
    return tokens.size();
}

public String getTokenAt(int position) {
    if (position >= 0 && position < tokens.size())
        return (String)tokens.elementAt(position);
    else
        return null;
}

public String getTokenAt(String label) {
    int index = findLabel(label);
    if (index < 0) {
        try {
            index = Integer.parseInt(label);
        } catch(NumberFormatException e) {
            return null;
        }
    }
    return getTokenAt(index);
}
```

```
    private int findLabel(String label) {
        int index;
        for (index=0; index < labels.length; index++)
            if (label.equals(labels[index]))
                return index;
        return -1;
    }

    public Vector getAllTokens() {
        return tokens;
    }

    public void setTokenAt(String text, int position) {
        tokens.setElementAt(text, position);
    }

    public String toString() {
        int i;
        String s = "";

        for (i=0; i < getTokenCount(); i++) {
            if (i > 0)
                s = s + "\n";

            s = s + "[" + getLabel(i) + "] = " + getTokenAt(i);
        }
        return s;
    }

}
```

The `PortScan` code itself is fairly straightforward. In truth, we probably do not need to create an object to perform the scanning operation, since this class only peforms a single function: scanning a range of ports.

The constructor is where we make use of the `Splitter` class that was discussed earlier. We build on a concept that was presented earlier, called stream layering. The biggest challenge in working with Java streams is to find the class that can perform a function that is needed. The `FileReader` class allows us to open a file for input. We layer a `BufferedReader` instance atop the `FileReader` so we can read a single line of input at a time, since the services file is an ASCII text file of a line-oriented nature. Once the line of input is read, the `Splitter` class is put to work, so a hash table of all predefined services can be built. `Hashtable services` maintains an association between a port number (contained in a character string) and a service name (also contained in a character string). That's all the constructor does.

The `scan()` method has been designed to allow multiple scans to be performed. An iteration is performed from the low to the high port values that were specified by the user. For each value, an attempt is made to open a socket to the service. This code is contained in a `try-catch` block, because many attempts are going to result in exceptions, since there is simply no service running on that port. When a `Socket` instance is successfully created, the port is looked up in `services`, and if the port is found, the name of the service is printed. If the port is not found, it is listed as an unknown service. In the case where a socket was successfully opened, the connection is closed at the end to ensure that system resources are not being wasted. (Sockets are IPC mechanisms, and most systems do have hard limits on how many of a particular resource can be used at a particular time, although the number is usually quite large.)

Example 11-4 **PortScan.java: scan a range of ports for standard (and other) services**

```
package com.toolsofcomputing.networking;

import com.toolsofcomputing.text.*;
import java.io.*;
import java.net.*;
import java.util.*;

public class PortScan {
    private Hashtable services;
    public static String[] serviceLabels = {"service","pinfo" };
    public static String[] portInfoLabels = { "port", "proto" };
    private Splitter lineSplitter;
    private Splitter portInfoSplitter;

    public PortScan(String servicesFile) throws Exception {
        FileReader fr = new FileReader(servicesFile);
        BufferedReader br = new BufferedReader(fr);
        String inLine;
        lineSplitter = new Splitter(serviceLabels," \t\n");
        portInfoSplitter = new Splitter(portInfoLabels,"/");
        services = new Hashtable();

        while (true) {
            inLine = br.readLine();
            if (inLine == null) break;
            if (inLine.startsWith("#")) continue;
            lineSplitter.setText(inLine);
            String service = lineSplitter.getTokenAt("service");
            String portinfo = lineSplitter.getTokenAt("pinfo");
            if (portinfo == null) continue;
            portInfoSplitter.setText(portinfo);
            String port = portInfoSplitter.getTokenAt("port");
```

```
            String protocol =
              portInfoSplitter.getTokenAt("proto");
            if (protocol.equals("tcp"))
                services.put(port,service);
        }
    }

    public void scan(String host, int lo, int hi) {
        int count=0;
        for (int port=lo; port <= hi; port++) {
            count++;
            if (count % 1000 == 0)
                System.out.println("Tested " + count + " ports.");
            try {
                Socket s = new Socket(host, port);
                String service = (String)services.get(port + "");
                if (service != null)
                    System.out.println(port + " -> " + service);
                else
                    System.out.println(port + "...unknown");
                s.close();
            } catch(Exception e) {
            }
        }
    }

    public static void main(String args[]) {
        try {
            PortScan ps = new PortScan("/etc/services");
            ps.scan(args[0],
              Integer.parseInt(args[1]),
              Integer.parseInt(args[2]));
        } catch(Exception e) {
            System.out.println(e);
            e.printStackTrace();
        }
    }
}
```

It is interesting to run this program to see the results against typical Windows and Unix configurations. We ran the program against our laboratory machines. The most obvious difference between the two is that more services are running on Unix than on Windows. This is not to insinuate that Windows is an inferior technology; however, out of the box, Windows definitely does not come configured with nearly as many useful services as Unix. The authors here are aware of a number of interesting claims made pertaining to Windows and Unix security, wherein Windows is claimed to have higher security. This argument certainly holds true if you limit the discussion to the number of services and ignore how the services are configured. The more services that there are running, the more susceptible you are to attack. Our Windows setup, however, is not representative of a truly typical Windows setup, wherein a few services are added, such as SMTP (provide by Microsoft Exchange Server), web service (provided by Internet Information Server), and a remote-terminal capability, usually provided by VNC or Citrix products.

Output on a Typical Linux Setup (Workstation)
```
22  -> ssh
23  -> telnet
25  -> smtp
80  -> www
98  -> linuxconf
111 -> sunrpc
113 -> auth
139 -> netbios-ssn
389 found but unknown service
515 -> printer
789 found but unknown service
794 found but unknown service
970 found but unknown service
Tested 1000 ports.
1024 found but unknown service
1025 found but unknown service
1029 found but unknown service
1033 found but unknown service
1034 found but unknown service
1035 found but unknown service
1036 found but unknown service
Tested 2000 ports.
Tested 3000 ports.
3306 -> mysql
Tested 4000 ports.
Tested 5000 ports.
```

In both cases, observe that a number of ports are registering as unknown services. This is not completely true.[2] Some of these services actually correspond to user programs that are listening on a particular port for incoming connections or possibly detached processes that

---

[2] PortScan differs from protocol analyzers and lower-level tools in that it does not actually look at protocol messages but simply well-known ports.

Output on a Typical Windows NT Setup (Server)
Example 11-5 Output Against a Windows NT 4.0 Setup
```
135 found but unknown service
139 -> netbios-ssn
Tested 1000 ports.
1032 found but unknown service
Tested 2000 ports.
Tested 3000 ports.
Tested 4000 ports.
Tested 5000 ports.
```

have allocated a port for a callback from a remote server. Thus, the port scanner should be construed as the "first call" to identify candidate ports for further exploration. To find out what is running (in general), you need to attempt to commnicate with the services that have been discovered by sending protocol messages or commands to perturb the service and (hopefully) get the service to "talk" to you.

A Kind and Gentle Introduction to the Server Side

Example 11-6 depicts a typical client–server networking setup. This setup represents the typical architecture of most message-passing schemes one will encounter that are based on sockets.

Example 11-6 Typical Client–Server Setup in Java

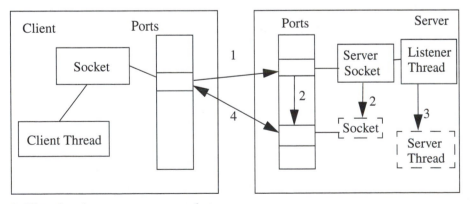

1. Client thread connects to server socket.
2. Connection automatically allocates a new port and socket on Server.
3. Listener thread allocates a server thread and hands it to the socket.
4. Client and server conduct their business.

There are four general steps to be performed in a typical clients–server environment:

1. The client initates contact with the server.

2. The server listens for and accepts client connections.

3. The server (optionally) allocates a thread to communicate with the client.

4. Business is conducted.

Iterative Servers

Example 11-7 contains the source code for a date-and-time server (class `DateTimeServer`), which is similar to the date-and-time service found in the Unix operating system. It is an example of an iterative server, which is a server that accepts requests one at a time and processes them fully, much like loop iterations in which each iteration of the loop passes through the body of the loop and executes fully (unless, of course, you have parallelized the iterations as we discussed in the chapter on parallel loops.)

Let us now consider the details of class `DateTimeServer`. This is the first example in which we make use of the `ServerSocket` class. `ServerSocket` is provided in the java.net package (with the `Socket` and `InetAddress` classes we presented earlier) and is a useful building block for building internet services. The `ServerSocket` class differs from `Socket` in its ability to accept incoming connections from clients. This is done using the `accept()` method, as shown in the code. When an incoming connection is accepted, a connection is obtained, and a reference to a `Socket` instance is returned. Once this reference is obtained, communication can be performed with the client and (once the communication has been completed), another connection can be accepted.

Example 11-7 Iterative Date-and-Time Server

```java
import java.net.*;
import java.io.*;
import java.util.*;

class DateTimeServer {
    public static void main(String[] args){
        if (args.length<1) {
            System.out.println("usage: java DayTimeServer port");
            System.exit(0);
        }
        try{
            int port = Integer.parseInt(args[0]);
            ServerSocket ssock=new ServerSocket(port);
            for(;;) {
                Socket s=ssock.accept();
                OutputStream os = s.getOutputStream();
                PrintWriter out=new PrintWriter(os);
                Date d = new Date();
                out.println(d);
```

```
            out.close();
            s.close();
        }
    } catch (IOException e) {
        return;
    }
  }
}
```

The real work in the code is done in a section known as the server loop. A server loop is almost always an infinite loop and is used in all distributed object systems, such as remote method invocation (RMI) and common object request broker architecture (CORBA). Let's study the details of the server loop a little more closely:

```
for(;;) {
    Socket s=ssock.accept();
    OutputStream os = s.getOutputStream();
    PrintWriter out=new PrintWriter(os);
    Date d = new Date();
    out.println(d);
    out.close();
    s.close();
}
```

The `for(;;)` loop header indicates that there is no initialization condition, no termination condition, and no increment peformed at the end of a loop iteration. This is the preferred way to setup infinite loops in Java (and C and C++ for that matter). You could equivalently do this with a `while(true)` loop header. The `accept()` method is called on the server socket *ssock* and is an example of a call that *blocks* indefinitely. We'll return to a discussion of blocking and its advantages and disadvantages shortly. Once the connection has been accepted, the `getOutputStream()` method gives you a handle for communication on the socket. Although we are not accepting input on this socket, note that there is no fundamental limitation on what you can do with respect to communication. Sockets in Java allow you to obtain both an `InputStream` and an `OutputStream` for communication. By obtaining an OutputStream (rememer that this is the server side of the picture), we are able to write output to the client. We layer a `PrintWriter` instance on top of the `OutputStream` in order to perform higher level output functions. `PrintWriter` is Java's way of giving you the ability to do formatted output in much the same fashion is C's `printf()` function, with the notable difference of being completely safe. We use `println()` to send the `Date` instance d to the output stream, which writes the string representation of d, followed by a newline.

The box "Strings and Java" provides a little insight on character strings and Java, since we are taking advantage of some tricks that may not be familiar to programmers who are coming from a C or FORTRAN background.

Iterative servers, such as the one shown in the `DateTimeServer` example, should only be used in situations where the body of the server loop executes very quickly. The date-and-time service happens to be a good example of such a service. Later, we will show

Strings and Java

Programmers who grew up on C or FORTRAN often find Java's built-in support for strings a bit confusing. Although Java makes string processing ever so much easier, its close integration with the language can be a bit disconcerting.

All Java classes are either direct or indirect descendents of the `Object` class. This means that a `toString()` method is inherited. The purpose of this function is to return a string representation of the class, which is ideal for debugging, as well as for easy conversion to a printable representation. In situations where a `String` is required, any attempt to pass an `Object` (or subclass thereof) will result in the `toString()` method being called. This is actually done in our `DateTimeServer` example, where the `Date` instance d is converted into a `String` when passed to the `println()` method.

The ability to convert any object to a string is also exploited in string concatenation. String concatenation is supported as an intrinsic operation in Java with a specially overloaded + operator. When any attempt is made to include an object in a concaenation expression, such as "s + object" or "object + s", the object will be converted to a string (using its `toString()` method). Then, the string representation will be concatenated with the other string.

`String` is just one of a few classes in Java that straddles the fine line between being a built-in primitive type and a part of the library. For all practical purposes, however, it will be necessary to learn the methods provided by the string class, since it is not possible to perform operations on strings as found in C, such as subscripting, with array-like syntax.

---

examples of where the amount of time to execute the body is either of longer duration or unknown, in which case it will be necessary to dispatch a thread to handle the incoming connection and perform the service. Example 11-8 shows how we can extend the iterative server to concurrently accept connections and perform the service. We realize that for such a simple service it does not make complete sense to create threads for this purpose; however, the intention is to demonstrate how to make the same code concurrent and exists primarily for pedagogical reasons. This same idea will be used to construct a much more general (and complex) services framework later, so we urge you not to rush to judgment quickly about this example being too simple minded in nature.

The `ThreadedDateTimeServer` class is very similar to the earlier example; however, a key difference is that we actually need to create an object for each connection made by clients. This example actually follows the general client–server scenario that was presented earlier in Example 11-6. We will now discuss the code in two parts. First, we discuss the details of the server loop, which is followed by a discussion of the `run()` method, which carries out the date-and-time service.

Example 11-8 Concurrent Date-and-Time Server

```java
import java.net.*;
import java.io.*;
import java.util.*;
```

```java
public class ThreadedDateTimeServer extends Thread {
    private Socket s;

    public ThreadedDateTimeServer(Socket s) {
        this.s = s;
    }

    public static void main(String[] args){
        if (args.length<1) {
            System.out.println
                ("usage: java ThreadedDateTimeServer port");
            System.exit(0);
        }
        try{
            int port = Integer.parseInt(args[0]);
            ServerSocket listener = new ServerSocket(port);
            for(;;) {
                Socket s=listener.accept();
                Thread server = new ThreadedDateTimeServer(s);
                server.start();
            }
        } catch (IOException e) {
            return;
        }
    }

    public void run() {
        try{
            OutputStream os = s.getOutputStream();
            PrintWriter out=new PrintWriter(os);
            Date d = new Date();
            out.println(d);
            out.close();
            s.close();
        } catch (IOException e) {
            return;
        }
    }
}
```

The server loop is always required when implementing a service. This is because requests must be accepted one at a time and processed:

```java
for(;;) {
    Socket s=listener.accept();
    Thread server = new ThreadedDateTimeServer(s);
    server.start();
}
```

As in the `DateTimeServer` iterative server, the `accept()` call is used to accept an incoming connection from the client. This time, however, instead of performing the service immediately, a thread is created to do the actual processing and return the date and time to the client. The `Socket` reference s is passed to the constructor used to initialize the thread reference (server).

You can inspect the code from the body of the iterative date server's server loop; the same exact code is used to return the results to the client. The only difference is that the entire body of the earlier loop (following the `accept()` call) has been moved into the `run()` method, with the only notable difference being a surrounding `try–catch` block.

```java
public void run() {
    try{
        OutputStream os = s.getOutputStream();
        PrintWriter out=new PrintWriter(os);
        Date d = new Date();
        out.println(d);
        out.close();
        s.close();
    } catch (IOException e) {
        return;
    }
}
```

The ability to easily make a concurrent server is what makes Java ideal for network programming. As we'll see shortly, this pair of examples can be used to generalize a services framework for doing client–server programming with sockets. The remainder of this chapter is dedicated to showing how we can build a general-purpose peer-to-peer messaging architecture that supports bidirectional communication. We'll use this messaging framework to reimplement the date-and-time service and then (in the next chapter) show how to evolve this framework in to a distributed framework and demonstrate the potential for scaling the techniques presented throughout the book to the network.

Before proceeding to the discussion of the services framework, it is important to consider when to use (and not to use) threads in a networked context. The challenge of using threads is that there is a trade-off to be made between the execution time of the service and the cost of creating a thread. Even without doing a performance analysis of the preceding code, it is abundantly clear that the cost of creating a date object and turning it into a string is very low. The cost of creating a thread is not so expensive on most operating systems; however, compared with the cost of computing and returning the date, it is expensive. Thus, it is very important to think about these costs and how to optimize. One way to strike a balance is to use the `RunQueue` abstraction presented in an earlier chapter. This allows you to create a working "pool" of threads that are responsible for performing the actual service without having to incur the cost of creating and destroying threads every time the service is performed. The code for a date-and-time server that employs a run queue to concurrently dispatch requests is shown in Example 11-9.

Example 11-9 `RunQueueDateTimeServer`

```java
import java.net.*;
import java.io.*;
import java.util.*;

class RunQueueDateTimeServer {
    public static void main(String[] args){

        if (args.length<1) {
            System.out.println("usage: java DayTimeServer port");
            System.exit(0);
        }
        RunQueue dispatchQueue = new RunQueue(10,5);
        try{
            int port = Integer.parseInt(args[0]);
            ServerSocket ssock=new ServerSocket(port);
            for(;;) {
                Socket s=ssock.accept();
                DateTimeRunnable dtr = new DateTimeRunnable(s);
                dispatchQueue.put(dtr);
            }
        } catch (IOException e) {
            dispatchQueue.terminate();
            return;
        }

    }

    private static class DateTimeRunnable implements Runnable {
        Socket s;

        public DateTimeRunnable(Socket s) {
            this.s = s;
        }

        public void run() {
            try{
                PrintWriter out;
                out = new PrintWriter(s.getOutputStream());
                out.println(new Date());
                out.close();
                s.close();
            } catch(Exception e) {
                return;
            }
        }
    }

}
```

In the foregoing example, the body of the loop is turned into the body of the `run()` method in a nested class (`DateTimeRunnable`) that implements the `Runnable` interface. The `main()` method of this example only differs in the following manner:

- The construction of a `RunQueue` instance: We have instantiated `RunQueue` dispatchQueue with a maximum number of threads (10) and maximum number of waiting threads (5).

- The construction of a `DateTimeRunnable` object that is placed on `dispatchQueue` using the `put()` method.

As finding the date and time is a very simple service, there really is no need to create so many threads. We have set values of 10 and 5 in anticipation of fairly light usage. Real services may need more control of these parameters. When we discuss the `MessageServer`, the service being implemented will be given more control of these parameters.

An interesting question arises: Is this a good use of the run queue? One of the goals in using the run queue was to minimize the cost of thread creation. We have only partly addressed this problem, since we still have the overhead of creating an instance of `DateTimeRunnable`. (Recall that in Example 11-8, we had to create an instance of `ThreadedDateTimeServer`.) Although we still have the overhead of object creation, we no longer have the additional overhead of starting a new thread and cleaning up after it, since the run queue maintains a working pool of threads.

Simple Messaging Architecture

The story of the Internet is fundamentally about client–server services. This is particularly apparent when you look closely at the most common services. In the foregoing discussion, we focused on the date-and-time service, which provides an excellent teaching example. Recognizing the importance of being able to develop Internet services easily, we have devised a simple framework for developing client–server networked applications, which you can use without modifications to make your own Internet services and clients. Example 11-10 shows an interaction diagram involving the various components of a client–server messaging system, which are as follows:

Message: A class used to describe a basic unit of communication. All communication between components is done via `Message` instances.

Deliverable: An interface implemented by any class (usually on the server side) to indicate that a particular object is interested in receiving messages. We refer to this relationship as a subscription, which is a common design pattern. Only classes that implement the `Deliverable` interface may subscribe to messages via a `MessageServer` instance.

MessageServer: A class used to factor out the common functionality of a server. The guts of this class are similar to the `DateTimeServer` but generalized for the purpose of accommodating a multitude of services.

MessageClient: A class used to factor out the common functionality of a client. The guts of this class are similar to the `DateTimeClient` but generalized as in the case of the `MessageServer`.

Example 11-10 Simple Messaging Architecture (Interaction Diagram)

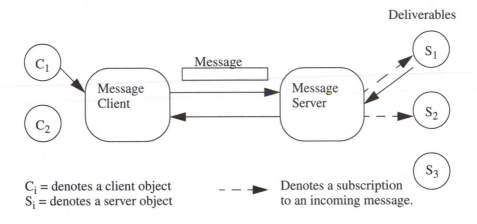

C_i = denotes a client object   Denotes a subscription
S_i = denotes a server object   to an incoming message.

Thus, simple messaging architecture (SMA) can be thought of as a very general-purpose set of class libraries for building your own client–server applications.

Let us now consider the various components in detail.

The **Message** *Class*

The core class used in SMA is the `Message` class.[3] A message is an abstraction that is built using a hash table, wherein the keys and values are `String` instances. Users of the `Message` class for all practical purposes think that they are working with something very similar to a hash table; however, a key difference between the `Hashtable` and the `Message` abstraction is that `Hashtable` instances can hold arbitrary objects as keys and values. This works very well for most applications, but can sometimes be very unfriendly for developing Internet services, which (to this day) predominantly make use of primitive data types (i.e., integer, float, and double) and character strings.

The `Message` class demonstrates an example of the power of OOP. OOP allows you to separate the interface from the implementation. Users think that a message is nothing more than a specialized hash table that allows them to work with data types that are commonly used. The implementation actually handles the details of translating the user view into a suitable representation for transmission on the network.

---

[3] An updated version of SMA that supports more data types and makes use of data streams can be found on the books Web site.

Example 11-11 presents the code for the `Message` class. The following attributes are defined in this class (there are others, however, but these are the essential ones):

- **parameters**: This is a `Hashtable` object of user-specified parameters. A parameter is nothing more than a <key,value> association.

- **type**: Every message has a type (an integer). This field is used to provide a quick way of determining what remote service is being accessed. By default, the value of zero is supplied.

- **tag**: Every message can also specify an optional tag (an integer). The concept of a tag is intended as a flag in case there is a need to have a second criterion (other than the `type` field) for selecting a message. We will not be making use of it in the examples of this chapter. Think of it as a field that is reserved for future use.

- **rep**: This is the packed representation of the `Message` (an array of characters). Method `pack()` is used to encode `parameters` into the packed representation.

- **length**: This is the number of characters in the encoded representation.

The key methods in the `Message` class include the following:

Constructors:

- **Message()**: This constructs an empty `Message` instance. The message has no type, no tag, and no parameters.

- **Message(char[] packedRep)**: This constructs a `Message` instance from a previously packed message representation. An invalid representation will result in an `Exception` being thrown.

- **pack()**: This prepares the representation of the message for transmission over the network. This representation will be accessible via the `rep` attribute.

- **unpack()**: This unpacks the representation presently being referenced by `rep` into `parameters`. This results in the previous value of parameters being completely clobbered.

There are a number of additional methods provided, such as accessor (get and set) methods, as well as a number of private methods (used for implementating the `pack()` and `unpack()` functions). These will not be discussed here; however, there are two rather important methods that will be discussed that are used to read and write methods from `Reader` and `Writer` character streams, respectively:

- **static Message getMessage(Reader in)**: This (factor) method allows us to return Message instances directly from an underlying stream. For this method to work correctly it is assumed that the stream has been written (using the companion method putMessage(), which writes the packed representation to a Writer stream).

- **void putMessage(Writer out)**: This method allows us to write the packed representation of a Message to a Writer stream to potentially be read again later via a call to getMessage().

These two methods can work in harmony to allow client–server communication in terms of messages, which is significantly easier than working with arrays of characters (the normal case for sockets programming). SMA uses Message instances for all communication between peers (the MessageServer and MessageClient classes).

Example 11-11 Message

```java
import java.util.*;
import java.io.*;

public class Message  {
    private static final int T_ANY = 0;
    private static final int T_INTEGER = 1;
    private static final int T_REAL = 2;
    private static final int T_STRING = 3;
    private static final int T_BOOLEAN = 4;
    private static final int T_UNDEFINED = 5;

    private Hashtable parameters = new Hashtable();

    private int type = 0;
    private int tag = 0;
    private int length = 0;

    private static final int HEADER_SIZE = 3;

    private char[] rep;
    private int repIndex = 0;

    private StringBuffer sb = new StringBuffer();

    public Message(char[] packedRep) {
        rep = packedRep;
        unpack();
    }
```

```java
public Message() {

}

public static Message getMessage(Reader in) throws IOException {
    int messageLength = (int) in.read();
    if (messageLength < 0)
        throw new IOException();
    char[] buf = new char[messageLength];
    int bytesRead = in.read(buf,0,messageLength);
    if (messageLength != bytesRead)
        throw new IOException();
    return new Message(buf);
}

public void putMessage(Writer out) throws IOException {
    pack();
    out.write(rep.length);
    out.write(rep);
    out.flush();
}
public void setParam(String key, String value) {
    parameters.put(key,value);
}

public String getParam(String key) {
    return (String) parameters.get(key);
}

public char[] getCharArray() {
    pack();
    return rep;
}

private void putInt(int value) {
    if (repIndex < rep.length)
        rep[repIndex++] = (char) value;
}

private void putParameter(String k, String v) {
    putString(k);
    putString(v);

}
```

```java
private void putString(String s) {
    putInt(s.length());
    putInt(T_STRING);
    char[] convertedText = s.toCharArray();
    for (int i=0; i < convertedText.length; i++)
        rep[repIndex++] = convertedText[i];
}

private int getInt() {
    if (repIndex < rep.length)
        return (int) rep[repIndex++];
    else
        return -1;
}

private String getString() {
    int paramLength = getInt();
    int paramType = getInt();
    sb.setLength(0);
    for (int i=0; i < paramLength; i++) {
        if (repIndex < rep.length)
            sb.append(rep[repIndex++]);
    }
    return sb.toString();
}

private int computeStorageSize() {
    int totalSize = HEADER_SIZE;
    Enumeration e = parameters.keys();
    while (e.hasMoreElements()) {
        String key = (String) e.nextElement();
        totalSize += (2 + key.length());
        String value = (String) parameters.get(key);
        totalSize += (2 + value.length());
    }
    return totalSize;
}

public void pack() {
    int totalStorage = computeStorageSize();
    rep = new char[totalStorage];
    length = totalStorage - HEADER_SIZE;
    repIndex = 0;
    putInt(type);
    putInt(tag);
    putInt(length);
```

```java
        Enumeration e = parameters.keys();
        while (e.hasMoreElements()) {
            String key = (String) e.nextElement();
            String value = (String) parameters.get(key);
            putParameter(key,value);
        }
    }

    public void unpack() {
        /* need to clear out the hashtable first */
        parameters.clear();
        repIndex = 0;
        type = getInt();
        tag = getInt();
        length = getInt();
        while (repIndex < rep.length) {
            String key = getString();
            String value = getString();
            parameters.put(key,value);
        }
    }

    public String toString() {
        return "Message: type = "
          + type
          + " param = "
          + parameters;
    }

    public static void main(String args[]) {
        Message m = new Message();
        m.setParam("v0","1.5");
        m.setParam("v1","2.0");
        m.setParam("person","Luiz");
        m.pack();

        Message m2 = new Message(m.getCharArray());
        System.out.println("v0 = " + m2.getParam("v0"));
        System.out.println("v1 = " + m2.getParam("v1"));
        System.out.println("person = " + m2.getParam("person"));
    }
}
```

So what happens when a `Message` object is packed? Consider the following code, which has been excised from the `main()` method of the code just presented (this is a test case that you can run standalone to get an understanding of what's going on):

```
Message m = new Message();
m.setParam("v0","1.5");
m.setParam("v1","2.0");
m.setParam("person","luiz");
m.pack();
```

This code creates a `Message` instance m and sets three parameters with the `setParam()` method call. Then, the message is packed. When the message is packed, it is translated into a representation (character array) that is suitable for network transmission. (See the `rep` variable discussion from before). Table 11–1 shows the contents of the representation after packing:

Table 11–1 The packed representation of the preceding `Message` instance

Position	Content	Description and Comments
rep+0	0	The `type` field
rep+1	0	The `tag` field
rep+2	N	The `length` field
rep+3	2	
rep+4	T_STRING	T_STRING is an integer constant to flag as a `String`.
rep+5	'v'	
rep+6	'0'	
rep+7	3	
rep+8	T_STRING	This version encodes everything as a `String`. Note that a float value may encode differently than `typed`.
rep+9	'1'	
rep+10	'.'	
rep+11	'5'	
rep+12		This will encode the parameter `"v1"` and `"2.0"`
rep+21		This will encode the parameter `"person"` and `"Luiz"`

MessageServer and Deliverable

At the center of SMA is the `MessageServer` class. `MessageServer` is designed to be a generic container-style class for building your own services. It extends the `Thread` class and is intended to run as a server. If you can ignore a few details for the moment and focus attention on the `run()` method, it should be clear that the `MessageServer` class is in one respect not much different that the `ThreadedDateTimeServer` class discussed earlier. Consider the server loop (found in the `run()` method):

```java
while (true) {
    try {
        Socket s=callListener.accept();
        MessageServerDispatcher csd;
        csd = new MessageServerDispatcher(this, s);
        csd.setDaemon(false);
        csd.start();
    } catch(Exception e) {
        log("Exception " + e);
        e.printStackTrace();
    }
}
```

A connection is accepted as always. A separate class, `MessageServerDispatcher`, is used to construct an instance that will actually handle the incoming connection. This technique was shown earlier in Example 11-8. The code for the `MessageServerDis-patcher` is shown in Example 11-13. We will return to a discussion of this code shortly.

Let us consider a few other aspects of the design of class `MessageServer`. Recalling the original figure showing the architecture of SMA, we see that objects that are interested in providing a service are called deliverables. Any class can provide service simply by implementing the `Deliverable` interface, which provides a single method:

```java
interface Deliverable {
    Message send(Message m);
}
```

This interface represents a contract of sorts. It says that a `Deliverable` object must provide a method `send()` that accepts an incoming `Message` m and returns a reply `Message` instance. Interfaces, by their very nature, are somewhat abstract, since they provide a mechanism for avoiding implementation details. After we have finished introducing all of the classes of SMA, there will be a concrete example that ties all of the principles together.

The `MessageServer` class contains two important methods that pertain to deliverables:

- **`public void subscribe(int messageType, Deliverable d)`**: This method allows a given `Deliverable` d to subscribe to a particular type of message. Recall that every message has a type, which is set via the `setType()` method provided in class `Message`.

- **public Deliverable getSubscriber(int messageType)**: This
method returns the deliverable that is subscribed to a particular type of message. If
there is no subscriber, null is returned.

The concept of subscription is a very powerful concept for building protocols. In real protocols, the complexity is in writing the handler code for different message types. SMA gives the protocol designer the capability of building a protocol incrementally by ensuring that each type of message has a particular (and hopefully unique!) response. There is one aspect of subscription that needs to be clarified, however. Subscription is limited to one subscriber per message type. This is done to ensure clean semantics. To understand this, consider that a deliverable must reply to a message that is sent to it. If multiple deliverables are subscribers, there would be multiple replies. Which one is returned to the `MessageClient`? It's possible to merge messages (we even provide a method for this capability); however, it can lead to confusion on the client side.

But now we digress. Let us consider the details of the `MessageServerDispatcher` code, shown in Example 11-13.

Example 11-12 MessageServer

```
import java.net.*;
import java.io.*;
import java.util.*;

public class MessageServer extends Thread {
    private ServerSocket callListener;
    private Hashtable subscribers;

    public static final boolean logging = true;

    public void log(String s) {
        if (!logging) return;
        System.err.println("MessageServer: " + s);
    }

    public MessageServer(int port) throws IOException {
        log("Simple Messaging Architecture (SMA) version 1.0");
        log("Copyright (c) 2000, George K. Thiruvathukal");
        callListener = new ServerSocket(port);
        subscribers = new Hashtable();
        log("Created MessageServer instance fully!");
    }

    public void subscribe(int messageType, Deliverable d) {
        subscribers.put(messageType + "", d);
    }
```

```
public Deliverable getSubscriber(int messageType) {
    return (Deliverable) subscribers.get(messageType + "");
}

public void run() {
    log("MessageServer thread started. run() dispatched.");
    while (true) {
        try {
            Socket s=callListener.accept();
            MessageServerDispatcher csd;
            csd = new MessageServerDispatcher(this, s);
            csd.setDaemon(false);
            csd.start();
        } catch(Exception e) {
            log("Exception " + e);
            e.printStackTrace();
        }
    }
}
}
```

The `MessageServerDispatcher` class is responsible for handling an incoming message (from the `MessageServer` we just discussed). It is important to note that there is a parenting relationship between the `MessageServer` class and the `MessageServerDispatcher` class. (We exploit this relationship to determine from the `MessageServer` the subscriber for a particular type of message. This is why a `MessageServer` reference is maintained in each instance of `MessageServerDispatcher` that is created.

The `run()` method (again) is where all of the action is for class `MessageServerDispatcher`. Let us focus on the loop in this method, which continuously accepts communications from a remote `MessageClient` and sends responses. This loop is excised and shown with annotations:

```
            while (true) {
```

`Message` provides a factory method, `getMessage()`, to read one `Message` at a time from an underlying stream. in refers to input from the socket.

```
            Message m = Message.getMessage(in);
            Message result = null;
            log("Received Message " + m + ".");
```

If a message is found with the "`$disconnect`" parameter (all variables beginning with "$" are reserved by SMA), the client has gracefully decided to end the session.

```
            if (m.getParam("$disconnect") != null) {
                log("$disconnect found in Message " + m);
                System.err.println("-> Disconnect");
                Message ack = new Message();
                ack.pack();
```

```
                    ack.putMessage(out);
                    socket.close();
                    return;
                }
            Deliverable d;
```

Find the subscriber that is interested in the type of message just received:

```
            d = callServer.getSubscriber(m.getType());
```

If there is a subscriber, deliver the message m and capture the reply in `result`; otherwise, there is no subscriber interested in this message. It is not a fatal error; however, we need to send an empty reply message back to ensure the client receives a reply:

```
                if (d != null)
                    result = d.send(m);
                else {
                    System.err.println("-> No subscribers found.");
                    result = new Message();
                }
```

The `pack()` method (as discussed earlier) is called to arrange the message as an array of characters for transmission via the underlying output stream. Once the message is packed, `putMessage()` can be used to send it to the client:

```
                result.pack();
                result.putMessage(out);
            }
```

And that's all there is to it.

Example 11-13 `MessageServerDispatcher`

```
import java.io.*;
import java.net.*;

public class MessageServerDispatcher extends Thread {
    MessageServer callServer;
    Socket socket;
    InputStreamReader in;
    OutputStreamWriter out;
    public static final boolean logging = true;


    public MessageServerDispatcher(MessageServer ms, Socket s)
        throws IOException {
        callServer = ms;
        socket = s;
        in = new InputStreamReader(socket.getInputStream());
        out = new OutputStreamWriter(socket.getOutputStream());
    }

    public void log(String s) {
        if (!logging) return;
        System.err.println("MessageServerDispatcher: " + s);
    }
```

```java
public void run() {
    log("Beginning of dispatch run() method.");
    try {
        while (true) {
            Message m = Message.getMessage(in);
            Message result = null;
            log("Received Message " + m + ".");
            if (m.getParam("$disconnect") != null) {
                log("$disconnect found in Message " + m);
                System.err.println("-> Disconnect");
                Message ack = new Message();
                ack.pack();
                ack.putMessage(out);
                socket.close();
                return;
            }
            Deliverable d;
            d = callServer.getSubscriber(m.getType());
            if (d != null)
                result = d.send(m);
            else {
                System.err.println("-> No subscribers found.")
                result = new Message();
            }
            result.pack();
            result.putMessage(out);
        }
    } catch (EOFException e1) {
        try {
            log("End of file exception." + e1);
            out.close();
            socket.close();
        } catch (Exception e2) {
            log("Unable to free open resources " + e2);
            e2.printStackTrace();
        }
    } catch (Exception e) {
        log("Unknown exception " + e);
        e.printStackTrace();
    }
}
}
```

The `MessageClient` object is used to establish a connection to a `MessageServer` object. The code for `MessageClient` is shown in Example 11-14. To connect to a `MessageServer` object, the host and port must be specified in the constructor.

Attempting to connect to anything other than a `MessageServer` object is likely to result in errors.

The key method of interest in the `MessageClient` class is the `call()` method. Much like making a telephone call, the idea is that the `MessageClient` object can send a message to a `MessageServer` object. This method basically puts the message on the wire (using the `putMessage()` method from the `Message` class). Then, the factory method `getMessage()` is used to read the reply (another `Message` instance) off the wire. Again, note that the client and server only think in terms of `Message` instances. (Recall our earlier discussion about how the entire Internet was built on top of message formats that are defined as arrays of character data.)

The other method of interest is the `disconnect()` method. When a `MessageClient` object no longer needs to interact with a remote `MessageServer` object, it is only polite to disconnect and give the server an opportunity to free up resources elegantly. Disconnection is handled by allocating a message and setting a reserved parameter named "`$disconnect`". When any message is seen by the server that contains this parameter, the session is ended.

This completes the tour of all of the classes that comprise SMA. We conclude by showing how SMA can be used to reimplement the working date-and-time example.

Example 11-14 MessageClient

```
import java.io.*;
import java.net.*;

public class MessageClient extends Thread {
    Socket socket;
    OutputStreamWriter out;
    InputStreamReader in;

    public MessageClient(String host, int port)
      throws IOException {
        socket = new Socket(host, port);
        out = new OutputStreamWriter(socket.getOutputStream());
        in = new InputStreamReader(socket.getInputStream());
    }

    public Message call(Message message) {
        try {
            message.putMessage(out);
        } catch(Exception e) {
            System.err.println("MessageClient (call): " + e);
            return null;
        }
```

```
    try {
        Message m = Message.getMessage(in);
        m.unpack();
        return m;
    } catch(Exception e) {
        System.err.println("MessageClient (reply): " + e);
        return new Message();
    }
}

public void disconnect() {
    Message m = new Message();
    m.setType(0);
    m.setParam("$disconnect","$disconnect");
    call(m);
    try {
        socket.close();
    } catch(Exception e) {
        System.err.println("MessageClient (disconnect): "+e);
    }
}
}
```

DateService *and* DateClient *SMA Style*

Example 11-15 shows the implementation of the DateService class. This class shows the ability of SMA to help you build a network service without needing to know the details of socket programming and streams. You simply think in terms of getting a message and doing something with its parameters.

SMA is somewhat different than programming with sockets. If you consider the earlier implementations of the date-and-time service (and its variants), as soon as the client opened a connection to the server, the server basically just writes the date to its output socket. The client immediately reads from its input socket until there is no more data. Then, the session is ended. SMA imposes *line discipline* on the application. A message must be sent by the client to initiate a response on the part of the server. The server sends a reply that must be read by the client. Then, the client can send another message. This request–reply scenario is almost identical to remote procedure call semantics; however, the intent of SMA is not to be an RPC system, but instead is a set of building blocks for RPC.

The DateService class implements the Deliverable interface. This means that it must provide a send() method that accepts a message and returns a reply. The incoming message m is actually ignored in the send() method, since the DateService object does not expect any parameters from the client. The message is modified by setting the date parameter with the String representation of today's date and then returned. The act of returning a message from the send() method is the first step toward

getting a result to the client. (The rest of the steps are handled in the
`MessageServerDispatcher` code, which was already discussed.)

To actually get a server running, it is necessary at some point to create a
`MessageServer` instance and subscribe at least one instance of the `DateService` to
it. It is also important to create a message type. In the `DateService` class, a number of
constants have been defined:

DATE_SERVICE_MESSAGE: This represents a constant that will be used to represent the
message type for communication with the `DateService`. The value is set to 100, but
could in fact be any number, as long as `DateClient` and `DateService` agree on it. In
`DateClient`, we have taken care to ensure that this constant is used as the message type.

DATE_SERVICE_PORT: This represents the TCP/IP port that will be bound when creating the `SocketServer` (in the `MessageServer` class). Again, the `DateService`
and `DateClient` objects must agree on this value.

In the `main()` method, the `DateService` instance is created as well as a
`MessageServer` instance. The following line of code shows how the `DateService`
instance becomes formally known to the `MessageServer`:

```
ms.subscribe(DATE_SERVICE_MESSAGE, ds);
```

Example 11-15 `DateService`

```java
import java.util.*;

public class DateService implements Deliverable {
    public static final int DATE_SERVICE_MESSAGE = 100;
    public static final int DATE_SERVICE_PORT = 1999;

    public Message send(Message m) {
        Date today = new Date();
        m.setParam("date", today.toString());
        return m;
    }

    public static void main(String args[]) {
        DateService ds = new DateService();
        MessageServer ms;
        try {
            ms = new MessageServer(DATE_SERVICE_PORT);
        } catch(Exception e) {
            System.err.println("Could not start service " + e);
            return;
        }
        Thread msThread = new Thread(ms);
        ms.subscribe(DATE_SERVICE_MESSAGE, ds);
        msThread.start();
    }
}
```

The `DateClient` class in fact is just a driver and only provides a `main()` method. The real work happens where you see `Message m` being instantiated. This message represents the `request` message that is being sent to the remote `DateService`. The `setType()` method is used to establish a type that corresponds to the value of the `DateService`, which is obtained from the `DateService` class, which defined a public static final variable `DATE_SERVICE_MESSAGE`. (Java makes this very convenient!) Just for show, we set a parameter named `person` to `george` and make the call. (This parameter, of course, will be ignored, since the `DateService` is just waiting for a message with the right type field and does not care about the parameters at all.) After the call is made, `date` is obtained by calling `getParam()` on the reply message, the value of which is subsequently printed.

To show that SMA recovers gracefully from human error, a second message is also sent by this client. This message has a hard-coded type of 75 (not equal to the type expected by `DateService`). This message results in an empty message as a reply. If you have not disabled logging on the server side, you'll notice that SMA provides detailed log messages to indicate that a message was received that "has no subscriber."

Example 11-16 `DateClient`

```java
public class DateClient {

    public static void main(String[] args) {
        if (args.length < 2) {
            System.out.println("Usage: DateClient host port");
        }
        String host = args[0];
        int port;
        try {
            port = Integer.parseInt(args[1]);
        } catch(Exception e) {
            port = DateService.DATE_SERVICE_PORT;
        }

        MessageClient conn;
        try {
            conn = new MessageClient(host,port);
        } catch(Exception e) {
            System.err.println(e);
            return;
        }

        Message m = new Message();
        m.setType(DateService.DATE_SERVICE_MESSAGE);
        m.setParam("person","george");
        m = conn.call(m);
        System.out.println("Date " + m.getParam("date"));
```

```
        m.setType(75);
        m = conn.call(m);
        System.out.println("Bad reply " + m);
        conn.disconnect();
}
```

Chapter Wrap-Up

This chapter has provided an introduction to computer networking principles with the intention of providing a sufficiently self-contained introduction and saving you from having to consult other textbooks to understand the advanced material in the remaining chapter (Coordination), wherein it is shown how to build a sophisticated process and thread coordination framework. As well, we have provided a glimpse into how network services are implemented. The emphasis on simplicity (as in the streams chapter) is intentional, since it is assumed that you will fully understand the basics of streams and networking before attempting to read the very last chapter.

SMA itself is being evolved to provide a very lightweight alternative to distributed object systems, such as RMI and CORBA, for building Internet services. There is good reason to believe such a (simplified) messaging framework may prove to be useful. At the time of writing, there is a flurry of activity to build new remote procedure calling (RPC) systems based on XML. One such system is called SOAP (Simple Object Access Protocol), which is an XML/RPC framework. XML is fundamentally a text based format, and so is SMA (although there is nothing to stop it from supporting binary data as well). The question then becomes one of overhead. XML is not a lightweight framework for structuring data. The data must be processed with an appropriate parser. Furthermore, while XML itself is fairly straightforward to learn (as is HTML), working with the parsers requires advanced programming knowledge, even when using the simple parsers. The ideas of SMA could actually be used to strike a balance between simplicity and flexibility. SMA "fields" could simply be XML data, when advanced structure is truly needed.

There is a revised version of the SMA class library available from the book web site. This version supports more data types, binary data, and also has a number of fixes to address bugs that we have encountered using the Reader and Writer classes in Java. The revised version is based on Java's data streams, which are based on byte streams and seem to work more reliably than the character streams.

Exercises

1. In the box entitled "Using Telnet to Contact sendmail: The Unix Mail Delivery Service" the telnet client was used to connect to SMTP and compose a message. Find out what your SMTP server is at your institution, and use it to compose a message to yourself. Does it work?

2.   Use telnet to connect to a site (preferably at your own institution) and interact with the World Wide Web server. You will more than likely need to specify the port numbered 80. Document the various commands that you can execute and what they do.

3.   The `PortScan` example suggests that there are a number of "unknown services" listening on a number of ports. Is it necessarily the case that the service is unknown? Or is this a limitation of the program? Explain.

4.   SMA as presented could also be extended to make use of `DataInputStream` and `DataOutputStream`. Explain why this would be better than packing an array structure and then writing to (or reading from) the underlying stream. Write a new version of SMA that makes use of `DataInputStream` and `DataOutputStream` to read and write `Message` instances. (You can also download the reworked version from the Java Web site.)

5.   Use the SMA classes to implement a basic `AuthenticationService` class. This service will accept messages with username and password parameters and maintain a list of sessions. The authentication will be performed against a password file, which you can assume is an association between username and a plaintext password. The reply message should indicate whether or not the authentication could be performed. Upon successful login, a session identifier should be returned to the user. Time and interest permitting, extend this service to support the notion of an expiration period (a period after which a session will be destroyed).

6.   Use SMA to extend the ideas of the previous question to create a general-purpose messaging system. After a user logs in, he or she can send messages to other users, retrieve incoming messages, etc. This type of service presents the possibility of a "denial of service" attack, since a user's incoming message list could grow without bound. How would you prevent such attacks from occurring? (Hint: You will need to keep some parameters with the user information!)

7.   In the `RunQueueDateTimeServer` example, we showed how to use the `RunQueue` class to service incoming network requests, thus alleviating the overhead of creating threads every time a connection is accepted on the `ServerSocket` object. Extend the SMA classes to make use of the same idea.

Chapter 12

Coordination

The networking classes found in the java.net package give you just about everything you need to build Internet services and other client–server applications, but is not quite what you need for doing parallel and distributed computing. This chapter addresses the basics of how to extend the ideas presented in the previous chapters to the realm of networking with an emphasis on coordination.

The topic of coordination has long been of interest to academic researchers and industry practicioners in the "field" of high-performance computing. The first notable ideas for coordination are found in the *Communicating Sequential Processes*, by Tony Hoare, one of two people behind the monitor concept presented in Chapter 4, and the Linda project done at Yale University. This chapter shows how to build a basic coordination model that is very similar to the seminal works but radically simplified

Before proceeding, we have not included here a discussion of other Java technologies that (in all fairness) allow us to venture beyond the client–server paradigm. These include RMI, CORBA, Java Spaces, and Jini. Of these four, Java Spaces is most similar to what we define as a coordination system. Java Spaces is a key component of the Jini architecture, and we believe that there are a number of excellent books in print that provide an excellent overview of these technologies. We have chosen not to cover these technologies in this book and focus on lighter and leaner frameworks that specifically address the need for (easily) writing parallel and distributed codes. For those who are interested in learning more about the relevant Java distributed computing technologies, we provide a comprehensive list of references at the end of the chapter.

The chapter begins with an overview of the generic mailbox invocation system (GMI). GMI is a simple remote procedure calling framework that makes use of Java object serialization. The GMI system is used to build Memo, which is a simple coordination model derived from the Linda project. The Memo system can be considered a remote interface to the shared table of queues abstractions presented in Chapter 9. This chapter presents a few examples of how to translate some codes presented earlier into versions that make use of the coordination facilities found in the Memo system. The examples presented include vector inner product (`VMpy`), trapezoidal integration (`IntegTrap`), and Warshall's algorithm (`Warshall`).

Generic Mailbox Invocations

GMI is a framework for peer-to-peer communication that we developed to facilitate the development and deployment of clustering software. It was developed somewhat as a response to remote method invocation (RMI). RMI is Java's built-in framework for doing remote procedure calling, which is accompanied by another framework called object serialization.

We will not discuss the details of RMI here, again leaving this discussion to books that have been written entirely on the subject. On the other hand, we will address the reasons why RMI does not work terribly well for clustered applications:

- **Serialization overhead**: The use of RMI virtually goes hand-in-hand with object serialization. Serialization is a very elegant framework that is designed to support the migration of tree-structured objects. Most clustered computing algorithms make little or no use of such complex data structures. In fact, the most commonly used data structures are scalars (boolean, character, integer, and floating point) and basic aggregations (one-, two-, and three-dimensional arrays of scalar). Java serialization does a particularly poor job of handling these basic cases, and a number of papers have been written that describe the problems in detail. Effectively, the Serialization facility supports call-by-copy semantics, which breaks the call-by-reference semantics that are Java's normal parameter passing scheme.

- **Registry**: The registry is a useful program for maintaining a semipersistent repository of objects that can be used remotely; however, it also adds a layer of indirection when it comes to communication. Latency is a major factor in the performance of any distributed communication system. TCP/IP sockets programming itself presents much unwanted latency in a clustered environment, since the assumption of the protocol is that the underlying network is not reliable. Adding more layers atop TCP/IP only exacerbates the problem of latency.

- **Sloppy Object Model**: Perhaps the worst aspect of the RMI system is its sloppy object model. Any class that is going to be used to create remote objects must inherit from one of Java's base classes, such as `UnicastRemoteObject`. This may not seem like a problem at first, but presents a great deal of difficulty if the class being served is actually a subclass of another class already. Unlike the `Threads` classes, which also have companion interfaces that can be implemented, RMI forces you to waste inheritance from a class that has no perceptibly useful functionality. This has also been discussed in a paper written by one of the authors.

There are more reasons; however, this list should be enough for anyone to think twice before trying to use RMI for an application that was never intended. RMI looks a little too much like a client–server paradigm, and what we need is a more peer-oriented paradigm.

GMI: Goals and Design Overview

GMI was thus created not as an alternative to RMI, but rather as a building block for building a peer-oriented communication system. It was also designed with extensibility in mind. The basic design of GMI consists of a very lean set of classes:

- **CallMessage**: This is an extension of the `Message` class. The key difference between the `CallMessage` and a `Message` is the ability to encode and decode. These functions can be useful to pack or unpack data structures that are sent as messages.
- **Callable**: This is an interface that can be implemented so an object can receive messages. The concept of `Callable` is very similar to the `Deliverable` concept presented in the discussion of SMA, but one level up.
- **RemoteCallServer**: This is a class that can be used to receive remote calls. The `RemoteCallServer` provides an API very similar to Java's naming framework (the interface to the rmiregistry). The difference here is that the `RemoteCallServer` also doubles as a registry for finding objects by name.
- **RemoteCallClient**: This is a class used to make remote calls.

Callable: *An Interface for Accepting Communication*

The notion of a `Callable` bears many similarities to the `MessageRecipient` presented in the SMA classes from the previous chapter. The callable notion refers to any object that can be called (remotely) with a `CallMessage` object.

```
package jhpc.gmi;

import java.io.*;

public interface Callable {
    Serializable call(CallMessage message) throws Exception;
}
```

CallMessage: *An Abstract Class for Marshalling and Unmarshalling!*

The CallMessage class is used to package parameters for a remote communication. It is usually subclassed. The CallMessage class provides a single instance variable (target) that is used to specify the remote invocation target. In GMI, the notion of an invocation target is a character string that uniquely represents the name of an object on the server side. A similar idea is found in Java's RMI with the addition of a special URL syntax. (RMI objects are referred to with a string of the form rmi://host:port/object-name.) We have not chosen this approach in GMI, since a client holds a reference to a remote call server (i.e., the host–port combintation is encapsulated in a connection), and thus a particular name can only refer to an object at a specific remote location. As we will demonstrate shortly, this framework is very transparent and easy to understand and minimizes much unwanted complexity (and overhead) that is found in RMI itself. Consider the following code:

```
package jhpc.gmi;

import java.io.*;

public abstract class CallMessage implements Serializable {
    protected String target;

    public CallMessage(String target) {
        this.target = target;
    }

    public void setTarget(String target) {
        this.target = target;
    }

    public final String getTarget() {
        return target;
    }

}
```

A couple of points are in order about the CallMessage:

1. **`Serializable`**: Any message must be serializable. Java object serialization is provided in the `ObjectInputStream` and `ObjectOutputStream` classes, which have the capability of reading and writing objects, respectively. We have not covered serialization in this book (again leaving the discussion to other books that already cover this material in detail), but make use of it only for exchanging objects between the client and the server (and vice versa).

2. **`CallMessage(String target)`**: All subclasses must call this constructor to ensure that the target object name field is properly initialized. It is permitted to have a null target object (acceptable only when a message is a reply from a remote call).

RemoteCallServer

Similar to the `MessageServer` class found in the SMA framework from the networking chapter, GMI provides similar classes with different names: `RemoteCallServer` (to provide basic registration facilities), `RemoteCallServerDispatcher` (to actually service the remote call), and `RemoteCallClient` (to allow clients to reach a `RemoteServer` to make calls).

The `RemoteCallServer` bears some similarities to RMI. There are two sets of methods: registration of `Callable` instances and serving remote calls.

Let us first consider the aspects of the `RemoteCallServer` that pertain to registration:

1. **`registeredObjects`**: All registrations are maintained in a Java Hashtable object. The key is simply a string that represents a user-defined name for contacting a `Callable` object remotely; the value is the `Callable` object itself.

2. **`bind()`**: This method is used to bind a given `Callable` instance to a user-defined name. This method simply uses the underlying `Hashtable put()` method to store the association in the `Hashtable`.

3. **`unbind()`**: This method allows a previous binding (done with `bind()`) to be remoted from the `Hashtable` of registered objects.

4. **`lookup()`**: This method looks up a previously defined binding.

Remember that this is not RMI! These functions are all intended to be called on the server side of the picture only. Clients are fully insulated from all details of registration and simply refer to remote objects by specifying the target object name in the `CallMessage`. We have chosen names similar to those found in the naming framework of RMI simply to ease the transition to GMI and not with the purpose of maintaining (or promising) any degree of compatibility.

Consider the following code:

```
package jhpc.gmi;

import java.net.*;
import java.io.*;
import java.util.*;

public class RemoteCallServer extends Thread {
    private Hashtable registeredObjects = new Hashtable();
    private ServerSocket callListener;

    public RemoteCallServer(int port) throws IOException {
        callListener = new ServerSocket(port);
    }

    public synchronized void bind(String target,
                                    Callable callable) {
        registeredObjects.put(target, callable);
    }

    public synchronized void unbind(String target) {
        registeredObjects.remove(target);
    }

    public synchronized Callable lookup(String target) {
        return (Callable) registeredObjects.get(target);
    }

    public void run() {
        while (true) {
            try {
                Socket s=callListener.accept();
                RemoteCallServerDispatcher csd =
                    new RemoteCallServerDispatcher(this, s);
                csd.setDaemon(false);
                csd.start();
            } catch(Exception e) { System.out.println(e); }
        }
    }
}
```

The rest of what you see in this class is dedicated to "being a server." This code is very similar to what is found in the SMA classes. This code is intended to be run as a thread. The run() method contains the familiar server loop. When a connection is accepted, a RemoteCallServerDispatcher instance is created to handle the incoming call. It is in this class where there are notable differences from the comparable SMA class `MessageServer`. The most important detail to notice in the server loop is that a reference to the `RemoteCallServer` instance `this` is passed to the `RemoteCallServerDispatcher` instance, thus making it possible for the various dispatcher instances to look up callables to perform the remote call.

`RemoteCallServerDispatcher`

The `RemoteCallServerDispatcher` class is similar to the `MessageServerDispatcher` class of SMA. The notable difference is that `DataInputStream` and `DataOutputStream` have been replaced with `ObjectInputStream` and `ObjectOutputStream` classes, which allow arbitrary Java objects to be exchanged between the `RemoteCallClient` and itself.[1]

The constructor initializes the `in` and `out` variables as done in the `MessageServerDispatcher` class, this time initializing the `ObjectInputStream` and `ObjectOutputStream` from the `InputStream` and `OutputStream`, respectively, associated with the incoming socket:

```
package jhpc.gmi;

import java.io.*;
import java.net.*;

public class RemoteCallServerDispatcher extends Thread {
    RemoteCallServer callServer;
    Socket socket;
    ObjectInputStream in;
    ObjectOutputStream out;

    public RemoteCallServerDispatcher(RemoteCallServer callServer,
      Socket socket)
      throws IOException {
        this.callServer = callServer;
        this.socket = socket;
        InputStream inRaw = socket.getInputStream();
        this.in = new ObjectInputStream(inRaw);
        OutputStream outRaw = socket.getOutputStream();
        this.out = new ObjectOutputStream(outRaw);      }
```

---

[1] We used serialization for pedagogical reasons. Although Java object serialization has been much maligned for having a multitude of performance and other implementation-related problems, it is (quite frankly) nice to be able to move data structures (even those as simple as subarrays) in the examples that follow. A version of GMI that does not use `Serializable` and that is similar to SMA is provided in the accompanying CD and on the book Web site.

```
public void run() {
    CallMessage message = null;
    try {
        while (true) {
            message = (CallMessage)in.readObject();
            if (message instanceof Goodbye) {
                out.writeObject(message);
                out.close();
                return;
            }
            Callable callTarget =
              callServer.lookup(message.getTarget());
            Serializable result;
            if (callTarget != null)
                result = callTarget.call(message);
            else
                result = null;
            out.writeObject(result);
            out.flush();
        }
    } catch (EOFException e1) {
        try {
            System.err.println(e1);
            out.close();
            socket.close();
            e1.printStackTrace();
        } catch (Exception e2) {
            System.err.println(e2);
            e2.printStackTrace();
        }
    } catch (Exception e) {
        System.err.println(e);
        e.printStackTrace();
    }
}
```

The run() method uses the readObject() method to read a CallMessage object from the underlying stream. We know for a fact that an object of type CallMessage or subclass thereof is the only type of object that can be read from the underlying stream. (You can verify this by studying the RemoteCallClient code in the next section, but trust us for the time being!) The following steps are done upon receiving a CallMessage (message):

1. The message is first checked to determine whether it is the reserved Goodbye message. The Goodbye message (which is a subclass of CallMessage) exists to

enable the client to politely (as opposed to rudely) go away. Connections with the client are persistent and thus only go away when either (a) the client sends the Goodbye message, or (b) an exception occurs. If the Goodbye message is received, the connection with the client is gracefully closed, and the dispatcher thread exits gracefully as well. Otherwise, continue to step 2.

2.   The message is then examined for the target object name. The target object name is not supposed to be null; however, if it is, the message simply cannot be delivered, and null is returned. The only condition by which null is returned is when no invocation takes place. The call server (i.e., the RemoteCallServer object that created this dispatch thread, or, more appropriately, the parent) is contacted to actually perform the call. It is entirely possible that the target name refers to an object that does not exist; however, this also results in a null return.

3.   Once the invocation is completed, a reply is returned. This reply must be sent to the RemoteCallClient object, using the writeObject() method. The flush() method is called every time an object is written to an ObjectOutputStream. This is, in general, necessary, because Java streams are buffered. Failing to flush() may result in the opposite end of this connection (a RemoteCallClient object) being blocked indefinitely on a readObject() call.

Thus, the RemoteCallServerDispatcher code is in many respects identical (in principle) to the MessageServerDispatcher code, with the notable difference being that serializable objects are involved. From the standpoint of the server side, the RemoteallServerDispatcher does virtually all of the work, except for managing the remote objects and actually performing the remote calls (both of which are left to the RemoteCallServer that created the RemoteCallServerDispatcher instance).

RemoteCallClient

The RemoteCallClient class is essentially the user interface that allows clients to easily send CallMessage objects to a remote object. An initial connection must first be made to a RemoteCallServer. The constructor for this class, much like the SMA MessageClient, allows a host and port combination to be specified. A socket is opened, and (as in the RemoteCallServerDispatcher) ObjectInputStream and ObjectOutputStream references are obtained for communication with the server.

The work done in the `call()` method is very similar to the work done by the `RemoteCallServerDispatcher` server loop shown earlier. The parameter to the `call()` method is a single `CallMessage` instance.[2]

```java
package jhpc.gmi;

import java.io.*;

import java.net.*;

public class RemoteCallClient extends Thread {
    Socket socket;
    ObjectOutputStream out;
    ObjectInputStream in;
    OutputStream debug = null;

    public RemoteCallClient(String host, int port)
      throws IOException {
        socket = new Socket(host, port);
        out = new ObjectOutputStream(socket.getOutputStream());
        in = new ObjectInputStream(socket.getInputStream());
    }

    public Object call(CallMessage message) {
        try {
            out.writeObject(message);
            out.flush();
        } catch(Exception e) {
            System.err.println(e);
            e.printStackTrace();
            return null;
        }

        Object result;
        try {
            result = in.readObject();
            return result;
        } catch(Exception e) {
            System.err.println(e);
            e.printStackTrace();
            return null;
        }
    }
```

---

[2] This is where the difference between GMI and RMI becomes very apparent. Our idea of a call is simply that a message is to be delivered. Our approach makes the call-by-copy semantics of RMI very obvious, thus resulting in a more transparent (and honest) abstraction for communication.

```
public Object call(String altTarget, CallMessage message) {
    message.setTarget(altTarget);
    return call(message);

}

public void disconnect() {
    try {
        out.writeObject(new Goodbye());
        out.flush();
        Object result = in.readObject();
        out.close();
        socket.close();
    } catch(Exception e) {
        System.err.println(e);
        e.printStackTrace();
    }
}
}
```

The `call()` method takes the `CallMessage` object (which is known to be of type `Serializable`) and writes it to the network. Then, the reply is read from the server, which must also be a `CallMessage`. This reply is then returned as the result of `call()`.

GMI is intended to be a simple remote procedure-calling framework. To be fair, let us say that there are a good number of things we have not done that you would find in the RMI framework from Sun. These details are summarized as follows:

1. No remote exceptions: This version of GMI does not handle remote exceptions. It is rather trivial to incorporate this enhancement, since it is merely a matter of reserving space for an `Exception` reference in `CallMessage`. An enhanced version of GMI can be downloaded from the course Web site.

2. No stubs and skeletons: Stubs and skeletons have been completely eliminated from this design. This is because we are less concerned with call transparency (i.e., the appearance that a remote call is just like calling a local function) than the potential for getting good performance. Supporting call transparency has the (undesirable) property of adding layers, which simply is not efficient. Since we are going to be adding a layer to GMI (`Memo`), the intent is to keep the number of layers to a minimum, while maintaining a sound design from an engineering and computing perspective.

3.   No forced subclassing: Classes used to make remote objects in RMI must subclass `UnicastRemoteObject,` and all methods must throw `RemoteException.` This is extremely cumbersome and almost makes the call transparency of RMI not worth the trouble, since you must be aware of so many details of the typing system in order to get the results. With GMI, any class can easily be made remote simply by implementing the `Callable` interface, providing a `call()` method, and providing an appropriate subclass of `CallMessage` to communicate to and from the remote object.

4.   Calls are not synchronized: When you open a connection between client and server, the calls are not synchronized. This capability has been provided strictly for the implementation of our higher level message passing systems, which require the ability to block (remotely). This means that calls must be explicitly locked that need to be atomic. Our implementation fully protects you on the server side, since a separate dispatcher is created to service each client, so you only need be concerned when creating client side threads that are all sharing a connection to a common `RemoteCallServer.` An alternative is to simply make separate connections to the `RemoteCallServer` using multiple `RemoteCallClient` instances (i.e., one instance of `RemoteCallClient` per thread).

Memo: A Remote Interface to `SharedTableOfQueues`

In Chapter 9, we presented the shared-table-of-queues abstraction, which represents a major building block of a coordination system. We created the shared table of (unordered) queues after observing that systems such as Linda (from Yale University) and Java Spaces are really nothing more than extensions of this fundamental principle that has been used in computing since the early days of operating systems. Linda and Java Spaces are both examples of tuple spaces.

The Memo system is an implementation of a tuple space; however, the concept of a tuple has been superseded by an object, which is a much more general concept than a tuple.

Design

The design of `Memo` is relatively straightforward. The GMI classes presented in the previous section are used to provide a remote interface to the `SharedTableOfQueues` class presented earlier. The following is a summary of the different key classes and their purpose:

1.   **MemoMessage**: This abstract class (derived from `CallMessage`) is used to request one of the various remote methods from the `SharedTableOfQueues` class. Since it is a subclass of `CallMessage`, a target object name must be specified. The additional method `go(SharedTableOfQueues stoq)` that allows the operation to be performed once the `MemoServer` has control of the `MemoMessage` is provided.

2. **MemoServer**: This class implements the `Callable` interface. It is used to accept the various instances of a subclass of MemoMessage (which is a subclass of CallMessage). When a given MemoMessage is received, an appropriate action will take place on the SharedTableOfQueues instance.

3. **MemoClient**: This class is used to provide the same methods for the client that are available in the SharedTableOfQueues class. Every method in this class has the same general implementation. The parameters are packed into one of the various MemoMessage subclass instances and sent to a remote MemoServer. Then, the result of the remote call is obtained as passed back to the client.

In the interest of conciseness, we will only discuss a few of the methods. As our examples in this chapter only make use of the basic methods (the put() and get() methods), we shall only discuss these two here and leave the rest for self-study (and a future book, an unresolved forward reference).

The following code shows the MemoMessage class:

```
public abstract class MemoMessage extends CallMessage {

    public MemoMessage(String target) {
        super(target);
    }

    public abstract Serializable go(SharedTableOfQueues stoq)
      throws Exception;

}
```

This class is marked abstract because instances of it are never created. The difference between CallMessage and MemoMessage is simply the go() method. The go() method must be overridden in the subclass to perform the operation on a remote SharedTableOfQueues (stoq).

The MemoGet subclass of MemoMessage is as follows:

```
class MemoGet extends MemoMessage {
    Serializable key;

    public MemoGet(String target, Serializable key) {
        super(target);
        this.key=key;
    }

    public Serializable go(SharedTableOfQueues stoq)
      throws Exception {
        return (Serializable) stoq.get(key);
    }
}
```

This class shows the essence of how GMI programming is done in practice. Typically, a constructor is provided that initializes the target object name and whatever parameters would normally be required to perform the remote call (thinking in RPC or RMI terms). Here the parameter that is needed is key. Why? Recall the method header from the `SharedTableOfQueues` class:

```
public Object get(Object key) throws InterruptedException
```

In the constructor for `MemoGet`, we translated key from `Object` to `Serializable`. This was to ensure that the message and any object references it contains are `Serializable`. This is not required, but rather is a matter of personal preference. It would have been perfectly acceptable to pass an `Object` as the parameter and allow an exception to occur if the key in fact proved not to be `Serializable`. As there was no loss of generality, we chose to make the interface safe from the end-user perspective.

Let us now consider the `MemoPut` message, which is used to access the `SharedTableOfQueues put()` function. Recall that the `put()` method has the following form:

```
public void put(Object key, Object value)
```

The following code shows the `MemoPut` class:

```
class MemoPut extends MemoMessage {
    Serializable key, value;

    public MemoPut(String target, Serializable key,
      Serializable value){
      super(target);
      this.key=key;
      this.value = value;
    }

    public Serializable go(SharedTableOfQueues stoq) {
      stoq.put(key,value);
      return new Ok(true);
    }
}
```

In this case, the constructor now has two parameters in addition to the target object name: key and value. Again, as a matter of preference and concern for the end user, we have chosen to make both of these parameters `Serializable`.

The operation is performed on the actual `SharedTableOfQueues` in the `go()` method. When writing remote interfaces to `void` methods, it is necessary to return a value. GMI provides a class for general-purpose acknowledgments (`Ok`) that can be set true or false to indicate success or failure. Here, we unconditionally indicate that the remote operation was successful (which will only occur when there is no exception caused by the put() call).

Let us now consider the case of the SharedTableOfQueues runDelayed() method, which allows a thread to perform a computation (asynchronously) that, when completed, leaves a result in the SharedTableOfQueues for subsequent retrieval.

The runDelayed() method has the following form:

```
public void runDelayed(Object key,Runnable r)
```

This is parsed as "start the Runnable r remotely as a thread, and leave the result behind as if MemoPut(key, r) had been performed."

The following code shows the MemoRunDelayed class:

```
class MemoRunDelayed extends MemoMessage implements Runnable {
    Serializable key;
    Serializable runnable;

    public MemoRunDelayed(String target, Serializable key,
                          Serializable runnable) {
      super(target);
      this.key = key;
      this.runnable = runnable;
    }

    public Serializable go(SharedTableOfQueues stoq) {
      stoq.runDelayed(key, this);
      return new Ok(true);
    }

    public void run(){
      if (runnable instanceof Runnable) {
        Runnable r = (Runnable)runnable;
        r.run();
      } else {
        // Strictly speaking, an exception should be thrown here.
      }
    }
}
```

This class shows some of the problems of working with interfaces (something you must know how to do, regardless of whether you use GMI, RMI, or CORBA). We want the ability to guarantee that both parameters (key and r) are Serializable. We also want the ability to guarantee that the parameter r is Runnable.[3] Ultimately, we decided in favor of enforcing the Serializable interface (which, if not checked, results in a great deal of trouble when working with object streams) and performing a run-time check just as we are about to run the Runnable.

Notice that the go() method simply calls the runDelayed() method of the SharedTableOfQueues class and returns an Ok message immediately. The runDelayed() method, in turn, creates a Thread instance from this message, hence the presence of the run() method. This run() method is simply a delegate that dispatches the actual Runnable r that was passed as part of the MemoRunDelayed message.

The remaining MemoMessage subclasses are all fairly straightforward. Here, we have presented the two easiest to follow (MemoGet and MemoPut) and the most difficult (MemoRunDelayed). All code is provided on the book CD and Web site.

The key thing to understand is that the go() method in the MemoMessage basically is where the remote operation is performed. This allows the messages themselves to play a role in carrying out the remote operation. It is for this reason that the MemoServer code will be fairly straightforward to understand, since the MemoServer instance simply takes a message that has been received and instructs it to perform the operation directly on a SharedTableOfQueues object.

MemoServer

Not surprisingly, the MemoServer code is straightforward and almost requires no additional information to be said about it. Nonetheless, we do offer a few words to tie a few loose ends together. The code is as follows:

```
public class MemoServer implements Callable {

    SharedTableOfQueues stoq = new SharedTableOfQueues();

    public Serializable call(CallMessage message)
        throws Exception {

        if (message instanceof MemoMessage) {
            MemoMessage mm = (MemoMessage) message;
            Serializable reply = mm.go(stoq);
            return reply;

        } else {
            return new Ok(false);
        }
    }
}
```

---

[3] Wish list for a language extension in Java: putDelayed(Serializable key, Serializable & Runnable r). The parameter r would take on the type Serializable; however, it would be staically known to having met the requirements of both interfaces. Java really needs this!

`MemoServer` is a class that implements `Callable`, which is required of any class that wants to act in a remote setting. It simply creates the `SharedTableOfQueues` instance (which will be used remotely) and provides a `call()` method. The code for performing the call on the server side is very straightforward. The message is checked to ensure that it is a `MemoMessage` (or a subclass). The downcast is performed, and the `MemoMessage` itself performs the operation on the `SharedTableOfQueues` instances `stoq`. In the unlikely event that the wrong type of message gets passed to the call, the general-purpose acknowledgment message `Ok` is returned with a status of false. This will, in fact, never occur.

A few words are in order about RPC in a parallel context. First, note that the `call()` method itself is not synchronized. Call synchronization is optional. If you need pure RPC semantics and have no need for the remote calls to block indefinitely (which we do in the case of the `put()` and `get()` methods), you should use the synchronized keyword accordingly.

Note that the `MemoServer` class, despite having the word "server" in its name, is not in fact the server. GMI provides `RemoteCallServer`, which contains the actual server loop. A `MemoServer` is created (trivially) by creating a `RemoteCallServer` instance and binding a name through which the `MemoServer` instance will be contacted:

```
RemoteCallServer server = new RemoteCallServer(port);
server.bind("memo", new MemoServer());
```

Any application may create a `MemoServer` simply by adding the preceding two lines. We provide an example server in the `MemoServer` class as an inner class.

MemoClient

The `MemoClient` is provided as a convenience class, so users of the `Memo` system do not need to make direct use of the various `MemoMessage` subclasses to perform `Memo` operations. Thus, users of the `Memo` system are completely isolated from the underlying communication system and simply make use of functions from the familiar `SharedTableOfQueues` class.

The code for `MemoClient` is as follows:

```
public class MemoClient {

    RemoteCallClient rc;
    String target;
    String host;
    int port;

    public MemoClient(String host, int port, String target)
      throws Exception {
        this.host = host;
        this.port = port;
        this.rc = new RemoteCallClient(host,port);
        this.target = target;
    }
```

```java
public void disconnect() {
    rc.disconnect();
}

public void goodbye() {
    rc.disconnect();
}

public void setTarget(String target) {
    this.target = target;
}

public Object get(Serializable key)
  throws InterruptedException {
    MemoGet mg = new MemoGet(target, key);
    return rc.call(mg);
}

public Object put(Serializable key, Serializable value) {
    MemoPut mp = new MemoPut(target, key, value);
    return rc.call(mp);
}

public Object getCopy(Serializable key)
  throws InterruptedException {
    MemoGetCopy mgc = new MemoGetCopy(target, key);
    return rc.call(mgc);
}

public Object getCopySkip(Serializable key) {
    MemoGetCopySkip mgcs = new MemoGetCopySkip(target, key);
    return rc.call(mgcs);
}

public Object getSkip(Serializable key)  {
    MemoGetSkip mgs = new MemoGetSkip(target, key);
    return rc.call(mgs);
}

public Object runDelayed(Serializable key, Runnable r)
  throws Exception {
    if (r instanceof Serializable) {
        Serializable rs = (Serializable) r;
        MemoRunDelayed mrd = new MemoRunDelayed(target, key, rs);
        return rc.call(mrd);
    } else throw new Exception("r not Serializable");
}
}
```

The code should be fairly straightforward to understand. To create this class, we essentially copied all of the methods from the `SharedTableOfQueues` class and added the following:

1. A constructor to initiate the remote connection via a `RemoteCallClient` object. The only aspect that is exposed to end users is the target object name. This is necessary to allow for the possibility of creating an arbitrary number of `MemoServer` instances and allowing clients the freedom to connect to them.

2. The various methods all correspond to existing `SharedTableOfQueues` methods, except for the `goodbye()` and `disconnect()` methods, which are used to politely disconnect from the `GMI RemoteCallServer` instance. For the most part, every method simply packages the parameters into a `MemoMessage` (or subclass thereof) and then issues a call via the `RemoteCallServer`.

The `MemoClient` provides a glimpse for how the GMI system could eventually become a transparent remote procedure-calling system, similar to RMI; however, this is well beyond the scope of this book. Our purpose has been to use the notion of remote procedure calling as a means to an end and not the end result itself. The `Memo` system is much more well-suited to thinking about parallel and distributed programming (where more than two entities are involved) than remote procedure calls (and RMI), and the rest of this section is dedicated to demonstrating the applicability of `Memo` to writing a few parallel codes.

Vector Inner Product

The first code example we shall consider is the vector inner product. The intention of this example is to show the basic capabilities that are possible with `Memo`. The vector inner product is not considered a computational grand challenge. Nonetheless, it is a good pedagogical example of how many interesting parallel problems are decomposed and solved using multiple processes running on one or more computers.

The idea of the vector inner product is very simple. Two vectors (arrays) of floating-point values are defined — v and w, with values $v=(v_0, v_1, ..., v_{N-1})$ and $w=(w_0, w_1, ..., w_{N-1})$. The inner product is computed by summing up the products of all corresponding elements in vectors v and w:

$$z = \sum_{I=0}^{N-1} v_I * w_I$$

The approach taken to compute the inner product is to decompose the problem (of size N) into smaller parts of size K, where N divides K evenly. Then the same algorithm is used to work on the smaller parts. Of course, the result obtained by solving each part is only a partial result, so the partial results must be collected at the end to obtain the total result.

In pseudocode,

> Let $P = N / K$, where P is the number of parts to work on.
>
> for j in 0..P-1 (this can be done concurrently)
>
> > partialSum[j] = sum(vI * wI), for I in 0..K-1
>
> partialSum[j] = 0, for all j in 0..P-1
>
> totalSum = 0;
>
> for j in 0..P-1 (this must be done sequentially)
>
> > totalSum += partialSum[j];

The ability to do identical tasks concurrently is something we refer to as a *job jar*. A job jar, much like a cookie jar, allows you to choose any task from the job jar and work on it. Here, the job jar will contain a pair of subvectors for which the (partial) inner product is to be computed.

The code presented next shows the general structure of the VMpy class, which only consists of static methods that actually coordinate the basic computation. We will then walk through the various methods and explain what is going on. In order for this program to work, it must be run *P* times, where *P* corresponds to the number of parts into which the vector inner product has been decomposed.

```
public class VMpy {

    public static void main(String[] args)

    public static void createWork(MemoClient memo, int dim, int N)

    public static void doWork(MemoClient memo, int partNumber)

    public static double mergeResults(MemoClient memo, int totalParts)

    public static class VectorPair implements Serializable { ... }
}
```

The VMpy class is where you will find the pseudocode just shown. In fact, the pseudocode is found in the main() method. We'll get to it shortly, but first we provide an explanation for the various static methods and other goodies found in this class:

1. **main()**: This is the actual driver for the entire computation. The command line is parsed here for the problem parameters and depending on the part being worked on,

the remaining functions are called: `createWork()`, `doWork()`, and `mergeResults()`.

2. **`createWork()`**: This function is only called by the process that is working on part 0. It is used to define entries in the `Memo` space.

3. **`doWork()`**: This function is called by all processes. This function will get entries from the Memo space and put partial results back into the `Memo` space.

4. **`mergeResults()`**: This function is only called by the process that is working on part 0. This function basically collects all of the partial results from the `Memo` space and prints the final result.

The nested `VectorPair` class is used as a "wrapper" to package the work to be done. It simply holds references to two arrays of `double` (`double[]`) for which the partial inner product is to be computed. We chose to bundle the two arrays together in a single object to make it clear that the inner product is a job to be done that is placed in the job jar. When a given process gets the job from the job jar, it can simply tell the object to perform its task with little or no concern about how to actually do the task. In the case of the task, the `innerProduct()` method is called, which returns a `Double` value. This value can then be inserted into the `Memo` space as a (partial) result for later accumulation.

```
public static class VectorPair implements Serializable {

        int partNumber;
        int dimension;
        private double[] v;
        private double[] w;

        public VectorPair(int partNumber, int dimension)
        public Double innerProduct()
    }
```

Let's now discuss the code from the top down, starting from the `main()` method. This is shown as follows:

```
    public static void main(String[] args) {
        try {
            if (args.length < 5) {
                System.err.println("VMpy host port dim part# N");
                return;
            }
            String memoHost = args[0];
            int memoPort = Integer.parseInt(args[1]);
            int dimension = Integer.parseInt(args[2]);
            int partNumber = Integer.parseInt(args[3]);
            int totalParts = Integer.parseInt(args[4]);
```

```
            if (dimension % totalParts != 0) {
                System.out.println("dimension % totalParts != 0");
                return;
            }

            MemoClient mc =
              new MemoClient(memoHost, memoPort, "memo");
            if (partNumber == 0) {
                createWork(mc, dimension, totalParts);
                doWork(mc, partNumber);
                double result = mergeResults(mc, totalParts);
            } else
                doWork(mc, partNumber);
        } catch (Exception e) {
            System.out.println(e);
            e.printStackTrace();
            return;
        }
    }
```

The main() method is called by every worker that will participate in the calculation of the vector inner product. A number of parameters must be passed on the command line to determine what this particular worker will do:

- **memoHost**: This is the hostname to use to contact a MemoServer.

- **memoPort**: This is the port number where the MemoServer is listening.

- **dimension**: This stores the dimension of each vector. This code does not ensure that both vectors in fact have the same dimension.

- **partNumber**: This holds the number the process will be responsible for working on.

- **totalParts**: This is the total number of processes that will be participating in the computation.

Once the command line parameters have been processed, the real work begins. The work to be performed depends on whether partNumber is zero. In parallel-computing applications, one of the parts usually has the added responsibility of creating the work to be done. By convention, this is usually part 0. The Memo system does not impose this requirement, unlike other message passing frameworks. Instead, Memo views process numbering as something beyond the scope of the framework that can be addressed by a process management framework.[4]

If the part number is zero (i.e., the "master"), the following methods are called:

- **createWork()**: This is used to decompose the work of the inner product into P parts and store them in the Memo space.

- **doWork()**: Although the master is responsible for creating the work to be done, the master also participates in doing the work.

- **mergeResults()**: The master will wait for all of the results to be computed by the various workers and put the final result together simply by adding up the partial sums.

If the part number is nonzero, the doWork() method is the only method that is called.

The createWork() method is as follows:

```
public static void createWork(MemoClient memo, int dim, int N)
{
    try {
        int blockSize = dim / N;
        for (int i=0; i < N; i++) {
            VectorPair vp = new VectorPair(i, blockSize);
            memo.put("pair" + i, vp);
        }
    } catch(Exception e) {
        System.out.println(e);
        e.printStackTrace();
    }
}
```

The createWork() method is given a reference to the MemoClient object, the dimension of the vector(s), and the number of parts (*N*). *N* VectorPair instances are created (randomly generated) and inserted into the MemoSpace. In the interests of safety, each of the entries in the Memo space is named "pair" + *i* (i.e., "pair0", "pair1", ... "pair*N*-1") to ensure that every worker gets precisely one unit of work to do. It is not required to do this. You could simply put all of the work into key pair, and the SharedTableOfQueues will be smart enough to ensure that all of the entries are stored safely in the queue named pair.[5]

The doWork() method is responsible for doing the actual work (the actual work being the inner product itself). The code is as follows:

---

[4] Many approaches exist for the management of processes. In this chapter, we will create all of the participant processes with a script. This script will allow you to start all of the processes locally (on the same computer) or on a list of computers. A separate framework is being developed by the JHPC research group (the computational neighborhood) that makes the management of parameters and process numbering completely transparent. See http://www.jhpc.org.

[5] The version that works this way is provided on the book Web site.

```
public static void doWork(MemoClient memo, int partNumber) {
    try {
        VectorPair pair;
        pair = (VectorPair) memo.get("pair" + partNumber);
        Double partialResult = pair.innerProduct();
        memo.put("partial" + partNumber, partialResult);
    } catch(Exception e) {
        System.out.println(e);
        e.printStackTrace();
    }
}
```

A `VectorPair` instance is retrieved from the `Memo` space. The worker uses its part-Number to determine which entry is to be retrieved. Now, the miracle of modern science occurs. The object is simply told to compute its inner product, and the result is stored in the `Memo` space under the name "partial" + partNumber. Thus, the inner product for the `VectorPair` contained in pair0 will be stored in partial0, pair1 in partial1, and so on. The `mergeResults()` code shows how the final result ultimtely is computed:

```
public static double mergeResults(MemoClient memo, int totalParts) {
    try {
        double result = 0.0;
        for (int i=0; i < totalParts; i++) {
            Double partialResult;
            partialResult = (Double) memo.get("partial" + i);
            result += partialResult.doubleValue();
        }
        return result;
    } catch(Exception e) {
        System.out.println(e);
        e.printStackTrace();
        return 0.0;
    }
}
```

Merging results together is actually very straightforward. A loop is established to `get()` the entries out of the `Memo` space. Recalling the original `SharedTableOfQueues` implementation, we see that the `get()` operation will block until the value actually becomes available—only this time the operation is working in a networked context. Although this step is sequential, everything leading up to this step was concurrent (and, in fact, parallel, if run on the network or a multiprocessor system). The result is returned and can be printed in the worker numbered zero.

The `VectorPair` class is used to create the basic unit of work. This code is shown next. The `VectorPair` object itself must be `Serializable`, since it will be transmitted over the network using object serialization. The `VectorPair` object contains a package of work, which is two arrays—*v* and *w*—both with a common dimension and corresponding to a part number. Strictly speaking, the part number instance variable (`partNumber`) appears here only for the purpose of debugging via the `toString()` method.

The nested `VectorPair` class is as follows:

```java
public static class VectorPair implements Serializable {
    int partNumber;
    int dimension;
    private double[] v;
    private double[] w;

    public VectorPair(int partNumber, int dimension) {
        this.partNumber = partNumber;
        this.dimension = dimension;
        v = new double[dimension];
        w = new double[dimension];

        for (int i=0; i < dimension; i++) {
            v[i] = Math.random() * 10.0;
            w[i] = Math.random() * 10.0;
        }
    }

    public Double innerProduct() {
        double result = 0.0;
        for (int i=0; i < dimension; i++)
            result += v[i] * w[i];
        return new Double(result);
    }

    public String toString() {
        int i;
        String result;

        result = "VectorPair: " + partNumber + " v: ";
        for (i=0; i < dimension; i++)
            result += " " + v[i];
        result = " w: ";
        for (i=0; i < dimension; i++)
            result += " " + w[i];
        return result;
    }
}
```

A few details are in order regarding the VectorPair class. The constructor uses the random-number generator from the the `Math` class (a standard language class) to generate random data for the subvectors *v* and *w*. The `innerProduct()` method is used to compute the actual vector inner product and returns a `Double` object. The reason that an object is returned instead of a scalar value is to address the requirement that a `Serializable` entity be `put()` in the `Memo` space as a result. Recall that `innerProduct()` is called on the pair that is retrieved from the `Memo` space with a `get()` in the `doWork()` static method; the result is `put()` back into the `Memo` space, and the result must be `Serializable`, which means that it must be an object that is `Serializable`. (All Java `Number` subclasses and arrays are `Serializable`.)

The following box explains how you can test this code:

Running the VMpy Code

Running a parallel code is somewhat of a pain. You need to take care to ensure that everything is started correctly.

First, the `Memo` server must be started. We have implemented a `MemoServer` that can be used to serve a `SharedTableOfQueues` to any application that wants to use it.

To start the `MemoServer` on port 2099 (you can start on ANY port desired), use

```
java jhpc.memo.MemoServerfServer 2099
```

Then, start *N* copies of the VMpy class. It does not matter how many copies you start, as long as you take care to ensure that each part is started correctly.

Suppose you want to compute the inner product of two vectors with dimension 1000 using 5 processes. You'd do the following:

```
java jhpc.memo.VMpy localhost 2099 1000 0 5
java jhpc.memo.VMpy localhost 2099 1000 1 5
java jhpc.memo.VMpy localhost 2099 1000 2 5
java jhpc.memo.VMpy localhost 2099 1000 3 5
java jhpc.memo.VMpy localhost 2099 1000 4 5
```

On the CD, we provide two scripts: `run-me-local` and `run-me-remote`. You can use these scripts to automate these tasks on Unix or Windows. (Windows scripts have a `.bat` extension.) The `run-me-local` script simply runs everything on a single host. (`localhost` may need to be replaced by `127.0.0.1`, the loopback address, in your environment.) The `run-me-remote` script can be used on Unix with **rsh** or **ssh** capability to start the various processes on different hosts.

Trapezoidal Integration

Earlier in the book, we presented trapezoidal integration. In trapezoidal integration, the goal is to find the area under the curve by subdividing the interval and approximating each subdivision as a trapezoid. The earlier version of this code essentially created a thread to compute the total area in a region. (The class `IntegTrapRegion` was used for this purpose and is reused here.)

Despite being a different problem than the vector inner product that was discussed in the previous section, there are striking similarities between how this problem and the vector inner product problem are attacked with the Memo system. As before, there is one part that is responsible for creating the work, doing the work, and merging the partial results together, while the other parts simply do their share of the work and write their partial results to the Memo space.

The complete code is available on the book CD and Web site in the class `IntegTrapMemo`. We now provide an overview of the key methods: the `main()` method (the driver) and the various methods that play a role in defining and doing the work.

The `main()` method is as follows.

```
public static void main(String args[]) {
    try {
        String usage;
        usage = "ITM host port part# parts start end gran"
        if (args.length < 7)  {
            System.err.println("usage: " + usage);
            return;
        }
        String memoHost = args[0];
        int memoPort = Integer.parseInt(args[1]);
        int partNumber = Integer.parseInt(args[2]);
        int numParts = Integer.parseInt(args[3]);
        double start = new Double(args[4]).doubleValue();
        double end = new Double(args[5]).doubleValue();
        int gran = Integer.parseInt(args[6]);

        MemoClient mc;
        mc = new MemoClient(memoHost, memoPort, "memo");
        if (partNumber == 0) {
            createWork(mc, numParts, start, end, gran);
            doWork(mc, partNumber);
            double result = mergeResults(mc, numParts);
            mc.disconnect();
        } else {
            doWork(mc, partNumber);
            mc.disconnect();
        }
    } catch (Exception e) {
        System.out.println(e);
        e.printStackTrace();
        return;
    }
}
```

As done in the vector inner product, (VMpy), the parameters are obtained from the command line. These parameters are now explained:

```
String memoHost = args[0];
```

- **memoHost (args[0])**: This stores the host where the Memo server has been started.

- **memoPort (args[1])**: This is the port on which the Memo server is listening.

- **partNumber (args[2])**: This worker is part "partNumber" of "numParts"

- **numParts (args[3])**: This holds the total number of workers.

- **start (args[4])**: This is the x-value to start integration.

- **end (args[5])**: This is the x-value to end integration.

- **gran (args[6])**: This is the granularity (number of trapezoids per worker)

Once the parameters have been obtained, a connection is made to the Memo server as before. Then, based on the value obtained for partNumber, a determination is made whether or not the partNumber is zero. If it is, the worker has the added responsibility of defining the work to be done and then proceeds to do the work, followed by a merge of the results. Otherwise, the worker simply does its share of the overall trapezoidal integration. These functions are virtually identical to the work done in vector inner product with the notable differences being the parameters from the command line and the actual computation performed. We'll get to this in a minute.

The createWork() function appears as follows:

```
    public static void createWork(MemoClient mc, int num_t,
      double start, double end, int gran) {
        function fn = new function();

        partition( mc, num_t, start, end, gran, fn );
    }
```

This function simply calls the partition() function, which was excised from the original program, after creating a function instance. Recalling the earlier discussion, we find that Java does not have function parameter passing as found in other programming languages (C and C++). The idiom is emulated in Java by creating an interface (F_of_x) and then creating a class that implements the interface (function):

```
    public static void partition( MemoClient space,
      int numThreads, double a, double b, int granularity,
      F_of_x fn )
    {

        try {
            if( numThreads < 1 )
                throw new BadThreadCountException();
```

```
        if( a > b )
            throw new BadRangeException();

        if( a == b )
            throw new NoRangeException();

        if( granularity < 1 )
            throw new BadGranularityException();
    }
catch( Exception e ) {
    System.out.println( e.toString() );
    System.exit( 1 );
}

long begin_time = 0;
long end_time = 0;

try {
    double range = b - a;
    double start = a;
    double end = a + ((1.0d)/numThreads * range);

    begin_time = System.currentTimeMillis();

    for( int i=0; i < numThreads; i++ ) {
        space.put("region"+i,
            new IntegTrapRegion(start,end,granularity,fn));
        start = end;
        end = a + ((i + 2.0d)/numThreads * range);
    }
}
catch( Exception e ) {
    System.out.println(e);
}
}
```

The code for the partition() function appeared in the original IntegTrap code. The notable difference appears in boldface. Where the original code would have created an IntegTrapRegion instance and then called the Thread start() method, this code simply uses the Memo put() function to create an entry in the Memo system. This entry is retrieved by one of the workers that calls the doWork() method, which appears as follows:

```
public static void doWork(MemoClient space, int partNumber)
   throws Exception{
     IntegTrapRegion region;
     region = (IntegTrapRegion)space.get("region"+partNumber);
     region.run();
     space.put("partial"+partNumber, region);
}
```

As done in the vector-inner-product example, every participant worker will get its work from the `Memo` space. This work will be an instance of `IntegTrapRegion` (which was `put()` in the `createWork()` method). Here, we do the work simply by calling the `run()` method explicitly. This was mostly done out of laziness; however, it also shows that with few code changes, we can modify a code that was never designed to work in a networked fashion to work with the `Memo` system.

Finally, we perform the now-familiar task of merging the results. Again, we rely on the `get()` method to block for each partial result and (once unblocked) simply accumulate the sum of partial values. The code is as follows:

```
public static double mergeResults(MemoClient space, int num_t)
   throws Exception {
     double totalArea = 0.0;
     for (int i=0; i < num_t; i++)  {
         IntegTrapRegion thisArea;
         thisArea = (IntegTrapRegion) space.get("partial"+i);
         totalArea += partialArea.getArea();
     }
     return totalArea;
   }
}
```

The `IntegTrapMemo` example shows that we can work almost exclusively with objects. In the vector-inner-product example, we computed a `Double` object value from the result of the inner product computed for a given `VectorPair` instance. This was, strictly speaking, not necessary. We could have simply computed the result as part of the object's state and then `put()` it under a different name in the `Memo` space.[6]

Running the `IntegTrapMemo` code is almost identical to running the VMpy code. Scripts are provided to ameliorate the task of starting up the various processes on your favorite operating system (Linux, other Unix environment, or Windows).

---

[6] We note here that it is very important to realize that when putting or getting something from the `Memo` space, you are making a copy. This is because serialization makes a copy of the object. We are working on other versions of `Memo` with distributed reference semantics; however, this is beyond the scope of the present effort. Most tuple space implementations in fact work in a manner similar to `Memo` (without the ease of use!).

Warshall's Algorithm

The third and final example we consider is Warshall's algorithm. Warshall's algorithm was also presented earlier in the book, and it represents one of the more difficult algorithms to make work in parallel. Here, we show how to extend the parallel version to use the Memo system.

The entire code for this example can be found on the book CD and Web site in class WarshallTQ. In the interests of conciseness, we highlight the design and leave the "rest of the story" to self-study and a future book.

To get this code to work with Memo, a bit of minor restructuring needed to be done. The first and foremost consideration is the assumptions made by the earlier code about shared memory. In particular, the boolean matrix a was assumed to be shared among all of the threads. In fact, only one thread (the master thread, part 0 again) really needs to know about this boolean matrix. All of the threads are computing a part of the closure, which is stored in the Block class. To ensure that no sharing occurred, we eliminated Block as an inner class in the original design; it now appears as a separate class.[7]

At the top level, the code appears to have much in common with the two previous examples. Part 0 basically creates work, does work, and merges results; the other parts simply do work. The key difference between this example and the previous ones is that this algorithm computes a very large result (the closure boolean matrix). The boolean matrix is decomposed into blocks, the closure is performed in parallel, and then a resultant matrix is obtained. Thus, we are not simply computing a scalar value as in the two previous examples, but rather a matrix.

Let us now consider the relevant methods of the WarshallTQ class, which will be followed by a discussion of the Block class, wherein the actual closure is computed.

The following is the main() method:

```
public static void main(String args[]) {
    String usage;
    usage = "ITM host port part# parts start end gran";
    if (args.length < 6)  {
        System.err.println("usage: " + usage);
        return;
    }

    try {
        int i,j;
        double probTrue = 0.3;
```

---

[7] This decision also makes sense because the Block class needs to be Serializable, but it is a shame for the containing class to be Serializable, since there is no need to send it over the network for any reason whatsoever.

```
            String memoHost = args[0];
            int memoPort = Integer.parseInt(args[1]);
            int partNumber = Integer.parseInt(args[2]);
            int numParts = Integer.parseInt(args[3]);
            int N = Integer.parseInt(args[4]);
            int bsize = Integer.parseInt(args[5]);

            boolean a[][]=new boolean[N][N];
            Random rand = new Random();
            for(i=0; i< N; i++ ) {
                for(j=0; j<N; j++ ) {
                    a[i][j] = (rand.nextDouble() <= probTrue);
                }
            }


            WarshallTQ w;
            w= new WarshallTQ(memoHost,memoPort,"memo",bsize);
            if (partNumber == 0) {
                w.connectToMemo();
                w.closureCreateWork(a);
                w.closureDoWork(partNumber,numParts);
                w.closureMergeResults(a);
                w.disconnect();
            } else {
                w.connectToMemo();
                w.closureDoWork(partNumber, numParts);
                w.disconnect();
            }
        } catch(Exception e) {
            System.out.println(e);
            e.printStackTrace();
        }
    }
```

As before, more than half of the code in this method is dedicated to obtaining parameters. The parameters include the following:

- **memoHost**: This is where the Memo server is running.

- **memoPort**: This stores the port where the Memo server is listening.

- *numParts*: This holds the total number of workers.

- **N**: This is the dimension of the matrix.

- **bsize**: This is the block size.

After the parameters are obtained, a boolean matrix is generated randomly. If you wanted to provide your own boolean matrix from an input file, you could replace the code that appears here. Then, a `WarshallTQ` object is created. Connections to `Memo` are actually managed by the `WarshallTQ` object via the `connectToMemo()` method, which uses the `memoHost`, `memoPort`, and `memo` Memo space name to make connections on demand.

The code in the `main()` method for the master (part 0) is very similar to the previous two examples:

1. A connection is made to the Memo system:
   ```
   w.connectToMemo();
   ```

2. The work is created, and a reference to the boolean matrix (a) is passed:
   ```
   w.closureCreateWork(a);
   ```

3. As in the two previous examples, the work is done. `partNumber` and `numParts` are needed to determine what `blocks` a worker will work on (it is not necessarily the case in this algorithm that the number of workers evenly divides the number of blocks, so this is done to keep the code general!):
   ```
   w.closureDoWork(partNumber,numParts);
   ```

4. The master is responsible for ensuring that all of the blocks have been computed. It will do this in the `closureMergeResults()` method and replace the original boolean matrix (a) with its closure one block at a time:
   ```
   w.closureMergeResults(a);
   ```

5. This is done to politely inform the Memo system that the work is done.
   ```
   w.disconnect();
   ```

The code in the `main()` method for the other parts simply performs steps 1, 3, and 5. Steps 2 and 4 are only done by part 0.

Let us now consider the details of some of these methods. The `closureCreateWork()` method is presented next and is a method of the `WarshallTQ` class:

```
    public void closureCreateWork(boolean[][] a) throws Exception
{
        int i,j,NR,NC;

        IndexedKey kthRows=IndexedKey.unique(0);
        IndexedKey kthCols=IndexedKey.unique(0);
        NR=a.length;
        NC=a[0].length;
        int nt=((NR+blkSize-1)/blkSize)*((NC+blkSize-1)/blkSize);
        for (i=0;i<NR;i+=blkSize)
            for (j=0;j<NC;j+=blkSize){
                Block b;
                b = new Block(a,i,j,kthRows,kthCols,blkSize);
                space.put("block", b);
                numBlocks++;
            }
        space.put("blockCount", new Integer(numBlocks));
    }
```

In the earlier version of the Warshall code, the lines that appear in boldface did not exist. The first of these two lines contained a call to the `Thread start()` method to actually start the computation on the block immediately. (The earlier version of `WarshallTQ` did actually make use of the `SharedTableOfQueues`, but only when evaluating the block itself. We use the `Memo` system to actually store the block, so multiple workers can contend for the different blocks and perform work.)

The second of these two boldfaced lines write a single entry, `blockCount`, that will be used by all parts of the computation to determine how many total blocks there are to be worked on. This global block count will allow us to demonstrate the power of `Memo` to address the need for global values, which can be obtained via the `getCopy()` method from the `SharedTableOfQueues` abstraction.

Once we have the work defined, we can think about actually doing the work. The `closureDoWork()` method does just that:

```java
public void closureDoWork(int workerNumber,
                          int numberOfWorkers)
    throws Exception{
    int numBlocksToWorkOn, remainder;
    Integer globalBlockCount;
    globalBlockCount = (Integer)space.getCopy("blockCount");
    Vector blocks = new Vector();
    Vector spaces = new Vector();

    int numBlocks = globalBlockCount.intValue();
    for (int j=workerNumber; j < numBlocks;
            j += numberOfWorkers)
    {
        Block b = (Block) space.get("block");
        MemoClient newSpace;
        newSpace = new MemoClient(memoHost,memoPort,"memo");
        spaces.addElement(newSpace);
        blocks.addElement(b);
        b.setMemoClient(newSpace);
        b.start();
    }

    Enumeration bEnum = blocks.elements();
    while (bEnum.hasMoreElements()) {
        Block b = (Block) bEnum.nextElement();
        try {
          b.join();
        } catch(Exception e) {}
    }
```

```
Enumeration sEnum = blocks.elements();
while (sEnum.hasMoreElements()) {
   MemoClient s = (MemoClient) sEnum.nextElement();
   try {
     s.goodbye();
   } catch(Exception e) {}
}
```
}

This method required a few enhancements from the original code. Boldface has been used to indicate the changes that needed to be performed. A block is retrieved from the Memo space. Then, a new connection is made to the Memo space to give each Block its own communication channel to the Memo system.[8] Then, (as before) the Block instance is started as a thread. Each worker creates threads to execute a subset of the Block instances that are needed to compute the closure.

Partitioning is a common technique that is used in parallel computing when multiple (numbered) workers are employed to do a set of numbered tasks. This is exemplified by the following loop that appears in closureDoWork():

```
for (int j=workerNumber; j < numBlocks; j += numberOfWorkers)
```

This is a particularly elegant way of dealing with the situation where the number of blocks does not evenly divide the number of workers. Consider what will happen when there are three workers (numberOfWorkers = 3) and 10 blocks (numBlocks = 10). The following values of j will be observed for workers 0, 1, and 2 (which represent all of the workers by number):

```
worker      j values observed
0           0, 3, 6, 9
1           1, 4, 7
2           2, 5, 8
```

This is precisely what would be expected. Because the total number of blocks to be worked on is 10, each worker is going to work on a minimum of three blocks. One worker will work on four blocks.

The rest of the code in this method is dedicated to joining all threads (to ensure that all of the Block instances have completed their part of the closure) and taking down the connections to the Memo space. The Vector instances that appear in this code (blocks and space) appear here for the purpose of keeping track of all of the blocks we're working on, as well as the connections that have been made, thus making for very easy bookkeeping.

Whew! The final step is to merge the results together in much the same fashion as done in the preceding examples. The code for closureMergeResults() is now shown:

---

[8] This version of Memo is intended to be simple. The MemoClient is not intended to accept calls from multiple threads. A more advanced version of Memo does address this concern and can be downloaded from the Web site.

```
public void closureMergeResults(boolean[][] a)
    throws Exception {
    for (int i=0; i < numBlocks; i++) {

        Block result = (Block) space.get("blockClosure");
        result.merge(a);
    }
}
```

That's it. It is just a matter of getting the `blockClosure` result that was written by the `closureDoWork()` method and then telling the object to replace its part of the boolean matrix (a) with its submatrix.

In the foregoing discussion, we made unresolved "forward" references to two aspects of the `Block` class, which exists for the sole purpose of holding part of the boolean matrix (a submatrix) and performing the closure.

The actual work of the closure is done in the `run()` method, which is shown next (the `Block` class is virtually unchanged from the original code, except that it now appears as a separate, unnested class):

```
public void run(){
    int i,j;
    int k;
    boolean IHaveRow, IHaveColumn;
    boolean[] row=null, col=null;
    try {
        for (k=0;k<N;k++) {
            IHaveRow = k-r>=0 && k-r < nr;
            IHaveColumn = k-c>=0 && k-c < nc;
            if (IHaveRow) {
                BooleanArray myRow;
                myRow = new BooleanArray(block[k-r]);
                space.put(rows.at(k+c*N), myRow);
                row = block[k-r];
            }
            if (IHaveColumn) {
                col=new boolean[nr];
                for (j=0;j<nr;j++) col[j]=block[j][k-c];
                BooleanArray myCol;
                myCol = new BooleanArray(col)
                space.put(cols.at(k+r*N), myCol);
            }
            if (!IHaveRow) {
                BooleanArray r;
                r = (BooleanArray) space.get(rows.at(k+c*N));
                row = r.getData();
            }
```

```
        if (!IHaveColumn) {
            BooleanArray c;
            c = (BooleanArray) space.get(cols.at(k+r*N));
            col = c.getData();
        }
        for (i=0;i<nr;i++)
            if (col[i])
                for (j=0;j<nc;j++)
                    block[i][j] |= row[j];
    }
    space.put("blockClosure", this);
}catch (InterruptedException iex){}
}
```

The differences between the original version of Block's run() method and this version are what would be expected. We are now interacting with Memo. A BooleanArray wrapper class has been used (but is not shown here). This was not strictly necessary; however, it made debugging somewhat easier.[9] Basically, instead of writing the data to a local SharedTableOfQueues, the data are written to the Memo space reference. Each Block has its own connection to the Memo server, which you can verify by studying the full source code. The changes are shown in boldface. The very last boldface line of code shows that the Block instance is saved as a different entry in the Memo space, once its part of the closure is completed (hence the presence of this as the subject of the put() method call).

The merge code was formerly a part of the Block run() method. It now appears separately, since the merging must be done where the boolean matrix a is located. It is provided as a method in Block, since a Block instance is the only place where the knowledge of where the data came from in the original boolean matrix. The following is the code for Merge():

```
public void merge(boolean[][] a) {
    for (int i=0;i<nr;i++)
        for (int j=0;j<nc;j++)
            a[r+i][c+j]=block[i][j];
}
}
```

And that's all there is to it.

---

[9] What we mean here is that we were able to print the class of what was being received using getClass() while testing the code. Sometimes, this is all that is needed to determine whether your code is working.

Chapter Wrap-up

It is impossibe to do complete justice to process coordination in a book that is largely dedicated to working with threads. The Memo system is really a very lightweight implementation of a tuple space that has more of a client–server flavor than a peer-to-peer one. We are actively engaged in other projects that are more peer oriented than client–server oriented. Nonetheless, Memo provides an excellent starting point for those who want to learn what is behind the various message passing systems that are out there. Memo has much in common with technologies as early as Linda and as recent as Java Spaces. It supports virtually all of the primitives that are found in tuple space systems.

The interested reader will want to read about the message passing interface (MPI) and Java virtual machine (JVM). These systems fall into the "oldies, but goodies" category. Despite being old and predominantly implemented in the C language, they address many other important factors in parallel programming. For example, Memo requires some hand holding to ensure that the various processes are all numbered correctly. (JVM and MPI have always provided a good amount of support for numbering at the expense of complexity. MPI has over 125 functions; Memo has fewer than 10 functions.) At present, this process must be done in a completely manual fashion. This decision has been made intentionally, because we are working on a research project called the Computational Neighborhood (we being J. Shafaee, G. Thiruvathukal, A. Singh, and T.W. Christopher) that addresses the issues of process management and job execution in a clustered environment. This framework makes use of the properties concept in Java and basically binds a set of properties for multipart jobs (Memo is just one variety of a multipart job). With relatively minor changes, Memo will be able to participate in the Computational Neighborhood without becoming a significantly more complex framework.

You are invited to stay tuned to our latest tools and techniques for parallel and distributed programming. Please visit our Web site at http://www.toolsofcomputing.com and http://www.jhpc.cs.depaul.edu (or http://www.jhpc.org) for the latest updates to the code presented in this book, as well as our other open-source and research projects.

Exercises

1. Using the ideas of the vector-inner-product example, write a program that performs matrix multiplication in parallel. You will find it useful to break up the work into rows of the first matrix and columns of the second matrix. (You may find it useful to further consider the possibility of breaking up the work of computing the inner product of the row and column vectors using a variation on the VectorPair class for large runs.)

2. Design a version of GMI that is more like SMA (thus eliminating the dependence on Serializable) where the CallMessage class allows you to set and get basic parameter types. Rewrite the Memo system to make use of the Message ideas

instead of `Serializable`. This could be a lot of work. (You may also find that it is desirable for scientific applications to extend SMA to have support for basic arrays of `int` and `float`.)

3. Write a `Memo` program that makes use of the `BigInteger` class found in Java to compute the factors of a very large number in parallel on a network of computers. (You might find this useful, say, for cracking public-key encryption schemes. We suggest limiting the key size to something tractable, say, 64 bits.)

4. Use `Memo` to rework some of the algorithms presented earlier in the book.

Index